Small Business Management

Small Business Management

Michael D. Ames
California State University—Fullerton

Norval L. Wellsfry
Sacramento City College

West Publishing Company
St. Paul / New York / Los Angeles / San Francisco

Copy Editor: Barbara Paul
Design: Rick Chafian
Cover Design: Taly Design Group
Composition: Carlisle Graphics

Library of Congress Cataloging in Publication Data

Ames, Michael D.
  Small business management.

  Bibliography: p.
  Includes index.
  1. Small business—Management.   I. Wellsfry,
Norval L.   II. Title.
HD62.7.A49   1983   658'.022   82-20139
ISBN 0-314-69631-8

To our families

Contents

Preface

This text on small business management focuses on the most common problems encountered by owners or managers of small enterprises. Written in a straightforward manner and using a problem-solving, step-by-step approach, it is a valuable guide to small business ownership for the college student studying entrepreneurship. It will also be useful to owners of small businesses, managers of small businesses, and people who want to start their own business.

Each of the problems presented in *Small Business Management* is identified and analyzed in depth. We have encountered these problems many times in our work with over 150 small businesses and we can assure you that good solutions to these problems, which we have offered here, will help the small business grow and prosper. We can also assure you that when these problems occur in a business, they cannot be safely ignored.

A unique feature of this text is the Case Problems, which serve to introduce the problems in an interesting manner. We feel the many cases included and the way in which they are presented will bring the subject matter to life. We also feel that the cases provide some inexpensive, risk-free experience in dealing with the problems they depict.

The chapters in this book are organized in a logical and efficient manner to help the student or the inexperienced small business operator identify and analyze each problem:

☐ **Key questions** open each chapter to stimulate interest and pinpoint the topics to be covered.

☐ A **Case Problem** introduces each chapter, illustrating key points which will be discussed and analyzed in the chapter. Each case is drawn from actual experience of entrepreneurs; most came from the experience of our consulting clients. Additional cases are also presented in the discussion questions following the chapter. Although the facts concerning each case have been modified somewhat to maintain client confidentiality, the problems actually occurred and were dealt with as described.

☐ **Problem Identification** sections focus on the major issues presented in each case.

☐ **Diagnosis** sections analyze the problems and help to identify where they may be present in your business.

□ **Understanding** sections discuss and analyze the theories behind the problems and explain how to effectively deal with the specific problems presented.

□ Detailed **Case Solutions** at the end of each chapter provide practical answers to the Case Problems.

□ A **Chapter Summary** follows each Case Solution and provides an easy way to check your understanding of the concepts discussed.

The problems addressed in this book have been grouped according to the five parts of the book. Part I deals with the issues to consider when starting a business, including how to decide if you should go into business, developing a plan for the business, and determining the legal structure of the business. Even an experienced entrepreneur will find valuable information presented here.

Part II focuses on how to control the financial aspects of a small business. The chapters in this section provide the tools to use to determine costs of doing business, how to monitor these costs over time, and how to determine how and when costs get out of hand. It also discusses how this data can help you determine what kinds of corrective actions are needed. The sources of funds needed to open, operate and expand a business are also explored, along with specific tools to help control and manage a small business's cash flow. The concluding chapter of the section provides techniques to evaluate major investments needed by your company, especially machinery and equipment.

Part III deals with the many problems a small business owner must solve to effectively market the company's goods and services. We show how to determine what products and services to sell, whom to sell them to, and how to sell to these customers by the use of promotion and personal selling. We also show how to price products and services to yield good profits.

Part IV explains common personnel problems that bedevil small business owners. In this part, we discuss how to attract good employees, how to hire the best, how to motivate them to maximum performance, and how to keep them working for you.

Part V explores several problems that have a number of good solutions, and analyzes how to pick the right solution for a particular business. Included in this part are chapters on taxes, insurance, and selecting a computer appropriate for a small business. This part concludes with a rethinking of the type of business you are involved in, or wish to be involved in, to ensure that you have dealt with all of its special problems.

We do not pretend that this book has a solution for every problem faced by a small business owner or manager. We have made an effort, however, to be thorough in our coverage of each problem we do analyze. Many specialized problems are dealt with in depth in appendices at the ends of selected chapters. In addition, if we found a problem to be too specialized, complex, or technical to deal with within the confines of these pages, we have pro-

vided references for your further research. These references have been selected after extensive review of the available literature on each subject. In addition, the Instructor's Manual contains an annotated bibliography which
expands on the references given in the book and which ranks the usefulness
of each work cited based on a number of criterion.

The Instructor's Manual which accompanies the text includes lecture
outlines for each chapter, teaching notes on how to best deal with the subject
matter, recommended answers to the discussion questions at the end of each
chapter, and a test bank.

We would like to express our appreciation to all of those who have
helped to make this book a reality—our students, our clients, our reviewers,
and the many competent people at West Publishing Company. Our special
thanks to our editors, Ron Harris, Denise Simon, and Marta Reynolds; and
to our reviewers Bruce E. DeSpelder, Wayne State University, Detroit,
Michigan, John Howe, Santa Ana College, Santa Ana, California, Ru-
dolph L. Kagerer, University of Georgia, Louis Mansfield, Kankakee Community College, Kankakee, Illinois, Larry Novick, Brookdale Community
College, Lincroft, New Jersey, Charles D. Phillips, Boise State University,
Joe Ryan, Saddleback Community College, Mission Viejo, California, Bob
Smith, University of Houston, Geoffrey A. Turnbull, Pasadena City College, Pasadena, California, D. Wayne Williams, California State Polytech-
nic University, Pomona, and Richard C. Winkler, Anne Arundel Community College, Arnold, Maryland, for their many insightful comments
regarding early drafts of this book; to Jill Rodriguez, Pat Sawada and Mi-
chele McEwen for their typing; to Jeff Calamusa for his work on the annotated bibliography in the instructor's manual; to Jack Carroll for his research
assistance; and to our wives and children for their encouragement and understanding about the many lost evenings and weekends of family time
which went instead to the writing of this book.

Small Business
Management

Getting Started

PART I

So You Want to Start a Business

1

□ **What are the advantages and disadvantages of going into business for yourself?**

□ **What qualities do you need to run a business?**

□ **What are the major barriers to success in your business?**

□ **How can you determine your business's chances of success?**

CASE
PROBLEM

Farber Child Care Centers

Joan Fargo and Edith Berger formed a partnership to provide child care services in suburban Boston. Joan had a background in elementary education. Edith brought a variety of business and financial skills to the partnership. Edith was to be in charge of the day-to-day operation and administration of the business, and Joan was to develop and manage the child care services. Although Joan and Edith knew that they wanted to provide day-care services, they were not certain of the steps they needed to follow in order to start such a business. They decided that before committing any financial resources to this venture, they would need to answer the following questions:

1. Was it feasible to start a profit-making child care service? Was there sufficient demand to support such a venture?
2. What would it cost to start such a business?
3. What were the licensing and financial requirements for a child care center?
4. Were funds available for the initial financing of the business? Where could they be obtained?
5. Was there any money available from grants, and what were the application requirements for those grants?
6. What kind of competition would they face?

PROBLEM
IDENTIFICATION

So you want to start a business. But where do you start? How can you determine whether or not you should go into business? Like Joan and Edith, you should begin by asking yourself some questions.

The first step is to look at yourself very carefully. You need to weigh the personal considerations of going into business for yourself. If you go into business, you will have to make some difficult choices. Your lifestyle will probably change. You need to decide whether or not you are willing and able to make the commitment that your business will demand. You have to decide whether you have the personal qualities needed to go into business. What does it take—intellectually, emotionally, and physically—to run a business?

Once you have answered these questions about yourself, you need to look at business. What is business? What do you need to know about running a business? Why should you go into business? Why shouldn't you? What will you be up against when you start your business? What are the common barriers to success, and how can you surmount them?

Are you still with us? Good! The next step is to look closely at the kind of business you want to start and decide whether or not your idea has a good chance of success. The best way to do this, without spending all of your hard-earned money on an experiment, is to do a feasibility study. A feasibility study will assess the need for your business, its potential location, the amount of money required to start, and the legal requirements for your type of business.

If your feasibility study convinces you that your business can be started and has a good chance of success, then you may decide to go ahead with it. However, your next step is not to start, but rather to plan.

DIAGNOSIS

Since you are reading this book, it seems a pretty safe bet that you want to start your own business or at least are thinking about it. Beyond your own wants and needs, however, there is the question of whether you should start your own business. For thousands of people every year, the answer to that question is yes. Unfortunately, for many people who go into business, the answer should have been no. For any number of reasons, a large proportion of new businesses fail before they ever get a chance to get going. The purpose of this chapter, and indeed of this whole book, is to help you to make the right decision about whether or not to go into business.

Are you the kind of person who can get a business going and make it succeed? As you evaluate the business that you want to start or buy, you also need to evaluate yourself. The following list of statements will help you in this self-evaluation. It will help you to think about yourself and how you will do in business. Do you agree or disagree with the following statements about yourself? Put a check in the appropriate column.

	Agree	Disagree
I have a strong need to achieve and be successful.	_____	_____
I am willing to take risks.	_____	_____
I am highly motivated.	_____	_____

	Agree	Disagree
I am totally committed to my business and am willing to put in long hours.	_____	_____
I have the discipline to get things done on time and to plan ahead.	_____	_____
I have confidence in myself and my ability to succeed.	_____	_____
I willingly accept responsibility.	_____	_____
I am willing and ready to make decisions and to live with the consequences of those decisions.	_____	_____
I have integrity and am honest in my dealings with others.	_____	_____
I am persistent and constantly strive to achieve my goals.	_____	_____
I take initiative and start things on my own.	_____	_____
I have the kind of personality needed to operate the kind of business that I want to start.	_____	_____
I can exercise restraint.	_____	_____
I am competitive.	_____	_____
I like people and am outgoing.	_____	_____
I am flexible.	_____	_____
I am in good health and have the stamina necessary to run my business.	_____	_____
I am mentally alert.	_____	_____
I understand stress and know how to handle it.	_____	_____
I have a high energy level.	_____	_____
I can analyze problems, determine their causes and arrive at solutions.	_____	_____
I exercise good judgment.	_____	_____
I have good organizational ability.	_____	_____
I understand the business that I want to start and have several years of experience in it.	_____	_____
I can communicate my ideas so that others understand them.	_____	_____

In order to decide whether you should go into business, you should think about four things:

1. Why should you go into business? What are the advantages?
2. Why shouldn't you go into business? What are the disadvantages?
3. What does it take to own and run a business? What personal qualities do you need?
4. What are you up against as you go into business? What are the barriers to success?

Advantages of Going into Business

Going into business for yourself has a number of advantages. First and foremost, it gives you independence. With your own business, you are the boss. Owning your own business is part of the "American dream." Individual ownership of business is at the foundation of a capitalist society.

One advantage of owning your own business is that you become directly involved in all of the decisions that affect your business. Instead of being in the position of recommending changes, you are in the position of listening to recommendations and acting on them. You are in a position to look at the whole business instead of only part of it.

As the owner of a business, you also have a lot of contact with people. You have the opportunity to interact with customers, employees, suppliers, and other business people. You *are* the business in the eyes of many people.

Another advantage is that owning your own business gives you an opportunity to be creative. You can put your ideas to work. You can try new things if you want to. You are not bound by a strict rulebook or procedures manual unless you write one yourself.

In addition, you might make a lot of money. As the owner of a business, the profits are yours. Your income is not limited to your salary.

Perhaps the biggest advantage of going into business is personal satisfaction. You have the opportunity to build something and watch it grow and develop. You can make your business an extension of yourself.

Disadvantages of Going into Business

Despite all of the advantages, there are a number of reasons for not going into business. The biggest reason is risk. All business ventures entail a certain amount of risk. As the owner of a business, you have a significant personal investment of time, energy and money in your business. If your business fails, you will lose this investment.

Small businesses are especially vulnerable to changes in the economy. Because they do not have the resources of large corporations, they may not be able to survive during a recession.

Another disadvantage of owning a business is that it is hard work. It usually requires long hours every day. Eight-hour days, paid overtime, two-week vacations, and paid holidays will become things of the past for you. Even when your business is not open, someone needs to keep the books, check inventory levels, and follow up on all of the details that keep your business operating.

When you are an employee, you need to know only your own job. As an owner, however, you need to know all of the jobs so that you can keep track of what your employees are doing and, if necessary, fill in for them.

Another disadvantage is that, as the owner of a business, you have no one to pass responsibilities on to. Harry Truman used to keep a small sign on his desk that said, "The buck stops here." As the owner of your own business, you may as well get a copy of that sign. You are responsible for all aspects of your business. Whenever employees, suppliers, customers, and creditors have problems, you must deal with them.

Dealing with these problems can be frustrating. You need to listen to the complaints of disgruntled customers and employees and still remain cordial and understanding. You need to accept the shortcomings of those you deal with and find ways to compensate when necessary. You also need to deal with the faceless bureaucrats of government and their rules.

You could probably add to the lists of advantages and disadvantages of owning a business, and it would be a good idea if you did. The reason for making these lists is to help you to recognize that the coin of owning a business has two sides. If you are going to play with that coin, you need to know both of its sides. Once you have an idea of the advantages and disadvantages of going into business, you should also start to think about what it takes to run a business.

Personal Qualities Needed for Success

Some of the qualities you need to go into business have already been implied in our discussion of the advantages and disadvantages of owning a business. These qualities and others needed to run your own business are listed below:

Drive.   In order to own your own business, you need to be a self-starter. You need initiative, perseverance, and stamina.

Intelligence.   You don't need to be a genius to own your own business, but you do need common sense. You need to be able to analyze a problem, evaluate the options available to you, and select the best course of action. You also need to be able to think quickly.

Personality.   A business is not run in a vacuum. It is run by people and for people. Therefore, as a business owner, you need to be able to handle people effectively. You need to be consistent, tactful, cooperative, sociable, friendly, and pleasant. You need to work with people to make your business a success.

Communication Skills.   People need to understand what you want if they are to do it. Therefore, your oral and written communications need to be clear, concise, and understandable.

Technical Background.   Although you may not have to be a technical expert in all phases of your business, you do need some familiarity with them. You need to understand your product—how it is made, what its characteristics are, and what it can and cannot be used for. You won't be much of a plumber, for example, if you don't know an elbow from a tee.

Business Knowledge.   Perhaps more than technical knowledge, you need a knowledge of general business practices. For example, you need to know about record keeping, finance, marketing, personnel, and budgeting. There are many examples of businesses that failed because although their owners knew their particular businesses, they did not know very much about business in general.

Experience.   Have you ever worked in the field that you want to start your business in? If you have, you have a much better chance of succeeding than someone with no experience. Through experience you get to know the ins and outs of an industry. You learn not only the quirks of a business but also its supply sources and its potential clients, customers, and employees. Anytime you start a new job, you need to learn about it. The more you know before you start, the faster you will learn. If you start a business without knowing very much about how it works, you will find you have invested in a very expensive education.

Now that we have discussed the personal qualities needed to be a successful entrepreneur, let's see how you did on the questionnaire in the "Diagnosis" section of this chapter. Did you agree or disagree with most of the statements? If you agreed, then you have the personal traits and knowledge necessary to own and operate your own business. If you disagreed with the majority of the statements, you will find that owning your own business will be rough going for you.

Major Barriers to Success

Building a business is a long and hard road. If you can avoid some of the barriers and pitfalls along that road, the going will be easier and quicker. The following are the factors that most frequently contribute to business failure.

Lack of Experience.   Lack of experience is one of the main causes of business failure. As mentioned earlier, there are two kinds of experience needed to start a business—technical experience in your particular field and general experience in business operations. For example, you will need some knowledge of the following:

The supplies and merchandise used by your business

Selling techniques

The product that you will sell

The financial aspects of the business

The competition and what it is doing.

Insufficient Money.   Another common reason for failure is that many businesses get started without enough money to keep them going. In today's complicated business world, it is very difficult to start a business with scanty funds. Your initial starting capital will be used for a number of purposes:

1. *Operating Expenses.* Cash is needed to cover the day-to-day expenses of operating the business. These include utilities, rent, payrolls, and an allowance for yourself.

2. *Inventory.* Your business will need an initial stock of merchandise. You won't sell anything if you don't have it on the shelves. You need sufficient cash to buy an initial stock plus some extra to replace inventory as it is sold.

3. *Furniture and Equipment.* You may need to acquire some furniture and display fixtures. Although some of these items can be leased, you need to make certain that your business is at least minimally equipped.

Poor Location.   An inappropriate location can also cause a business to fail. You should not select your business site on the basis of the rent alone. Although you do not want to pay too much for your location, you do want to pay enough to get what you need. If you select a site because of its low rent, you may find yourself in a location with no traffic. If no one comes into your business, you will find your cheap rent very expensive. The location that you select for your business should be appropriate for the type of business that you start and should be in an area that attracts customers. It should also be large enough to give you some room for growth as your business expands.

Poor Inventory Management.   The inventory that you stock in your business must be the right type for your market. You also need the right amount of inventory. If you do not have enough, your customers will become frustrated when they cannot find what they want. On the other hand, if you have too much inventory, you may be tying up valuable space and money that could be used more profitably.

Overinvestment in Fixed Assets.   Fixed assets can use up a large amount of your invested capital. Although they are often necessary, fixed assets sometimes limit your business's ability to grow. As you are getting your business started, you might consider renting or leasing the fixed assets that you need. In this way, you can conserve your cash yet still have the facilities you need.

Poor Credit Arrangements Management.   Granting credit to your customers is an excellent way to increase your sales. However, it can also be a good way to get your business into serious trouble. There are three questions that you should answer before you decide to grant credit:

1. Do you have enough capital to afford to grant credit? As you begin to grant credit, you will not have cash flowing into the business. However, you will still need to pay your bills. Therefore you will need to invest enough capital to maintain normal operations.

2. Do you have a set of guidelines to help you to decide who should get credit and who should not? Before you grant credit to any of your customers, you need to reassure yourself that they will pay you what they owe.

3. Do you know how to collect? Some of the people that you grant credit to will pay late or not at all. You need to have the persistence and skills necessary to collect these debts.

Personal Use of Business Funds.   The reason that you are in business is to make a profit for yourself, but your business may also need that money. You should not take more money out of the business for yourself than the business can stand. When deciding how much to take out for yourself, you should remember two things:

1. You cannot take out more than you make in profits. If you do, you will be depleting your invested capital. This is similar to taking money out of your savings account. If you take out only the interest you have earned, your investment remains. When you draw out more than your interest, however, your investment decreases, along with the interest that it could be earning.

2. You need to look at your business's needs as well as your personal needs. If your business is growing, you may need to reinvest your profits in additional inventory, equipment, or other assets. You may also need to increase your equity in the business to put it on a more secure financial foundation. You have to decide whether these needs of your business are more important than a new car for you.

Unexpected Growth.   If your business does extremely well, you may be tempted to expand. This is fine as long as the expansion is planned. If you jump into an expansion without carefully planning it and looking at all of its implications, however, you may find that you have overextended the resources of your business. Instead of increasing your business's profitability, you could endanger it.

Conducting a Feasibility Study

Up to this point, this chapter has helped you to determine whether or not you should go into business. If you have done a careful analysis and looked at all of the pros and cons of going into business, you will have made a decision. If you have decided that you want to start your own business, the next step is to conduct a feasibility study. A feasibility study is designed to help you to determine whether it is possible to open your business and whether its chances of success are good. A feasibility study looks at the following four factors:

1. The market for your product
2. The location for your business
3. The financial requirements for your business and your ability to meet them
4. The legal requirements for your business

In the following sections we give a brief outline of a feasibility study. In later chapters we will discuss in more detail specific portions of the feasibility study. You can then come back to the outline in this chapter and use it to develop a comprehensive feasibility study for your business.

Market Study.   Your market study looks at your product or service and examines how it fits into the market that you are entering. Your market study should have three parts: a product description, a market analysis, and an analysis of the competition.

Product.   What specific product or service do you plan to offer in your business? Your product description should describe your product or service and explain how it is different from that offered by your competition. It should highlight any advantages your product has over that generally available in the marketplace.

Market Analysis.   Your market analysis describes the overall market for your product and identifies the specific target market that you are going to try to capture. Your overall market is the area in which you are planning to locate your business. Your analysis of this market should include a description of the demographics of the population, such as income level, educational level, age, and family size. This information is available in publications of the Department of Commerce and Census Bureau at the library. Your local Chamber of Commerce and local newspaper are also excellent sources.

Your target market is the specific group to whom you plan to sell your product. Your target market can be described as a specific geographic area or age group or income group. You should examine your target market to determine whether there is a demand for your product and, if so, whether this demand is great enough to justify an investment.

Competition.   Your market study should also look at your competition. It should identify who your competitors are, what their strengths and weaknesses are, and how successful they are. If you have a competitor who offers a good product but who is barely surviving, you might conclude that there is insufficient demand for the product. If, on the other hand, your competition is overwhelmed by the market, you may be able to find a place for your business. A solid knowledge of your competition can help you to define your business and select the best products for it.

Location.   Once you have completed your market study, you are ready to start looking for a location for your business. Choosing a location is one of your most important decisions. The Appendix to chapter 12 discusses locating your business in more detail, but some of the key considerations are discussed briefly here. Different types of business have different requirements that determine whether or not a location is appropriate. For instance, a manufacturing plant will have problems if it is located in the middle of a residential neighborhood. No matter what your business is, however, you should consider the following factors as you look for a location.

Nearness to your target market

Accessibility of labor (the right type at the right price)

Availability and cost of utilities

Attitude of potential neighbors toward business and the local tax structure

Character of the neighborhood (does it reflect the "image" of your business)

Room for expansion

As you narrow down the possible sites for your business, you will want to look at the physical requirements of your business and the availability of appropriate facilities in the area. This could affect whether you will be able to lease facilities or need to build or buy your own. As you consider potential sites, you will also want to find out the following:

Zoning restrictions

Cost of facilities and terms of leases

Availability and reliability of materials and supplies

Appropriateness of facilities and the potential costs of remodeling the site to your specifications

Accessibility of storage and parking facilities

If you are going to start a retail or service business, you should also consider the following factors:

Availability of transportation, parking, loading and unloading facilities, lighting, waste and rubbish disposal

Recent trends in population in the surrounding area, especially as they relate to your target market

Proximity to your major competition and similar businesses

General orientation of the neighborhood (regarding property values, cleanliness, crime rate, etc.)

Expected quality of this site five to ten years from now

These are some of the factors that you will want to examine in your search for a location. There may be others that you want to include because of the unique needs of your business. No matter what factors you consider, your feasibility study should tell you whether an appropriate site is available and what it will cost you.

Financial Requirements.   The third step in your feasibility study is to determine how much it will cost you to start your business and how much money your business will need to generate to meet your living expenses. This part of your study should include a personal financial analysis and a statement of start-up costs.

Personal Financial Analysis.   Your personal financial analysis consists of a statement of your monthly living costs and a personal balance sheet listing your assets and debts.

Your monthly living expenses should be broken down into two categories. Some of your expenses will be fixed, and some will be variable. You might find the following lists helpful in developing your statement of expenses:

Fixed Expenses:	House payment or rent
	Car payments
	Installment payments
	Insurance payments (health and life)
	Taxes
	Other
Variable Expenses:	Utilities (telephone, water, gas, electricity, etc.)
	Food
	Personal expenses (cleaning and repairs, dues, automobile gas and oil, subscriptions, charitable contributions, etc.)
	Other expenses

One of the advantages of listing your expenses in terms of fixed and variable costs is that if you need to restrict spending because of the needs of your business, you will be able to see where the cuts can most easily be made.

A personal balance sheet lists your assets and debts and the difference between these two totals, your personal equity. This amount is important because it tells you what you have available to invest in your business or to fall back on if necessary. Your personal balance sheet might take the form of Figure 1.1.

Item	Amount (Market Value)	
Assets		
Residence	$_____	
Automobiles	$_____	
Furniture and Fixtures	$_____	
Tools and Equipment	$_____	
Savings Accounts	$_____	
Stocks and Bonds	$_____	
Insurance (Cash Value)	$_____	
Other Investsments	$_____	
Other Business Investments	$_____	
Other Assets	$_____	
TOTAL ASSETS		$_____
Liabilities		
Home Mortgage	$_____	
Installment Debt	$_____	
Taxes Payable	$_____	
Car Payment Balance	$_____	
Credit Card Balances	$_____	
Other Debts	$_____	
TOTAL LIABILITIES		$_____
Personal Equity (Assets − Liabilities)		$_____

Figure 1.1 Personal Balance Sheet

Start-up Cost.   One of the most important steps in your feasibility study is to determine the cost of going into business. You need to determine all the expenses you will incur as you get ready to open your business. Your list should include the following:

Lease deposit or down payment of facility

Costs of remodeling and site preparation

Opening inventory

Equipment

Utility deposits and hookup charges

Supplies and stationery

Taxes, licenses, and professional fees

Advertising and opening promotional costs

Operating expenses

Other expenses

This list should help you to determine how much money you need to open the doors of your business. However, we advise that you double your estimate, as your expenses may well be twice as much as you expect them to be.

Legal Requirements

There are many local, state, and federal laws that control the conduct of business. Before you start your business, you should become familiar with those regulations that apply to your business and estimate what they will cost you. Keep in mind that the legal requirements for your business will vary, depending upon your legal form of organization. Chapter 3 discusses in more detail what impact your decision to be a sole proprietorship, partnership or corporation has on the legal requirements for your business.

Local Requirements.   Each community has a unique set of rules and regulations that control business. You may find that there are both city and county regulations that affect you. Generally, the following kinds of regulations are controlled at the local level.

Business Licenses and Permits.   Each locality establishes its own system of licenses and permits. The fee and rate structures also vary from one area to another. You should check with your local city hall or county offices to find out what the licensing system and fee structure in your area are.

Special Permits.   Special regulations adopted by cities and counties to cover a wide range of activities may affect you. When you do your research for a business license, you should also find out if any of the following special regulations apply to you:

Zoning compliance and parking permits

Building code compliance

Health permits, especially for food handling and preparation

Law enforcement permits, especially for entertainment establishments

Fire permits

Personal property and inventory tax registration

Special local taxes, such as bed taxes for motels

Fictitious name registration. Many areas require that you register the name of your business with the county clerk and publish a notice of your business's name in a local newspaper.

Other regulations. Localities may also have regulations regarding certain legal forms of business organization, such as limited partnerships, or environmental regulations regarding energy conservation, air and water pollution, and noxious and nuisance emissions.

State Requirements.   Most state regulations that deal with business relate to taxes and employees. The following kinds of regulation generally require you to take some special action:

Sales Taxes.   Since most states have some type of sales tax, you need to collect that tax and forward it to the state tax department. Generally, this will require that you obtain a certificate. You may also qualify for a resale certificate, which permits you to buy merchandise from another merchant without paying the sales tax if you plan to resell it. You could be required to post some type of security deposit on your sales tax remissions. Since the laws governing taxes are usually quite rigid, you should pay careful attention to these regulations.

State Excise Taxes.   If your state has special excise taxes on certain products, you should find out if you are subject to them.

Income Taxes.   State income taxes affect you in two ways. First, depending on the legal form of your business, you may be required to file an income tax return for your business. Second, if you have employees you need to withhold taxes from their wages and forward them to the state tax department. Because the penalties for not complying with these regulations are quite serious, you should take special care to comply with these rules.

Employee Regulations.   If you have any employees, there are a number of regulations that you are subject to:

Unemployment insurance, disability insurance, and withholding taxes are required of most employers in most states. You will need an employer identification number.

Many states also have Workers Compensation requirements. State regulations regarding minimum wages, hours, and working conditions generally correspond to federal regulations. State rules regarding fair employment practices and discrimination on the basis of sex, race, age, or ethnicity also generally follow federal guidelines.

Federal Requirements.   Like state regulations, most federal regulations deal with taxes and employees.

Taxes.   Income taxes are not assessed directly against a business unless it is a corporation. However, if you choose to become a sole proprietorship or partnership, your profits will be taxed as personal income on your annual tax return. In addition to these taxes, businesses are required to collect and make payments for the following:

> FUTA (Federal Unemployment Taxes)
>
> FICA (Social Security): You are responsible for both your employees' deductions and your matching contribution.
>
> Federal Income Tax Withholding

All of these taxes need to be reported on a regular basis, and prompt payment is an absolute necessity. Delay in payment can result in the closing down of your business by the Internal Revenue Service.

In addition to tax regulations, there are a number of federal regulations that deal with wages, hours, discrimination, safety, and other matters. Much of the information regarding these regulations can be obtained from the IRS or the Wage and Hour Division of the United States Department of Labor.

CASE
SOLUTION

Farber Child Care Centers

Joan and Edith started off on the right foot by asking the right questions before going into business. Their feasibility study provided the following information:

The program plan for Farber Child Care Centers needed to address three issues—the educational program, the physical facilities, and the staff. The educational program needed to have certain goals, with a unique program designed for each age group they planned to serve. Activities needed to address the child's total development. The center itself needed to be licensed. It should be physically attractive and equipped with appropriate equipment and toys. It would need to have areas for both indoor and outdoor activities as well as quiet areas, including an isolation room for sick children. Menus needed to be balanced and nutritious. Formal procedures for the release of the children had to be developed. The facility would also have to be safe and clean, with provisions for fire protection, clean water, and toilet facilities.

The staff needed to be adequate in both size and quality for a child care center. Staff members needed to be appropriately trained and sensitive to the needs of both the children and their parents.

In assessing the need for a child care center, Joan and Edith discovered that there was a need and support for the creation of child care facilities. The city planning staff had recognized this need and had planned for the establishment of apppropriate facilities. The city planning office was also able to provide a list of existing day-care facilities in the area.

A realtor was able to provide the partners with some estimates of the cost of appropriate facilities in the areas they were interested in. Further investigation indicated that several companies in the area were interested in a cooperative venture, with child care being one of several options offered to employees in a flexible benefit package. Under this arrangement, Joan and Edith would be able to secure appropriate facilities at a lower cost.

One financing option that Joan and Edith discovered through their research was the possibility of operating the centers as a nonprofit organization. Nonprofit status would permit them to solicit funds from foundations and other charitable organizations. It would also allow them to gain experience in the operation of a business while limiting their financial risk.

The partners discovered that there were several franchise operations for day-care centers. Although these franchises required a substantial capital investment, they did offer helpful services and information that would increase the probability of success for the business. The franchise companies would provide all of the materials needed to open a facility and professional help in site selection and lease negotiations, promotion, insurance, training, compliance with regulations, bookkeeping, and certification.

They were able to develop a set of financial forecasts based on the costs of establishing and operating a child care center meeting minimum requirements. These estimates helped the partners to determine their fee structure.

Based on their feasibility study, Joan and Edith decided to hold back on their plans to start a center for one year. In the meantime, they decided to take the following preparatory actions:

1. They would both secure the appropriate credentials required to operate a day-care center.
2. They would acquire firsthand experience by working in a day-care center.
3. They joined several civic organizations that promoted day-care operations to make professional contacts and make their names known in the community.

They decided that their initial start would be as a nonprofit day-care center. During the period prior to starting, they would research the grants available and apply when the time was right.

CHAPTER SUMMARY

This chapter has explored some of the advantages and disadvantages of going into business for yourself. It has also looked into what it takes from you, both personally and financially, to start a business and has warned you about the pitfalls that you will face.

Going into business for yourself has many advantages. It gives you independence and the ability to make all of the decisions about the business. It also gives you the opportunity to have a lot of contact with people and to be creative. In addition to personal satisfaction, your business may also provide you with a good profit.

However, the coin of going into business for yourself has two sides. In addition to the advantages, there are disadvantages. First and foremost, going into business is risky. You are very vulnerable to uncontrollable changes in the economy. Also, going into business requires a significant investment of time, energy, and money. You need to know all of the jobs in the business, and you are held personally responsible for everything that happens. You run up against countless frustrations. After it is all over, you may well find that you could have made substantially more money by working for someone else and putting your money into a sound financial investment.

To be successful in business, you need a unique combination of personal qualities. You need drive, intelligence, personality, communications ability, a sound technical background, business knowledge, and experience.

You will also find that there are numerous barriers to success. Do you have enough experience in the business that you are going into? Do you have a good understanding of general business practices? Do you have enough money to get started and keep going? Where are you going to locate your business? Other potential pitfalls for your business include mismanagement of your inventory, over investment in fixed assets, credit mismanagement, unexpected growth, and taking too much money out of the business for your personal needs.

If you have looked at all of the pros and cons of going into business, then you need to start a feasibility study. A feasibility study examines the market for your product or service, the potential location of your business, the financial requirements for your business, and the legal regulations that affect your business. Your market study examines the product that you plan to sell, analyzes the overall market and the target market for your product, and reviews the competition that you face. Your location analysis begins with a preliminary search for a suitable site for your business. Among the important considerations are proximity to your target market and appropriateness for your type of business. Your financial analysis includes an analysis of your personal financial status as well as the potential cost of starting your business. The legal part of your feasibility study reviews the local, state, and federal laws and regulations that apply to your business. You might also want to acquire the forms and applications that you need to complete before you can start your business.

The feasibility study is only a first step. If you conclude from your study that you have the necessary personal and financial resources to start a business and that the kind of business you want to start has a good chance to succeed, then you are ready to develop a plan for your business. A business plan uses the feasibility study as a starting point. It provides you with a detailed blueprint of how to start and build your business. The next chapter will demonstrate how to develop a business plan.

DISCUSSION QUESTIONS

1. What are the factors that will make you successful in your own business?
2. List several advantages of going into business. Then list an equal number of disadvantages.
3. What qualities do you need to be successful in business?
4. What are some of the factors that will make it difficult for you to succeed in your business?
5. What should you include in a feasibility study before you start your business?
6. Select a commercial site and evaluate it as a potential site for your business.
7. Prepare a personal financial analysis.
8. Determine the rules and regulations in your locality that affect your business.
9. Acquire copies of the forms that you need in order to comply with your state tax laws. These include applicable forms for sale taxes, excise taxes, employee taxes, and income taxes.

REFERENCES

Bank of America. *Steps to Starting a Business*. San Francisco: Small Business Reporter, 1976.

DeCarlo, J. F., and Lyons, P. R. "A Comparison of Selected Personal Characteristics of Minority and Non-Minority Female Entrepreneurs." *Journal of Small Business Management* 17 (1979): 22–29.

Hull, D. L.; Bosley, J. J.; and Udell, G. G. "Renewing the Hunt for the HEFFALUMP: Identifying Potential Entrepreneurs by Personality Characteristics." *Journal of Small Business Management* 18 (1980): 11–18.

Jackson, P. B. *A Guide to Starting a Business, Buying a Business, Financing a Business*. Sacramento: Office of Small Business Development, State of California, 1979.

Powell, J. D., and Bimmerle, C. F. "A Model of Entrepreneurship: Moving Toward Precision and Complexity." *Journal of Small Business Management* 18 (1980): 33–36.

Small Business Administration. *Checklist for Going into Business*. Small Marketers Aid number 71. Washington D.C.: U.S. Government Printing Office, 1975.

State of California, Commission for Economic Development. *Doing Business in California: A Guide to Establishing a Business*. Sacramento, 1979.

Planning for Success | 2

☐ How do you develop a budget that works for you?

☐ How do you develop a long-range plan for your business?

☐ Why should you develop a business plan?

CASE
PROBLEM

George's Foreign Car Service Center

George Paulson had always wanted to be a mechanic. In high school he had taken all of the shop courses that he could. You could count on finding him under someone's car every weekend. George spent several years working as a mechanic in a used car lot. While there, he noticed that there were more and more foreign cars available. Therefore, he decided to specialize in foreign cars, especially economy models such as Volkswagons and Japanese cars. When he felt that he had enough experience, he leased an old gas station and opened up George's Foreign Car Service Center. His first customers were people who had purchased their cars on the used car lot. Eventually word got around about George's skill and honesty, and his business slowly grew. Eventually, George was able to hire his younger brother as a part-time helper.

However, as George's business grew, he ran into some problems. He found that although his business was successful, he wanted it to grow even more. One weekend, while watching a football game, he started to sketch out a list of some of the problems that he was having and some of the goals that he wanted to achieve:

1. He found that he frequently missed payments and deadlines. He had been late making payments to his vendors several times and had already missed one sales tax payment. He also seemed to be unable to put some of his ideas into action. He would get a good idea, but somehow it kept being put off.

2. He found it difficult to keep track of his inventory of parts and supplies. Several times recently he had found that he did not have the parts needed to complete a job. This had resulted in unnecessary delays and several backlogs of work.

3. George wanted to add another service bay to his shop. Although he had the space, another bay would require that he invest in a new door and hydraulic lift.

4. George felt that he would soon be able to hire another mechanic if his work volume continued to increase.

5. George wanted to increase his sales. Although they had been growing steadily, he wanted them to grow even faster. He realized that an increase would be necessary if he were going to add a new bay and hire another mechanic.

It is very difficult to identify the planning problems in a business. This is because the biggest planning problem of many businesses is that they do not do any planning. Although it is a critical step in developing a successful business, it is the one most frequently overlooked.

PROBLEM IDENTIFICATION

Do you have a plan for your business? Your answer to that question should be yes. If you do not have a plan, you should develop one immediately. If you are just starting out, a plan will help you to plot the direction that your business will develop in. It will outline the steps that you need to take to be successful. It will help you to avoid costly mistakes, and it will help you to become more profitable.

George took the first step by sitting down and writing out his problems and goals. However, his list illustrates his lack of planning. Missing payments to his creditors and the government shows that he has not anticipated and planned for these expenditures. His stock problems could be solved by implementing an inventory plan that insures both a basic stock of common parts and an arrangement with a parts supplier to obtain special parts quickly. However, the greatest indicator of a lack of planning is reflected in his goal to add another bay and hire a mechanic. Has he analyzed the need for another lift? Why does he need another mechanic? Is his current work load too much or is he going to add the mechanic in the hope that this will generate additional business? A last question that George needs to ask is what will the impact be on his business if his sales do increase? George is an example of a common problem of small businesses. They tend to move forward without any real idea of where they are going, and often no idea of where they have been. Good planning will help to alleviate this problem.

Are you good at planning? This section will help you to diagnose your planning skills. As you read through the business plan outline below, ask yourself how many of the planning questions you have already thought about. If you have already begun to develop ideas in most of the areas covered in the outline, you are on the way to becoming a good planner. If you have not at least thought about these questions, you need to now. This chapter will show you what it takes to plan for success.

DIAGNOSIS

Planning is one of the most important, and most frequently overlooked, steps in developing a successful and profitable business. Can you start a business without a plan? Unfortunately, yes. You can also be very successful without a plan—maybe. What a plan does is to increase your chances of success. Since statistics indicate that your chances of failing are better than your chances of succeeding, you should take advantage of anything you can that puts you on the success side of the scale. The two most important things a plan does are to help you to determine where you are going and to alert you to the problems that you might encounter along the way. Problems will always occur in your business; but if you reduce the number of unexpected problems, you will be able to keep your business on the track to success. A plan is like a gas gauge in a car. If it is working, you know what you need to get where you are going. If it is broken, you are never quite sure of what you need. That may be fine—until the day you are crossing the desert right after someone has siphoned the gas out of your full tank.

A plan for your business does not need to be elaborate to be useful and effective. The following simplified business plan outline should help you to begin to develop a plan for your business:

What kind of business do you want to be in?

Where do you want your business to be?

What do you want to accomplish with your business?

What is your market?
   Whom do you want to sell to?
   What is your competition?
   What product do you sell?
   How can you reach your market?

What is your marketing strategy?
   What is your pricing policy?
   What sales terms will you offer—cash and/or credit?
   What methods will you use for selling and distributing?

How will you organize your business?
   How many employees do you need, and what qualifications do they need?
   What form will your organization take?

Does your financial plan have—
   a sales forecast?
   a cash forecast?
   an expected return on your investment?

UNDER-STANDING

Now that you have some idea of what the planning process is, let's take a closer look at planning and its benefits to you. This chapter is a guide to creating a workable business plan. The model plan at the end of the chapter directs you to other chapters that focus on specific parts of the plan.

A business plan has several benefits:

1. *It is a map for your business*. It tells you where you are going and how to get there. It helps you to get your business where you want it to be.

2. *It can be used as a communications tool*. You can use it to keep your employees, suppliers, bankers, and anyone else who needs to know about your business informed about its direction and goals. These people need to know where you are going in order to help you to get there, and they can help more if they know where you are going.

3. *It will improve your ability to predict the future*. These predictions can help you to take advantage of opportunities and avoid pitfalls.

4. *It can help you with bankers and creditors*. If they know what your intentions are, they may be more willing to grant you favorable terms. The information in your plan helps them to decide whether to grant you credit. A business that has a clear idea of where it is headed, as shown in a plan, is a much better credit risk.

The length and detail of a business plan are up to you. However, a plan that is too short or which contains little detail is not very useful. On the other hand, a book takes too long to write and may bog you down. The most important aspect of a plan is its usefulness.

Your business plan should be divided into the following major sections corresponding to the major considerations in starting and operating a business:

1. A definition of the business

2. A marketing plan for the business, including a market analysis, a description of the product or service that is offered, and the marketing strategies that will be used

3. An outline of your inventory and how you will handle it

4. A description of the organization of your business

5. The financial requirements and data of your business

The above outline represents the minimum amount of information to include in a business plan. You may decide that you want more information in your plan.

There are also two additional factors related to developing a business plan.

1. You should make a provision for feedback and control so that you will know whether things are going according to plan. Feedback will help you to make any necessary adjustments.

2. The plan should be updated on a regular basis. A plan should not be an ironclad document that cannot be changed. Instead, it should be adjusted to take into account new developments and changes that occur naturally over time.

The business plan is your tool for achieving success in your business. The remainder of this chapter is designed to help you to develop each part of the business plan.

Business Definition

What business are you in, or what business do you want to get into? That is the fundamental question that you need to ask yourself as you begin developing your business plan. You might say to yourself, "Of course I know what business I'm in. I'm a mechanic (or builder or plumber or children's clothing store retailer)." But is that an adequate definition of your business?

You should start to develop your definition by writing a brief description of the industry that you feel your business is a part of. You should then describe how you see your business fitting into that industry. Once you have a broad view of the business you want to get into, you should begin to narrow your focus and make the definintion of your business more personal and specific. You can do this by asking yourself a series of questions:

What is your business trying to do?

How much of it do you want to do?

Who else is doing it?

What is different about the way that you do it?

As you answer these questions, the real definition of your business will start to come alive. Your answers will enable you to do the following:

List the main services or product lines that your business provides.

Determine what you expect your most profitable activities to be and rank them in their order of profitability.

Determine what you do not do that similar businesses might do.

Your thoughts on the above issues will help you to focus in on the actual definition of your business. After you have come to a set of conclusions about your business that you are happy with, you will be able to complete this statement:

My business is _____

_____

Your answer can be as long or as short as you want, but is should be a clear, concise, and specific statement of the purpose and goals of your business.

Marketing Plan

Once you have developed a solid definition of your business, you will be in a position to develop the meat of your business plan. The first step in this development is to plan the marketing aspects of your business. The marketing section of your plan is a good starting point because it will give direction and proportion to the rest of your plan.

A marketing plan has three parts: a market analysis, an analysis of your product or service, and a description of the marketing strategies you will use.

Market Analysis.   A market analysis or market study gives you a clear picture of where you stand in the marketplace that you are about to enter. Your market analysis should focus on four issues: the overall market, the target market, the competition, and the industry trends.

Overall Market.   What is the overall market that you are trying to reach? How would you describe it?

The overall market is the area in which you plan to locate your business and from which you will draw your customers. A description of your overall market should include the following:

Location of the market

Population of the market area

Age of the population of the market

Distribution of earnings in the market

General description of the major industries or employers in the market area

General level of economic activity and expected trends in the local economy

There may be additional factors that you want to include in your description. What is important is that you give an accurate and clear description of the overall market that you intend to enter.

Target Market.   Your target market is that group of customers within the overall market from which you expect to attract your primary customers. Your target market can be described in several ways. For example, it can be a geographic area. Most grocery stores expect to draw the majority of their customers from an area within a certain radius of the store. Neighborhood phone books reflect geographic target markets. Age can also define target markets. A children's wear store will probably want to focus its efforts on parents with young children. However, an excellent secondary target market might be grandparents. Income can also describe a target market. Some boutiques try to attract customers with above-average earnings. Therefore, the products that they sell are those that fall within the taste and affordability ranges of this market. You might also describe your target market in terms of a particular industry. For instance, most of the businesses around an airport are there to service either the airplanes or their passengers.

As you can see, you can describe your target market from several different perspectives. What is important is that you define that particular part of the overall market that you are going to focus your marketing efforts on. If you define your target market too broadly, you may find that your promotional efforts are spread too thinly and do not have the desired impact. On the other hand, too narrow a definition may limit your efforts and restrict the potential of your business to succeed.

Competition.   Whom are you going to compete against when you attempt to sell to your target market? A good knowledge of who the other sellers in your marketplace are will help you to determine what strategies you should use and how you should use them. It can also tell you which markets have unmet needs and which are completely filled. Since the nature of your competitors will help to determine what you do, you need information about them. For instance, you might want to know the following about your competitors:

How many other sellers are in the market, and how large are they? Is the competition prosperous, barely surviving, or swamped by excess demand? What is the growth rate of your competitors? How many of them have recently entered the market, and how fast has their volume increased? Which of your competitors do you expect to be your biggest rival?

A thorough knowledge of your competition can help you to decide whether you should enter a particular market, how to enter it, and when to enter it. It can also help you to determine the potential for success.

Industry Trends. What direction is your particular industry headed in? Is it a growing industry with increasing demand and rising sales? Or is it at maturity or declining? Calculators and computers, for example, have been strong in the 1980s. Many industries, however, have declined during the same period. Nineteen eighty-one was generally not a good time to open a new car dealership.

Product Plan. The product section of your marketing plan should describe your product, list its special advantages, compare it with products of competitors, and provide sources of supplies.

Description. A complete description of your product or service is a necessary part of your plan. If you are selling or manufacturing a product, you should include a description of what your product is and what it does. A retail store's product description will outline the various kinds of goods stocked by the store. If you are opening a service business, you should list the kinds of service that you will provide.

Special Advantages. If your product has any special advantages, you should describe them in your plan. For example, patents or copyrights, technological advances, or particular expertise or special credentials can give you a competitive edge that should be highlighted in your plan.

Comparison to Competitors. Your plan should describe your position in relation to your competitors, focusing on your strengths or advantages over them. However, you need to look realistically at the advantages that your competitors hold. A realistic appraisal of your position can help you to exploit your strengths and improve in areas where you are weak.

Supply Considerations. Where are you going to get your merchandise and supplies? The supply section of your plan should indicate who your suppliers are, where they are located, and what arrangements you have with them for purchasing and shipping materials. You need to decide whether you are going to buy from wholesalers or directly from manufacturers. You also need to assess the reliability of the distribution system that you are going to use.

Marketing Strategies.   The first two sections of the marketing plan—the market analysis and the product plan—indicate where you are going to sell your products, whom you are going to sell it to, and exactly what it is you are going to sell. The marketing strategies section of your plan details *how* you are going to sell your product.

Your overall marketing strategy begins with your image, or how you want or expect people to perceive your business. To a large extent, your image needs to reflect your target market because your image is what will attract customers to your business. Your image also will determine the kinds of promotional technique you use. An exclusive boutique will rely on tasteful decor and personal service, while a discount variety store will use utilitarian decor, self-service, and quick check-out.

You should keep in mind that image is more important to some businesses than others. Retail stores and service businesses, for example, rely more on image than manufacturers and junk yards. A manufacturer's image is more apt to be reflected in the quality of the product than in the quality of the front office.

Once you have decided what kind of image you want your business to have, you will use this image to develop a marketing strategy to reach your customers. A marketing strategy focuses on four factors: pricing, customer service, advertising, and promotion.

Pricing.   Product pricing is related to both the cost that you pay for products and the quantity that you sell. Of these two factors, cost is more important. You must charge enough for your products to cover their cost and leave you something for overhead and profit. Therefore, an important part of your pricing plan will be to acquire merchandise which has a price range that is consistent with the image and target market of your business.

The amount that you add to your cost to cover overhead and profit is your markup. The actual amount that you mark a product up is partially determined by the volume that you expect to sell. If you expect a high sales volume, your marketing strategy may call for a smaller markup than if you expect a low sales volume.

Customer Services.   The second component of your marketing strategy is to offer customer services. Although customer services will cost you money, they will also encourage sales for your business. You need to determine what services you will offer based on the type of business you are in and your own desires.

One of the most important services is your sales terms. Are you going to sell on a cash basis, or will you grant credit? If you grant credit, will it be through an in-house system or will you use a bank card like VISA or Mastercard? If you are going to grant credit, it will have a cost, and you will need to cover this cost in your pricing structure.

Some of your customer services will be determined by the type of business you are in. For example, a jewelry store cannot be run on a self-service basis, and a variety store will probably not offer a high level of personal service. You should provide the kinds of customer service normally expected in your type of business.

You should also assess the types and levels of service that your competition provides and determine which, if any, you want to provide. You should decide whether you want to add any services not provided by your competitors. These unique services could give you a competitive edge. They could also help you to establish the image of your business.

A small bank was recently started. It offered the full range of banking services in order to compete with the established banks in town. In an effort to gain an edge, it added two unique services. One was a 24-hour teller, the first one in town. The other service was sit-down banking: all customers were able to sit at table height when conducting business with the tellers. Both of these services were unique and contributed to the bank's image of friendly service.

Advertising. You need to announce your product if you expect anyone to buy it. Therefore, your advertising plan is also an important dimension of your marketing strategy. Your advertising plan should have two parts. First, it should state what you want to say about your business. Second, it should describe how you will communicate this message.

The first step in developing your advertising plan is to set goals for your advertising campaign. To develop a focus for your plan, you should ask yourself several questions:

What are the strongest points of my product or business?

What makes my business and product different from those of my competitors?

What facts do I want my customers to know about my business and its products?

The second part of the advertising plan is to determine where your advertising will be placed. There is a wide variety of media that you can use for advertising. It includes TV, radio, newspapers, direct mail, door-to-door flyers, point-of-sale displays, such as your business's sign, and other media. Not all of these media will be appropriate or effective for your business. Therefore, this part of your advertising plan should determine which media are effective for your business and the cost of using them.

Because your advertising funds are limited, you can do only a limited number of things with them. Your plan should show how you are going to use the most effective combination of advertising media within your budget.

Promotional Methods. While the purpose of advertising is to get customers into your business, the purpose of promotion is to get them to buy once they are in. Your promotional strategy will include some combination of the following:

Layout

Merchandise displays

Signs

Price markings (or the lack of them)

Personal selling

You may want to add to the list. Each type of business has unique promotional factors. One of the most important promotional factors is you. Don't forget that most people will see your business in you.

Once you have decided what promotional methods you are going to use, you should deterine how much each will cost you. You may need to acquire display counters, racks, and other special equipment to show your merchandise. You may also need to hire appropriate sales personnel. The cost of these items becomes a part of your plan.

Inventory Plan

Retail and manufacturing businesses need to plan for inventory. There are two dimensions of inventory planning—buying and handling. Buying includes selecting and purchasing those materials needed in your business. Handling includes arrangements for receiving, storing, and preparing merchandise. It also includes controlling your stock so that you have enough to meet your needs.

Buying. You should have already decided what kind of material to buy when you chose your business's target market and image. The next step in your buying plan is to decide where you will get your merchandise. Depending on the kinds of merchandise that you stock, you may need to acquire your materials from a number of suppliers. In compiling your list of suppliers, you should list the items that you need and the names and addresses of potential suppliers. You may find that your suppliers are product manufacturers. However, in many instances, you will need to purchase merchandise from jobbers and wholesalers or even other retailers.

You should also compile a list of the terms offered by each potential supplier. This can help you to determine the best supplier for your needs. You should get the following information for each supplier:

The sales terms that are offered (credit, discounts, etc.)

The delivery schedule

The cost of delivery (freight charges) and who pays it

Minimum order quantities

This information will also help you to plan the cost of your inventory and to schedule your ordering so that you have sufficient inventories to meet your sales requirements.

Handling.　Once you have determined where you are going to get your materials, you need to plan how you are going to receive and store the merchandise. You will need a system for receiving merchandise. This system will help you to keep an account of what has been received and when. This will enable you to keep a running inventory and insure that you pay only those invoices for which you have received materials.

The complexity of your receiving system will depend on the volume of merchandise that you receive. If you get only a few shipments, you can get by with a simple manual system. As the size and complexity of your inventory increases, however, you may need a more complicated system to keep track of things.

Your storage system should accomplish several tasks. It should keep your materials secure, usable, and available. This means that your receiving and storage area needs to be well organized. Different kinds of storage system are available for these purposes. Your plan should include a provision for a storage area and appropriate shelving or bins to keep materials sorted and accessible.

You should also plan the level of staffing needed to operate your receiving and storage area. You may be able to do it yourself on an as-needed basis. However, as your business grows, you may need to hire a special staff.

Organizational Plan

Your organizational plan helps you to do what you are in business for—to make a profit. It tells you who does what and why with whom. The organization part of your business plan should include an organizational chart, a method to determine how many employees are needed, and a job description for each position in the business.

An organizational chart shows whom people report to and who is primarily responsible for which functions in the operation. It should make your business work better. If you have a small organization with only two or three employees, your organizational chart will show everyone reporting to you. However, as a business grows in size and complexity, it is no longer feasible for the owner to direct everyone. Therefore, an additional structure is added to the business to make certain that it operates efficiently. A simple organizational chart is illustrated in Figure 2.1.

Your organizational plan should also include some way of planning how many employees you need in your business. If you have a retail store, you will need enough sales people to cover all of your business hours. You will also need staff to provide additional coverage during your busy periods. As your sales staff increases, you may also need to make provisions for office help. You need to remember that your job is to manage the business. If you spend all of your time in the office posting your books or on the floor making your product, you may not be making the best use of your time. Your staffing formula can be quite simple. However, its main function is to help you to decide when to add to or reduce your staff.

A job description is a simple outline of the tasks that each person in the business needs to perform. The easiest way to prepare a job description is to make a listing of the jobs that need to be done in your business and then assign those jobs to the people that you have. The following is an example of a simple job description for a sales clerk:

JOB DESCRIPTION: Sales Clerk

Sells merchandise to customers

Arranges display shelves and keeps them stocked

Cleans sales area

Takes inventory at appropriate times

Receives, unpacks, and counts merchandise that is received and checks it against invoices

Other tasks as needed

The main purpose of the job description is to help you to assign your staff to the most important tasks in your business. You should also make provisions in your organizational chart and job descriptions for cross-responsibility so that employees will be able to do fill-in work when someone is gone or when the demands on a certain area are excessive. For instance, your holiday office staff might help on the sales floor during sales and holiday rush periods.

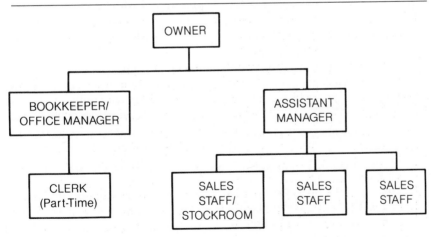

Figure 2.1 Organizational Chart—Anderson's Variety Store

Financial Requirements

Up to this point, your business plan has been expressed in words. Now it is necessary to express those words in dollars and cents. The financial part of your business plan should consist of a listing of your start-up costs, a budget, and pro forma financial statements.

Start-Up Costs. How much money do you need to get going? This question has two answers. First, you need enough to get a place for your business and a starting inventory. Second, you need to make certain that you have enough money to keep you going until your business is on its feet.

In order to plan for the start-up costs of your business, you should make a list of those expenses that you will incur before you ever open your door. For most businesses, they will probably include the following:

Fixtures and equipment

Starting inventory

Equipment installation

Rent deposit or down payment on facilities

Initial utility deposits

Decorating expenses

Licenses and permits

Advertising

Professional fees (accountants and lawyers)

Operating expenses

You may have additional expenses, but this list should give you a good idea of your start-up costs. The last expenditure, operating expenses, may be the most difficult to estimate. How do you know how much your business is going to cost to operate before you even open your doors? The best way to estimate this is to develop a budget.

Budget. A budget is a plan that converts ideas about operating a business into dollars. Your budget should be based on your expectations of sales and expenses. Although budgeting will be discussed in more detail later, you should be able to sit down right now and make some estimates as to how much your business will cost to run. Figure 2.2 can help you to organize your estimates.

As you develop your budget, you should keep several things in mind:

1. Your budget should be realistic. Do not estimate hugely optimistic sales figures that guarantee a profit. On the other hand, you should not make unnecessarily low projections.

2. Use as many sources as possible to develop your budget. The obvious first source is yourself, but you should also ask your suppliers and your bank-

er for advice. They should have comparable figures for businesses like yours. Since they also have a stake in your success, they should be willing to help.

3. Remember that businesses go through cycles of peaks and valleys of activity. Make provisions for these cycles in your budget.

4. Keep in mind what your plan is telling you. If you find that you will have a cash deficiency, make provisions for it in your start-up budget.

5. Use the other parts of your plan to develop your budget. For example, your marketing plan can help you to develop reasonable sales projections. Your buying plan can help you to plan inventory costs. Your organizational chart lays out personnel costs. Since your business plan is an overall view of your business, you should use it as one: its parts are not isolated from one another.

Pro Forma Statements.   A pro forma financial statement is an estimate of what you expect your business's financial picture to be at some point in the future. It has two benefits for you. First, it helps you to see where your business is headed. Second, it helps to reassure your banker and creditors that

	Month 1	Month 2	Month 3
Net Sales			
Cost of Goods Sold			
Gross Profit			
OPERATING EXPENSES			
Salaries			
Sales Staff			
Owner Manager			
Advertising			
Utilities			
Rent			
Maintenance and Repairs			
Insurance			
Telephone			
Interest			
Taxes			
Delivery Expenses			
Other Expenses:			
__ __			
__ __			
TOTAL EXPENSES			
Net Profit			

Figure 2.2 Operating Budget

you are planning where your business is going, rather than letting things happen as they will. Your accountant and banker should be able to help you to develop pro forma statements.

If you develop an operating budget along the lines of Figure 2.2, you will have an *estimated income statement*. A pro forma balance sheet lists your assets, liabilities, and equity. Although chapter 4 goes into more depth on how to develop a balance sheet. Figure 2.3 shows what one looks like.

Your accountant and banker should be able to help you develop a pro forma statement. It has two benefits for you. First, it will help you to see where your business is headed. Second, it will help to reassure your banker and creditors that you are planning where your business is going, rather than letting things happen as they will.

Feedback and Control

The best way to find out whether your plan is working is to use feedback. One source of this feedback is your financial statements. These provide you with an ongoing picture of what is happening to your business. Besides showing you what your profits are, they can provide a broad variety of other information on the status of your business. Future chapters will explain in more detail how you can use financial statements.

One drawback to financial statements is that they can be used only after they have been developed. Sometimes there is a lag between the end of a fiscal period and the preparation of the statements. Another difficulty is that fi-

ASSETS			
Current Assets:			
Cash	$$$		
Accounts Receivable	$$$		
Inventory	$$$	$$$$	
Fixed Assets:			
Buildings and Land	$$$		
Equipment	$$$		
Furniture and Fixtures	$$$	$$$$	
Total Assets			$$$$$
LIABILITIES			
Accounts Payable	$$$		
Notes Payable	$$$		
Long Term Debt	$$$		
Total Liabilities		$$$$	
EQUITY		$$$$	
Total Liabilities and Equity			$$$$$

Figure 2.3 Balance Sheet (Pro Forma)

nancial statements may not be prepared as often as you need them for feedback and control.

You can also use budget comparison reports for feedback on the effectiveness of your planning.

A budget comparison report compares the actual results of your business with your budget. For instance, by comparing your weekly or monthly sales with your budgeted sales for the period, you can get a quick reading on how you are doing. You can also total your expenses each month and compare them to your expense budget. These comparisons tell you very quickly whether you are performing to your expectations. This kind of feedback will help you correct any problems that appear before they become too serious. It might also tell you what you are doing right so that you can continue to do it.

Another quick feedback device is your cash level. Your budget will give you an idea of how much cash you should have left every month. If most of your sales are for cash, this surplus, or deficit, will be very close to your profits. Therefore, by keeping a close eye on your cash balance, you will have an ongoing picture of your performance. However, one word of caution: Do not make the mistake of thinking that your cash balance is your profit. It isn't. Your cash balance is a barometer that you can use to check how your performance compares with your plan. Like a barometer, it does not tell you whether it is raining or shining. It tells you only what the chance of rain or sunshine is. To find out what condition your business is in, you'll have to check by reading your financial statements.

Figure 2.4 illustrates a budget comparison report for the Smarte Sette, the business illustrated in the sample business plan at the end of this chapter. The budget comparison report indicates that the business sold $2,000 more than forecast but overall lost $100 more than it expected to. A quick glance at the expenses shows that both salaries and advertising were substantially higher than budgeted. Since these accounts are readily controllable, they should be carefully reviewed by the store's owner. The higher-than-normal professional services may be due to initial start-up problems that will not be recurring items. This kind of budget comparison allows you to focus quickly on problems and discover possible strong points that you can use to increase your profits.

Updating

A business plan is a living document. It is not cast in bronze forevermore. It can, and should, be changed when necessary. One of the few things that will be constant about your business is that it will change.

There are many factors that can cause the conditions that affect your business to change. The most obvious is the state of the economy. Most small businesses will quickly reflect any economic changes that occur in their surrounding communities. For instance, if a new company moves into your area or an old one closes up, your business's sales might be affected. Changes within your company might also prompt you to change your plans. For instance, you might hire some especially capable sales people who cause your sales to surge, or you might see your normal customers start to change in age or income. The technology that affects your business might also shift. Imagine what might happen to you if you were in the office supply business and continued to sell rotary calculators in a world where electronic calculators and microcomputers are readily available at low prices.

In order to keep your plan effectively updated, you should follow these suggestions:

Be alert to change, and recognize it when it occurs.

Determine how the change will affect your business.

Make any necessary adjustments in your plan so that further changes can be spotted and adjusted for.

Your plan will change as your business grows and matures. After you have been in business for a while, you will no longer need to put as much emphasis on the definition of your business, and start-up costs will not be as important. However, it will be more important to update other areas of your plan.

You will also need to make changes in your plan to reflect significant changes in the environment around your business. There may be a shift in your target market. For instance, if your business is in a rural area, you have defined your target market in one way. If a major new industry comes into your community, you may find that you will need a new target market to prosper. You will also find that your plan needs to be modified as old com-

MONTH ___September___

YEAR ___1982___

ITEM	BUDGET AMOUNT	ACTUAL AMOUNT	DIFFERENCE
Sales	40,000	42,000	2,000
Cost of Goods Sold	24,000	25,200	1,200
Gross Profit	16,000	16,800	800
Salaries	5,900	6,300	400
Advertising	1,800	2,400	600
Taxes	680	680	–0–
Supplies	1,100	1,000	(100)
Professional Services	800	1,300	500
Insurance	750	750	–0–
Rent	2,550	2,550	–0–
Other Operating Expenses	3,400	2,900	(500)
Depreciation	490	490	–0–
Total Operating Expenses	17,470	18,370	900
Operating Income (Loss)	(1,470)	(1,570)	100

Figure 2.4 Budget Comparison Report

petitors leave the market and new ones enter. The methods you use to reach your market need to be kept flexible in order to adapt to change. For instance, if a small weekly newspaper that you use for the majority of your advertising closes, you will have to shift your advertising dollars to another medium, such as direct mail, to continue to reach your customers. Your pricing policy, credit policy, and the methods that you use to sell and distribute your product may also need to be modified as the community and the market that you are in change over time.

All of these changes will have an impact on your business plan. The most obvious part of your plan that you will need to change is the organizational plan. As your business grows and matures, new employees will be brought in. Therefore, you will need to modify your organizational chart and job descriptions to reflect the changing structure of your business and the changing responsibilities of your employees.

The financial part of your plan will also change constantly and therefore require frequent updating. As you gain experience, you will develop more accurate and useful sales forecsats. You will have a better understanding of the cycles that your business goes through, and you will be able to predict growth and decline more accurately. Experience will also help you to develop a better operational budget. Your previous financial statements and your budget comparison reports will help you to make more accurate forecasts of your expenses. Both the sales forecast and the operating budget will help you to develop more accurate and timely cash forecasts. Your plan will also include a capital budget plan as you expand your business and replace aging or outdated equipment.

A business plan is useful. It can help you to put your business on a profitable footing quickly. Therefore, the best thing that you can do for your business is to develop a plan and use it.

George has taken the crucial first step in managing his future and the direction of his business. He has written down a list of his problems and ideas. Working from this list, George should next take steps, such as those suggested below, to get his business going in the right direction:

1. George should set up a calendar to keep track of his deadlines and due dates. For instance, if his taxes are due on April 15, he might write "prepare tax return" on March 15 on the calendar. The calendar can also be used to set deadlines. For example, George might put a definite date down to investigate the cost and availability of a new door. The calendar could also help George to schedule his daily work flow. He should already have a pretty good idea of how long it takes to do a particular kind of job. Therefore, if a customer wants an engine overhauled, the calendar can be used to make the appointment. It can also alert George not to schedule any other large jobs for that day so that he will be able to finish the overhaul schedule. It can also alert him to order the required parts.

CASE
SOLUTION

*George's
Foreign Car
Service
Center*

2. George should also use a tickler file, which is a file that keeps track of due dates. For example, when a bill that is due on the tenth of the month comes in, he would just stick it into the slot for the tenth. Then on the tenth, he would check that slot to see what needs to be done on that day.

3. George should set aside a secure area for parts storage. Each kind of part should have its own storage area. If necessary, a card should be kept on each item so that he can readily see when a particular item is low in stock. He should also make arrangements with a parts supplier so that he can get special parts quickly and has a ready supplier for his normal inventory.

4. George should get a cost estimate on the new service bay. Once he has an estimate, he can determine how much new business he needs to pay for the equipment.

5. Before George hires a new mechanic, he should determine the sales level that will be necessary to keep this mechanic busy and generate enough money to pay his wages.

6. George should determine the best ways to attract new customers and increase business from his current customers. He should set up a customer account card with the name and address of each customer and a list of the dates and types of service rendered. He could then send these customers follow-up cards reminding them of suggested services or announcing periodic specials, such as a discount on tune-ups. He could also come up with a sales gimmick, such as a free lube job, to get the names of new customers and to build goodwill.

This is only a short list of the kinds of steps George could take to improve his business. What is important is that he review his problems and ideas and develop specific plans to deal with them.

CHAPTER SUMMARY

Developing a business plan is the first and most important step to take when starting a business. A plan has several important benefits for you and your business. It serves as a map that tells you where your business is going and as a communications tool that tells those you depend on about your business. It also helps you to predict problems and opportunities.

Your business plan has several important sections:

1. A definition of what your business is and how it fits into the industry that it is part of.

2. A marketing plan, which describes and analyzes the market that your business is in, the product that you are selling, and the strategies that you will use to sell that product.

3. A description of your inventory, how you will buy it, and how you will handle it.

4. An organizational plan, which describes the structure of your business and the jobs of all employees and how they relate to one another.

5. A financial plan, which includes a list of the start-up costs of your business, an operating budget detailing what it will cost to run your business, and pro forma financial statements illustrating the expected financial picture of your business.

Your business plan also helps you to set and control the destiny of your business. It provides feedback on how well you are doing in relation to what you had expected. It also helps you to control your business so that the direction it takes is the one you want it to.

DISCUSSION
QUESTIONS

1. What are the major issues that should be addressed by your business plan?
2. What are the major sections of a business plan? List and describe each of them.
3. Write a clear and concise definition of the business that you would like to start.
4. Describe the target market of the business that you would like to start.
5. Describe the competition that you will face in your selected market.
6. Prepare two organizational charts for your planned business. The first should reflect how it is organized on the day you open. The second should represent its organization three years after you opened.
7. Prepare job descriptions for three employees (including yourself) that you expect to have in your business.
8. Develop an operating budget for three months for your business.
9. Develop a pro forma balance sheet for your business for the day you open.

REFERENCES

The following publications of the Small Business Administration will be of use in developing a business plan:

Basic Budgets for Profit Planning. Management Aid Number 220

Breaking the Barriers to Small Business Planning. Management Aid Number 179

Business Plan for Retailers. Small Marketers Aid Number 150.

Business Plan for Small Construction Firms. Management Aid Number 221.

Business Plan for Small Manufacturers. Management Aid Number 218.

Business Plan for Small Service Firms. Small Marketers Aid Number 153.

Planning and Goal Setting for Small Business. Management Aid Number 233.

These publications are available through the Small Business Administration, P. O. Box 15434, Fort Worth, Texas 76119, or a Government Printing Office outlet.

Appendix A

MODEL BUSINESS
PLAN OUTLINE:
THE SMARTE
SETTE

This chapter has explored the process of developing a business plan. What follows is a sample of what a business plan looks like. If you use this model plan in conjunction with the other sections of this book, you will be able to develop a workable plan for your business that greatly increases your probability of success. When you prepare your business plan, use this outline as your table of contents.

I. BUSINESS DESCRIPTION/DEFINITION (See chapter 9)
   A. Place within Larger Industry
   B. Purposes/Goals
   C. Main Services/Products
   D. Most Profitable Activity
   E. Similarities to/Differences from Competition

II. MARKETING (See chapters 9–10)
   A. Market Analysis
      1. Overall Market
         a. Location
         b. Population
         c. Age
         d. Earnings
         e. Major Industries/Employers
         f. General Economic Activity Level/Expected Trends
      2. Target Market
      3. Competition
         a. Number of Competitors
         b. Relative Prosperity
         c. Growth Rate
         d. Number of New Competitors
         e. Biggest Rival
      4. Industry Trends
   B. Product (See chapter 10)
      1. Description
      2. Advantages
      3. Comparison with Competitors
      4. Supply Considerations
   C. Marketing Strategies
      1. Image (See chapter 11)
      2. Pricing (See chapter 13)
      3. Advertising (See chapter 11)
         a. Message
         b. Media Placement
      4. Promotion (See chapters 11–13)
         a. Layout
         b. Merchandise Displays
         c. Signs/Price Markings
         d. Personal Selling (See chapter 12)
         e. Customer Services
            1. Sales Terms
            2. Personal Services
            3. Competitors' Services

III. INVENTORY (See chapter 6)
    A. Buying
    B. Handling (Receiving/Storage)

IV. ORGANIZATION (See chapter 3, 14–16, 19)

V. FINANCIAL REQUIREMENTS (See chapters 4–8)
    A. Start-Up Costs
        1. Fixtures
        2. Starting Inventory
        3. Facilities
        4. Decorating
        5. Licenses/Permits
        6. Advertising
        7. Professional Fees
        8. Operating
    B. Operating Budget
        1. Sales Forecast
        2. Cash Forecast (See chapter 8)
    C. Pro Forma Statement

Business Description and Definition

BUSINESS PLAN FOR THE SMARTE SETTE

The Smarte Sette is a women's retail clothing store offering better-to-high-quality name-brand and designer merchandise. It focuses on the kinds of clothing worn by professional women, wives of professional men, and women who want to emulate this group. Its principal product lines are office wear, such as suits and better dresses; sport and casual wear; and evening wear. It is expected that the suits and better dresses will be the most profitable product line and account for the greatest volume of sales. Evening wear is expected to be the least profitable. Sport and casual wear will carry a modest markup. The casual wear line will be the source of most store specials and loss leaders. The store will carry some seasonal merchandise, such as swim suits in the summer and coats in the winter; however, the selection will be limited. The store will not carry any speciality sportswear, such as tennis outfits, or any shoes. Merchandise will be carefully selected to reflect the store's image of high quality.

Marketing

Market Analysis.   The store is located in Jonesville. This is a moderate-sized city with a population of 45,000. It is part of a metropolitan area with an overall population of 135,000 within a 40-mile radius. Because the city is the largest urban area within the region, it functions as the retail trade center for the metropolitan area. It is approximately 60 miles from a major urban area with a population of 650,000. The age distribution of the population is normal. However, there is a fairly large group in the 30-to-50-year age range. This is due to the type of industrial complex in the area.

The area has three major industrial complexes. One is a large chemical research facility with a large number of professional employees. The second is an electronics assembly and research company. The third industrial complex is a relatively new industrial park in the northeast section of the city. This area has attracted a number of small-to-moderate-sized manufacturing companies. It is also the location of several warehousing and distribution facilities.

The city is also in the center of an established farming district. Agriculture has been a basic industry for the area for many years. However, because of the presence of a major highway and rail line, manufacturing has been becoming progressively more important in the last fifteen years.

Target Market.   The store's target market is women from the age of 25 to 50 who come from families with average incomes of $25,000 to $50,000 per year. Approximately 30 percent of the population falls into this category because of the community's industrial mix.

Competition.   There are currently five women's wear stores in the area. One will be in direct competition with this store. A second carries a better quality line; however, it carries a slightly less expensive line overall and tends to cater to a clientele older and more conservative than this store's target market. The other three stores tend to carry a less expensive line of goods and cater to a broad spectrum of shoppers.

The store that will be in direct competition appears to be doing quite well. Its shelves are well stocked with current and seasonal merchandise. It has a steady clientele. Although the store has grown in the past few years, it appears to have reached the limit of its expansion in its current location. The second store also appears prosperous, but it too appears to have maximized the potential of its location. The other stores have enjoyed mixed success. They have all been in existence for at least five years, but two of the stores have changed hands at least once during that period.

Because of the prosperity of the existing stores and their limited potential for expansion, it is felt that there is adequate demand for another store. Because only one of the existing stores caters to the selected target market, it is felt that there is more than sufficient demand to make this venture successful.

There is no major regional shopping center in the area. Therefore, there are no main line department stores selling merchandise similar to this store's to compete with. Because the population in the area is relatively stable at present, there is not sufficient demand for a regional shopping center with main line department stores. Although it is possible that such a shopping center could be established within the next five years, it is felt that there is adequate time for this store to develop a regular clientele and get established in the market.

Industry Trends. The trend for the store's product line and target market appears to be strong. More women are selecting professional careers than in the past.

The store's product line will include better quality women's clothing. A special emphasis will be placed on natural fabrics, such as wool, silk, and cotton. The advantages of these fabrics lie in their wearability, durability, and comfort.

Contacts have already been established with appropriate manufacturers and wholesalers to provide the product line desired.

Marketing Strategies. The store will project an image of conservative sophistication. Where possible, this will be conveyed through the use of antiques and Victorian decor. The use of antique items will be selective to provide a tone rather than an overwhelming presence. The entire shop will be carpeted in a neutral shade.

Pricing. The merchandise lines that will be carried will be in the medium-to-high price range. The average markup will be 40 percent of the retail price. Sportswear will average slightly less (30-35 percent) and evening wear slightly more (45 percent).

Customer Services. The store will accept credit sales. Most credit sales will be made with bank credit cards, such as Mastercard and VISA. Some preferred customers will be granted in-house credit through special accounts. It is expected that 45 percent of sales will be for cash and the remainder for credit. The following personal services will be offered:

Low cost alterations

Free parking

Personal selling (There will be at least two sales personnel on the selling floor at all times. All customers will be addressed by a sales person within one minute of entering the store.)

Customer lounge (There will be a comfortable seating area in the center of the store. Free coffee, tea, and wine will be available).

Advertising. Store advertising will emphasize the following points:

Quality of merchandise

Advantages of natural fabrics

Personal attention

Because of the particular nature of the market for the store, the majority of the advertising will be done in the following media:

Two major newspapers: 60 percent of advertising budget

Flyers and direct mail: 10 percent of advertising budget

Three major radio stations: 20 percent of advertising budget

Other media: 10 percent of advertising budget (special ads in school yearbooks, company magazine, church news-letters, etc.)

Promotional Strategies. The front window will be used for special displays, such as seasonal clothing. The sales desk will be located in the front of the store to simplify security against shoplifting. The general merchandise layout is illustrated below.

Merchandise will be displayed on open racks and in glass display cabinets. Racks will be high enough to keep merchandise off of the floor. Each item of merchandise will have a price tag attached, with an inventory control number as well as the size and price. Merchandise will be displayed so that customers can browse freely. Display racks will be adequately separated so that the store has an uncrowded appearance.

Inventory

Buying. Merchandise will be bought by the store owner. Arrangements have been made to attend three merchandise conventions during the next six months. In addition, a major merchandise mart is within 150 miles. This merchandise mart has offices for manufacturers and wholesalers, including the manufacturers of all the major lines to be carried in this store. Initial investigations have indicated that most items can be delivered to the store within two weeks of placing an order. Small orders and fill-ins are available through the merchandise mart. It is expected that one buying trip will be made to the merchandise mart each month to keep the inventory balanced.

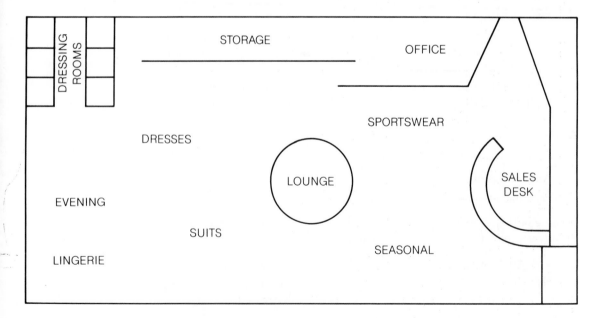

Receiving and Handling. Merchandise will be received and prepared for sale in the stockroom of the store. The stockroom will be equipped with appropriate marking equipment. A small press and iron will also be available to steam wrinkles out of merchandise. A cleaning plant is nearby to take care of more serious problems. A discount of 30 percent has been arranged with the plant owner.

A cash register with a built-in inventory control system will be used. This will permit daily monitoring of stock levels.

Organization

An organization chart is presented below. The principal responsibilities of each person are as follows:

Owner/Manager—administers all management aspects of the business, buys merchandise, arranges advertising, maintains customer relations

Sales Supervisor—supervises sales staff, arranges merchandise displays, sells to customers, schedules sales clerks

Office Manager—serves as bookkeeper, inventory manager, payroll clerk, supervisor of stock clerks, and credit manager

Sales Staff—sells to customers, keeps track of merchandise, maintains sales floor

Stock Clerk—unpacks and prepares merchandise for display, checks merchandise receipts against invoices, manages stockroom, performs general janitorial services.

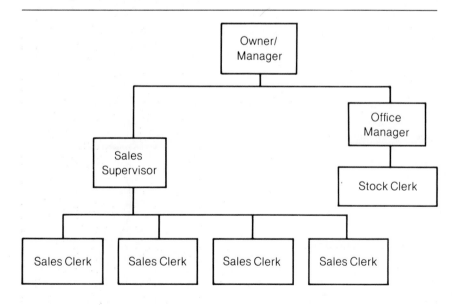

Figure 2.5 Organization Chart for The Smarte Sette

All personnel will do general tasks required around the business. The basic responsibility of all employees will be to provide services to customers.

During the initial stages of the business, it is expected that only five employees will be full-time: the owner, sales supervisor, office manager, stock clerk, and one sales clerk. All others will be part-time.

The owner has had extensive experience in retail clothing. For the past twelve years she has worked for a major West Coast department store chain. She has worked as both a department manager and a buyer for women's clothing. She also has a bachelor's degree in marketing with a concentration in merchandising.

The sales supervisor has six years of retail clothing experience. She has been on the sales staff of a major department store and has most recently been the department manager for women's wear. She has an associate degree in retail management.

Financial Requirements

The following charts and tables illustrate the many financial requirements and considerations necessary when starting your own business.

Table 2.1   Start Up Costs

Fixtures & Equipment		
Sales Racks	$8,000	
Furniture	4,500	
Storage Shelves (Stock)	2,000	$ 14,500
Starting Inventory		120,000
Equipment Installation		3,000
Rent (6 months at $2,550/mo. + deposit		20,400
Decorating/Store Setup		12,000
Licenses, Permits, Deposits		800
Advertising (6 months at $1,200/mo.)		7,200
Professional Fees (100 hrs. at $60/hr.)		6,000
Initial Operating Expenses (6 months)		
Office Manager		9,000
Sales Supervisor		7,200
Sales Staff		8,000
Stock Clerk		3,800
Utilities		2,400
Other Operating Expenses		6,000
Cost to Start		$220,300
Owner Living Expenses (6 mos. at $1,500/mo.)		9,000
Contingency		60,000
Funds Required for Starting Business		$289,300

Table 2.2   One-Year Sales Projection

	SALES FORECAST	
	Monthly Sales	*Total Sales*
September	$40,000	$ 40,000
October	45,000	85,000
November	50,000	135,000
December	80,000	215,000
January	70,000	285,000
February	60,000	345,000
March	50,000	395,000
April	40,000	435,000
May	50,000	485,000
June	50,000	535,000
July	40,000	575,000
August	40,000	615,000

Table 2.3   Operating Buget for Four Months

		OPERATING BUDGET			
		September	*October*	*November*	*December*
Net Sales		$40,000	$45,000	$50,000	$80,000
Cost of Goods Sold (60 %)		24,000	27,000	30,000	48,000
Gross Profit		16,000	18,000	20,000	32,000
	Industry				
Operating Expenses:	*Average*				
Salaries	15.3%	5,900	7,700	8,840	12,140
Advertising	2.9	1,800	1,500	1,600	1,800
Taxes	1.7	680	765	850	1,360
Supplies	2.2	1,100	1,100	1,100	1,100
Professional Services	1.4	800	800	800	800
Insurance	1.2	750	750	750	750
Rent	5.0	2,550	2,550	2,550	2,550
Other Operating Expenses	8.5	3,400	4,050	4,250	6,800
Depreciation/Amortization		490	490	490	490
Total Operating Expenses		17,470	19,705	21,230	27,790
Operating Income (Loss)		(1,470)	(1,705)	(1,230)	4,210

Table 2.4 Cash Flow Worksheet

CASH FLOW WORKSHEET

Receipts	Sept	Oct	Nov	Dec	Jan	Feb	March	April
Cash Sales	18,000	20,250	22,500	36,000				
Collections on Account	4,400	13,550	23,475	39,275				
Other Receipts								
Total Receipts	22,400	33,800	45,975	75,275				
Cash Payments								
Inventory Purchases		25,000	30,000	25,000				
Salaries	5,900	7,700	8,840	12,140				
Taxes	680	765	850	1,360				
Rent	5,100	2,550	2,550	2,550				
Insurance	2,250			2,250				
Supplies	1,100	1,100	1,100	1,100				
Advertising	1,800	1,500	1,600	1,800				
Overhead	3,400	4,050	4,250	6,800				
Equipment								
Note Payments	2,600	2,600	2,600	2,600				
Other Cash Payments	1,600		800	800				
	24,430	45,265	52,590	56,400				
Net Cash Flow	(2,030)	(11,465)	(6,615)	18,875				
Beginning Cash	5,000	5,000	5,000	5,000				
Balance (Shortage)	2,970	(6,465)	(1,615)	23,875				
Loan Requirement	2,030	11,465	6,615	---				
Loan Repayment	---	---	---	18,875				
Ending Cash	5,000	5,000	5,000	5,000				
Potential Excess Cash	---	---	---	---				

Table 2.5 Balance Sheet

BALANCE SHEET (PRO FORMA)

September 1, 1983

Assets

Cash – Checking		5,000	
– Savings		20,000	25,000
Accounts Receivable			–0–
Inventory			120,000
Prepaid Rent			7,650
Prepaid Insurance			3,600
Total Current Assets				156,250
Furniture & Fixtures			14,500
Leasehold Improvements			15,000
Investment (Long-Term)			80,000
Total Fixed Assets				109,500
TOTAL ASSETS				265,750

Liabilities & Equity

Note Payable				140,000
Owner's Investment				125,750
TOTAL LIABILITIES & EQUITY				265,750

Legal Forms of Organization

3

□   Which legal form of organization is best for you?

□   Can you avoid the most common partnership pitfalls?

□   Should you incorporate?

CASE
PROBLEM

*Oh So
Good!, Inc.*

Three midcareer professional men, Paul, Harry, and Fred, had met at a tennis club they all belonged to and became good friends. They often talked about starting a business with their combined savings and hiring an experienced manager to run it for them. In 1975 opportunity knocked. An experienced, energetic restaurant manager named Mary joined the tennis club and expressed an interest in leaving her present job for a new position. Mary had no desire to own her own business but did want to work at a good restaurant location where her hard work could pay off with year end bonuses. Shortly after meeting Mary, Fred learned that a new shopping center was opening in the neighborhood and had space available for a restaurant. Fred reported this to Paul and Harry. The three of them talked to Mary. She liked the location and said she would be willing to manage the restaurant. She even provided the three men with a list of needed equipment and a proposed layout for the restaurant.

At this point Paul, Harry, and Fred were very excited. However, they knew that owning a restaurant was a risky business. They didn't mind risking a portion of their savings on the business, but they didn't want to gamble everything. Harry had heard that if a corporation were formed to operate the business, owners of the stock could not lose any more than what they had paid for the stock if things went badly. This sounded good to all three of them. They went to an attorney, who prepared the incorporation papers. In a few weeks Oh So Good!, Inc.[1] was born. Paul, Harry, and Fred each owned one-third of the stock. Each had paid $10,000 for his stock to provide the capital to get the company started.

Next, the three men approached the owner of the shopping center. The owner was willing to lease to them but insisted that each of the three sign the lease personally in addition to signing as a corporate officer. This dismayed the three because it made them each personally liable for five years of lease payments. Still, no other locations in the area appeared nearly as good; so they decided to take the chance.

Next, the three men approached their bank to get a loan to buy the cooking equipment and furniture for the restaurant. They ran into the same problem. The bank would not lend anything unless each of them personally signed the corporation's promise to repay the loan. Further, the bank would lend only 50 percent of the value of the equipment and insisted that the three pay cash for the rest. Since the equipment cost $70,000, this meant each man had to contribute another $11,667 to the corporation. At this point, Paul and Harry were beginning to have some reservations about the whole matter but decided to go along with Fred, who was still enthusiastic, because they were already hooked on the lease and needed to do something fast with the rented space.

For the next few months things went well. The restuarant improvements were completed rapidly, and the store opened on schedule. Mary proved to be a competent manager. At the end of the first six months the store showed a small profit. At Fred's urging, this was reinvested in more equipment.

Then things went sour. Business dropped off. Losses grew over the next three months. Over Fred's objections, Paul and Harry made it clear to Mary that they blamed her for the losses. Mary got angry and within two weeks quit to take a better position with a restaurant chain.

At this point the restaurant was losing $2,000 per month. By the end of the year the restaurant had had four managers and had lost $24,000. Fred was convinced the most recent manager was the spark that the business needed and could turn the business around. Paul and Harry were not so sure.

Things came to a head when the three stockholders met with their tax accountant to have their taxes done for the first year of operation. Their accountant noted that the corporation's tax loss could not be deducted on the men's personal returns. Paul and Harry were upset about this. When the accountant told the three they would have to contribute still more capital to the corporation to keep it going, Paul and Harry rebelled. They said they would put no more of their money into the business, even if that meant it would go broke, and stormed out of the room.

Fred was stunned. He was convinced that the restaurant had good prospects, but he owned only one-third of the stock. If Harry and Paul wanted to quit, he was powerless to do anything about it. He knew that if the restaurant were closed immediately, the bank would foreclose on the equipment and probably leave nothing for Paul, Harry, and Fred to split. Further, who was going to make the lease payments? Fred wondered how he had gotten himself into this mess and how he could get himself out.

PROBLEM IDENTIFICATION

The problems of Oh So Good!, Inc. should make it clear that the choice of the legal form of organization for your business is a serious matter. A good choice can help your company to grow while an inappropriate one can cause severe problems.

The choice you make will affect all facets of your business—from the amount of red tape you have to deal with to the motivation of your employees. Your choice will determine your degree of liability for your business's debts. It will affect the amount of control you have over the business. It will affect your ability to raise money and the taxes you pay. It will even affect how much you or your heirs can sell the business for in the future.

Your company's legal form of organization should not be selected hastily as you rush to get your business started. Invariably, taking the time to think this matter through carefully will benefit you greatly. The choice of your legal form of organization is an important part of your business plan.

DIAGNOSIS   How do you figure out which legal form of organization is best for you? The answer is that you must first determine your needs. Then you must evaluate how each legal form of organization helps you or hurts you in trying to satisfy these needs.

In this section we present several questions that will help you to determine what you need from your legal form of organization. We will also help you determine the relative importance of these needs to you. In the next section we will discuss how well each of these needs can be met by each legal form of organization. Reviewing your answers to the questions in this section will then permit you to choose the best legal form of organization for you. Your final choice should be double-checked with legal and tax experts to insure that you have taken all of your important needs into consideration and understand clearly how your needs are served by the legal form of organization you have in mind. Exhibit 3.1 presents the questions designed to determine what you need from the legal form of your business. Answer these questions before reading further.

Once you have answered the questions in Exhibit 3.1, the next step is to rank them in order of importance to you. To do this, assume you have 100 points to distribute among the eight questions. All 100 points must be assigned, with the most points going to the question that is most important to you, the second greatest number of points going to the second-most impor-

---

Exhibit 3.1   What Do You Need From Your Legal Form of Organization?

Instructions: Answer each question by choosing one of the five responses shown.

1. Does it matter to you if the legal form of organization you choose requires a lot of paperwork to organize and operate? Minimizing red tape . . .

Is of No Importance To Me	Is of Little Importance To Me	Is of Medium Importance To Me	Is Very Important To Me	Is Extremely Important To Me
_____	_____	_____	_____	_____

2. Does it matter to you if the legal form of organization you choose protects your nonbusiness assets from being sold to pay business debts if your business goes broke? Minimizing my personal liability for business debts . . .

Is of No Importance To Me	Is of Little Importance To Me	Is of Medium Importance To Me	Is Very Important To Me	Is Extremely Important To Me
_____	_____	_____	_____	_____

3. Do you care whether or not your business continues to operate after you withdraw from its management or die? Continuation of the business after my withdrawal or death . . .

Is of No Importance To Me	Is of Little Importance To Me	Is of Medium Importance To Me	Is Very Important To Me	Is Extremely Important To Me
_____	_____	_____	_____	_____

4. Do you care whether or not you or your heirs are able to sell your interest in your business for a fair price should you die, decide to retire, etc.? Getting a fair price for my interest in the business . . .

Is of No Importance To Me	Is of Little Importance To Me	Is of Medium Importance To Me	Is Very Important To Me	Is Extremely Important To Me
_____	_____	_____	_____	_____

5. Will you need to raise a lot of money to get your business started and make it grow? The ability to raise money for my business . . .

Is of No Importance To Me	Is of Little Importance To Me	Is of Medium Importance To Me	Is Very Important To Me	Is Extremely Important To Me
_____	_____	_____	_____	_____

6. Is it necessary that you personally control the business, making all the important decisions that guide the company's progress? Management control . . .

Is of No Importance To Me	Is of Little Importance To Me	Is of Medium Importance To Me	Is Very Important To Me	Is Extremely Important To Me
_____	_____	_____	_____	_____

7. Will it take more than one highly motivated individual to make your business prosper? Will having your employees feel they have a long-term stake in your business be helpful? Making my employees feel they have a personal stake in my business . . .

Is of No Importance To Me	Is of Little Importance To Me	Is of Medium Importance To Me	Is Very Important To Me	Is Extremely Important To Me
_____	_____	_____	_____	_____

8. Is one of the reasons you are starting this business that you want to shelter some of your present income from taxes? Reducing my current income taxes . . .

Is of No Importance To Me	Is of Little Importance To Me	Is of Medium Importance To Me	Is Very Important To Me	Is Extremely Important To Me
_____	_____	_____	_____	_____

tant question, and so on. For example, if question 2 is the only one of importance to you, you might give it 100 points and each of the other seven questions no points. Perhaps questions 2 and 8 are of high, and about equal, importance to you, while the rest of the questions are of low importance. You might then give 35 points each to questions 2 and 8 and 5 points to each of the other six questions. Assigning points is your choice, but they must add up to 100 for the eight questions. If one question is twice as important to you as another, it should get twice as many points.

UNDER-STANDING   In this section we will discuss several legal forms of organization and explain the major advantages and disadvantages of each. Our objective is to give you an understanding of the nature of the choice you face when deciding which legal form is best for you.[2] At the end of the chapter we will summarize the pros and cons of each form of organization in a convenient chart. Reference to this chart will help you to solve the difficult problem of choosing an organizational form.

Attributes of Legal Forms of Organization

In discussing the advantages and disadvantages of the major legal forms of organization, it is helpful to think in terms of eight attributes:

1. Red Tape
2. Liability
3. Continuity
4. Transfer of Interest
5. Ability to Raise Money
6. Management Control
7. Motivation
8. Taxation

Each of these attributes corresponds to a business need or problem that you may want your legal form of organization to address. In the "Diagnosis" section you estimated how important each of these needs is to you. We will now discuss each attribute in detail to give you a more precise idea of its importance to you and how it is affected by your legal form of organization. This will give you a better understanding of the advantages and disadvantages of the various organizational forms.

Red Tape.   The first attribute, red tape, refers to special procedures or paperwork that you have to complete. This includes the paperwork involved in setting up your business, reports required by government bodies, tax returns, and reports to investors. Generally speaking, the more passive certain owners of your business are, and the more dependent they must be on your business judgment, the more red tape you will have to generate to prove you are acting in their best interest. Also, if an organizational form has special tax advantages, the red tape required to prove you deserve those advantages increases markedly. Red tape consumes your money and your valuable time. Just how significant a cost the extra red tape for a more complex business form is cannot be judged without looking at its benefits also. For example, many small business owners with modest incomes find that the benefits they derive from being incorporated are not worth the $1,000 or so they spend per year in the extra red tape costs of a corporation.

Liability.   Liability is the second attribute. All of us, of course, are liable for our actions. If we commit a crime or fail to live up to our word, the parties we injure have a right to seek legal recourse from us.

When going into business, owners can in some cases limit their liability for the money they will owe if their business fails to the amount of their investment in the business. In other words, with the right legal form, if your business goes broke despite your best efforts to make it work, your business creditors can claim only the assets of your business for repayment. They cannot force you to sell your home to pay off your business debt. This concept of limited liaiblity is quite attractive. Many business owners consider incorporating in order to get limited liability protection. The trouble is that most creditors know how limited liability works and will not grant you credit as the principal owners of a small corporation unless you personally pledge to honor the debt. Therefore, in most cases, corporate limited liability does not really offer much protection to a small business owner.

Still, if you can offer limited liability to your investors, it makes your business a much more attractive investment for them. With limited-liability protection, the most they can lose is the money they invest. Even though you may lose your house if the business fails, they know they cannot lose theirs. We will come back to this point when we discuss the fifth attribute, the ability to raise money.

Certain legal forms of organization increase your liabilities. This occurs when you take on a partner. Unless your liability is otherwise limited by the nature of your legal form of organization, having a partner increases your liability because you become liable for your partner's business-related acts as long as your partner has the real or apparent authority to act. In other words, your partner can, in some cases, commit you to contracts when he/she has no business doing so. You also can be responsible for any acts of fraud, negligence, or deceit that your partner commits while transacting company business. You can even be held criminally liable for your partner's acts in certain instances. It is no wonder that the issue of liability is a major consideration when establishing a partnership.

Continuity.   The third attribute that you can use to evaluate organizational forms is continuity. Continuity refers to the ability of a legal form of organization to continue to function if an owner dies or drops out of the business.

Of course when the key person in a small business dies or becomes disabled, the business may simply cease to function no matter what it's form of legal organization. In many cases, however, once your business is well established, others are ready and able to fill your shoes; and your business can live a healthy life after you are out of the picture if you make adequate provisions for continuity in advance.

If you share ownership of a business with others, you need to pay especially careful attention to the issue of continuity. Otherwise, after you leave the business, your family may lose all of its interest in a valuable company and receive little or nothing for it.

The question of continuity also arises when one of several owners wants to drop out, perhaps to move on to bigger or better things. The legal form of organization and the way you have handled red tape will determine whether this change in ownership leads to routine paper shuffling or to accusations, recriminations, and lawsuits.

Transfer of Interest.   Transfer of interest is the fourth attribute you should consider when evaluating legal forms of organization. In some regards, this attribute is similar to continuity since it refers to the ability of owners to sell their interest in a company at a fair price while the company continues operation. What we are really getting at when we talk about transfer of interest is the ease with which investors in your company can sell their ownership interests to others. These investors, or silent partners, have little or no interest in running your business. They rely on you to do that. They are interested, however, in how easily they can get their investment out of your company if they need their money for an emergency. The legal form of your organization can make transfer of ownerhsip easy or hard. The easier it is for investors to buy and sell ownership interests in your company at a fair price, the more attractive your company will be as an investment. If you are trying to raise money for your company, transfer of interest is a very important consideration.

Ability to Raise Money.   The fifth attribute that distinguishes legal forms of organization is the ability to raise money. Your ability to raise money depends on several other attributes of your organizational form. We have already discussed liability, continuity, and transfer of interest. These attributes color the perceptions investors and lenders have of your organization and therefore affect your ability to raise money. The attributes of management control and taxation, which will be discussed below, also affect your ability to raise money.

What are investors and lenders looking for? What does it take to attract their money? Invariably, lenders and investors want to feel they will get back any money they put into your business, along with a fair return, or profit. They need to be convinced that you have the ability to repay them. For lenders, this can mean calculating the forced-sale value of your assets to make sure it is more than the money you want to borrow. For investors, it can mean deciding whether or not you will be around long enough to turn your dreams for your company into reality. Both lenders and investors, of course, want you to be fully committed to your business. The harder they feel you work and the smarter they feel you are, the more willing they will be to trust you with their money.

If you look at your organization from the standpoint of the people who put up the money, it is not too surprising that your legal form of organization can make a big difference to them. If your business is a sole proprietorship, they worry that one mishap, such as your death, will destroy the company. If your business is a corporation, they worry that your limited liability will also limit your commitment to the company's success; but at the same time they are happy about their own limited liability as stockholders. If your business is a partnership, they may like the idea that several partners are pooling their resources to build the company.

There is another way your form of organization affects your ability to raise money. If you want to raise money for your business from several passive investors, government regulations governing securities offerings require that you offer them clearly defined ownership interests. As a practical matter, limited partnerships and corporations are the best ways to pool the capital of several passive investors since these organizational forms offer investors clearly defined ownership interests, in addition to limited liability.

Management Control.   Management control, the sixth attribute, is also affected by your legal form or organization. Depending on the legal form of organization you choose, you may have absolute control over your company or be only a minority where the majority rules. Often control means more than simply guiding the company to profitability. It can also mean acting to prevent fraud or other questionable acts by those representing the company. Even if you are in control, your legal form of organization determines the degree to which you must listen to the management suggestions of those who own small pieces of your company.

Motivation.   The seventh attribute that can be used to evaluate organizational forms is motivation. The way you set up your organization will have a significant impact on your ability to motivate those who work for you. The issue of motivation centers on how ownership is held in your company and on how easy it is for an employee to become an owner. An owner is motivated by having a stake in the business. Depending on your legal form of organization, it can be easy or difficult to offer employees ownership interests in the business as payment for a job well done.

Taxation.   The eighth, and final, attribute that distinguishes the various types of legal organization is taxation. The amount and timing of taxes to be paid are the principal issues. Individuals have higher tax rate schedules than ordinary corporations. Consequently, you might have more money available after taxes to finance company growth if it is a corporation than if it is a sole proprietorship. However, if you take your money from the corporation to spend on yourself, you will have to pay taxes on it again. Your form of organization also affects your ability to write off business losses against your personal income.

Concerning the timing of tax payments, there may be real advantages to having your personal tax year end at a different time from your company's tax year. This is possible when you and your business are not one and the same. For example, in a partnership or a corporation, if your business has a good year, a little tax planning can permit you to use a good part of the money for up to eleven months before you pay taxes on it.

Major Forms of Legal Organization

Now that we have discussed each of the eight attributes, the next step is to define the common legal forms of organization and to evaluate each in terms of the eight attributes. You will then understand the pros and cons of each organizational form and be ready to decide which is best for you.

There are five distinctive types of legal organization for you to choose from: sole proprietorship, general partnership, limited partnership, corporation, and S Corporation.

Sole Proprietorship.   The sole proprietorship has often been called the simplest form of legal organization. You are the sole owner. You have total management control. You make all the major decisions and are responsible for everything. The legal red tape involved in setting up a sole proprietorship is minimal. You may, for example, have to buy a business license; or if the name of your business does not include your own name, you may have to file a ficticious name statement and publish this statement in the paper.

When you operate a sole proprietorship, you are personally liable for all the debts of your company and for any misdeed committed in the company name. Still, since you are the only owner in the business, you don't have to worry about being responsible for the acts of co-owners.

Continuity can be a problem since when you die, the legal life of your business ends. However, there is a variety of ways to get around this problem, particularly if you have an experienced employee who is eager to buy the business. If arrangements to sell are made in advance, your customers may hardly notice that you no longer own the business.

The problem of transfer of interest is difficult for any small business, no matter what its legal form of organization. Generally, your sole proprietorship will have very little value to your heirs if you have not made provisions for transferring your interest to an interested buyer before your death. Lessors and creditors, through painful experience, have learned to move in quickly when a sole proprietor dies. They are less interested in continuing the business than in recovering their money by selling the assets. If a well-qualified buyer with a proven track record is not ready to fill your shoes, creditors would indeed be foolish to wait for your heirs to try to pick up the pieces. The hard fact is that you cannot expect your heirs to get anything near the real value of your sole proprietorship unless you plan ahead. You simply have no interest to transfer if you die before providing for continuity.[3]

Generally, the only way a sole proprietor can raise money is through a collateral loan. Your promise to repay each dollar must be backed up with pledged collateral, such as equity in real estate, stocks, bonds, life insurance policies, inventory, or accounts receivable, which the lender can turn into cash if you fail to repay your loan. If you do not have enough collateral, the lender may require you to find someone to cosign your loan. Cosigners are not easy to come by. You may have to give cosigners part of your business to get them to sign. Even when you get the money from the lender, it may have several strings, or restrictions, attached. These restrictions can require you to do such things as buy insurance, maintain the property, keep your cash or working capital above a minimum level, or maintain inventories at a certain level.

As you may have gathered from the above, although you have total management control in a sole proprietorship, you may find it difficult to grow without conceding some management control to people like cosigners or lenders. Also, the advantages of total management control may be more than offset by the difficulties of having to deal with many problems outside your areas of expertise. In other words, although you control everything, you may not make the best decisions in all areas. Generally, the areas you don't like or are unfamiliar with will suffer. Employees hired to handle these areas may not do as good a job as a co-owner of the business would do.

Since you are the only owner, you will be the only one who has a long-term stake in the company. You may be highly motivated, but are your employees? You can pay them well, but they still know you can fire them any time you want. They know the business will die when you do. Chapters 15 and 16 discuss how to deal with the problem of employee motivation.

Sole proprietorship earnings are simply added to your personal income for tax calculation purposes. Your business income and expenses are summarized on Schedule C of your Form 1040. If your business shows a loss, the loss can be deducted from your gross income. When you go into business for yourself, certain tax deductions become more available to you than they are for salaried employees. You should check with your tax advisor to make sure you keep track of all tax deductions that are rightfully yours.

General Partnership.   The second major form of legal organization is the general partnership. A general partnership is a voluntary association of two or more people to operate a business for profit as co-owners. Each partner contributes capital, labor, skill, or some combination thereof, to the business.

The red tape involved in forming a partnership can be minimal, consisting of that required for a sole proprietorship plus a handshake between the partners. However, since a partnership is basically a contract between the partners, we strongly recommend that you put the contract in writing with the help of an attorney. If you can't agree on such matters as how profits and losses are to be split, how decisions will be made, or how to assess each partner's interest in the partnership, it is better to find out in advance. The general rule, is that, unless otherwise agreed, each partner has an equal right to share in management and profits.

As noted earlier, liability is of special concern in a partnership because you are liable not only for your own acts but also for the acts of your partners. In addition to the unlimited liability you have as a sole proprietor, you are also liable for the actions of partners when they act as agents for the partnership in business activities. This problem can be partially dealt with by a well-written partnership agreement that specifies each partner's scope of authority. If these authority limits are also communicated to those you do business with, nasty surprises should be minimized. Still, there is no way you can completely protect yourself if you select a "bad apple" for a partner. Be very, very careful when you select partners.

Continuity is somewhat easier for a partnership than for a sole proprietorship. If one partner dies or quits, the other partners are usually ready-made buyers for the business. Partnerships are legally terminated by the death or withdrawal of one partner or the addition of a new partner, but it is relatively simple to form a new partnership to continue a business if the original partnership agreement includes a carefully structured buy-sell agreement. Such an agreement specifies the terms under which partnership interests may be bought and sold, in effect detailing what the new partnership will look like once it comes into existence. Even when buy-sell agreements have been carefully drafted, problems can arise with continuity. For example, the remaining partners may not have enough money to pay off the heirs of a deceased partner under the terms of the partnership agreement. This can force the business to close so that assets can be liquidated. Various strategems can be used to fund buy-sell agreements. For example, buying life insurance on a partner can provide the money needed to buy out the partner's heirs should he or she die. Installment notes can also be substituted for cash to make funding easier.

The buy-sell clause in partnership agreements also serves to facilitate the transfer of interest. In effect, a good buy-sell agreement creates a marketplace for your ownership interest in the company. If you make sure that your buy-sell agreement is funded by company cash, life insurance on partners, or by installment notes, you will have some assurance that your heirs will get a fair price for your ownership interest in the partnership. The same applies if you retire. On the other hand, severe problems can arise in a partnership if the ownership interest must be sold outside the partnership. Since the buyer must buy both your ownership in the business and your partners, you may find no buyers available. As with the sole proprietorship, the only recourse may be liquidation of company assets at a fraction of their value.

General partnerships have an easier time raising money than sole proprietorships. This is simply because there are more business owners to sign the note if money is borrowed, and lenders have more people and assets to look to for repayment. Attracting investors may still prove troublesome, however, since the only way investors can share in the business is to assume the liabilities of a partner.

Management control can be both helped and hindered by a move from a sole proprietorship to a general partnership. If your partnership includes partners with complementary interests and abilities and the authority and responsibility of each partner are clearly spelled out in writing, the results can be dramatic. A specialist committed to your organization's success will oversee each aspect of its operation. Your company can grow quickly and provide each partner with high profits. Perhaps the main management control problem is that there is money involved. The marriage of managerial talent can easily end in a messy divorce unless the partners have a clear understanding about who does what and who decides what. It is difficult when you own part of something to keep your nose out of another partner's job. You tend to feel left out if you are not included in all decisions. When your money is at stake, it is hard to be understanding and forgiving when mistakes are made.

Motivation for employees can be somewhat better in a partnership than in a sole proprietorship. The presence of more than one owner gives the employees the impression the company will be around for a while. Also, an employee may be motivated by the possibility of becoming a partner some day, particularly if the current partners are not from the same family. On the other hand, if the partners have not clearly divided management responsibilities, employees' morale can be destroyed by inconsistent work assignments and rule enforcement. A sole proprietor may be hard to get along with, but at least there is only one boss giving the orders.

Taxation for a general partnership is similar to that for a sole proprietorship. Each partner pays individual taxes on his or her share of partnership earnings and can deduct his or her share of losses from personal gross income. The tax year of a partnership can be set up so that it differs from the personal tax year of the individual partners. This can lead to tax advantages. However, it can also lead to problems if the majority of partners decide on a tax year that does not meet your needs. Another point to be careful about is that individual partners are taxed on their share of partnership profits even if this income is not distributed. You need to insure that you will not end up with taxes to pay but no income from the partnership to pay them with.

Partnerships are required to file a Partnership's Form 1065 tax return even though no tax is ever paid by a partnership. The Form 1065 is an informational return detailing who the partners are, each partner's share of profits and losses, and what the partnership made or lost during the year. Each partner includes his or her share of the partnership's gains or losses when filing the individual Form 1040.

Limited Partnership. The third major legal form of organization is the limited partnership. A limited partnership is made up of one or more general partners and one or more limited partners. The general partners have almost exclusive control over the management of the limited partnership. They also have the same unlimited liability as they would in a general partnership. The limited partners are what make a limited partnership special. They cannot share in the management or the control of the partnership, and, as a result, their liability for the partnership is limited to the amount of their investment in the partnership. The general partners are the managers, and the limited partners are the investors, or silent partners.

The red tape involved in setting up a limited partnership is significant. There are two reasons for this. First, if certain partners want limited liability they must give due notice to the public that this is the case. This is accomplished by careful drafting of a limited partnership agreement and by recording a Certificate of Limited Partnership, which spells out the essential details of the partnership and details the rights of the partners. Second, the limited partners are at the mercy of the almost total managerial power of the general partners. Because of this, it is essential that the contract between the general and limited partners be clearly thought out and written down. Even if a written agreement were not required to assure limited liability for the limited partners, they would be foolish if they did not demand a written agreement. The laws of each state concerning limited partnerships vary. You should check with your attorney to insure that you have complied with your state's laws before promising anything to a limited partner. Since seemingly insignificant actions like including the surname of a limited partner in the partnership's name can destroy the partner's limited liability, the need to consult with legal counsel cannot be overemphasized.

In regard to continuity, there are both advantages and disadvantages to forming a limited partnership rather than an ordinary partnership. On the positive side, limited partnership agreements can be drafted to permit continuance of the partnership in the event of death or withdrawal of a limited partner. This can be very helpful if an investor becomes dissatisfied and wants to sell out. On the negative side, the death or withdrawal of a general partner, which legally terminates the partnership, is never a simple matter for a limited partnership to overcome, even if a carefully structured buy-sell agreement exists. This is because the limited partners, who are only investors, have a different attitude toward the business than do the general partners, who are managers and owners. Limited partners are like bankers. They may try to withdraw their capital from your business if a significant change in management or ownership occurs. Usually the last thing they want to do is to get actively involved in managing your business.

In regard to the transfer of investor interests, limited partnerships offer the general partners about the same flexibility as other partnerships if proper documentation is created and the continuity problems noted above are overcome. Limited partnerships can also offer the limited, or silent, partners an opportunity to sell or transfer their ownership interests to outsiders without disrupting a profitable business. Of course, they still have to persuade a prospective buyer to invest in your management skills. Also, you may not like the prospective buyer, even as a limited partner. As a result, from your standpoint as a general partner, it is advisable to retain the right to buy a limited partner's share at a reasonable price when death or withdrawal occurs.

Limited partnerships can be an excellent vehicle to raise money, especially if the general partners are good credit risks or the company owns real estate or other assets of established value. As we noted above, limited partners are like bankers and look for collateral. What makes limited partners different is that you pay them a percentage of profits rather than loan payments. Payments to limited partners will not climb with the prime rate, and limited partners cannot foreclose if you miss payments. These differences can be critical if your business is growing rapidly and is short of cash. Having limited partners, of course, does not prevent you from borrowing money from a bank.

You should be very careful about how you go about raising money through solicitation of limited partners. Strict laws have been enacted in most states to prevent the defrauding of unwary investors. Check with your legal counsel to see how these laws apply to you. In some cases even a newspaper advertisement offering limited partnership interests in your business can be a violation of the law if you have not taken the proper steps to register your offerings with regulatory authorities.

As noted above, the management control of a limited partnership rests with the general partners. For the most part, the limited partnership offers the same control advantages and disadvantages to the general partner as does the general partnership. The limited partners cannot be ignored, however, even though their role is limited. As a general partner you have a duty to look out for the limited partners' interest. This means you have to deal with them fairly honestly, and in good faith. You cannot put yourself ahead at the expense of the partnership or the limited partners. In addition, you must disclose any personal dealings that might compete with the partnership.

A limited partnership has the same strengths and weaknesses as a partnership in motivating employees. One additional weakness is that employees may see less of a chance of obtaining an ownership interest. Profit-sharing arrangements, as discussed in chapter 15, can be used to deal with this problem.

A limited partnership receives the same tax treatment as a general partnership unless it is viewed as having too many of the attributes of a corporation. Assuming that reasonable care has been taken to avoid having your limited partnership look like a corporation, you can pass partnership losses on to your limited partner investors. In many cases these losses provide significant tax deferral benefits for your investors even though they may not be real losses. For example, for tax purposes depreciation of equipment can exceed the actual loss in value due to wear and tear. Such tax advantages make limited partnership interests relatively attractive compared to ownership of stock in a corporation, where losses cannot be passed on to stockholders. S Corporations, also allow losses to be passed on but limit the number of investors there can be. No such limits apply to the number of limited partners in a limited partnership.

Corporation.   The fourth major legal form of organization is the corporation. A corporation is a legal entity created by its owners but considered a separate and distinct being for legal purposes. The method of creating a corporation is governed by the state. Once created, the corporation possesses many of the rights of a person, such as the right to buy and sell property, to enter contracts, to manage one's own business affairs, and to borrow money.

The existence of a corporation as a separate legal entity has several implications as far as you are concerned. The property of a corporation is owned by the corporation, not its shareholders. Debts of the corporation are its own debts, not the debts of the shareholders. The death of a stockholder does not affect the existence of a corporation. It simply means the stock will now be owned by someone else. The corporation lives on until it is terminated by legal action of the stockholders. The corporation can even sue and be sued in its own name with respect to corporate rights and liabilities.

If the corporate form interests you, prepare yourself for a significant amount of red tape. Application must be made to the state to create the corporation, and the state must approve the corporation and grant its charter or certificate of incorporation. Once the corporation exists, it must file tax returns, pay taxes, and provide the state with current information on its owners. In most states at least three people must sit on the board of directors that manages a corporation. This board must meet regularly and keep minutes of its meetings. The sale of corporate stock is regulated, and care must be taken to conform to existing law. Most small business owners wisely choose not to tackle this red tape themselves. They hire attorneys to help them to write the legal documents and accountants to do the tax returns. There are many advantages to the corporate form, but the red tape involved is not one of them.

Limited liability for the owners, including those who are active and those who are only investors, can be a major advantage of the corporate form. Unless you personally pledge to honor corporate debt, the lender can look only to the corporations's assets for repayment of corporate debt. Although you may have to make a personal pledge in order to get money for your business, at least your investors will be protected.

The corporation also offers excellent assurances of continuity. It can continue to function regardless of the death or withdrawal of its management.

If you share ownership of your corporation with a few other key owners, you should remain cautious concerning transfer of interest, however. Getting fair value for your ownership interest can still be a real problem. Even though you may want to sell your shares, you may not be able to find anyone willing to buy. This is because the people who own the majority of the stock control the corporation. Therefore, you are in the same situation as a partner who tries to sell out. Even though the corporation continues its existence, the only way you can assure getting a fair price for your stock is to have a stockholder's agreement with a buy-sell clause.

The corporate form provides a great deal of flexibility for raising money. How much you will be able to take advantage of this depends on how solvent your company is. Still, even if you have to back up corporate notes personally, raising money through the sale of shares can work out well. In fact, in some cases small corporations can offer stock with special tax advantages to investors. Internal Revenue Code Section 1244 provides that owners of small business stock will enjoy lower capital gains tax rates if the stock is sold at a profit. If it is sold at a loss they can write the loss off as an ordinary loss to shelter other ordinary income.

The red tape involved in selling stock to raise money for your business is considerable. You must conform to state regulations to protect investors. You may also have to conform to federal regulations. If you want to offer Section 1244 stock to your investors, a written plan will have to be prepared and submitted to the IRS. The amount of money you are trying to raise must be significant to justify the time and expense involved in a stock offering. Still, if you have a good thing going and need a lot of money to grow, the opportunity to issue stock that a corporation gives you may be what you need.

Management control of the corporation rests with the board of directors. If you own the majority of the stock, you control who sits on the board. Although you have a duty as a controlling stockholder not to give yourself benefits at the expense of other stockholders, the rights of small stockholders are less than the rights of limited partners, for example. As a result, knowledgeable potential investors will pay careful attention to the governing documents of the corporation and shareholder agreements. This is another good reason to have these documents drafted by an attorney.

Because of perceived continuity and stability, employee motivation can be quite good in a corporation as long as stockholders are actively involved in management. As any company grows, employees can become too far removed from the owners to keep up their motivation to work hard. They simply will not work as hard as they would if they owned a piece of the business. In a growing corporation this problem can often be avoided by offering stock in the company or options to buy stock based on performance to key employees. You and the other company founders can, of course, still be the majority stockholders and can control the direction of the business. Offering ownership to key employees helps to insure that they will work hard in the direction you specify.

Corporate taxation can work for or against the small-business owner. The corporation is taxed as a separate and distinct entity from its owner. Its profits are taxed at different, often lower, rates than your income. If you leave profits in the corporation, only the corporation's lower taxes are paid on it. However, if you then distribute what is left to yourself as dividends, you must also pay the higher taxes on it. This double taxation is obviously undesirable. One way to avoid it is to withdraw money as salary, which is an expense to the corporation and ordinary income to you. If the corporation needs money to grow, however, you will then have to lend money back. After taxes there will be precious little left for the corporation to use. Another way to avoid double taxation is to agree to defer your salary until a later date. If properly done, this permits the corporation to use its profits after tax right away and to pay you a big salary check later. Payday can't be put off forever, however, since the IRS limits the amount of capital a small corporation can accumulate unless there is a good business reason. The IRS wants you to pay taxes on the money, even though the corporation has already paid taxes on it. It figures that the taxes it gets from you will be larger than the refund it gives to the corporation. If you can't prove that the money is back salary, the IRS has dividends, which are taxed at a higher personal tax rate than regular income. Thus, a profitable corporation can be a tax trap.

An unprofitable corporation can also be a tax trap. This is because losses of the corporation are not deductible by the stockholder until the stock is sold at a loss. The corporation gets the deduction, of course, but this is small consolation. You may have big taxes to pay on your personal income at the same time that your corporation is absorbing all your spare cash.

What then are the tax advantages of a small corporation? Actually, they can be quite significant if yours is the right kind of business. For example, a corporation that operates on a cash basis can defer taxes during a growth phase by paying its bills just before the end of the tax year and deferring collection of money owed to it until just after the beginning of the next tax year. This makes year end net income low and can keep corporate taxes minimal. Also, tax-deferred pension plans and deductions such as group insurance are available to owner/managers of small corporations. These can add up to significant tax savings. It should be clear that the issue of corporate taxation is complex and that you will require expert tax counsel to help you to decide whether or not incorporation is a good tax decision for you.

S Corporation. The final major legal form of organization is the corporation that elects Subchapter S status. A corporation can elect to be an S Corporation under provisions of the Internal Revenue Code known as Subchapter S that allow qualified small corporations to be taxed as partnerships. This allows corporate losses to be passed directly to the shareholders and avoids the double taxation mentioned above. If properly handled, an S Corporation can provide significant tax advantages for a closely held corporation and its shareholders. It is not, however, an unmixed blessing.

The red tape for an S Corporation exceeds that of a conventional corporation since certain qualifications must be met regarding classes of stock, number of shareholders, and type of income. You have to prove to the IRS that you meet these qualifications when you apply for Subchapter S status and periodically thereafter.

The liability of the stockholders in an S Corporation is the same as that in a regular corporation. Continuity is also the same. Transfer of interest is somewhat constrained due to the limitations on the number and types of stockholders.

Ability to raise money can also be affected by the limitations on the number of stockholders and by the fact that for tax purposes all profits are considered distributed to stockholders and are taxed at personal tax rates. This latter aspect of an S Corporation can present a real problem to the small corporation that needs to reinvest its profit to finance its growth. It often leads to termination of the Subchapter S status so that the corporation can pay lower corporate tax rates on its income and hold on to its cash to finance its own growth.

The S Corporation has the same advantages and disadvantages regarding management control as a regular corporation. Motivation issues are also the same, except that the number of employees who can become shareholders is limited.

The taxation aspects of an S Corporation have already been discussed. Whether these tax aspects are advantages or disadvantages for you will depend on whether your company is just starting up, has survived the start-up period and is now growing rapidly, or has reached maturity.[4] It also depends on the tax brackets of the stockholders relative to the corporation and on whether or not the stockholders can benefit from being treated as employees of the corporation. The list of considerations goes on and on. Expert tax counsel is needed if you are considering Subchapter S status. Also, your decision should be reviewed with your experts annually since changes in your business situation can materially affect the value of the Subchapter S election to you.

Special Forms of Legal Organization

You have probably heard of several other kinds of organizations in addition to the five major types discussed above. For example, joint ventures, syndications, holding companies, and trusts are often mentioned in the business section of your newspaper. These organizational types are other names or special cases of the five major legal forms of organization. We describe each below, along with one additional form of organization we call a management agreement.

Joint Venture.   A joint venture is a relationship in which two or more persons or corporations combine their labor or property for a single business undertaking. The actual difference between a joint venture and a partnership is inconsequential since partnerships can also be created for a single undertaking, such as the building of a house. As far as the law is concerned, a joint venture is really another name for a partnership.

Syndications.   A syndication, or syndicate, is an association of persons formed to conduct a particular business transaction, generally of a financial nature, such as underwriting issues of stocks and bonds or real estate. A syndication can be organized in several different ways. It can be a corporation, a general partnership, or a limited partnership.

Holding Companies.   A holding company is a corporation that holds a controlling interest in the stock of another corporations, or subsidiary. The holding company may engage in its own business, or it may be organized solely for the purpose of controlling subsidiary companies which are the breadwinners. Holding companies are required to be fair in their dealings with the corporations they control. Small businesses rarely use the holding company approach unless they deal in banking, real estate, mortgage lending, or a similar business in which it is to coordinate the financial aspects of the separate operating companies.

Trusts.   A business trust is created when the owners of a business property transfer their ownership of the property to trustees. The trustees manage the business for the benefit of the owners. A business trust is a lot like a corporation. The owners get trust certificates, or shares, in return for their property, and the trust is sometimes taxed and regulated like a corporation. The big difference between a corporation and a trust is that the holders of the trust shares do not have control of the trustees running the trust. They cannot vote them in or out of office as stockholders can with the board of directors of a corporation. If all control over management of the company is given to the trustees, the holders of the trust certificates typically enjoy limited liability for the debts of the business trust.

Management Agreement.   One additional type of organization worth mentioning is the management agreement. Often a small businessperson has special management skills that an investor needs in his or her business, but the small businessperson is hesitant to form a partnership with the investor because of the large amount of money involved. If the investor's business fails, the small businessperson does not want to be liable for the large debts that the business will generate. A limited partnership will not work, of course, since the small businessperson's contribution is management skill rather than money. Further, the small businessperson does not want to go to work for the investor as an employee.

The solution to this type of problem is a management agreement. A management agreement is a contract between a small businessperson and an investor that establishes the small businessperson as an independent contractor performing management services for the investor for a fee. If properly worded, management agreements can be for long periods of time and can compensate small businesspersons with a share of the profits without making them liable for anything other than the acts they carry out under the contract. The investor, of course, retains full ownership of the business until it is sold.

Choosing Your Organizational Form

The three questions at the beginning of this chapter do not have universal answers. The best answers for you will depend on your particular business situation. Given your present situation, there is one best legal form of organization for you.

The process of selecting the best legal form of organization boils down to comparing the pros and cons of each form for you. For each form, all of the advantages must be weighed against all of the disadvantages. As you proceed with your analysis, you may find it difficult to determine whether advantages outweigh disadvantages.

Exhibit 3.2 summarizes the pros and cons of each organizational form. This exhibit will help you to analyze each form systematically. A few suggestions, to be used in conjunction with Exhibit 3.2, are given below.

Keeping Things Simple.   First, it pays to keep things as simple as possible when starting your business. If you plan to start on a small scale, do not want partners, have sufficient cash to get started, and have a proven track record in your kind of business, you probably are best advised to stay a sole proprietor. The ability to make quick decisions and the avoidance of unnecessary red tape can easily outweigh the tax and legal advantages of the corporate form, for example. As you grow in size and profitability, raising money to finance your growth and tax planning will become more important. You may then want to consider the more complicated organizational forms needed to solve the new problems of your business.

Don't Oversimplify.   Second, it is all too easy to keep things too simple. If you are forming a partnership, you need to spell out the partnership relationship in writing. As noted above, a well-written partnership agreement considers factors such as who gets what and the scope of authority and responsibility of each partner. Our experience has been that a clear, written understanding among all the partners strengthens the working relationship and avoids explosive conflicts and misunderstandings that can blow your business apart.

Exhibit 3.2   The Pros and Cons of Each of the Five Major Forms of Legal Organization

Form	Pros and Cons in Regard to Each Attribute
SOLE PROPRIETORSHIP	1. Red Tape—Little or none.
	2. Liability—You are personally liable for all business debts and misdeeds you commit in the company name. Since there are no co-owners, you are not liable for their misdeeds.
	3. Continuity—Your company dies with you unless you have arranged to be bought out.
	4. Transfer of Interest—None, even for your family, if continuity has not been provided for.

Form	Pros and Cons in Regard to Each Attribute
	5. Raising Money—Usually limited to collateral loans. Cosigners often required.
	6. Management Control—You are the only controlling owner, but this can be a disadvantage if you are not expert in the way you exercise your control.
	7. Motivation—You are the only one with a long-term stake in the company. Can employees be expected to work as hard as an owner?
	8. Taxation—Profits are simply added to your other personal income. Losses are deductible. This can be a help if you have other income.
GENERAL PARTNERSHIP	**1.** Red Tape—Can be minimal, but major problems can be avoided by having a written partnership agreement.
	2. Liability—You are personally liable for all business debts and misdeeds you commit in the company name, *and* you are liable for certain acts of your partners. Be very, very careful when you select partners.
	3. Continuity—Somewhat better than for sole proprietorship, if a written buy-sell agreement exists between the partners. Although partnership is terminated when a partner withdraws or dies, under such an agreement other partners agree to buy out the existing partner's interest and continue business as a new partnership.
	4. Transfer of Interest—Can be good for you and/or your heirs if a written buy-sell agreement exists and is funded.
	5. Raising Money—Usually easier than for sole proprietorship since more owners are available to sign the note.
	6. Management Control—Has to be shared with partners, but this may not be too bad if partners have complementary expertise and the duties of each partner are clearly spelled out.
	7. Motivation—More than one owner has a long term stake in the business. Employee sees more permanence and may have the possibility of becoming a partner as an incentive. However, the partners have to avoid giving conflicting orders to employees.
	8. Taxation—Each partner adds his/her share of profits to personal income whether or not profits are distributed and deducts his/her share of losses. The tax year of the partnership can be different from that of the partners.
LIMITED PARTNERSHIP	**1.** Red Tape—Significantly more than general partnership due to state filing requirements and necessity to protect interests and limited liability of limited partners.
	2. Liability—Same as for general partnership for general partners. Limited partners' liability is only for capital invested.
	3. Continuity—Can be better or worse than for general partnership. The limited partnership can continue if a limited partner withdraws, but the existence of limited partners complicates matters if a general partner dies or withdraws.

Form	Pros and Cons in Regard to Each Attribute
	4. Transfer of Interest—About the same as a general partnership for general partners. Limited partners can sell interests, etc. without disrupting the business. It is in the general partners' best interest to control transfers of interest by limited partners.
	5. Raising Money—Can be excellent since the company can raise needed cash today in return for a percentage of tomorrow's profits. However, strict laws govern solicitation of money from limited partners. Check with legal counsel.
	6. Management Control—For general partners, same advantages and disadvantages as in general partnership. Limited partners have little or no control, but they are protected by the law.
	7. Motivation—Same as for general partnership, except employees may see less chance to become partners. Limited partners tend to think more like bankers than owners. This can lead to conflict if the company experiences difficult times or a general partner dies.
	8. Taxation—Same as for general partnership unless viewed as a corporation for tax purposes. Income and tax losses can be passed on to limited partners.
CORPORATION	**1.** Red Tape—Significant in both the creation and operation of the corporation since it is a separate and distinct legal entity.
	2. Liability—Limited to invested capital for stockholders. However, major stockholders may have to personally pledge that corporate debt will be repaid or that other corporate obligations will be fulfilled, thereby losing limited liability for practical purposes.
	3. Continuity—Excellent.
	4. Transfer of Interest—Excellent in theory, but nobody may want to buy the stock. When the corporation's stock is owned by a few major stockholders, stockholder agreements are essential to assure a fair price for your stock on sale.
	5. Raising Money—Sale of stock can work well and provide special tax advantages for the new stockholders. However, the sale of stock is stringently regulated, making sale of corporate stock at least as complicated as the sale of limited partnership interests.
	6. Management Control—If you own the majority of stock, you control the corporation. Rights of minority stockholders are less than the rights of limited partners unless written stockholder agreements protect them. (Remember, if you and two partners form a corporation, you may be a minority stockholder with only one-third of the stock!)
	7. Motivation—Good for stockholder/managers. Offering stock to key employees can be a good incentive. On the other hand, employees may see little chance to ever own a piece of the company.
	8. Taxation—Corporate income can be taxed at lower rates and at different

Form	Pros and Cons in Regard to Each Attribute
	times than personal income, leaving more money available for the company. However, double taxation can occur. Also, losses can be bottled up in a corporation when it would be more advantageous to deduct them from personal taxes.
S CORPORATION	1. Red Tape—Exceeds that of a conventional corporation.
	2. Liability—Same as for regular corporation.
	3. Continuity—Excellent.
	4. Transfer of Interest—Constrained by the limits on the number and types of stockholders.
	5. Raising Money—More difficult than in regular corporation due to limits on number and types of stockholders, although opportunity to pass on losses may attract those seeking tax shelters. Tends to drain off money needed by a growing company.
	6. Management Control—Same as for a regular corporation.
	7. Motivation Issues—Similar to a regular corporation, but the number and type of potential employee stockholders are limited by regulations.
	8. Taxation—Can provide savings for a new or mature company. Tends to be disadvantageous for a rapidly growing company. Involves complex pros and cons that require annual review with tax counsel.

The best time to write things down is before the partnership begins business, when there are no profits to fight over or losses to blame one another for. Possessiveness about certain job functions is less, and each partner is more willing to agree to do what he or she can do best rather than what he or she wants to do. Also, drawing up a contract clarifies each partner's commitment to the new business. This helps to avoid the tragedy of pouring your money, heart, and soul into a business only to discover that your partner is less committed to it than you are. The effort spent to draft a good partnership agreement is well worth it if it causes you to get out of an unfair situation before getting trapped.

Consult Legal and Tax Advisors. The third suggestion we offer to you is to consult your legal and tax advisors. Once you have reviewed Exhibit 3.2 and have noted how each of the pros and cons might affect your business plan, you should double-check your impressions with your advisors. They will point out a number of subtleties that will affect your assessment of the pros and cons. Remember, however, their advice will be good only if you give them a complete picture of your business plan. Also, their advice is just that—advice. You will have to make the final decision.

Do Your Homework.   Before venturing into the more complicated legal forms of organization (partnerships and corporations), we suggest you do your homework. Careful study of this chapter is a good starting point. Next, go to a library, preferably one with sections designed for attorneys and accountants. Look up the form of organization you are contemplating in a textbook for business law students. Your reference librarian will help you choose a good one. After getting the basics from the business law book, look up the organizational form in a textbook written for attorneys—one dedicated to the continuing education of the bar. Also refer to the specialized legal and tax law references used by attorneys and accountants. Some present suggested wordings for partnership agreements, corporate by-laws, and other legal documents, and explain what the wording is supposed to accomplish. These references also explain specific matters such as how to incorporate or set up a limited partnership in your state. Other references are designed for accountants and explain the tax laws affecting partnerships and corporations and give up-to-date information about state and federal taxes.

Doing your homework will pay off since you will develop a clearer understanding of the legal and tax implications of your chosen organizational form. You will enter your first meetings with your attorney and your accountant armed with a set of good questions to ask. When they suggest something that sounds different from what you have read, you will be able to ask intelligent questions and learn from their answers. Also, once your legal organization is set up, you will be aware of the proper procedure to follow to avoid legal and tax pitfalls, or at least you will be able to recognize a pitfall for what it is and know to consult your attorney or accountant.

Review Your Choice.   We have one last suggestion. Once you decide on an organizational form, review your choice at least once a year. As noted in the "Understanding" section, even if your company is a corporation, it might pay to switch to or from Subchapter S status or to dissolve the corporation if the costs have turned out to outweigh the benefits. Similarly, partnership agreements often need amendment to reflect the changing contributions of partners, and sole proprietorships often must mature into more complex legal forms in order to grow.

Paul, Harry, and Fred had picked the wrong legal form of organization for their restaurant. Because of this, they stood to lose their entire investment plus the cost of the lease payments. This fact was particularly distressing to Fred, who was sure that the restaurant could recover given a chance. In terms of what has been discussed in this chapter, Paul, Harry, and Fred actually made two major mistakes in setting up their organization.

CASE
SOLUTION

Oh So Good!, Inc.

First, they should have formed either an S Corporation or a limited partnership instead of a regular corporation. Subchapter S status would have allowed them to deduct probable early losses on their personal tax returns. If Fred were really the driving force behind the restaurant, he might have been better off as the general partner in a limited partnership, with Paul and Harry as limited partners. In this way, he could have controlled the situation better.

The second mistake Paul, Harry, and Fred made was not spelling out their business relationship in a written agreement. If they had designated one person to oversee the day-to-day restaurant operations, for example, the confrontation with Mary might never have occurred. If they had had a buy-sell agreement, Fred might have been able to continue the business by buying Paul and Harry's stock according to a prearranged formula.

What actually happened? Paul and Harry were true to their word. They put no more of their money into the business. Fred wanted to but realized it would be foolish to do so unless he could buy Paul and Harry's stock. He did not have the money to pay them cash. They would not sell on credit because they expected the business to fail and ruin Fred along with it. The restaurant closed its doors two weeks after the meeting with the accountant and never reopened. The bank auctioned the equipment, recovering about what it had lent to the three men. The only luck the three men had was that a local real estate firm looking for more office space liked the location and agreed to take over the lease. Paul, Harry, and Fred each lost over $20,000. Once the corporation was legally dissolved, they were finally able to deduct this loss on their personal tax return. Needless to say, Paul, Harry, and Fred are no longer friends.

The solutions to Oh So Good!, Inc.'s problems were hardly gratifying. The only ones not to lose money were the bank and the landlord. Once the business started to go sour, the series of events was all too predictable, given the defects in the legal form of organization chosen and the lack of a clear, written understanding among the stockholders. The lessons of this chapter should help you to choose an appropriate organizational form for your company—one that helps you rather than hurts you when the going gets rough.

CHAPTER SUMMARY

Choosing the legal form of organization for your business is a serious matter. Your choice can work for you or against you in a variety of ways. It affects the amount of red tape you have to deal with, your degree of liability for your business debts, whether or not your business will survive you, how much you or your heirs can sell the business for, your ability to raise the money necessary to grow, the amount of control you will have over the conduct of your business, the motivation of your employees, and the taxes you will pay.

There are five basic types of legal organization: sole proprietorships, general partnerships, limited partnerships, corporations, and S Corporations. In addition, there are variations on the basic types. These include joint ventures, syndications, holding companies, trusts, and management agreements. Each organizational form has a different impact on your business. When choosing an organizational form, keep the following suggestions in mind: keep it as simple as possible, put agreements in writing, get expert legal and tax advice, do some research, and review your decision. Choosing a legal form is one of the most important decisions you will make about your business.

1. **Short Case: J. Albrecht and Co.**

   J. Albrecht and Co. is a mini-chain of three meat markets founded and operated by John Albrecht. John is now 55 years old. He would like to open more stores but cannot seem to raise the money. He would also like his son and daughter to take over the business when he retires. J. Albrecht and Co. is currently a sole proprietorship. Based on what you have read in this chapter and on what you know about the company, is the company's present form of legal organization appropriate? Explain.

2. One observer has argued that all high technology start-ups, or new businesses starting up in high technology industries, should be corporations. Do you agree? Why or why not?

3. Trinity Rodriguez is planning on opening a boutique in a Spanish neighborhood. Trinity has had considerable sales experience in clothing stores but knows little or nothing about how to go about buying the clothing needed to stock the store. Which legal form of organization do you suspect would be the best for Trinity? Why?

4. Eric Powell is basically a loner, but he is considering taking on a partner in his metal-finishing business. He needs more working capital. He also needs someone he can trust to manage the employees when he is not there. Right now he does not feel he can afford to pay the going wage for such a person. This is why he thinks taking in a partner would be a good idea. How would you counsel Eric? If Eric does decide to take in a partner, what advice would you give him at that point?

5. Harvey Jamison has completed the eight questions in Exhibit 3.1 and, as described in the "Diagnosis" section, has divided 100 points among the eight questions as follows:

1 – 30		5 – 0	
2 – 30		6 – 30	
3 – 0		7 – 0	
4 – 0		8 – 10	

   Which legal form of organization should be the most attractive to Harvey?

REFERENCES   Cavitch, Zolman. *Business Organizations With Tax Planning*. New York: Matthew Bender & Co., Inc., 1982. A ten-volume work with frequent supplements which is part of a multiple volume series on Business Organizations.

Clarkson, Kenneth W.; Miller, Roger L.; and Blaire, Bonnie. *West's Business Law*. St. Paul: West Publishing Company, 1980.

Concise Explanation of the Subchapter S Revision Act of 1982. Englewood Cliffs, N.J.: Prentice-Hall, Inc. 1982.

Giacomino, Edward D.; Hargrove, John O.; and Small, Winslow O. *Organizing Corporations in California*. Berkeley: California Continuing Education of the Bar, 1973. Most recent supplement: Noelke, Carl B. *Organizing Corporations in California—Supplement June, 1982*.

Giacomino, Edward D.; Hargrove, John O.; and Walker, John R. *Advising California Partnerships*. Berkeley: California Continuing Education of the Bar 1975. Most recent supplement: Krause, Herbert. *Advising California Partnerships—Supplement June, 1982*.

1982 U.S. Master Tax Guide, 65th ed. Chicago: Commerce Clearing House, Inc. 1981. Updated at least annually.

FOOTNOTES   1. This case was prepared by one of the authors based on information collected during a small-business consulting project. In order to maintain client confidentiality, the information presented here differs somewhat from the original case.

2. Three sources that were particularly helpful in the preparation of this review are: Ronald A. Anderson, *Business Law,* 7th ed. (Cincinnati: South-Western Publishing Co., 1972), pp. 717–840; Richard A. Mann and Barry S. Roberts, "When the Corporate Form Doesn't Make Cents: Alternative Forms of Business Organization," *Journal of Small Business Management* 17, no. 2 (April 1979): 47–52; and *1981 U.S. Master Tax Guide*, 64th ed. (Chicago: Commerce Clearing House, Inc., 1980).

3. One practical discussion of how to arrange to sell your business can be found in Cliff Messinger, "My Managers Are Buying Me Out," *Inc.* 3, no. 4 (April 1981): 61–66.

4. The discussion in this paragraph owes much to the analysis of Marvin J. Dickman, "A Business Approach to Subchapter S," *Journal of Small Business Management* 19, no. 1 (January 1981): 16–21. The start-up, growth, and maturity phases of a Subchapter S corporation are discussed on page 17. Many of Dickman's observations remain valid under The Subchapter S Revision Act of 1982. However, the exact implications of this act for your situation should be discussed with your tax counsel.

Financial Tools for Business Success

PART II

Financial Statements 4

□ How can you determine what the equity of your business is?

□ What does the "bottom line" really mean?

□ Do you know what your working capital is?

□ Do you have enough working capital, or too much?

CASE
PROBLEM

Clothing Recycle Center

Sally Johnson's Clothing Recycle Center has been doing a great business since she opened six months ago. She takes in used garments and sells them on a consignment basis. Her shop has grown quickly, largely as the result of word-of-mouth advertising. It is known as a great place to pick up good clothing at bargain prices.

Sally started the shop with some loans from friends and some savings. Now she must face two problems. She needs to pay back the loans, and she needs to prepare a tax return. Both of these problems have convinced Sally that she needs to step back and determine whether her business has been as successful in the past six months as she thinks. She knows she has money in the bank; but what is the condition of her business, and has she made a profit?

Sally knew when she started the shop that she would need to keep some kind of financial records; so she went down to the stationery store and bought a bookkeeping kit. She also opened a checking account for her business. Although she has faithfully recorded all of the checks she has written and has kept receipts on everything, she does not know where to go now. Is there some way all of her records can be sorted out and summarized so that she can make better sense of them?

PROBLEM
IDENTIFICATION

Sally has confronted the same problem that faces all business owners. She has collected a substantial amount of information about her business but she doesn't know what to do with it. In the normal course of operations, businesses collect data, whether or not they do so intentionally. Receipts, invoices, cancelled checks, contracts, and deeds all say something about a business. But the information is often confusing and unrelated. Sally needs to pull all of this data together in a logical and useful manner so that she can determine where the business is going.

Sally's problem of collecting and organizing data goes beyond her own personal needs. She has creditors who want to be repaid. She needs to prepare a tax return. Therefore, outside agencies are also interested in seeing that her business records are orderly and useful.

In addition to organizing her financial information, Sally needs to know where she is and how she has done. Once she has organized her data she needs to arrange it in a way to answer these questions. The data on "where she is" is normally found in a *balance sheet*. This document will tell her how much she owes to her creditors, how much is owed to her, how much her business is worth, and what the business owns. Information on "how she has done" is contained in the *income statement*. This will tell her how much she has sold and what her operating expenses have been. The difference between these items is her profit.

Therefore Sally's problem, and indeed the problem facing all business owners, is to organize her financial information so that she can determine for herself and all interested parties outside her business what her current status is and how she has performed in the operation of her business. The information that she derives from her statements will help her make decisions in running her business. It will also help her to get the assistance she needs from outside agencies. Lastly, her financial statements will enable her to comply with the regulations and requirements of others, especially the government.

DIAGNOSIS

Anyone who has ever looked at a shoebox full of receipts and canceled checks at tax time will appreciate the need for a business to have a logical and organized summary of all of its transactions. Financial statements provide this summary. They are a concrete statement of the facts about a company's operations. These facts are much more valuable than hunches when crucial decisions have to be made.

Financial statements, and the records needed to prepare them, are not a popular aspect of running a business for most entrepreneurs. In fact more often than not it's a problem that most would prefer to be able to avoid entirely. However here are some questions that you should ask yourself.

How much of the data for your business do you carry around in your head? Can you recall it quickly, completely, and accurately? Is your head a place where records are kept permanently and systematically?

Is information about your business available to others who need it when you are away from your business?

How well do you control the activities of your business and how quickly can you take corrective action? Do you know what your sales are, how much your customers owe you, and when your expenses are getting too high?

How do you evaluate the performance of your business? How do you determine how well you are doing in relation to your expectations?

Do you have the information needed to complete tax returns and meet other government reporting requirements? Will your records adequately support your claims if you are audited? Can you complete your reports quickly and easily?

Do you meet all of your obligations to your creditors and customers? Do you pay your debts on time? Do your customers pay their debts to you on time? Are your customer services functioning in the way that you want them to?

Do you have the data that you need to prepare, update, and monitor your performance as you outlined in your business plan?

These questions should point out the need for complete, accurate, and up-to-date record keeping for your business. You cannot expect to keep your business on a profitable course with a few loose scraps of paper. Keeping a good set of accounting records can be one of the most important things that you do in your business. As a Chinese fortune cookie once warned:

"It is easy to open a business. The hard part is keeping it open."

Your accounting records, along with your business plan, will help you to keep that business open. You should also understand that your accounting records do not need to be extensive or complicated to be useful. What is important is that they be complete, accurate, and up-to-date.

UNDER-STANDING   The data collected by a firm falls into two general categories. Some of it reflects the *condition* of the company. This information is put into a *Balance Sheet*, which is a picture of the company's status at a particular point in time. The other type of information collected by a business shows the *results* of its operations for a certain period of time. This information is put into an *Income Statement*. The "bottom line" of the income statement is the profit from the business's operations.

Financial statements can tell you much more about your business than its condition and the results of its operations. Because all financial statements follow certain general rules, one firm's statements can be compared with those of other firms and with its own past statements. They will show trends that can be used to gauge your success or spot developing problems.

The balance sheet shows a firm's financial position on any given date. It shows the company's *assets* (what the company owns) and its *liabilities* (what the company owes to its creditors). The difference between the assets and liabilities is the *equity*, or capital, which is that part of the company that belongs to the owner. The equity is what the owner has invested in the company plus the profits that have accumulated over time and have not been taken out as drawings or dividends.

The income statement shows the results of the operations of a business over a period of time, usually one year. Income statements are also done for shorter periods, such as a month or quarter. The income statement shows the company's *revenues*, or sales, (what the company has taken in as a result of its operations) and its *expenses* (the costs of operating the business). The difference between the revenues and expenses is the *profit*, or income, for the given period.

Each of the general categories mentioned above is divided into *accounts*. Each account is used to summarize similar information, such as accounts receivable, or salaries. These accounts are the building blocks of financial statements.

Balance Sheet

The balance sheet is the oldest of the financial statements used today. In the past it was used to determine the position of a firm and to examine changes in equity. Although it no longer has the dominant position it once had, the balance sheet is still important. Everyone who owns or manages a business should understand the structure of a balance sheet and be able to interpret one.

The foundation of the balance sheet is the accounting equation. The accounting equation is:

$$\text{Assets} = \text{Liabilities} + \text{Equity}$$

As was mentioned earlier, assets are what the firm owns, liabilities are what it owes, and equity is what is left, or the assets owned by the owner of the business. The two sides of the accounting equation are equal, or balance. It is this relationship that gives the balance sheet its name. In order to give you a better understanding of the balance sheet, its components will be examined in more depth.

Assets. The total of a company's assets shows what the firm owns. Assets are part of what generates sales and profits. The assets section of the balance sheet is broken down into three categories: current assets, fixed assets, and other assets. We will use these subclassifications to analyze and interpret the balance sheet.

Current Assets. Current assets consist of cash and those assets that can be converted into cash quickly. Current assets are generally listed in order of liquidity, or the ease with which they can be converted into cash. The following four accounts are the most common of the current assets:

1. Cash. The cash accounts of a firm show how much cash is readily available for the firm's immediate needs. Some of it may be held in a change fund or petty cash. The bulk of the cash available to the business, however, should be held in a checking account for convenience and safety as well as the control such an account provides. A savings account or similar interest-bearing account should also be used so that any surplus cash generates additional income.

2. Receivables. The total owed to a company by its customers is shown in accounts receivable, or trade receivables. From time to time a business may give customers long-term credit advancements, supported by written contracts, or notes. These are separately classified as notes receivable.

3. Inventories. Items stocked for resale to customers are presented in the inventory accounts. Inventory includes completed merchandise held on

display shelves and in the stockroom. A manufacturing business also has inventories of raw materials and work in process.

4. Prepaid Expenses. Certain expenses, such as a year's worth of premiums on an insurance policy, are paid in advance. Because the benefits of these payments extend beyond the date of the statement, these prepaid expenses are reflected as assets rather than expenses.

Fixed Assets.   Those assets that are held for more than one year and are less liquid than current assets are classified as fixed assets. They are normally broken down into three accounts: equipment, buildings, and land. Long-term notes and investments (those with over one year to maturity) are also listed as fixed assets.

1. Equipment. The equipment account summarizes the personal property assets of a firm. Included are such items as display shelves, office furniture and equipment, machinery, small tools, automobiles, and trucks. Personal autos are *not* included here, however.

2. Buildings. The acquisition cost of buildings is listed under this account. Only buildings that are owned are listed here.

3. Land. The cost of land owned by a business, including land on which buildings have been located, is listed separately from the buildings account. This separation is required because a building can be depreciated whereas land cannot.

Other Assets.   The other assets classification is generally used for intangible assets, such as copyrights, patents, and goodwill. These are assets that have a value to a business and provide benefits but do not fit well in any of the other categories.

Liabilities.   Liabilities are the financial obligations of a firm to outside creditors. As with assets, liabilities are classified as current or fixed (long-term). Liabilities inform the owner and his or her creditors of the extent of the firm's financial obligations. Additionally, the difference between the total assets of a firm and its liabilities is the owner's equity.

The *current liabilities* of a business are those obligations that will be paid within one year. The following two accounts are current liabilities:

1. Accounts Payable. Accounts payable reflect a business's obligations to other firms. These obligations are generally incurred through the use of trade credit in normal operations and are usually paid within 30 to 90 days.

2. Notes Payable. During times of tight cash or rapid sales expansion, a business may borrow short-term funds from a bank or other financial institution. If these notes are for less than one year, they are included with the current liabilities. Longer-term obligations are listed as long-term liabilities, long-term debt, or fixed liabilities.

Those financial obligations that will be paid more than one year from the date of the balance sheet are considered *long-term liabilities*. For example, a mortgage on a company's building and land or a four-year note on a truck is long-term liability.

Owner's Equity.   The owner's equity, or capital, is the difference between the total values of the assets and the liabilities of a firm. The two main components of the owner's equity are capital investment and undistributed earnings.

When a business owner makes an investment in the firm from sources outside of the firm, the investment is considered a *capital investment*. For example, if a business owner takes an inheritance from Aunt Martha and invests it in a hot dog stand, the amount of that investment would be considered the equity. If additional capital contributions are made, such as more cash or other assets, these would be added to the capital investment.

The name of the account representing capital investment on the balance sheet is determined by the legal form of the business. In a sole proprietorship, the initial and all subsequent investments of the owner are shown in the *owner's capital* account. In a partnership, there is a separate *partner's capital* account reflecting the individual investment of each partner. In a corporation, capital investment is expressed in terms of shares of stock. The total dollar amount of stock sold by the corporation is its capital investment and is shown in an account called *capital stock*.

A business owner will not necessarily draw all of the profits out of a firm. That part of profits not withdrawn is called undistributed earnings. These earnings are reinvested to help the business to grow. Every year the *undistributed* earnings of a business are added to its equity.

Again, the presentation of the undistributed earnings on the balance sheet depends on the legal form of the business. Sole proprietorships and partnerships add any profits directly to the capital account of the owner or each partner. Any withdrawals made by the owner or any partner are then subtracted to determine the equity on the date of the balance sheet. A corporation accumulates its undistributed earnings in an account called *retained earnings*. The retained earnings account is the total of all of the corporation's profits less any dividends paid to stockholders.

Valuation Accounts.   Two special accounts, called valuation accounts, are used in conjunction with assets. These valuation accounts are allowance for bad debts and accumulated depreciation.

Allowance for Bad Debts.   The allowance for bad debts account is used in conjunction with accounts receivable to compensate for accounts that might not be collected. Although it is an estimate, the allowance account assures that the net amount of accounts receivable will not be overstated but rather reflect the expected amount of collections.

Accumulated Depreciation. Over the time that a business holds a fixed asset, it decreases in value because of physical wear and declining usefulness. Annual depreciation charges are made on the income statement to reflect this expense. As the annual charges for depreciation are assessed, they are totaled in the accumulated depreciation account. The initial cost of the fixed assets less the accumulated depreciation is called the book value of the assets. The book value is used to determine the value of total fixed assets.

A balance sheet for the Cormar Company is presented in Figure 4.1. This balance sheet represents the Cormar Company's financial position on December 31, 1981.

ASSETS			
Current Assets:			
Cash		4,000	
Accounts Receivable	13,000		
Less:Allow for Bad Debts	500	12,500	
Merchandise Inventory		23,100	
Prepaid Expenses		800	
Total Current Assets			40,400
Fixed Assets:			
Equipment	23,400		
Less: Accumulated Deprec	14,600	8,800	
Building	162,000		
Less: Accumulated Deprec	19,300	142,700	
Land		24,000	
Total Fixed Assets			175,500
Other Assets:			
Patent Rights			4,000
Total Assets			219,900
LIABILITIES AND EQUITY			
Liabilities			
Current Liabilities:			
Accounts Payable	5,300		
Notes Payable	6,700		
Total Current Liabilities		12,000	
Long-Term Liabilities:			
Mortgage Payable	70,000		
Notes Payable	8,000		
Total Long-Term Liabilities		78,000	
Total Liabilities			90,000
Owner's Equity			
Capital Investment		45,000	
Undistributed Earnings		84,900	
Total Owner's Equity			129,900
Total Liabilities and Owner's Equity			219,900

**Figure 4.1 The Cormar Company Balance Sheet,
December 31, 1981**

Income Statement

One of the main reasons for going into business is to make a profit. The income statement reports the results of a business's operations over a period of time, a fiscal period. If a business is successful, the result of its operations will be profit. But what exactly is profit, or the "bottom line," so often referred to? The profit equation is:

$$\boxed{\text{Revenue} - \text{Expenses} = \text{Profit}}$$

To understand profit, it is first necessary to understand what revenue is and what expenses get subtracted from revenue to determine profit.

Revenue.   Revenues are the funds received by a firm for services rendered or goods sold during the fiscal period. Often they are stated on the income statement as sales. If more detailed information is needed, sales can be subdivided into major categories, such as service revenue and parts sales.

Not all of the funds that come into a business are revenues, however. For instance, if you take out a loan or use money from your personal savings to build up your inventories, that amount would not be revenue but rather an addition to capital. A good rule of thumb is to consider only money received as the result of the operations of the business as revenue.

Cost of Goods Sold.   The cost of goods sold is used by businesses that sell a product, including retail, wholesale, and manufacturing firms. It is the net cost of the products sold by the business during the period of the income statement. Rather than being a single account like the other items that we have discussed so far, cost of goods sold is a calculation. The cost of inventory purchases, including freight charges, is added to the beginning inventory of the period to give the cost of goods available for sale. Then, the ending inventory or whatever is left on the shelf at the end of the period, is subtracted from the cost of goods available for sale to yield the cost of goods sold. The calculation is illustrated in Figure 4.2.

Gross Profit.   Gross profit is the difference between sales and cost of goods sold. It is the markup that covers the cost of overhead items, such as selling and administrative expenses, and may also provide some profit. Although it is called gross profit, it is far from the bottom line: quite a few expenses will still be subtracted.

Selling and Administrative Expenses.   Selling and administrative expenses are those costs incurred in the operation of the business. Selling expenses are those directly connected with product sales, such as sales salaries and commissions, advertising, and rent or depreciation on sales floor space and display furniture. Administrative expenses are those costs related to the overall operation of the business, such as office salaries, office equipment costs,

Beginning Inventory		$ 35,000
Purchases (Net)	$ 82,000	
Freight-in	+ 1,200	
Net Cost of Purchases		83,200
Cost of Goods Available for Sale		118,200
Less: Ending Inventory		23,100
Cost of Goods Sold		95,100

**Figure 4.2 Statement of Cost of Goods Sold For Year
Ending December 31, 1981**

management salaries, and all operating expenses not directly associated with sales.

Operating Income.   Operating income is the difference between the gross profit and the selling and administrative expenses. It is important because it represents the profit from the actual operation of the business.

Other Income and Expenses.   Income and expense items not directly related to the operation of your business are included under other income and other expenses on the income statement. Other income includes interest from savings accounts or notes, rent from surplus property, and similar income. Other expenses include interest charges on loans and other expenses not directly related to operations.

Net Income.   At last we have reached the bottom line—net income or profit. Profit is the difference between a company's revenue and expenses. We have already noted that not all of the money that comes into a business is income and not all of a business's expenditures are expenses. It is also important to recognize that the money left over in the cash account is not profit, but just cash. Far too many companies fail because their owners falsely believe that as long as there is cash in the bank, the companies are prospering.

A detailed income statement for the Cormar Company is presented in Figure 4.3. This income statement tells us the results of the Cormar Company's business operations during the fiscal year. This kind of statement is called multiple step because it contains substantial detail. Its detail makes it very useful to someone trying to interpret the health and vitality of the company. Figure 4.4 illustrates a simplified single step income statement. Although it contains the same information as Figure 4.3, much of it is condensed. Often more detail is contained in supporting schedules.

Cash or Accrual Accounting.   There are two ways to recognize revenue and expenses—the *cash basis* and the *accrual basis*. All large companies use the accrual basis because it is much more accurate than the cash basis in determining profits. However, many small firms find that the cash basis is easier and requires a less complicated record-keeping system.

Sales		$224,200
COST OF GOODS SOLD		
Merchandise Inventory, 1/1/81		$ 35,000
Purchases	$82,000	
Freight	1,200	
Net Costs of Purchases		83,200
Cost of Goods Available for Sale		118,200
Merchandise Inventory, 12/31/81		23,100
Cost of Goods Sold		95,100
Gross Profit		129,100
SELLING AND ADMINISTRATIVE EXPENSES		
Selling Expenses		
Sales Salaries and Commissions	48,000	
Advertising	6,000	
Depreciation, Store Equipment	3,500	57,500
Administrative Expenses:		
Office Salaries	24,800	
Depreciation, Office Equipment	1,800	
Utility Expense	3,600	
Insurance	900	
Supplies	1,200	
Taxes	2,500	34,800
Total Selling & Administrative Expense		92,300
Net Operating Income		36,800
OTHER EXPENSES		
Interest Expense		800
Net Income		$ 36,000

**Figure 4.3 The Cormor Company Income Statement For
The Year Ended Dec. 31, 1981**

Under the cash basis of accounting, revenue and expenses are recognized when the cash is collected for a sale or paid out for an expense. The cash basis uses the concept of constructive receipt for recognizing income. This means that revenue is recognized when it is effectively received: in other words, it is income as soon as you gain the use of it. For instance, if you receive interest on a savings account, it is income whether or not you withdraw it. Also, if a check is received from a customer in payment of an account, it is recognized as revenue, even if it is not cashed or deposited.

Under the cash basis, most expenses are recognized in the year that they are paid. The exception is expenses that carry benefits for more than one year, such as expenditures for capital assets. These expenses are spread out over the life of the asset as an annual depreciation expense.

Sales	224,200
Cost of Goods Sold	95,100
Gross Profit	129,100
Selling and Administrative Expenses	92,300
Operating Income	36,800
Other Income and Expenses	(800)
Net Income	36,000

**Figure 4.4 The Cormar Company Income Statement For
The Year Ended Dec. 31, 1981**

Accrual system accounting recognizes revenue and expenses when they are earned or incurred rather than when the cash is actually received or paid out. For instance, under the accrual system, if your company makes a credit sale, you record the sale and recognize the revenue immediately. Under the cash system, on the other hand, you have to wait until the payment is received to record the revenue. The rules for expenses are similar. If you incur a liability to pay an expense under the accrual system, you recognize it immediately; and under the cash system you wait until it is paid.

Manufacturing Expenses.   A manufacturing firm encounters a unique set of problems when it prepares its income statement. A manufacturer has three kinds of inventories to account for, and they directly affect the calculation of the cost of goods sold. Because a manufacturing firm is actually making products as well as selling them, it will, at any given time, have three kinds of inventory: an inventory of raw materials; an inventory of partially completed products, called a work-in-process inventory; and an inventory of goods completed but not yet sold called the finished goods inventory. There are also three costs involved in making the final product: direct labor, materials, and overhead. In order to determine accurately the cost of the products sold, a manufacturer must consider these three costs as well as the three kinds of inventory.

A statement of cost of goods manufactured is used to determine product cost for a manufacturer. Figure 4.5 illustrates how this statement is presented. Once the cost of goods manufactured has been calculated, it is included in the calculation of the cost of goods sold, as shown in Figure 4.6.

Limitations of Financial Statements

If financial statements are carefully prepared, following generally accepted accounting practices, they provide extremely useful and valuable informa-

Work in Process Inventory, 1/1/81		$ 25,000
MANUFACTURING COST		
Materials:		
Materials Inventory, 1/1/81	$ 18,000	
Purchases (Net)	120,000	
Materials Available	138,000	
Less: Materials Inv., 12/31/81	16,000	
Cost of Materials Used	$122,000	
Direct Labor	320,000	
Manufacturing Overhead	130,000	
Total Manufacturing Cost		572,000
Total Cost of Work in Process		597,000
Less: Work-in-Process Inventory, 12/31/81		21,000
Cost of Goods Manufactured		$576,000

Figure 4.5 Ames Manufacturing Company Statement of Cost of Goods Manufactured For The Year Ended Dec. 31, 1981

Finished Goods Inventory, 1/1/81	$ 20,000
Cost of Good Manufactured	576,000
Cost of Goods Available for Sale	596,000
Less: Finished Goods Inventory, 12/31/81	25,000
Cost of Goods Sold	571,000

Figure 4.6 Ames Manufacturing Company Statement of Cost of Goods Sold For The Year Ended Dec. 31, 1981

tion for making business decisions. However, there are limits to what statements can do. First, financial statements provide only a fair picture of a company, not a 100 percent accurate one. They cannot be completely accurate because there are judgments made regarding many components of the statements. For instance, a company could show very different profits if it chose to report its income and expenses on the cash basis rather than the accrual basis. Correspondingly, the amount of annual depreciation and hence both the depreciation expense and the book value of the assets are directly affected by the economic life chosen for the assets and the method employed to make the calculation. Second, it must be remembered that all accounting entries are made based on historical cost. Therefore, a building purchased ten years ago is listed at its purchase cost less accumulated depreciation. Its actual fair market value, however, might easily be more than double that amount.

When interpreting financial statements, remember that they are based on judgments and may not accurately reflect the actual market value of the firm. However, if statements are carefully prepared following generally accepted accounting practices, they provide extremely useful and valuable information for making business decisions.

Working Capital

Working capital is the difference between a company's current assets and its current liabilities. It is a crucial measure of the liquidity of a firm. Since liquidity is vital to the successful operation of a business, a good understanding of working capital will help to insure success.

Working capital is the amount of funds available to a business for its day-to-day operations. Most firms will have a minimum amount of working capital available, called the permanent working capital. From time to time, some excess liquidity may occur, in which case temporary excess working capital may develop. Since working capital may make up a substantial amount of a company's total equity, for maximum efficiency it should be carefully controlled.

One of your primary concerns about working capital is that you need enough to take care of day-to-day requirements. This means that you need at least enough current assets to cover current liabilities. Anything less than that will make it very difficult to borrow needed funds. Working capital is also needed to insure that the company can operate during slack periods of activity. Obligations, such as payment of debts and employee salaries, will continue even when sales decline. Further, a strong working capital enables you to take advantage of opportunities, such as acquiring inventory at an especially attractive price, without borrowing.

Working capital is different from owner's equity, or owner's capital. Equity includes both working capital and fixed assets. Fixed assets are the basic investment providing a return for a business. Working capital keeps a business running from day to day. Working capital and equity work hand-in-hand to keep a business profitable.

Basic Business Records

So far we have discussed the financial statements and the basic building blocks of those statements, the accounts. But how do you get the information from a business transaction, such as a sale, into the accounts? Your accounting system handles this in four steps:

1. A transaction occurs, such as a sale or the payment of an expense. This transaction is supported by a *source document*, such as a cash register tape, a sales slip, or a check.

2. The transaction is recorded in a *journal.*

3. The data is transferred from the journal to a *ledger,* which contains the accounts. This process is called *posting.*

4. The accounts are balanced and the data is summarized in the financial statements.

All transactions should be supported by a source document. A source document is some kind of written evidence that a transaction occurred. Source documents include cash register tapes, canceled checks, invoices, sales slips, and vouchers. All of these documents indicate that some kind of business transaction has taken place, such as a sale, a payment of an expense, or the purchase of a piece of equipment or inventory item.

Once a transaction has occurred, the source documents are recorded in a journal. The journal is a chronological diary of the events that affect a business. A simple accounting system uses two journals, a cash receipt and sales journal and a cash payments journal.

A cash receipt and sales journal is used to record all of the sales and receipts of cash for a business. Figure 4.7 is a sample of this kind of journal. All credit sales and cash receipts are recorded in it at least daily. As can be seen from the illustration, credit sales are recorded in one column and cash sales in the next. When a credit customer makes a payment on an account, it is also recorded in this journal. The last column is a catchall column. It is used for nonroutine cash collections, such as the sale of an asset or receipt of a loan.

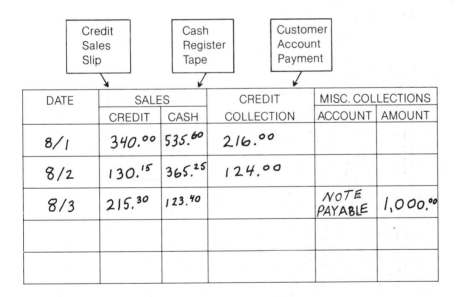

DATE	SALES		CREDIT COLLECTION	MISC. COLLECTIONS	
	CREDIT	CASH		ACCOUNT	AMOUNT
8/1	340.00	535.60	216.00		
8/2	130.15	365.25	124.00		
8/3	215.30	123.40		NOTE PAYABLE	1,000.00

Credit Sales Slip → *Cash Register Tape* → *Customer Account Payment* →

Figure 4.7 Cash Receipt and Sales Journal

At the end of each month, each column is added. The total is then transferred to the appropriate account.

The simplest form of cash payments journal is your checkbook. However, a simple columnar journal can also be developed for cash payments, as illustrated in Figure 4.8. A column is set aside for each account with frequent charges made to it, and a miscellaneous column is added for those accounts used infrequently, such as equipment purchases.

Both types of journal can be set up inexpensively using readily available multicolumn accounting paper, or you may wish to use one of the ready-made accounting systems, which you can purchase at most stationery and office supply stores. The important point is to set up and use a system quickly and easily.

The use of columnar journals is straightforward. Entries are recorded in the journal each day. For instance, the cash register totals should be entered

DATE	PAYEE	CK no.	amount	Inven. Purch	Supplies	Wages	Taxes FICA	W.H.	Other	Utility	Misc. Payments amount	Acct.

Figure 4.8 Cash Payments Journal

in the cash sales column of the sales and cash receipts journal. The cash payments journal should have an entry for each check that you issue. As a check is written, the date, payee, check number, and amount are recorded in the journal. Then the amount is also recorded in the column for the appropriate account. For example, payment of the electric bill would be recorded under "Utility." At the end of each month, each column is added. The total of the checks written should equal the total of all of the other columns. You can also quickly identify the total amount spent for each expense by looking at the total for that column.

Posting is the process of transferring accounting data from the journals to the ledger. The ledger is the collection of all of the accounts. We will use a three column account that allows you to keep a running balance for that account. As was mentioned earlier, an account is a place where you collect data. You may have as many accounts as you wish. However, at a minimum, you should have one account for each item that appears on your financial statements. Therefore, you will need a separate account for each of your assets, liabilities, and equity. You should also have a separate account for each of your revenue sources and expenses. A simple account is illustrated in Figure 4.9. One column is used for increases, one for decreases, and the last column is used to keep a running balance. The account illustrated is cash. The balance in this account is the same as the balance in your checking account.

Many businesses keep a list of their accounts. This list is called a chart of accounts. Usually the accounts are numbered. If you switch to any kind of computerized system in the future, you will need to have all of your accounts numbered. Figure 4.10 is a sample chart of accounts for the Cormar Company.

The accounts for assets, liabilities, and owner's equity are carried from one year to the next. The revenue and expense accounts are closed at the end of the fiscal year and reopened with a zero balance for the new fiscal year. The net result of all income and expenses is the profit for the year. That amount is transferred to the undistributed earnings account.

Once all of the accounts have been balanced, it is an easy matter to develop financial statements. The chart of accounts tells you which category

CASH				01
Account Name –				No.
Date	Description	Increases	Decreases	Balance
8/1	Open Account	5,000.00		5,000.00
8/12	Cash Payments Jour		2,400.00	2,600.00
8/15	Loan	2,000.00		4,600.00

Figure 4.9 Simple Account

each account belongs in. All you need to do is transfer the account balance to that account in the financial statement. You can do this monthly if you desire. At a minimum, financial statements should be prepared yearly. We suggest you do statements quarterly so that you are able to keep in touch with the pulse of your business.

The system that has been described above is a *single-entry system*. That means that each transaction is recorded in one account. An alternative system is called a *double-entry system*. In a double-entry system, all transactions are recorded in two accounts simultaneously, which allows for balance. However, a double-entry system requires that you have advanced knowledge of bookkeeping. Since we wish to illustrate a simple system here, we will not attempt to explain the double-entry system.

	Account Title	Number
ASSETS	Cash	100
	Accounts Receivable	104
	Allowance for Bad Debts	105
	Merchandise Inventory	110
	Prepaid Expenses	115
	Equipment	120
	Accum Depr, Equipment	121
	Building	125
	Accum Depr, Building	126
	Land	130
	Patent Rights	140
LIABILITIES	Accounts Payable	201
	Notes Payable	205
	Mortgage Payable	220
	Notes Payable (L.T.)	230
OWNER'S EQUITY	Capital Investment	300
	Undistributed Earnings	305
REVENUE	Sales	401
	Other Income	450
EXPENSES	Merch Purchases	501
	Freight-in	502
	Sales-Salaries	510
	Advertising	512
	Deprec, Store Equip	514
	Office Salaries	520
	Deprec, Office Equip	522
	Utilities	525
	Insurance	526
	Supplies	528
	Taxes	530
	Interest	540

Figure 4.10 Cormor Company Chart of Accounts

Sally Johnson has already taken the first step in solving her record-keeping problem by getting a checking account and keeping a record of where she spends her money. If she sorts the data that she has collected into the general categories described in this chapter, she will be on her way to generating sound financial statements. Cash receipts should be classified as revenues or investments. Payments should be classed as expenses or purchases of assets. She should also determine her outstanding obligations and class these as liabilities. Schedule C of the 1040 Tax Return can help her to develop an income statement.

Two columnar journals that Sally could use are illustrated in Figures 4.11 and 4.12. The data in these journals will be the basis for her financial statements. With this data she will be able to complete her tax return, control her business on a day-to-day basis, and insure that her prices allow her to make a profit.

In the next chapter, we discuss how financial statements can be used to provide even more information about a business.

**CHAPTER
SUMMARY**

Businesses need accurate, complete, and timely financial statements. These financial statements and the accounting system used to develop them perform five major functions for business owners. Financial statements help owners to control their businesses, evaluate their performances, comply with government regulations, insure that obligations to creditors and customers are met, and plan for the future. Accounting records do not need to be elaborate or complex. Even a simple system that gives you timely and

| DATE | DESCRIPTION | SALES | | OTHER CASH RECEIPTS | |
		Credit Card	Cash	Amount	Description

**Figure 4.11 Sales/Cash Receipts Journal
Clothing Recycle Center**

complete information on the status of your company can be a tremendous boon to your business's survival and success.

There are two major financial statements—the balance sheet and the income statement. The balance sheet tells you the condition of a business on any given day. It gives the balances of the assets, liabilities, and owner's equity accounts. The income statement describes the results of a business's operations over a period of time. It shows the profits of the business for that period.

Financial statements can be developed using either the cash or accrual basis of accounting. Although complicated, the accrual basis gives you a more complete and accurate picture of your company. The cash basis is easier to use.

Working capital is the amount of funds available to meet the day-to-day requirements of a business. It measures the liquidity of the business, or the business's ability to pay its debts.

There are four steps to developing financial statements. The first step is to document each business transaction with a source document, such as a cash register tape or canceled check. Second, the data from the souce document is transferred to a journal, which is a diary of the business. Third, data from the journal is posted to ledger accounts. Finally, these accounts are balanced, and the balances are used to develop the financial statements.

DATE	PAYEE	CHECK NUMBER	EXPENDITURE DISTRIBUTION							
			Consignment Payments	Utilities	Rent	Supplies	Taxes		Other Payments	
							Amount	Type	Amount	Description

Figure 4.12 Cash Payments Journal
Clothing Recycle Center

1. What is the purpose of an income statement, and what does it tell you?
2. What is the purpose of a balance sheet, and what does it tell you?
3. Classify the following accounts as assets, liabilities, equity, revenue, or expenses and briefly define each:

Commissions paid	Office supplies used
Property taxes payable	Depreciation, equipment
Sales	Delivery expense
Accounts payable	Bad debts expense
Advertising expense	Sales returns
Accumulated depreciation, building	Cash
	Prepaid insurance
Supplies inventory	Rent
Equipment	Capital investment
Purchases	Office salaries

4. Prepare a balance sheet for Jones's Book Store based on the following:

Cash	$ 4,200
Accounts Payable	5,000
Capital Investment	?
Retained Earnings	5,000
Merchandise Inventory	12,000
Office Supplies	500
Fixtures	6,000
Accumulated Depreciation, Fixtures	2,000
Notes Payable	4,000

5. Prepare an income statement for Harper's Card Shoppe from the following information:

Utility Expense	$ 3,200
Bad Debts Expense	1,300
Office Supplies Expense	450
Sales	147,200
Interest Expense	1,900
Cost of Goods Sold	84,000
Depreciation Expense, Fixtures	6,000
Tax Expense	2,100
Sales Returns	2,800
Wage Expense	24,000
Insurance Expense	1,200

6. From the following information, prepare an income statement and balance sheet for White's Repair Service.

Sales	$90,000
Accounts Receivable	10,000
Cash	6,000

Repair Parts Expense	40,000
Depreciation Expense, Equipment	950
Accounts Payable	8,000
Rent Payable	200
Advertising Expense	500
Delivery Expense	2,300
Supplies Used	1,100
Wage Expense	32,000
Wages Payable	1,200
Equipment	10,000
Tax Expense	2,800
Taxes Payable	700
Owner's Withdrawals	10,000
Bad Debts Expense	250
Undistributed Earnings	13,000
Other Operating Expenses	3,600
Capital Investment	?

7. Your former bookkeeper left the following balance sheet with you. Prepare a corrected Balance Sheet from this information. You can assume that the account balances are correct.

ASSETS		LIABILITIES AND EQUITY	
Cash	9,000	Interest Payable	10,600
Accounts Receivable	15,200	Wages Payable	600
Equipment	1,600	Undistributed Earnings	30,800
Inventory	40,000	Accounts Payable	18,400
Prepaid Insurance	1,000	Capital Investment	9,000
Supplies Inventory	3,000	Accum. Deprec., Equipment	1,000
Interest Receivable	600		
Total Assets	70,400	Total Liabilities & Equity	70,400

REFERENCES

Abraham, A. B. *Analyze Your Records to Reduce Cost.* Small Marketers Aid No. 130. Washington, D.C.: Small Business Administration, 1977.

Cotton, J. *Keeping Records in Small Business.* Small Marketers Aid No. 155. Washington, D.C.: Small Business Administration, 1974.

Small Business Administration. *Cash Flow in a Small Plant.* Management Aid No. 229 for Small Manufacturers. Washington, D.C., 1976.

Small Business Administration, *A Handbook of Small Business Finance*, Small Business Management Series No. 15, Washington, D.C., 1975.

Small Business Administration. *Recordkeeping Systems, Small Store and Service Trade*, Small Business Bibliography No. 15, Washington, D.C., 1973.

Accounting Textbooks:

Brock, H., and Palmer, C., *Accounting: Principles and Applications*, 4th ed., Norcross, Ga.: McGraw-Hill, 1981.

Meigs, W. B., and Meigs, R. F., *Accounting: The Basis for Business Decisions*, 5th ed., Norcross, Ga.: McGraw-Hill, 1981.

Neely, L. P., and Imke, F., *Accounting: Principles and Practices*, 2nd ed., Cincinnati: South-Western Publishing, 1982.

Analyzing and Interpreting Financial Information

5

☐ How can you use financial statements to learn more about your company's profitability and efficiency?

☐ Is there an easy way to compare your company with others?

☐ How can you use debt to be more profitable?

☐ What is your business worth?

☐ How has your company's financial position changed over time?

CASE PROBLEM

Varga's Sewing Machines

Anthony Varga established Varga's Sewing Machines in 1973. He had been in the sewing machine industry since the late forties as a mechanic and salesman for a major sewing machine manufacturer. At present his market is in the southern half of the state, with about 30 percent of his business in one major city. Most of his business is with established accounts.

The company is in the business of selling, renting, and servicing industrial sewing equipment. Mr. Varga controls all of the daily operations and assigns daily work schedules to his staff of three service technicians and two clerks.

This past year he obtained a large loan to increase his working capital. He also considered expanding his operations. He had lost some of his established customers as their businesses failed. He had also lost some of his customers to competition.

As he considered an expansion of his business, he was concerned about his overall financial position. He did not know how well he was doing. Although he was making a profit, he had a feeling of dissatisfaction with the performance of his business. He was especially concerned about several factors. His overall debt was increasing, primarily because of the large loan. He was also concerned about the control of his inventory and the cash flow of his accounts receivable. His profit performance, especially in regard to his cost of goods sold, seemed to be decreasing.

Mr. Varga needed to make a decision. However, he was not sure that he had all of the information that he needed to insure that it was the right decision. A financial statment can provide valuable information which can help you assess the financial health and vitality of your business. However, some of this information may not be readily apparent without careful financial statement analysis.

Mr. Varga had expressed some concern about his company's overall financial health. He was concerned about his debt, inventory control, and accounts receivable. However, he did not know how to focus on these problem areas and determine exactly what his problems were.

The techniques of financial statement analysis will help Mr. Varga in two ways. First, they can help him determine where his potential financial problems are. Second, they can be used to focus on the nature and extent of the specific problems. With this knowledge, Varga can then take appropriate corrective action. Once Varga learns how to assess his problems, he will be able to chart the future course of his business with more confidence.

**PROBLEM
IDENTIFICATION**

You have spent a lot of time and energy developing your financial statements. Now, how do you get the most out of them? There are a number of ratios and other calculations that can help you interpret your financial statements and make them tell you what is happening to your company. The interpretation of these ratios and other calculations can help you to improve the financial health and profit potential of your business.

There are two aspects of financial statement interpretation that you should keep in mind as you read this chapter. First, you need to know which calculations are most useful and how to make them. Second, and even more importantly, you need to know how to interpret these calculations and how to use the information to your advantage. The "Understanding" section of this chapter will explain the calculation of the critical ratios and some other important and useful measures. It will also demonstrate the uses and applications of these calculations.

As you analyze your financial statements, you should ask yourself some questions. For example:

DIAGNOSIS

What is my company's liquidity? Am I able to pay my bills on time?

How profitable is my company? What return am I earning on my investment, and what is my profit rate on each sales dollar?

How well do I manage my receivables, inventory, and payables? How long do I carry my customers' accounts? Does my inventory turn over fast enough, or is it spending too much time on the shelf? How many days' worth of purchases am I carrying in my payables?

How much debt am I carrying in relation to my assets and equity? Is it too much? Could I carry more debt and still be secure and profitable?

How am I doing in relation to last year? Am I effectively managing all of my accounts?

How is the competition doing, and am I doing better or worse?

The answers to these questions will help you manage your business better.

UNDER-STANDING
There are ten important ratios used to analyze financial statements. These are divided into four general categories: liquidity tests, profitability tests, activity tests, and leverage tests. Each test measures a different aspect of your business's financial health. Monitoring these ratios should make it easier for you to keep a finger on the financial pulse of your business. They can alert you to opportunities for success as well as warn you about developing problems that could lead to financial difficulties.

Ratio analysis is a two-step process. The first step is the calculation of the ratio. The second, even more important, step is the interpretation of the ratio.

As an aid in explaining the financial ratios and their interpretation, sample balance sheets and income statements from the Williams Company are presented in Figures 5.1 and 5.2 for the years 1981 and 1982. Examples of the ratio calculations will be made using these statements.

Liquidity Tests

Liquidity tests are used to assess your ability to pay your current obligations as they become due. They are a quick way of testing your day-to-day ability to continue operating. They can also alert you to developing credit problems. Liquidity ratios are also used to prevent you from becoming too liquid, or holding too much in current assets when the funds might be more profitably invested elsewhere.

Current Ratio. The current ratio is one of the most commonly used ratios in business. It is a measure of a firm's ability to pay its debts as they become due. Anyone interested in the financial solvency of a business will be interested in this ratio. It is calculated by dividing the current assets by the current liabilities.

$$\text{Formula:} \quad \text{Current Ratio} \quad \frac{\text{Current Assets}}{\text{Current Liabilities}}$$

	1981	1982	EXAMPLE
Current Assets / Current Liabilities	$\dfrac{\$80,000}{\$32,000} = 2.5$	$\dfrac{\$88,000}{\$40,000} = 2.2$	

The general rule of thumb for the current ratio is that it should be about 2 to 1 (2.0). The Williams Company appears to be comfortably above the rule. If

ASSETS		1981		1982
Current Assets:				
Cash		$ 12,000		$ 12,800
Accounts Receivable	$ 14,000		$ 12,700	
Less: Allow for Bad Debts	500	13,600	600	12,100
Inventory		53,000		61,600
Prepaid Expenses		1,400		1,500
Total Current Assets		80,000		88,000
Fixed Assets:				
Equipment	65,000		68,000	
Less: Accum Deprec	13,000	52,000	19,500	48,500
Buildings	202,000		202,500	
Less: Accum Deprec	30,300	172,200	35,400	167,100
Land		83,000		83,000
Total Assets		$387,200		$386,600
LIABILITIES				
Current Liabilities:				
Accounts Payable	$ 21,500		$ 29,800	
Notes Payable	8,000		7,500	
Other Payables	2,500		2,700	
Total Current Liabilities		32,000		40,000
Long Term Liabilities:				
Mortgage Payable		198,000		196,500
Total Liabilities		230,000		236,500
EQUITY				
Owners Capital	127,500		127,500	
Undistributed Earn	29,700		22,600	
Total Equity		157,200		149,100
Total Liabilities & Equity		$387,200		$386,600

**Figure 5.1 The Williams Company
Balance Sheet, December 31**

the ratio is too low, your business might be unable to pay its bills as they come due. This could cause a decline in your credit rating, which might make it difficult for you to get credit when you need it. However, you can also have too much liquidity. If the ratio is substantially above the rule of thumb, you might have too much of your equity tied up in current assets. You might

Sales	$166,830		$167,787	
Less: Sales Returns	3,720		2,967	
Net Sales		163,560		164,820
Cost of Goods Sold:				
Beginning Inventory	55,000		53,000	
Purchases (net)	118,000		132,200	
Cost of Goods Available	173,000		185,200	
Ending Inventory	53,000		61,600	
Cost of Goods Sold		120,000		123,600
Gross Profit		43,560		41,220
Selling and Administrative Expenses:				
Selling Expenses:				
Sales Salaries	8,710		4,634	
Advertising	4,420		5,200	
Other Selling Expenses	800		270	
		13,930		10,104
Administrative Expenses:				
Office Salaries	2,560		1,500	
Depreciation	11,400		11,600	
Bad Debts	330		350	
Misc. Admin. Expense	620		690	
		14,910		14,140
Total Selling and Admin. Expense		28,840		24,244
Net Operating Income		14,720		16,976
Other Expenses:				
Interest Expense		800		700
Net Income		13,920		16,276
Taxes		2,780		3,255
After Tax Income		11,140		13,021

Figure 5.2 The Williams Company Income Statement
For The Year Ending Dec. 31

find it more efficient to invest your funds in assets that earn higher profits. It is important to have enough liquidity, but too much liquidity can result in less than optimum profits.

Acid Test Ratio.   The acid test ratio is a stricter liquidity measure than the current ratio. Some current assets, especially inventories and prepaid expenses, are difficult to convert into cash easily on short notice. Therefore, the acid test measures liquidity without these accounts. The acid test ratio is:

> Acid Test Ratio
>
> Formula: $\dfrac{\text{Current Assets} - (\text{Inventories and Prepaids})}{\text{Current Liabilities}}$

The rule of thumb for the acid test ratio, also called the quick ratio, is that it should be 1 to 1 (1.0). An acid test ratio of less than 1.0 indicates that the firm might have a difficult time paying its bills on time. The following examples from the Williams Company illustrate the calculation.

EXAMPLE

$$\frac{\text{CA} - (\text{INV} + \text{PREPD})}{\text{CL}}$$

1981
$$\frac{\$80,000 - (53,000 + 1,400)}{\$32,000} = 0.8$$

1982
$$\frac{\$88,000 - (61,600 + 1,500)}{\$23,600} = 1.05$$

Inventory to Working Capital.   A measure that is closely tied to the liquidity measures is the ratio of the inventory to the working capital. As you will recall, the working capital is the difference between the current assets and the current liabilities. The ratio of inventory to working capital should not exceed 0.80. A higher ratio indicates that the day-to-day operating capital might become inadequate. If a firm has too much of its operating capital tied up in inventory, its liquidity is endangered, and it loses much of the flexibility provided by the working capital.

> Inventory to Working Capital
>
> Formula: $\dfrac{\text{Inventory}}{\text{Working Capital}}$

EXAMPLE

$\dfrac{\text{Inventory}}{\text{Working Capital}}$

1981
$$\frac{\$53,000}{\$48,000} = 1.10$$

1982
$$\frac{\$61,600}{\$64,400} = 0.96$$

Summary of Liquidity.   Liquidity measures help you to determine your ability to pay your bills as they come due. They can alert you to potential credit problems before they become serious. They can also indicate when you are using your assets inefficiently. The examples of the Williams Company are useful in illustrating the application and interpretation of liquidity ratios. The current ratio for 1981 to 1982 indicated that the company was in a good liquidity position, although the 1981 liquidity was somewhat above the norm. However, the acid test indicated that a potential liquidity problem existed. In 1981, even though the current ratio was high, the acid test ratio was somewhat below the norm of 1.0. By 1982, however, the acid test ratio had improved somewhat to 1.05. The company's liquidity problem was also indicated by the ratio of the inventory to working capital. This ratio was 1.10 in 1981, quite a bit above the 0.80 maximum suggested. However, the ratio was improving in 1982. Overall, the liquidity position of the Williams Company improved over the year.

Profitability Tests

Profitability tests are an excellent way to determine and evaluate the performance of your company. The actual bottom line of your income statement might look satisfactory. By subjecting it to the following tests, you will be able to determine whether you are doing as well as you think you are, and as well as you should be.

Operating Margin. The operating margin is an expression of the profitability of your sales dollars. It tells you how much of a profit you are making on each sales dollar. The operating margin is calculated by dividing the net income (before taxes) by net sales. The operating margin can also be calculated using the net operating income as the numerator. This ratio reveals the profitability of the business as a result of the operations of the business. The difference between the two ratios is that using the net income may include some nonoperating income in the calculations. However you choose to do the calculation, make certain that you do it the same from year to year so that you do not confuse the interpretation of the ratio.

$$\text{Formula:} \quad \frac{\text{Operating Margin}}{\text{Net Operating Income (before taxes)}} \Big/ \text{Net Sales}$$

EXAMPLE

	1982		1982	
Net Operating Income / Net Sales	$\dfrac{\$14{,}720}{\$163{,}560}$	= 9.0%	$\dfrac{\$16{,}976}{\$164{,}820}$	= 10.3%

Return on Investment. The return on investment is a measure of the profitability of your tangible net worth. It is calculated by dividing net profits by net worth. It measures the rate of return on the money that you have invested in your business. It is considered one of the best measures of profitability. This ratio indicates how much may be available for future growth as well as payments to owners for their investment return. If the return on investment is below a minimum or target rate, there may be better uses for the funds that you have invested in the business.

$$\text{Formula:} \quad \frac{\text{Returns on Investment}}{\text{Net Profits (after taxes)}}{\text{Net Worth}}$$

EXAMPLE

	1981		*1982*	
Net Profits (after taxes)	$11,140	= 7.09%	$13,021	= 8.73%
Net Worth	$157,200		$149,100	

Net Profit on Working Capital.   Working capital is what is available to the business for its day-to-day financing, including buying inventory and carrying receivables. This ratio measures the contribution that the profits make to working capital and to the liquidity of the firm. This ratio is calculated by dividing the net income (before taxes) by the working capital.

$$\text{Formula:} \quad \frac{\text{Net Profit on Working Capital}}{\text{Net Income (before taxes)}}{\text{Working Capital}}$$

EXAMPLE

	1981		*1982*	
Net Income (before taxes)	$13,920	= 29%	$16,276	= 25.3%
Working Capital	$48,000		$64,000	

Summary of Profitability.   The three profitability tests measure different things and therefore must be interpreted differently. The operating margin is a measure of the efficiency of each sales dollar. In many cases it may be lower than you would expect. A high rate of return on sales is not necessary, nor is it always a sound business practice. Before you can fully evaluate the significance of your operating margin, you must also look at other factors, such as sales volume, total capital or assets invested, and the rate of turnover of receivables and inventory. These factors can have a great effect on the operating margin. For instance, a company with a low rate of return may do quite well if it has a large sales volume in relation to its assets or if it has a high rate of inventory turnover. However, a company with a low investment in assets, such as a service firm, may need a much higher operating margin to achieve satisfactory earnings for the owner.

As was mentioned earlier, the return on investment is one of the best measures of a company's profitability. It measures the return that you are earning on your investment dollar. As such, it gives you a ready measure of the efficiency of your money. However, you must show care when using this ratio. If you own a service business with a low capital investment, you might be lulled into complacency with a high rate of return on investment. You must recognize that even a modest profit can yield a high rate of return on a low capital investment. Therefore, you need to return to the operating margin to evaluate your efficiency.

The best way to evaluate the net profit on working capital is to compare it with that of similar companies in the same industry. Some businesses have a higher rate than others. This ratio depends on the composition of your current assets as well as your profits. More will be said later in this chapter about industry comparisons.

Activity Tests

The activity tests measure how hard your investment is working for you. Generally, the higher the ratio, the harder the investment is working, or the more you will get out of each dollar you have in the business.

Net Sales to Net Worth.   The ratio of net sales to net worth measures the turnover of the capital invested in the business. It is directly dependent on your investment in the business. Two companies with identical sales can have very different ratios depending on the amount of the owner's capital. If a company has a lot of debt, it will tend to have a higher turnover. Therefore, care is necessary in evaluating this ratio. It is calculated by dividing the net sales by the net worth of the business.

> Net Sales to Net Worth
>
> Formula: $\dfrac{\text{Net Sales}}{\text{Net Worth}}$

EXAMPLE

	1981	1982
$\dfrac{\text{Net Sales}}{\text{Net Worth}}$	$\dfrac{\$163,560}{\$157,200} = 1.04$	$\dfrac{\$164,829}{\$149,000} = 1.11$

Net Sales to Working Capital.   The ratio of net sales to net worth measures how hard the total investment is working. Similarly, the ratio of net sales to working capital measures how hard the working capital is working. It measures your company's ability to turn over its working capital and operating funds. Since working capital is the day-to-day operating capital of the business, this measure is a good test of your daily operating efficiency. This ratio is calculated by dividing the net sales by the working capital.

> Net Sales to Working Capital
>
> Formula: $\dfrac{\text{Net Sales}}{\text{Working Capital}}$

EXAMPLE

	1981	1982
$\dfrac{\text{Net Sales}}{\text{Working Capital}}$	$\dfrac{\$163,560}{\$\ 48,000} = 3.41$	$\dfrac{\$164,829}{\$\ 64,400} = 2.56$

Leverage Tests

Debt is a fact that all companies face. It occurs in the normal transaction of business. A business that refuses to use any debt may find that it cannot compete effectively. Therefore, the critical question that you should ask yourself is how much debt you should carry. Debt can be used to increase your profits. If you are able to earn a higher rate of return on borrowed money than it costs you in interest, you can increase your company's rate of return on investment. The leverage tests will help you determine the proper or permissible level of debt.

Current Liabilities to Net Worth. The ratio of current liabilities to net worth measures the claim of the current liabilities on the owner's net worth. It is important because it represents the immediate claims of creditors. Current liabilities mature in one year. If the business's current liabilities equal or exceed its net worth, there could be a problem. A guideline of 0.80 is used for this ratio. It is calculated by dividing the current liabilities by the net worth.

> Current Liabilities to Net Worth
> Formula: $\dfrac{\text{Current Liabilities}}{\text{Net Worth}}$

	1981	1982	EXAMPLE
$\dfrac{\text{Current Liabilities}}{\text{Net Worth}}$	$\dfrac{\$32,000}{\$157,200} = 2.04$	$\dfrac{\$40,000}{\$149,100} = 2.68$	

Total Liabilities to Net Worth. The ratio of total liabilities to net worth is a measure of the proportion of the company owned by creditors. If this ratio exceeds 1.0, then the creditors of the business own the majority interest. The importance of this ratio is in its absolute value. As the ratio gets large, over 3.0, for example, the owner might find that obtaining additional needed funds becomes more and more difficult. Close monitoring of this ratio will help to insure enough flexibility to enable you to borrow funds if and when they are needed. This ratio is calculated by dividing the total liabilities by the net worth.

> Total Liabilities to Net Worth
> Formula: $\dfrac{\text{Total Liabilities}}{\text{Net Worth}}$

	1981	1982	EXAMPLE
$\dfrac{\text{Total Liabilities}}{\text{Net Worth}}$	$\dfrac{\$230,000}{\$157,200} = 1.46$	$\dfrac{\$236,500}{\$149,100} = 1.59$	

Summary of Critical Ratios

The ten ratios mentioned above are the most important measures used in ratio analysis. They are valuable tools in the efficient and profitable management of your business. By carefully watching these ratios, you will be able to spot potential problems before major surgery is required. Other ratios that can help you to direct your company down the most profitable path are discussed in the next section.

Other Important Measures

The measures presented here are intended to help you to get even more information out of your financial statements. These ratios and other techniques go beyond the critical ratios. They will help you to control your accounts receivable and inventory. Other topics include how to do a common size statement, the horizontal analysis of statements, and more on leverage and debt.

Accounts Receivable Analysis. There are two activity measures of accounts receivable, the accounts receivable turnover and the average collection period. Both measure the amount of time it takes to collect from your customers. Both measures are presented here so that you can choose which you would like to use.

The accounts receivable turnover measures the number of times per year the receivables are collected. Each account takes a different amount of time to be collected, but this measure gives you an average of how long it takes. The accounts receivable turnover is calculated by dividing the credit sales by the average accounts receivable. The average accounts receivable is calculated by adding the beginning and ending accounts receivable and dividing by two.

$$\text{Accounts Receivable Turnover}$$
$$\text{Formula:} \quad \frac{\text{Sales}}{\text{Average Accounts Receivable}}$$

EXAMPLE

	1981	1982
$\dfrac{\text{Sales}}{\text{Avg. Accounts Receivable}}$	$\dfrac{\$163,560}{\$ 14,100} = 11.6$	$\dfrac{\$164,820}{\$ 13,400} = 12.3$

The average collection period for accounts receivable is calculated in two steps. Step 1 is the calculation of the average daily credit sales by dividing the total net credit sales by 365. In step 2 the average daily credit sales are divided into the accounts receivable. The average collection period is an average of the amount of sales in receivables and, as such, is an estimate of the average amount of time needed to collect on accounts.

> Average Collection Period
>
> Formula: Step 1: $\dfrac{\text{Sales}}{365}$ = Average Daily Sales
>
> Step 2: $\dfrac{\text{Accounts Receivable}}{\text{Average Daily Sales}}$

	1981	1982	
			EXAMPLE

Step 1: Average daily credit sales

	1981	1982
$\dfrac{\text{Sales}}{365}$	$\dfrac{\$163,560}{365}$ = $448.11	$\dfrac{\$164,829}{365}$ = 451.59

Step 2: Average Collection Period

	1981	1982
$\dfrac{\text{Accounts Receivable}}{\text{Average Daily Sales}}$	$\dfrac{\$14,100}{\$448.11}$ = 31.46	$\dfrac{\$13,400}{\$451.59}$ = 29.67

As was mentioned, both ratios yield the same information. For instance, in the examples presented, if you divide the turnover into 365, you will get the average collection period, as illustrated below:

	1981	1982
Comparison	$\dfrac{365}{11.6}$ = 31.46	$\dfrac{365}{12.3}$ = 29.67

Comparisons for the average collection period or turnover should be made with your company's collection and credit policy. If there is a wide variance between your normal credit terms and the average collection period, you will need to review your credit and collection policies. An average collection period longer than your normal credit period means that your credit collections are lagging. If the term is too long, you may be tying up more of your assets in accounts receivable than you want to, with the result that your assets are not being used efficiently.

Inventory Analysis.   The two measures of inventory activity are the inventory turnover and the number of days sales in inventory. Both are measures of the activity of your inventory and the efficiency with which you use it. the major limitation is that you may have an inventory of hundreds or even thousands of items, but the inventory analysis figures yield an average only.

The calculation of inventory turnover is similar to accounts receivable turnover. The company's sales are divided by the average inventory (beginning inventory plus ending inventory divided by 2). The important comparison to be made is between your inventory turnover and the industry average. If your turnover rate is near the industry average, then you can feel confident that you are not carrying excessive inventory, which would reduce your efficiency and profits. Too *low* a turnover rate indicates that you have too much invested in inventory or that your inventory is too large a proportion of your working capital. If your turnover rate is too *high,* you may be carrying insufficient inventory. This could result in lost sales and frustrated customers.

$$\text{Inventory Turnover}$$
$$\text{Formula:} \quad \frac{\text{Sales}}{\text{Average Inventory}}$$

EXAMPLE

	1981	1982
$\dfrac{\text{Sales}}{\text{Average Inventory}}$	$\dfrac{\$163,560}{\$\ 55,000} = 3.09$	$\dfrac{\$164,820}{\$\ 57,300} = 2.88$

The days sales in inventory is the corollary measure to the inventory turnover. As its name suggests, it tells you how many average days of sales you have available in your inventory. It is a convenient way to control inventory and its related costs. If you know how long it takes to order and receive inventory, you can use this ratio to minimize your in-store stocks. The general test of inventory is to have enough to meet your day-to-day needs but not so much that an excessive amount of your capital is tied up. This ratio is calculated in two steps. First, the average daily sales are determined by dividing the total annual net sales by 365. Then, this figure is divided into the inventory to determine the days sales in inventory.

$$\text{Days Sales In Inventory}$$
$$\text{Formula:} \quad \text{Step 1: } \frac{\text{Sales}}{365} = \text{Average Daily Sales}$$
$$\text{Step 2: } \frac{\text{Inventory}}{\text{Average Daily Sales}}$$

EXAMPLE

	1981	1982
Step 1:		
$\dfrac{\text{Sales}}{365}$	$\dfrac{\$163,560}{365} = \$448.10$	$\dfrac{\$165,820}{365} = \$451.60$

	1981	1982
Step 2:		
$\dfrac{\text{Inventory}}{\text{Average Daily Sales}}$	$\dfrac{\$53,000}{\$448.10} = 118.3$	$\dfrac{\$61,600}{\$451.60} = 136.4$

Both of the inventory activity ratios measure the average activity of inventory. The important limiting factor is that the ratio yields only the average for all inventory items. However, these calculations could be applied to different classes of inventory, or even individual items, if adequate information were available. However, for a company with a large number of items in inventory, a computer would be necessary to keep track of all of the information. These ratios can be an important aid in controlling your investment in inventory.

Common Size Statements.   One of the quickest and easiest ways to compare different-sized financial statements is to reduce them to a common size. This is especially useful when trying to control expenses in a growing company. Despite the fact that the absolute numbers in financial statements change from year to year, the relationships between the various accounts should stay fairly constant. If there is a wide variation in some aspect of a financial statement, it could indicate a problem area that needs attention.

The calculations for common size statements are essentially the same for both the income statement and the balance sheet. Common size statement analysis is also known as vertical analysis. For both statements, each of the accounts is divided by a common number. All figures on the income statement are divided by the net sales figure. The total assets figure is the common denominator for the balance sheet. The resulting decimal is multiplied by 100 to change it to a percentage. The statements are considered "common size" because all of the figures are expressed as a percentage of a common number, either net sales or total assets. Because all of the figures on the statements are expressed as a percentage, they are readily comparable even though the absolute numbers that went into the calculations were different and used a different base number.

Balance Sheet:	1981		1982		EXAMPLES
Cash	$\dfrac{\$12,000}{\$387,200}$ =	3.1%	$\dfrac{\$12,800}{\$386,600}$ =	3.3%	
Equipment	$\dfrac{\$65,000}{\$387,200}$ =	16.8%	$\dfrac{\$68,000}{\$386,600}$ =	17.6%	
Income Statement					
Beginning Inventory	$\dfrac{\$55,000}{\$163,560}$ =	33.6%	$\dfrac{\$53,000}{\$164,820}$ =	32.2%	

Complete common size statements for the Williams Company are presented in Figures 5.3 and 5.4.

Horizontal Analysis.   Horizontal analysis is used to calculate the percentage change in the figures presented in financial statements from one year to the next. Regardless of the statement, the process used is the same. Step one is to subtract the amount of the first year from the amount of the second. This difference can be either positive or negative. The second step is to divide the difference by the amount of the first year. The decimal is then multiplied by 100 to get the percentage. Sample calculations are presented below.

Balance Sheet:	1981	1982	diff.	% change	EXAMPLE
Cash	$12,000	$12,800	$ 800	6.7%	
Accounts Receivable	$14,100	$12,700	$(1,400)*	(9.9%)*	

*( ) parentheses are used to denote negative numbers.

ASSETS		1981	%		1982	%
Current Assets:						
Cash		$ 12,000	3.1		$ 12,800	3.3
Accounts Receivable	$ 14,000		3.6	$ 12,700		3.3
Less: Allow for Bad Debts	500	13,600	0.1	600	12,100	0.2
Inventory		53,000	13.7		61,600	15.9
Prepaid Expenses		1,400	0.4		1,500	0.4
Total Current Assets		80,000	20.7		88,000	22.8
Fixed Assets:						
Equipment	65,000		16.8	68,000		17.6
Less: Accum Deprec	13,000	52,000	3.4	19,500	48,500	5.0
Buildings	202,000		52.2	202,500		52.4
Less: Accum Deprec	30,300	172,200	7.8	35,400	167,100	9.2
Land		83,000	21.4		83,000	21.5
Total Assets		$387,200			$386,600	
LIABILITIES						
Current Liabilities:						
Accounts Payable	$ 21,500		5.5	$ 29,800		7.7
Notes Payable	8,000		2.1	7,500		1.9
Other Payables	2,500		6.5	2,700		0.7
Total Current Liabilities		32,000	8.3		40,000	10.3
Long-Term Liabilities:						
Mortgage Payable		198,000	51.1		196,500	50.8
Total Liabilities		230,000	59.4		236,500	61.2
EQUITY						
Owners Capital	127,500		32.9	127,500		33.0
Undistributed Earn	29,700		7.7	22,600		5.8
Total Equity		157,200	40.6		149,100	38.8
Total Liabilities & Equity		$387,200			$386,600	

Figure 5.3 The Williams Company
Balance Sheet, December 31

		%			%
Sales	$166,830	102	$167,787		101.8
Less: Sales Returns	3,720	2	2,967		1.8
Net Sales		163,560	100		164,820	100.0
Cost of Goods Sold:						
Beginning Inventory	55,000	33.6	53,000		32.2
Purchases (net)	118,000	72.2	132,200		80.9
Cost of Goods Available	173,000	105.8	185,200		112.4
Ending Inventory	53,000	32.4	61,600		37.4
Cost of Goods Sold		120,000	73.4		123,600	75.0
Gross Profit		43,560	26.6		41,220	25.0
Selling and Administrative Expenses:						
Selling Expenses:						
Sales Salaries	8,710	5.3	4,634		2.8
Advertising	4,420	2.7	5,200		3.2
Other Selling Expenses	800	0.5	270		0.2
		13,930			10,104	
Administrative Expenses:						
Office Salaries	2,560	1.6	1,500		0.9
Depreciation	11,400	6.9	11,600		7.0
Bad Debts	330	0.2	350		0.2
Misc. Admin. Expense	620	0.4	690		0.4
		14,910			14,140	
Total Selling and Admin. Expense		28,840			24,244	
Net Operating Income		14,720	9.0		16,976	10.3
Other Expenses:						
Interest Expense		800	0.5		700	0.4
Net Income		13,920	8.5		16,276	9.9
Taxes		2,780	1.7		3,255	2.0
After Tax Income		11,140	6.8		13,021	7.9

Figure 5.4 The Williams Company Income Statement
For The Year Ending Dec. 31

A complete horizontal analysis of the Williams Company balance sheet for 1982 is presented in Figure 5.5.

Debt Financing Ratios. There are two debt financing ratios that are of use in analyzing financial statements. They are the debt to assets ratio and the times interest earned ratio. Both of these ratios add to the knowledge of the debt position of the company and complement the leverage ratios presented earlier.

ASSETS		1981		1982	Change
Current Assets:					
Cash		$ 12,000		$ 12,800	6.7%
Accounts Receivable	$ 14,000		$ 12,700		9.9*
Less: Allow for Bad Debts	500	13,600	600	12,100	20.0
Inventory		53,000		61,600	16.2
Prepaid Expenses		1,400		1,500	7.1
Total Current Assets		80,000		88,000	10.0
Fixed Assets:					
Equipment	65,000		68,000		4.6
Less: Accum Deprec	13,000	52,000	19,500	48,500	50.0
Buildings	202,000		202,500		0.2
Less: Accum Deprec	30,300	172,200	35,400	167,100	16.8
Land		83,000		83,000	–0–
Total Assets		$387,200		$386,600	0.15*
LIABILITIES					
Current Liabilities:					
Accounts Payable	$ 21,500		$ 29,800		38.6%
Notes Payable	8,000		7,500		6.3*
Other Payables	2,500		2,700		8.0
Total Current Liabilities		32,000		40,000	25.
Long-Term Liabilities:					
Mortgage Payable		198,000		196,500	0.8
Total Liabilities		230,000		236,500	2.8
EQUITY					
Owners Capital	127,500		127,500		–0–
Undistributed Earn	29,700		22,600		23.9*
Total Equity		157,200		149,100	5.2*
Total Liabilities & Equity		$387,200		$386,600	0.15%*

*Negative number

**Figure 5.5 The Williams Company Balance Sheet,
December 31**

The debt to assets ratio indicates how much of the assets is financed by creditor funds. It is calculated by dividing the total liabilities by the total assets.

$$\text{Debt to Assets} \quad \text{Formula:} \quad \frac{\text{Total Liabilities}}{\text{Total Assets}}$$

EXAMPLE

	1981	1982
Total Liabilities	$\dfrac{\$230,000}{\$387,000} = .594$	$\dfrac{\$236,500}{\$386,600} = .612$
Total Assets		

The times interest earned ratio is useful when considering new debt. It is especially interesting to bankers and other lenders when they attempt to determine your ability to repay a loan. It is calculated by dividing the earnings before interest and taxes (EBIT) by the fixed charges (usually interest). From a lender's perspective, the larger this ratio is, the greater your ability to repay a loan. Therefore, you are a better risk when this factor is high.

$$\text{Time Interest Earned} \quad \text{Formula:} \quad \frac{\text{EBIT}}{\text{Fixed Charges}}$$

EXAMPLE

	1981	1982
EBIT	$\dfrac{\$14,720}{\$\;\;800} = 18.4$	$\dfrac{\$16,976}{\$\;\;700} = 24.2$
Fixed Charges		

Applications of Ratio Analysis

There are two tools that we can use to expand our interpretation of financial ratio data. They are Trend Analysis and Industry Comparisons.

Trend Analysis. A financial ratio, in and of itself, provides limited information about a company. To be able to interpret a ratio adequately, you must look at its trend over the life of your company. For instance, a current ratio of 2.3 would indicate that the firm slightly exceeded the norm and therefore seemed to be in a good liquidity position. However, if the current ratio had shown a steady downward trend over the past several years, the liquidity position might be deteriorating. Therefore, it might be a good idea to examine this situation more carefully before a more serious condition arose.

Another use of trend analysis is as a feedback device to check on the results of some actions you have taken. For instance, you may have determined that your current ratio was too high and taken some action to decrease it. The situation described above would confirm that the results you desired were occurring. Therefore, in the same way that ratio analysis helps you to get more information out of your financial statements, trend analysis helps you to get more information out of a ratio analysis.

An excellent way to do a trend analysis is to graph it. A graph of the ratios will give you a quicker, more readable picture of the trend of a ratio than looking at the actual numbers. Although it is not necessary to use graph paper, you will probably find it easier to draw the graphs if you do. The vertical axis of the graph should be used for the numbers represented by the ratio. The horizontal axis should be used for time. The time intervals that you use should be equally spaced.

Figure 5.6 is a trend graph based on the information given below:

Current Ratios—The Williams Company, 1975 to 1982

1975	3.5
1976	3.4
1977	3.2
1978	2.9
1979	2.8
1980	2.6
1981	2.5
1982	2.2

To construct the graph, current ratios are first transferred to the graph shown in Figure 5.6. Once the points have been plotted on the graph, they can be connected with a line. Some prefer bar charts to line graphs. If you desire a bar chart, just draw a bar up to the point that you have plotted. Either way you will have a graph that can be easily read. If you desire, you can add a target that you want to achieve to the graph. All you need to do is plot the target with a dotted line as was done in Figure 5.6. Then you will have a ready reference point on the graph to gauge your performance.

Industry Comparisons. How can you determine whether your target for a ratio is a good one? You can set a personal goal for something like a return on investment. However, the realities of the marketplace might make it difficult to reach your goal. Also, for some ratios you may have no idea of what a good goal would be. In either case, you may find that the performance of companies similar to yours in the same or a similar industry will give you some guidance. These performance guidelines can help you to define your goals.

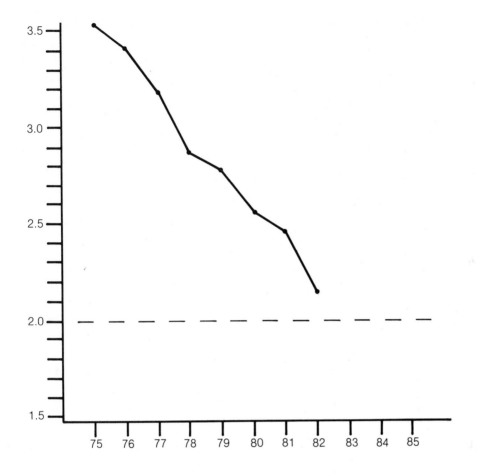

Figure 5.6 Current Ratios—The William's Company

There are a number of agencies that collect and make available common industry ratios. The two most common sources are private industry trade groups that concentrate on one trade or industry and those agencies that collect data for a number of different industries. A partial listing of trade associations that provide industry ratios is included in Appendix A. The best known of the specialized data collection agencies are Dun and Bradstreet, Inc. and the Robert Morris Associates. Some private companies, such as the National Cash Register Company, and governmental agencies also provide information. Appendix B includes the kinds of information provided by these agencies and their addresses. Appendix C shows some examples of the data provided by these groups.

CASE
SOLUTION

Varga's Sewing Machines

A financial analysis of Varga's Sewing Machines yields some interesting and conflicting data. Many factors indicate that the company is doing well or exceptionally well compared to industry standards. The result of a three-year trend analysis of the critical ratios plus some additional measures is presented in Table 5.1. Some of the ratio trends have also been plotted to create a clearer picture of the company's position.

The liquidity position of Varga's Sewing Machines appears to be satisfactory. The current ratio, acid test, and inventory to working capital are at or near the industry average. However, in 1981, the acid test jumped up as the inventory to working capital ratio declined. These factors should be watched carefully to insure that the company does not become overly liquid.

The company's profitability appears to be excellent. Although the operating margin had dipped below the industry average, both the return on investment and the net profit on working capital are substantially above the industry standard.

The activity ratios are near the standards. However, the net sales to working capital lags slightly behind the industry average. This factor should be watched carefully.

The company's leverage position has increased substantially. This reflects the recent loan. The company is currently carrying quite a bit more debt than the industry average, and the times interest earned ratio is lagging behind the industry. Both of these factors point to a need to monitor the debt position of the company carefully.

Table 5.1   Ratio Analysis

	VARGA'S SEWING MACHINES			
Ratio	1979	1980	1981	Industry Average
Current Ratio	2.25	1.7	2.0	2.0
Acid Test	1.06	.848	1.56	1.0
Inventory to Working Capital	.952	1.22	.434	108.8
Operating Margin	6.2%	6.9%	4.4%	5.0%
Return on Investment	66%	57%	42%	15%
Net Profit on Working Capital	58.4%	99.3%	32.4%	7.4%
Net Sales to Net Worth	9.4	14.3	7.4	5.34
Net Sales to Working Capital	8.1	14.3	7.4	10.7
Current Liabilities to Net Worth	.904	.820	1.31	.887
Total Liabilities to Net Worth	1.96	1.44	2.62	1.507
Times Interest Earned	5	7	5	8
Debt to Assets	.24	.34	.30	.33
Average Collection Period	25.5	24.2	36.65	20.0
Inventory Turnover	9.9	11.7	16.4	9.0

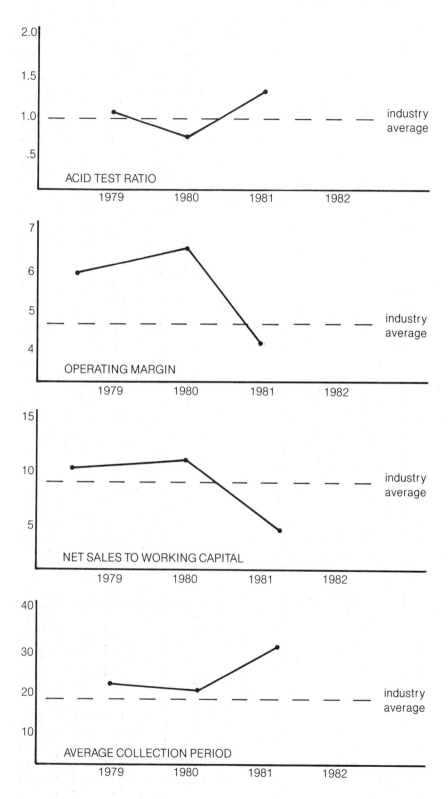

The average collection period is substantially above the industry average. In fact, it is almost double the average. This indicates a serious collection policy problem. If this situation is not attended to immediately, there could be some serious cash flow problems that could endanger the company's own credit rating.

There are several ratios that should be watched carefully, as they may indicate developing problems. The operating margin is lower than the industry average. However, this seems to be counterbalanced by the return on investment. The ratio of net sales to working capital has also dropped. The only time that it was above the industry average was right after the working capital loan was received. This could indicate an inefficient sales operation. Even though sales levels are satisfactory, the working capital is not generating enough activity compared to the industry standard. The times interest earned ratio suggests a need to watch the debt position of the company carefully. The average collection period's high levels are indicative of a serious collection problem that needs to be addressed immediately.

Mr. Varga should delay any expansion plans that he has for the near future. He is already in a weak position as far as debt is concerned. Two performance measures, his operating margin and his ratio of net sales to working capital are below industry averages. His liquidity is also unsettled, and his credit operation needs improvement. Varga should get his normal operations more stabilized before he embarks on any significant expansion, especially one which would require that he incur additional debt.

CHAPTER SUMMARY

Financial statements provide essential information about the economic health of your business. By using the tools of financial analysis, you can get much more from your statements than your equity and profit. Financial analysis is carried out in two steps. The first step is a calculation to determine a particular ratio. The second, and more important, step is to interpret the ratio.

Financial ratios can be grouped into four general categories. Liquidity ratios measure the ability of your company to pay its maturing obligations and continue to operate. Profitability tests help you to evaluate the overall performance of your company. Activity ratios measure how hard your investments are working for you. Leverage tests are useful in determining the impact and efficiency of debt in your business. Other important tests help you to determine the efficiency of your accounts receivable and inventory investments.

Another aspect of financial analysis revolves around the comparison of data. Vertical analysis is used to compare different-sized statements by reducing them to a common base, a percentage. Vertical analysis is valuable in interpreting the amount of change in your financial statements from one year to the next. Debt financing ratios are used to monitor the status of your debt and insure that it does not exceed your ability to repay. Horizontal analysis helps you to compare the relative changes in your financial accounts from one year to the next.

Financial ratios can also be compared with ratios from prior years in order to demonstrate trends. This trend analysis is used to give you feedback on the overall performance of your company and to analyze your performance over time. Another valuable technique is to compare your business with other similar businesses using standard industry ratios.

1. What would you suggest as a target current ratio for the following businesses?

   Kid's Klothing Haus
   Brandelson's Fine Furniture
   Arnson's Jewelry
   Joe's Stereo Shop
   Black's Shoe Store

2. What does "liquidity" mean, and what is its importance to a business?

3. What is the difference between accounts receivable turnover and inventory turnover?

4. Operating margin and return on investment both measure a company's profitability. How are these two measures different?

5. The Castle Company has current assets of $100,000 and current liabilities of $75,000. Compute its current ratio. What would the current ratio be if the following events occurred? Treat each event separately.

   a. Payment of $6,000 of accounts payable
   b. Receipt of $5,000 as a loan to be repaid in 10 years
   c. Purchase of additional inventory for $10,000 cash
   d. Purchase of additional inventory for $10,000 on credit (short-term account payable)
   e. Receipt of payment from customers of $12,000 on their accounts
   f. Purchase of a new piece of equipment for $2,000
   g. Payment of $6,000 in weekly wages (not recorded as wages payable)

DISCUSSION QUESTIONS

Kroncke, C. O.; Nemmers, E. E.; and Grunewald, A. E. *Managerial Finance: Essentials*, 2nd ed. St. Paul: West Publishing 1978.

Moyer, R. C.; McGuigan, J. R.; and Kretlow, W. J. *Contemporary Financial Management*. St. Paul: West Publishing Company 1981.

Sanzo, Richard, *Ratio Analysis for Small Business* Small Business Administration, Washington, D.C., 1970.

Weston, J. F., and Grigham, E. F. *Essentials of Managerial Finance*, 5th ed., Hinsdale, Ill: Dryden Press, 1979.

REFERENCES

Appendix A

TRADE ASSOCIATIONS

Specialized Industry Sources

The most important specialized industry sources for ratio data are trade associations. In addition, however, accounting firms, trade magazines, universities, and some large companies publish ratio studies.

National trade associations which have published ratio studies in the past include the following:

Air-Conditioning & Refrigeration Wholesalers, 22371 Newman Avenue, Dearborn, Mich. 48124

Air Transport Association of America, 1000 Connecticut Avenue NW, Washington, D.C. 20036

American Bankers Association, 90 Park Avenue, New York, N.Y. 10016

American Book Publishers Council, One Park Avenue, New York, N.Y. 10016

American Booksellers Association, 175 Fifth Avenue, New York, N.Y. 10010

American Carpet Institute, 350 Fifth Avenue, New York, N.Y. 10001

American Institute of Laundering, Doris and Chicago Avenues, Joliet, Ill. 60433

American Institute of Supply Associations, 1505 22d Street NW, Washington, D.C. 20037

American Meat Institute, 59 East Van Buren Street, Chicago, Ill. 60605

American Paper Institute, 260 Madison Avenue, New York, N.Y. 10016

American Society of Association Executives, 2000 K Street, NW, Washington, D.C. 20006

American Electric Association, 16223 Meyers Street, Detroit, Mich. 48235

American Supply Association, 221 North LaSalle Street, Chicago, Ill. 60601

Automotive Service Industry Association, 230 North Michigan Avenue, Chicago, Ill. 60601

Bowling Proprietors' Association of America, Inc., West Higgins Road, Hoffman Estates, Ill. 60172

Florists' Telegraph Delivery Association, 900 West Lafayette Boulevard, Detroit, Mich. 48226

Food Service Equipment Industry, Inc., 332 South Michigan Avenue, Chicago, Ill. 60604

Laundry and Cleaners Allied Trades Association, 1180 Raymond Boulevard, Newark, N.J. 07102

Material Handling Equipment Distributors Association, 20 North Wacker Drive, Chicago, Ill. 60616

Mechanical Contractors Association of America, 666 Third Avenue, Suite 1464, New York, N.Y. 10017

Menswear Retailers of America, 390 National Press Building, Washington, D.C. 20004

Motor and Equipment Manufacturers Association, 250 West 57th Street, New York, N.Y. 10019

National-American Wholesale Lumber Association, 180 Madison Avenue, New York, N.Y. 10016

National Appliance and Radio-TV Dealers Association, 1319 Merchandise Mart, Chicago, Ill. 60654

National Association of Accountants, 525 Park Avenue, New York, N.Y. 10022

National Association of Building Owners and Managers, 134 South LaSalle Street, Chicago, Ill. 60603

National Association of Electrical Distributors, 600 Madison Avenue, New York, N.Y. 10022

National Association of Food Chains, 1725 Eye Street, NW, Washington, D.C. 20006

National Association of Furniture Manufacturers, 666 North Lake Shore Drive, Chicago, Ill. 60611

National Association of Insurance Agents, 96 Fulton Street, New York, N.Y. 10038

National Association of Music Merchants, Inc., 222 West Adams Street, Chicago, Ill. 60606

National Association of Plastic Distributors, 2217 Tribune Tower, Chicago, Ill. 60611

National Association of Retail Grocers of the United States, 360 North Michigan Avenue, Chicago, Ill. 60601

National Association of Textile and Apparel Wholesalers, 350 Fifth Avenue, New York, N.Y.10001

National Association of Tobacco Distributors, 360 Lexington Avenue, New York, N.Y. 10017

National Automatic Merchandising Association, Seven South Dearborn Street, Chicago, Ill. 60603

National Beer Wholesalers' Association of America, 6310 North Cicero Avenue, Chicago, Ill. 60646

National Builders' Hardware Association, 1290 Avenue of the Americas, New York, N.Y. 10019

National Electrical Contractors Association, 1200 18th Street, NW, Washington, D.C. 20036

National Electrical Manufacturers Association, 155 East 44th Street, New York, N.Y. 10017

National Farm and Power Equipment Dealers Association, 2340 Hampton Avenue, St. Louis, Mo. 63130

National Home Furnishing Association, 1150 Merchandise Mart, Chicago, Ill. 60654

National Kitchen Cabinet Association, 918 Commonwealth Building, 674 South 4th Street, Louisville, Ky. 40204

National Lumber and Building Material Dealers Association, Ring Building, Washington, D.C. 20036

National Office Products Association, Investment Building, 1511 K Street, NW, Washington, D.C. 20015

National Machine Tool Builders Association, 2071 East 102d Street, Cleveland, Ohio 44106

National Oil Jobbers Council, 1001 Connecticut Avenue, NW, Washington, D.C. 20036

National Paper Box Manufacturers Association, 121 North Bread Street, Suite 910, Philadelphia, Pa. 19107

National Paper Trade Association, 220 East 42d Street, New York, N.Y. 10017

National Parking Association, 1101 17th Street, NW, Washington, D.C. 20036

National Restaurant Association, 1530 North Lake Shore Drive, Chicago, Ill. 60610

National Retail Furniture Association, 1150 Merchandise Mart Plaza, Chicago, Ill. 60654

National Retail Hardware Association, 964 North Pennsylvania Avenue, Indianapolis, Ind. 46204

National Retail Merchants Association, 100 West 31st Street, New York, N.Y. 10001

National Shoe Retailers Association, 200 Madison Avenue, New York, N.Y. 10016

National Sporting Goods Association, 23 East Jackson Boulevard, Chicago, Ill. 60604

National Stationery and Office Equipment Association, Investment Building, 1511 K Street, NW, Washington, D.C. 20005

National Tire Dealers and Retreaders Association, 1343 L Street, NW, Washington, D.C. 20005

National Wholesale Druggists' Association, 220 East 42d Street, New York, N.Y. 10017

National Wholesale Jewelers Association, 1900 Arch Street, Philadelphia, Pa. 19103

National Wholesale Hardware Association, 1900 Arch Street, Philadelphia, Pa. 19103

Northamerican Heating & Airconditioning Wholesalers Association, 1200 West 5th Avenue, Columbus, Ohio 43212

Optical Wholesalers Association, 222 West Adams Street, Chicago, Ill. 60606

Paint and Wallpaper Association of America, 7935 Clayton Road, St. Louis, Mo. 63117

Petroleum Equipment Institute, 525 Dowell Building, Tulsa, Okla. 74114

Printing Industries of America, 711 14th Street, NW, Washington, D.C. 20005

Robert Morris Associations, Philadelphia National Bank Building, Philadelphia, Pa. 19107

Scientific Apparatus Makers Associates, 20 North Wacker Drive, Chicago, Ill. 60606

Shoe Service Institute of America, 222 West Adams Street, Chicago, Ill. 60606

Super Market Institute, Inc., 200 East Ontario Street, Chicago, Ill. 60611

United Fresh Fruit and Vegetable Association, 777 14th Street, NW, Washington, D.C. 20005

United States Wholesale Grocers' Association, 1511 K Street, NW, Washington, D.C. 20005

Urban Land Institute, 1200 18th Street, NW, Washington, D.C. 20036

Wine and Spirits Wholesalers of America, 319 North Fourth Street, St. Louis, Mo. 63102

Dun & Bradstreet Key Business Ratios & Cost of Doing Business

Appendix B

DATA COLLECTION
AGENCIES

Key Business Ratios

Retailing

Children's and infants' wear stores
Clothing and furnishings, men's and
  boys'
Department stores
Discount stores
Discount stores, leased departments
Family clothing stores
Farm equipment dealers
Farm and garden supply stores
Furniture stores
Gasoline service stations
Grocery stores
Hardware stores
Household appliance stores
Jewelry stores
Lumber and other building materials
  dealers
Miscellaneous general merchandise
  stores
Motor vehicle dealers
Paint, glass and wallpaper stores
Shoe stores
Tire, battery and accessory stores
Variety stores
Women's ready-to-wear stores

Wholesaling

Air conditioning and refrigeration
  equipment and supplies
Automotive equipment
Beer, wine and alcoholic beverages
Chemicals and allied products
Clothing and accessories, women's and
  children's

Clothing and furnishings, men's and
  boys'
Commercial machines and equipment
Confectionery
Dairy products
Drugs and druggists' sundries
Electrical appliances, TV and radio sets
Electrical apparatus and equipment
Electronic parts and equipment
Farm machinery and equipment
Footwear
Fresh fruits and vegetables
Furniture and home furnishings
Groceries, general line
Hardware
Industrial machinery and equipment
Lumber and construction materials
Meats and meat products
Metals and minerals
Paints and varnishes
Paper and its products
Petroleum and petroleum products
Piece goods
Plumbing and heating equipment and
  supplies
Poultry and poultry products
Scrap and waste materials
Tires and tubes
Tobacco and its products

Manufacturing and Construction

Agricultural chemicals
Airplane parts and accessories
Bakery products
Blast furnaces, steel works and rolling
  mills

Blouses and waists, women's and
misses'
Books; publishing and printing
Broad woven fabrics, cotton
Canned and preserved fruits,
vegetables and sea foods
Commercial printing except
lithographic
Communication equipment
Concrete, gypsum and plaster products
Confectionery and related products
Construction, mining and handling
machinery and equipment
Converted paper and paperboard
products
Cutlery, hand tools and general
hardware
Dairy products
Dresses: women's, misses' and junior's
Drugs
Electric lighting and wiring equipment
Electric transmission and distribution
equipment
Electrical industrial apparatus
Electrical work
Electronic components and accessories
Engineering, laboratory and scientific
instruments
Fabricated structural metal products
Farm machinery and equipment
Footwear
Fur goods
General building contractors
General industrial machinery and
equipment
Grain mill products
Heating apparatus and plumbing
fixtures
Heavy construction, except highway
and street
Hosiery
Household appliances
Industrial chemicals
Instruments, measuring and
controlling
Iron and steel foundries
Knit outerwear mills
Malt liquors
Mattresses and bedsprings
Meat packing plants

Metal stampings
Metalworking machinery and
equipment
Millwork
Miscellaneous machinery, except
electrical
Motor vehicle parts and accessories
Nonferrous foundries
Office and store fixtures
Outerwear, children's and infants'
Paints, varnishes, lacquers and
enamels
Paper mills, except building paper
Paperboard containers and boxes
Passenger car, truck and bus bodies
Petroleum refining
Plastics, materials and synthetics
Plumbing, heating and air conditioning
Sawmills and planing mills
Screw machine products
Shirts, underwear and nightwear,
men's and boys'
Soap, detergents, perfumes and
cosmetics
Soft drinks, bottled and canned
Special industry machinery
Suits and coats, women's and misses'
Suits, coats and overcoats, men's and
boys'
Surgical, medical and dental
instruments
Toys, amusement and sporting goods
Trousers, men's and boys'
Underwear and nightwear, women's
and children's
Wood household furniture and
upholstered
Work clothing, men's and boys'

Cost of Doing Business

Retailing

Apparel and accessories
Automotive dealers
Building materials
Drug and proprietary stores
Eating and drinking places
Farm equipment dealers
Furniture and home furnishings
Gasoline service stations
General merchandise

Manufacturing
Apparel and other finished products
Food and kindred products
Lumber and wood products, except
   furniture
Machinery, except electrical
Printing, publishing and allied
   industries

Construction
General trade contractors
Special trade contractors

Services
Accounting, auditing and bookkeeping
Automotive
   Automobile repair shops
Business
Educational
Engineering and architectural
Legal
Lodging services
Grocery stores, meat, fish, fruit and
   vegetable markets
Hardware stores
Liquor stores
Tire, battery and accessory dealers

Wholesaling
Farm products—raw materials
Groceries and related products

Other wholesale trades
   Medical services
      Dentists and dental surgeons
      Physicians and surgeons
   Personal services
      Beauty and barber shops
      Laundries, cleaning and dyeing
         plants
   Recreational
   Repair, except automotive

*Transportation, Communication and
   Sanitary Services*
Motor freight transportation and
   warehousing

Finance, Insurance and Real Estate
Insurance agents and brokers
Real estate operators (except
   developers) and lessors
Security and commodity brokers and
   dealers

Mining
Agriculture, Forestry and Fisheries

Source: Dun & Bradstreet, Inc.
            Business Information Systems
            99 Church Street
            New York, NY 10007

Robert Morris Reports

Manufacturing
Advertising displays and devices
Apparel and other finished fabric
   products:
      Canvas products
      Children's clothing
      Curtains and draperies
      Furs
      Hats
      Men's and boys' sport clothing
      Men's work clothing
      Men's, youths' and boys' separate
         trousers
      Men's, youths' and boys' shirts,
         collars and nightwear

      Men's, youths' and boys' suits, coats
         and overcoats
      Women's dresses
      Women's suits, skirts, sportswear
         and coats
      Women's undergarments and
         sleepwear
Beverages:
      Flavoring extracts and syrups
      Malt liquors
      Wines, distilled liquor and liqueurs
Caskets and burial supplies
Chemicals and allied products:
      Drugs and medicines

Fertilizers
Industrial chemicals
Paint, varnish and lacquer
Perfumes, cosmetics and other toilet
preparations
Plastic materials and synthetic resins
Soap, detergents and cleaning
preparations
Food and kindred products:
Bread and other bakery products
Candy and confectionery supplies
Canned and dried fruits and
vegetables
Dairy products
Flour and other grain mill products
Frozen fruits, fruit juices, vegetables,
and specialties
Meat packing
Prepared feeds for animals and
poultry
Vegetable oils
Furniture and fixtures:
Mattresses and bedsprings
Metal household furniture
Store, office, bar and restaurant
fixtures
Wood furniture—except upholstered
Wood furniture—upholstered
Jewelry, precious metals
Leather and leather products:
Footwear
Luggage and special leather products
Tanning, currying, and finishing
Lumber and wood products:
Millwork
Prefabricated wooden buildings and
structural members
Sawmills and planing mills
Veneer and plywood
Wooden boxes and containers
Machinery, equipment and supplies—
electrical:
Electronic components and
accessories
Equipment for public utilities and
industrial use
Household electrical appliances
Lighting fixtures
Radios, TV and phonographs

Radio and TV transmitting,
signaling and detection equipment
Machinery, except electrical
equipment:
Ball and roller bearings
Construction and mining machinery
and equipment
Farm machinery and equipment
General industrial machinery and
equipment
Industrial and commercial
refrigeration equipment and
complete air conditioning units
Machine shops—jobbing and repair
Machine tools and metal working
equipment
Oil field machinery and equipment
Special dies and tools, die sets, jigs
and fixtures
Special industry machinery
Metal industries—primary:
Iron and steel forgings
Iron and steel foundries
Non-ferrous foundries
Metal products—fabricated (except
ordnance, machinery, and
transportation equipment):
Coating, engraving, and allied
services
Cutlery, hand tools and general
hardware
Enameled iron, metal sanitary ware
and plumbing supplies
Fabricated structural steel
Heating equipment, except electric
Metal cans
Metal doors, sash, frames, molding
and trim
Metal stampings
Miscellaneous fabricated wire
products
Miscellaneous non-ferrous
fabricated products
Screw machine products, bolts,
nuts, screws, rivets and washers
Sheet metal work
Valves and pipe fittings, except
plumbers' brass goods
Paper and allied products:

Envelopes, stationery and paper bags
Paperboard containers and boxes
Pulp, paper and paperboard
Printing, publishing and allied industries:
Book printing
Bookbinding, and miscellaneous related work
Books: publishing, and printing
Commercial printing, except lithographic
Commercial printing, lithographic
Newspapers: publishing and printing
Typesetting
Professional, scientific, and controlling instruments:
Engineering, laboratory and scientific and research instruments
Photographic equipment and supplies
Surgical, medical and dental equipment and supplies
Rubber and miscellaneous plastics products:
Miscellaneous plastics products
Rubber footwear and fabricated rubber products
Stone, clay and glass products:
Brick and structural clay tile
Concrete brick, block and other products
Minerals and earths, ground or otherwise treated
Pressed and blown glass and glassware
Ready-mixed concrete
Textile mill products:
Broad woven fabric—cotton, silk and synthetic
Broad woven fabric—woolens and worsteds
Dyeing and finishing
Hosiery—anklets—children's, men's and boys'
Hosiery—women's—full fashioned and seamless
Knitting—Cloth, outerwear and underwear

Narrow fabrics and other smallwares
Yarn—cotton, silk, and synthetic
Toys, amusement, sporting and athletic goods:
Games and toys, except dolls and children's vehicles
Sporting and athletic goods
Transportation equipment:
Aircraft parts (except electric)
Motor vehicle parts and accessories
Motor vehicles
Ship and boat building and repairing

Wholesaling

Automotive equipment and supplies:
Automobiles and other motor vehicles
Automotive equipment
Tires and tubes
Beauty and barber supplies and equipment
Drugs, drug proprietaries and druggists' sundries
Electrical equipment:
Electrical supplies and apparatus
Radios, refrigerators and electrical appliances
Flowers and florists' supplies
Food, beverages and tobacco:
Coffee, tea and spice
Confectionery
Dairy products and poultry
Fish and sea foods
Frozen foods
Fruits and vegetables
General groceries
Grain
Meats and meat products
Tobacco and tobacco products
Tobacco leaf
Wine, liquor and beer
Furniture and home furnishings:
Floor coverings
Furniture
General merchandise
Industrial chemicals
Iron, steel, hardware and related products:

Air conditioning and refrigeration
equipment and supplies
Hardware and paints
Metal products
Metal scrap
Plumbing and heating equipment
and supplies
Steel warehousing
Lumber, building materials and coal:
Building materials
Coal and coke
Lumber and millwork
Machinery and equipment:
Agricultural equipment
Heavy commercial and industrial
machinery and equipment
Laundry and dry cleaning equipment
and supplies
Mill supply house
Professional equipment and supplies
Restaurant and hotel supplies,
fixtures and equipment
Transportation equipment and
supplies, except motor vehicles
Paper and paper products:
Printing and writing paper
Wrapping or coarse paper and
products
Petroleum products:
Fuel oil
Petroleum products
Scrap and waste materials:
Textile waste
Sporting goods and toys:
Textile products and apparel:
Dry goods
Footwear
Furs
Men's and boys' clothing
Women's and children's clothing
Wool

Retailing

Aircraft:
Aircraft—new and used
Apparel and accessories:
Family clothing stores
Furs
Infants' clothing
Men's and boys' clothing

Shoes
Women's ready-to-wear
Books and office supplies:
Books and stationery
Office supplies and equipment
Building materials and hardware:
Building materials
Hardware stores
Heating and plumbing equipment
dealers
Lumber
Paint, glass and wallpaper stores
Cameras and photographic supplies
Department stores and general
merchandise:
Department stores
Dry goods and general merchandise
Drugs
Farm and garden equipment and
supplies:
Farm equipment
Feed and seed—farm and garden
supply
Flowers
Food and beverages:
Dairy products and milk dealers
Groceries and meats
Restaurants
Fuel and ice dealers:
Fuel, except fuel oil
Fuel oil dealers
Furniture, home furnishings and
equipment:
Floor coverings
Furniture
Household appliances
Radio, television and record players
Jewelry
Liquor
Luggage and gifts
Marine hardware, boat and supply
Motor vehicle dealers:
Autos—new and used
House trailers
Tire, battery, and accessories
Trucks—new and used
Musical instruments and supplies
Road machinery equipment
Sporting goods

Vending machine operators,
merchandise

Services

Advertising agencies
Auto repair shops
Auto and truck rental and leasing
Bowling alleys
Business and management consulting
Commercial research and
development laboratories
Engineering and architectural services
Equipment rental and leasing
Funeral directors
Insurance agents and brokers
Intercity bus lines
Laundries and dry cleaners
Linen supply
Local trucking and storage—
including household goods
Local trucking—without storage
Long distance trucking
Motels, hotels and tourist courts

Nursing homes, sanatoria,
convalescent and rest homes
Real estate holding companies
Refrigerated warehousing, except
food lockers

Contractors

Oil well servicing contractors
Oil and gas well drilling

Not Elsewhere Classified

Bottler—soft drinks
Commercial feed lots
Poultry, except broiler chickens
Radio and/or TV stations
Seed companies (vegetable and
garden)

Source: Robert Morris Associates
Philadelphia National Bank
Building
Philadelphia, PA 19107

Table 5.2   National Results—Profit and Loss Statement
All Dealers Reporting

Appendix C

SAMPLE DATA

SHEETS

	Average	25% With Highest Profit
Total Sales	100.00	100.00
Cost of Goods Sold	61.95	59.75
Gross Profit	38.05	40.25
SELLING EXPENSES		
Wages–Store Clerks	4.50	5.23
Wages–Outside Salesmen	4.89	4.32
Wages–Sales Manager(s)	1.33	1.43
Wages–Designers	.82	.55
Travel & Entertainment	.28	.24
Auto Expense	.59	.46
Advertising	.95	.85
Other	.31	.33
Total	13.67	13.41

OCCUPANCY EXPENSES		
Wages–Janitorial & Maintenance	.20	.20
Rent	1.88	1.63
Light, Heat & Power	.55	.51
Depreciation & Amortization	.44	.45
Insurance	.40	.36
Other	.30	.30
Total	3.77	3.45
WAREHOUSE & DELIVERY EXPENSES		
Wages–Delivery & Warehouse	2.59	2.69
Vehicle Expense	.69	.62
Depreciation	.27	.26
Outside Cartage	.31	.43
Other	.15	.14
Total	4.01	4.14
OFFICE EXPENSE		
Wages–Office Personnel	2.21	2.21
Telephone & Telegraph	.53	.49
Postage	.23	.23
Stationery & Supplies	.32	.29
Other	.17	.21
Total	3.46	3.43
COMPUTER EXPENSE		
Wages–D.P. Personnel	.52	.39
Rental and Maintenance	.30	.29
Depreciation	.30	.16
Oustide Services	.40	.39
Supplies	.09	.07
Other	.13	.04
Total	1.74	1.34
ADMINISTRATIVE EXPENSES		
Wages–Owners & Officers	4.55	4.43
Travel & Entertainment	.25	.24
Bad Debts	.18	.16
Professional Services	.33	.30
Insurance & Pension Plans	1.16	1.14
Other	.33	.30
Total	6.80	6.57
TAX EXPENSE (Except Federal)		
Payroll Taxes–Compensation Insurance	1.44	1.49
Property Taxes–Except Vehicles	.17	.15
Other Taxes	.27	.29
Total	1.88	1.93

OTHER EXPENSE		
Discounts Allowed......................	.14	.11
Interest Expense......................	.77	.49
Miscellaneous.........................	.18	.09
Total.................................	1.09	.69
OTHER INCOME		
Discounts Earned	.87	.84
Consignment Income	.25	.26
Interest Earned	.16	.19
Miscellaneous.........................	.32	.27
Total.................................	1.60	1.56
NET PROFIT (Before Income Tax)	3.50	7.59

Note: Profit and loss statements will not add to the net profit shown.
All figures are medians and not intended to total.

Source: NOPA Dealer Operating Results (annual) National Office Products Association,
301 N. Fairfax St., Alexandria, VA 22314

Table 5.3   Sales Volume Size of All Home Centers

Income Statement Data	Sales Under $1,000,000	$1,000,000 To $2,999,999	Sales $3,000,000 Or More
Number of Stores	56	88	30
Net Sales Volume	$756,328	$1,843,823	$4,919,539
Current Year's Sales vs. Previous Year*	− .33%	− 1.65%	− 5.40%
Gross Sales...	102.55%	102.18%	102.33%
Less: Total Deductions	2.55	2.18	2.33
Net Sales...	100.00%	100.00%	100.00%
Cost of Goods Sold	66.42	69.84	72.22
Margin	33.58	30.16	27.78
Payroll and Other Employee Expense			
Salaries—Owners, Officers, Managers	5.34	4.52	3.25
Salaries—Other Employees	10.78	10.39	10.12
Federal and State Payroll Taxes	1.24	.95	.89
Group Insurance......................................	.47	.57	.32
Benefit Plans	.44	.67	.84
Total Payroll and Other Employee Expense	18.27	17.10	15.42
Occupancy Expense			
Heat, Light, Power, Water	1.03	.68	.41
Repairs to Building	.35	.52	.41
Rent or Ownership in Real Estate**	3.34	2.63	2.04
Total Occupancy Expense	4.72	3.83	2.86

Income Statement Data	Sales Under $1,000,000	$1,000,000 To $2,999,999	Sales $3,000,000 Or More
Other Costs of Doing Business			
Advertising	2.14	2.01	1.26
Delivery (Other than Wages)	.53	.57	.71
Insurance (Other than Real Estate and Group)	.76	.63	.41
Taxes (Other than Real Estate and Payroll)	.28	.51	.30
Interest on Borrowed Money (Other than Mortgages)	1.38	1.03	.93
Depreciation (Other than Real Estate)	.69	.58	.71
Store and Shop Supplies	.49	.30	.15
Total Other Costs of Doing Business	9.28	8.01	7.24
Total Operating Expense	32.27	28.94	25.52
Net Operating Profit	1.31	1.22	2.26
Other Income	1.24	1.54	1.24
Net Profit (Before Income Taxes)	2.55	2.76	3.50
Financial Performance			
Profit on Investment	8.51%	14.13%	16.23%
Active Owner's Return	26.38%	37.30%	31.00%
Current Asset Ratio	3.71×	2.63×	2.34×
Quick Asset Ratio	1.26×	.94×	1.22×
Total Debt to Tangible Net Worth	76.90%	81.10%	90.00%
Stock Turn Times	2.51×	4.04×	5.06×
Sales to Inventory Ratio	3.77×	5.78×	7.00×
Average Inventory per Sq. Ft. Sales Area	$21.92	$28.14	$50.26
Net Sales to Accounts Receivable	12.26×	18.41×	10.14×
Net Sales to Total Assets	1.89×	2.83×	2.43×
Net Sales to Net Worth	3.35×	5.13×	4.62×
Net Sales to Net Working Capital	3.37×	6.02×	5.93×
Other Operating Data			
Incoming Freight—% of Purchases	.81%	.30%	.36%
Credit Sales—% of Total Gross Sales	36.55%	38.27%	62.52%
Consumer Sales—% of Total Gross Sales	84.62%	74.58%	42.53%
Inventory—% Stored in Central Warehouse	.00%	48.75%	25.00%
Selling Area—Square Feet	11,359	14.011	14,108
Sales Per Square Foot—Selling Area	$66.58	$131.60	$348.71
Total Area—Square Feet	17,400	23,090	31,348
Sales Per Square Foot—Total Area	$43.47	$79.85	$156.93
Sales Per Person Employed	$61,370	$89,534	$120,133
Sales Per Customer	$11.44	$12.89	$60.17

Source: "The Bottom Line" Retail Hardware Association/Home Center Institute, 1981 Edition, 776 North High School Road, Indianapolis, Ind. 46224

Table 5.4   Key Business Ratios—Retailing

Line of Business	Current assets to current debt	Net profits on net sales	Net profits on tangible net worth	Net profits on net working capital	Net sales to tangible net worth	Net sales to net working capital	Collection period	Net sales to inventory	Fixed assets to tangible net worth	Current debt to tangible net worth	Total debt to tangible net worth	Inventory to net working capital	Current debt to inventory	Funded debts to net working capital
	Times	Percent	Percent	Percent	Times	Times	Days	Times	Percent	Percent	Percent	Percent	Percent	Percent
Auto & Home Supply Stores	3.29	4.26	12.96	25.00	6.12	8.48	**	7.5	12.3	28.3	68.2	67.7	49.4	9.8
	1.98	1.54	7.04	12.50	4.01	6.07	**	5.7	29.4	74.3	85.1	93.0	89.7	44.5
	1.48	0.38	2.48	2.84	2.64	3.61	**	4.0	57.4	122.0	184.7	150.4	172.4	92.4
Children's & Infants' Wear Stores	5.22	3.36	14.08	19.25	5.26	6.82	**	6.7	28.3	72.7	55.7	39.3		17.9
	2.57	1.68	6.67	8.29	4.21	4.40	**	5.4	18.9	51.6	97.1	102.1	67.4	32.1
	2.07	0.32	1.77	1.61	2.92	2.90	**	2.8	31.3	71.7	175.6	127.9	88.6	52.0
Clothing & Furnishings, Men's & Boys'	5.46	4.18	13.50	15.12	4.75	5.68	**	6.6	4.9	21.9	59.0	60.2	37.3	18.2
	3.15	1.72	5.85	7.16	3.26	3.58	**	4.5	13.1	44.6	117.2	89.1	66.3	35.7
	1.85	0.51	1.29	1.52	2.23	2.58	**	3.3	29.5	104.0	216.5	131.9	101.7	53.7
Department Stores	4.31	2.88	9.56	12.91	4.86	6.22	**	6.7	14.1	24.1	54.0	56.8	42.9	19.1
	2.81	1.61	5.47	7.09	3.64	4.42	**	5.7	33.0	45.3	88.9	80.2	69.4	39.1
	2.05	0.36	1.24	1.69	2.58	3.11	**	4.3	60.1	74.9	134.6	110.5	96.7	67.5
Discount Stores	3.00	2.67	14.52	20.87	7.99	11.09	**	7.0	14.2	41.6	71.2	98.4	51.1	19.1
	2.18	1.42	9.04	10.60	5.84	6.76	**	5.3	30.9	70.0	123.1	130.9	62.9	36.5
	1.70	0.35	3.11	4.11	4.23	4.63	**	4.0	57.4	118.0	183.0	186.7	85.6	69.0
Discount Stores, Leased Departments	3.32	3.25	13.81	17.15	8.16	9.35	**	7.0	10.0	42.7	94.3	86.3	53.9	20.4
	2.20	1.17	6.53	7.86	5.88	5.69	**	5.4	25.9	93.7	139.4	121.0	62.3	32.6
	1.84	0.02	0.08	0.06	4.17	4.52	**	3.7	38.0	128.8	187.4	184.5	89.2	55.9
Family Clothing Stores	5.89	4.55	12.60	14.69	4.45	5.40	**	6.8	3.5	18.2	44.6	49.5	41.1	16.9
	3.41	2.06	6.24	8.37	3.01	3.53	**	4.6	11.3	38.5	77.3	76.8	64.2	34.3
	2.20	0.30	0.41	1.24	2.04	2.41	**	3.2	27.9	69.8	98.1	112.8	105.6	52.7
Furniture Stores	5.52	4.46	11.36	11.49	4.78	4.87	29	6.4	5.1	23.3	62.1	33.3	47.2	10.6
	2.82	2.00	5.66	6.00	2.94	2.89	83	4.5	12.0	53.1	111.8	69.5	75.6	25.7
	1.98	0.28	1.41	1.03	1.72	1.75	177	3.5	27.4	99.2	213.2	113.0	114.9	59.9
Gasoline Service Stations	2.88	8.36	25.51	77.62	5.44	16.10	**	22.7	26.1	25.8	41.1	55.4	91.1	16.3
	1.73	4.97	15.67	44.06	3.72	9.44	**	10.9	38.6	44.1	68.9	88.5	133.9	39.5
	1.41	1.56	7.54	23.31	2.40	5.34	**	6.5	61.4	72.3	103.1	146.1	219.8	92.7
Grocery Stores	2.21	1.49	18.78	41.61	18.60	41.53	**	21.0	50.5	47.7	87.3	98.6	70.6	30.3
	1.63	0.94	12.78	23.27	12.30	21.62	**	16.1	77.2	77.7	117.3	155.9	96.3	63.0
	1.25	0.49	5.21	10.31	8.49	13.82	**	12.3	105.2	120.5	188.0	257.1	123.4	128.6
Hardware Stores	6.25	5.25	16.38	20.45	4.55	5.02	**	5.7	5.2	16.0	41.0	60.1	27.3	9.3
	3.36	3.27	8.41	10.82	3.08	3.74	**	4.7	15.1	36.4	69.4	81.8	55.5	36.7
	2.03	1.49	4.63	5.48	1.97	2.48	**	3.2	33.2	68.3	159.0	114.0	82.2	67.3
Household Appliance Stores	2.97	3.36	12.60	15.08	8.85	9.24	16	7.4	6.4	42.9	108.6	62.8	60.6	10.7
	2.00	1.20	7.26	7.37	5.34	5.74	26	4.7	19.7	88.7	150.7	108.8	83.4	33.6
	1.45	0.29	1.83	1.72	2.77	3.47	57	4.0	50.0	174.3	316.1	185.1	121.1	66.5
Jewelry Stores	4.99	6.23	13.16	13.90	2.84	3.07	**	4.0	2.5	24.0	49.5	56.8	35.1	10.2
	3.46	3.79	7.46	8.19	1.87	2.00	**	3.0	8.0	36.2	81.8	80.3	57.5	17.0
	2.38	1.57	3.36	3.79	1.52	1.63	**	2.2	15.0	65.0	130.6	107.9	85.0	37.9
Lumber & Other Bldg. Mt's. Dealers	4.20	4.01	13.79	17.41	5.08	7.04	30	9.7	14.3	23.6	50.9	54.8	42.8	22.1
	2.86	2.27	7.43	8.75	3.52	4.90	48	5.9	28.1	44.6	93.8	80.7	71.6	32.7
	2.15	0.97	3.48	4.47	2.36	2.97	61	4.0	45.5	69.4	138.2	105.2	121.5	50.6
Miscellaneous General Mdse. Stores	6.68	4.36	14.17	17.95	5.46	6.88	**	6.7	6.6	15.3	47.3	60.2	33.3	9.6
	3.25	2.34	8.70	12.30	3.24	4.05	**	4.1	17.2	42.4	104.5	93.5	46.0	29.4
	2.03	1.30	4.86	4.74	1.98	2.36	**	3.2	33.4	70.6	155.3	148.3	80.9	59.5
Motor Vehicle Dealers	1.79	2.17	17.75	30.04	11.66	17.96	**	7.9	10.4	80.4	127.7	152.2	76.1	10.4
	1.43	1.02	9.09	14.63	8.95	14.13	**	6.6	30.8	126.8	198.3	188.4	95.4	33.0
	1.25	0.42	4.41	6.75	6.52	10.48	**	5.0	60.7	235.5	263.9	275.5	120.3	76.4
Paint, Glass & Wallpaper Stores	6.17	6.85	17.44	51.47	5.25	6.82	**	9.0	11.4	17.9	38.9	47.3	31.3	15.2
	3.70	3.13	8.57	14.29	3.45	4.33	**	7.0	30.4	29.2	80.6	71.9	51.7	30.1
	2.10	1.31	4.62	7.86	2.45	3.73	**	5.4	74.1	66.1	158.0	117.2	109.3	68.4

Line of Business	Current assets to current debt	Net profits on net sales	Net profits on tangible net worth	Net profits on net working capital	Net sales to tangible net worth	Net sales to net working capital	Collection period	Net sales to inventory	Fixed assets to tangible net worth	Current debt to tangible net worth	Total debt to tangible net worth	Inventory to net working capital	Current debt to inventory	Funded debts to net working capital
	Times	Percent	Percent	Percent	Times	Times	Days	Times	Percent	Percent	Percent	Percent	Percent	Percent
Radio &	3.45	3.90	23.34	25.35	8.94	11.31	**	6.7	10.7	33.6	100.9	96.8	37.5	17.3
Television	2.28	1.48	10.17	15.88	4.79	5.86	**	4.8	22.7	71.7	143.3	126.1	60.0	40.8
Stores	1.61	0.70	5.63	6.95	3.78	4.14	**	3.1	36.2	153.8	319.1	187.5	93.4	65.7
Retail Nurseries,	3.41	7.02	24.51	44.10	5.98	12.06	**	10.5	16.2	25.4	55.8	58.1	50.7	24.0
Lawn & Garden	2.00	3.86	12.33	29.34	3.82	6.26	**	6.9	36.1	59.8	84.3	89.4	88.4	37.6
Supp. Stores	1.40	1.53	6.72	9.00	2.53	4.41	**	5.4	54.3	96.9	134.6	145.2	154.4	46.3
Shoe	4.69	3.38	9.26	12.53	5.22	5.97	**	4.9	5.6	24.9	64.1	71.5	33.3	12.3
Stores	2.69	1.34	4.45	5.00	3.45	3.98	**	3.7	13.2	49.3	106.7	104.1	54.3	24.5
	1.99	0.12	0.56	0.83	2.28	2.68	**	2.9	31.6	94.1	201.3	147.2	78.5	60.5
Variety	4.06	3.06	13.61	16.33	6.16	7.52	**	5.1	11.4	27.5	65.0	96.0	32.2	17.1
Stores	4.88	2.20	8.80	10.94	3.98	5.13	**	4.0	28.4	48.6	89.8	128.9	44.8	30.2
	2.05	1.33	5.13	6.32	3.06	3.52	**	3.4	46.2	70.9	129.4	162.3	66.1	63.6
Women's Ready-	4.63	3.57	14.18	17.90	5.93	7.55	**	9.6	6.8	24.0	61.9	48.1	53.8	13.7
to-Wear Stores	2.68	1.82	6.68	7.31	3.89	4.62	**	7.1	29.4	49.6	109.4	72.5	84.6	32.3
	1.87	0.42	1.45	1.66	2.77	3.19	**	5.0	46.1	89.3	172.6	103.5	126.7	72.2

**Not computed. Necesary information as to the division between cash sales was available in too few cases to obtain an average collection period usage as a broad guide.

Reprinted by permission of Dun & Bradstreet Credit Services

Controlling Costs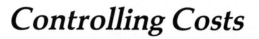

□ **How much do you need to sell to break even?**

□ **How can you determine how much inventory to carry?**

□ **When you need to buy equipment or expand your business, what financial questions do you need to ask yourself?**

□ **How much does it cost you to make your products, and how do you allocate costs to different products?**

CASE
PROBLEM

Washington Molding Company[1]

The Washington Molding Company manufactures plastic injection moldings in the Southeast. John Washington, the founder of the firm, has had extensive experience in the plastics industry. The Washington Molding Company has been in existence for three years and currently has three employees.

At the present time, the company services fifteen accounts. Half of its business is with a small aircraft manufacturer, and 30 percent is with a drug manufacturer. The remainder of the business is spread among the other thirteen accounts. John is also negotiating with a midwestern aerospace concern for a contract that could significantly expand his business. He has a good chance of securing the contract because the aerospace firm is looking for more minority subcontractors.

As John prepares for this potential growth in his company, he is becoming concerned about how he will control his costs. Specifically, he wants to know how much each job he completes costs him and how much he needs to sell at what price in order to make a profit.

Most of Washington Molding's business is acquired through the bidding process. The company responds to bid requests submitted by potential customers along with blueprints and product specifications. In order to respond to these requests with bids low enough to be competitive and high enough to allow for a satisfactory return, John needs accurate data on his costs. He needs a system for collecting and analyzing this data in order to determine whether a bid will yield a profit.

John's problem is similar to that of many business people. Often they have a good knowledge of the product they manufacture or sell but have a difficult time determining a good price for it. They avoid detailed cost calculations, although they recognize that good management demands them. Instead, they make haphazard guesses on costs and hope that the prices they set based on their guesses will yield a profit.

    Good management, however, requires a solid understanding of costs. This chapter will give you the understanding you need to control costs, make pricing decisions, and plan for profit.

PROBLEM IDENTIFICATION

Cost control is a matter of concern for all businesses. Although many cost control techniques are oriented toward the manufacturer, retail and service companies can also use some of the techniques.

    The first question that you should ask yourself when considering cost control is: Do I want to increase my profits? Since the obvious answer to this question is yes, the next step is to focus on some specifics that might help you.

    The following questions can help you to determine which cost control techniques are appropriate for you:

DIAGNOSIS

Do you know which of your costs are fixed, i.e., are constant regardless of how much you produce or sell?

Can you identify which of your costs are variable, i.e., vary directly with how much you produce or sell?

How much does your total cost increase as your sales or production level increases?

Do you know what your breakeven volume is? Do you know how many units you need to sell before you start making a profit?

Can you divide your costs into direct materials costs, direct labor costs, and overhead costs? Do you know how to calculate these costs?

Which of your operating costs need to be reduced?

Can you divide your company into centers that can earn a profit? How do you define a center, and how do you assign costs and revenues to that center?

Which costs should be assigned to one department or center? Which costs should be allocated to several departments, and how do you do the allocation?

Can you identify the costs, revenues, and profits of the various jobs that you complete?

Is there an easy way to determine whether your costs are exceeding your estimates before it is too late?

How can you use cost information to set your prices?

UNDER-
STANDING

Controlling your costs is one of the best ways to increase your profits. To some extent, you can control your costs through careful observation. Inefficient labor, wasted materials, and other careless and costly practices can be stopped or reduced through prompt action on your part. However, observation alone is not enough to control your costs. Effective cost control also requires a systematic review of your cost structure and the procedures that you develop to control costs. Specific tools of cost control are needed.

In this chapter, we will discuss several techniques of cost control, including breakeven analysis, cost classification, identification of excessive costs, cost allocation, standard costing, job costing, and inventory control.

Breakeven Analysis

Breakeven analysis is one of the tools used in cost control. It is used to determine the breakeven point, or that sales or production level at which total cost equals total revenue. The breakeven point is important because it indicates when a company can make a profit. If the sales level is less than the breakeven point, the company will suffer a loss. Beyond the breakeven point, the company can make a profit. The breakeven point is affected by several factors—fixed and variable costs, the sales price, and the sales volume.

Costs can be broken down into two types—fixed and variable. Fixed costs are those that remain constant regardless of use or production level. Variable costs are those that vary directly with use. For example, your car payment is a fixed cost because it remains the same regardless of how much you drive your car. Gas, however, is a variable cost because the amount you spend on it is directly related to how much you use your car. Fixed costs include depreciation, insurance, property taxes, and rent. Variable costs include supplies, hourly wages, electricity, and sales commissions.

There are several ways to determine whether a cost is fixed or variable. The easiest way is by intuition. However, the accuracy of this method depends on your own experience and knowledge. In general, if you can determine the amount of a particular cost at the beginning of the year, it is probably a fixed cost. For instance, depreciation is calculated at the beginning of the year and does not change through the year. If a cost fluctuates throughout the year, it is probably a variable cost.

In breakeven analysis fixed and variable costs can be expressed in terms of each unit sold. Each unit sold has both fixed and variable costs, which represent its share of the total fixed and variable costs. The variable cost of each unit sold is a constant amount. For example, each gallon of gasoline costs $1.30, regardless of how many gallons you use. However, the fixed cost of each unit is directly dependent on the production or sales volume. As the sales volume increases, the fixed costs have less of an impact on the cost of each item sold.

Figure 6.1 illustrates what happens to unit costs as the volume changes. As can be seen, the unit variable cost remains the same regardless of the sales volume. However, the unit fixed cost drops steadily as the sales volume increases, while the total fixed cost is constant. Fixed costs are related to a span of time. Variable costs, on the other hand, are related to some volume factor.

As you would expect, as you increase your volume, your total costs increase. However, as you can see in Figure 6.1, the total unit cost steadily decreases as your volume increases. This is a major factor in calculating the breakeven point. Assuming that your price covers at least all of your variable costs, there should be some point where the total revenue equals the total cost. This point is the breakeven point.

One way to determine the breakeven point is by using a cost/volume graph. A sample graph for the Acme Manufacturing Company is shown in Figure 6.2. We will assume that each unit of Acme's product sells for $6.60. Therefore, the total revenue for any sales volume can be determined by multiplying that sales volume by $6.60. The dotted line on Figure 6.2 represents the revenue generated. The solid line represents the total costs. The point where these two lines intersect is the breakeven point. As can be seen from the graph, the breakeven point is either 7,500 units or $49,500 in sales. At a sales volume of less than 7,500 units, the revenue is less than the total cost. When the volume is over 7,500 units, however, the revenue is greater than the cost, and the company can make a profit. The vertical distance between the two points is the amount of profit or loss.

Variable Costs:

Materials	$3.00/unit	
Labor	2.00/unit	
Total Unit Variable Cost		$ 5.00/unit

Fixed Costs:

Depreciation	$8,000/year	
Interest	1,500/year	
Insurance	500/year	
Property Taxes	2,500/year	
Total Fixed Costs		$12,000/year

Sales Volume (Units)	Total Variable Costs	Unit Variable Costs	Total Fixed Costs	Unit Fixed Costs	Total Cost	Unit Cost (Total)
3,000	$15,000	$5.00	$12,000	4.00	$27,000	$9.00
6,000	30,000	5.00	12,000	2.00	42,000	7.00
9,000	45,000	5.00	12,000	1.33	57,000	6.33
12,000	60,000	5.00	12,000	1.00	72,000	6.00

**Figure 6.1 Acme Manufacturing Company—
Unit Manufacturing Cost Summary**

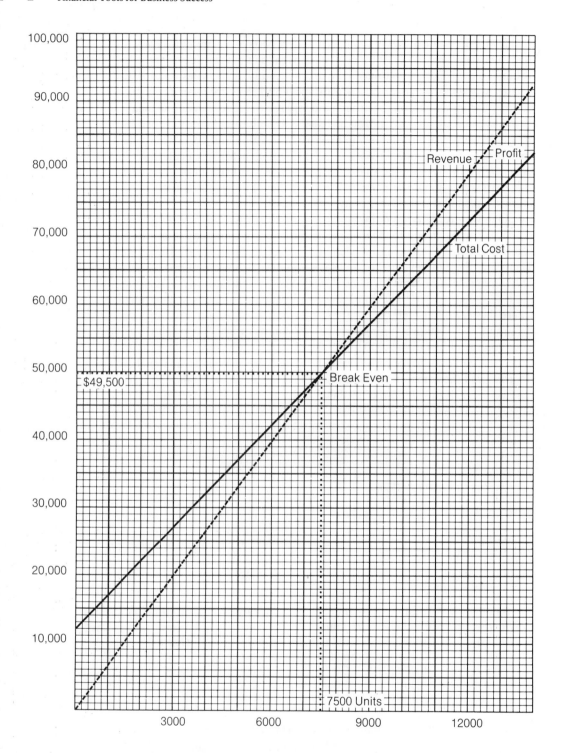

Figure 6.2 Sample Graph for Acme Manufacturing Company

The graph shows that at a sales volume of zero (-0-), the loss is equal to the fixed costs of $12,000. You can also see that as the sales volume increases, the amount of the loss constantly decreases, until eventually a profit is earned. The loss decreases because each sales dollar contributes to both fixed and variable costs. Since the unit variable cost remains the same as sales volume increases the difference between the variable cost for each unit and the selling price for each unit is the amount that can go toward covering the unit's fixed cost. Once all of the fixed costs have been covered, this difference can then contribute to the profits.

The difference between the sales price and the variable cost for each unit is called the contribution margin. This contribution margin can be used to calculate the breakeven point mathematically. The contribution margin can be expressed as either a dollar amount or as a percentage of a sales dollar. The following example illustrates how the contribution margin is derived:

Breakeven Point—Contribution Margin		
Sales Price (unit)	$6.60	100%
Variable Cost (unit)	5.00	75.8%
Contribution Margin	$1.60	24.2%

In the above example, 24.2 percent of every sales dollar, or $1.60 of the sales price of every unit sold, contributes to either covering the fixed costs of the company or adding to the profits. Because the profit at the breakeven point is zero, if we divide the total fixed costs by the contribution margin, we get the breakeven point. The general formula for the breakeven point is:

$$\text{Breakeven Point} = \frac{\text{Fixed Costs}}{\text{Contribution Margin}}$$

The breakeven point is expressed as units of sales if the dollar amount contribution margin is used. If the percentage contribution margin is used, the breakeven point is expressed as dollars of total revenue. The following example illustrates the calculation of the breakeven point for the Acme Manufacturing Company.

Breakeven Point—Units of Sale

$$\frac{\text{Fixed Costs}}{\text{Contribution Margin}} = \frac{\$12,000}{\$1.60} = 7,500 \text{ units}$$

Breakeven Point—Revenue

$$\frac{\text{Fixed Costs}}{\text{Contribution Margin}} = \frac{\$12,000}{24.2\%} = \$49,587^*$$

*Difference attributable to rounding

The two breakeven points are interchangeable as illustrated below:

$6.60 × 7,500 = $49,500 (unit sales price × units = BEP)
$49,500 ÷ $6.60 = 7,500 (total revenue ÷ unit sales price = BEP)

The breakeven point can also be used to help you in profit planning. If you want to find out how many units you need to sell to achieve a given profit, all you need to do is add the desired profit to the fixed cost and calculate the breakeven again. The following example illustrates this calculation:

Profit desired: $4,000

Calculation: $\dfrac{\text{Fixed Cost} + \text{Desired Profit}}{\text{Contribution Margin}} = \begin{array}{c} \text{Sales level} \\ \text{needed} \end{array}$

$\dfrac{\$12,000 + \$4,000}{\$1.60} = 10{,}000 \text{ units}$

Proof: Sales: 10,000 × 6.60 $66,000

Costs:

Variable Cost 10,000 × 5.00 = $50,000

Fixed Cost   12,000

Total   62,000

Net Profit $ 4,000

You can also use breakeven analysis to set prices. You can readily see that any price must be at least high enough to cover the variable cost. The amount of the contribution margin that is added to this variable cost will help to determine the breakeven point.

You can also determine the impact of a price change using breakeven analysis. For instance, what would be the impact on the breakeven point of a ten-cent increase or decrease in the sales price? The following example illustrates how to determine this effect:

EXAMPLE

	10¢ Increase	10¢ Decrease
Current sales price	$6.60	$6.60
Price change	+ .10	− .10
New sales price	6.70	6.50
Variable cost	5.00	5.00
Revised contribution margin	1.70	1.50

New Breakeven calculations:

10¢ Increase

$\dfrac{\$12,000}{\$1.70} = 7{,}059$

10¢ Decrease

$\dfrac{\$12,000}{\$1.50} = 8{,}000$

A change in the variable cost would have the same effect on the breakeven point as a price change since the contribution margin would be changed in the same way. A ten-cent increase in variable costs would decrease the contribution margin by ten cents, and a ten-cent decrease would increase the contribution margin by ten cents.

Cost Control

Once you have analyzed your cost structure using the breakeven calculations, you can focus on actual cost control.

There are three steps to cost control. The first is to classify costs. The second is to identify those costs that are excessive or out of control. The third, is to assign responsibility and accountability for controlling those costs identified as excessive.

Cost Classification.   Costs are classifed into three general areas—direct materials, direct labor, and overhead. Direct materials are those materials that are identifiable in the final product. For instance, the wood and other materials used in the manufacture of a chair are direct materials. A piece of sandpaper used to finish the chair, however, is an indirect material, and as such, is classified as an overhead cost rather than a direct materials cost. Direct labor is the labor that actually goes into the manufacture of a product. An example of a direct labor cost would be the wages of all production line workers. Overhead costs are all of those costs that are not included in direct materials or direct labor costs. These include indirect materials, indirect labor (such as the maintenance crew), supplies, repairs, heat and light, depreciation, and insurance. Any cost that cannot be readily identified with a particular product is included in overhead.

Identification of Excessive Costs.   Once costs have been classified, those that are excessive need to be identified. One way of doing this is to use common size financial statements, which were described in the previous chapter. Common size statements can be used to identify excessive costs in two ways. First, you can use them to compare your current performance with your performance in a prior period. Second, you can use them to compare your performance with industry averages.

If you were satisfied with your performance in a prior period, you can use that performance as a control standard. For instance, if your production wages were 30 percent of your total costs and you find that level acceptable, then that 30 percent becomes your control standard. As long as the production wages for your company are 30 percent or less, then you can consider that you are controlling your costs.

If you do not have a history of your cost behavior, or if you do not want to use it as a standard, then the averages for your industry can serve as cost standards. As long as your costs stay close to the average for your industry, you are controlling your costs. If you have costs that far exceed the standards, then you have identified excessive costs and know where to take corrective action.

Another way to identify excessive costs is to set cost objectives or performance goals and measure actual performance against them. Techniques for setting these standards will be described later when standard costing is discussed.

Assignment of Responsibility. After identifying excessive costs, the next step is to assign responsibility for controlling them. Setting up profit centers and cost centers is a good way to do this. A profit center is a part of a business that incurs costs and generates sales. Because it is capable of generating profits, it is designated as a profit center. A cost center is a part of the company that incurs costs but does not have a revenue-generating capability. Both profit centers and cost centers are important because they allow you to identify costs and assign responsibility for their control.

A cost or profit center can be defined in a number of ways. The following are some of the more common methods for assigning responsibility.

Department: Many businesses are divided into departments. For example, a retail store might have departments for children's toys, stationery, and women's clothing. These departments are natural responsibility centers because costs and revenues can be easily assigned.

Location: Some businesses operate at a number of locations. For instance, a dry cleaning business might have a number of small shops scattered around a city. Each of these locations can be used to accumulate revenue and costs.

Product Line: If a business has several distinct product lines or services, each of these can be considered a responsibility center, or similar products or services can be combined. You can then evaluate the cost and profit structure of each. This information is especially useful if you are considering expanding or dropping a product or service.

Responsibility centers can help you to determine and control your costs. However, determining actual costs can be a difficult process because some costs are not directly assignable to a particular department, location, or product. Therefore, in order to determine the full cost of operating a department, it may be necessary to develop a way of allocating some costs to it.

Cost Allocations. If you are going to use responsibility centers to control costs and profits, you need to assign costs to each center accurately. To do this, you need to distinguish between direct and indirect costs. A direct cost is one that is incurred by one department for its operations only. An indirect cost is one that is incurred by the operation of the company as a whole and cannot be directly identified with a particular department.

Direct costs are assigned to the appropriate department, location, or product line. For instance, if the shoe department in a store has $4,500 in wage costs, those costs are assigned to the shoe department. You will probably have little difficulty in determining and assigning direct costs.

However, indirect costs are more difficult to assign. Instead of being assigned to one department, they are distributed among the various responsibility centers using some reasonable basis of allocation. For example, allocations can be made based on sales, square footage, number of people, value of property, or labor hours. Whatever basis is used, the allocation is an estimate of each department's share of the total cost. It is important to remember that all allocations are estimates rather than precise measurements. The following example illustrates how a particular cost can be allocated to several departments.

Cost Allocation—Rent Total Rent Expenses = $9,000				
Department	Square Footage	Percentage of Total	Total Cost	Allocated Cost
A	500	12.5	9,000	$1,125.00
B	1000	25	9,000	2,250.00
C	1250	31.25	9,000	2,812.50
D	750	18.75	9,000	1,687.50
E	500	12.5	9,000	1,125.00
TOTAL	4000	100.00		9,000.00

It is also important to note that cost allocations are primarily useful in profit planning. When the indirect costs are allocated to the various departments, you can determine whether a department is covering its direct costs and indirect costs and still showing a profit. However, if a department is not showing a profit after allocations, you should not jump to the conclusion that it needs to be eliminated. There are several important factors to remember. First, the department may have had no control over its allocated costs. Second, the allocation technique used may not have treated the department fairly. Third, and most important, the elimination of the department may not eliminate all of the expenses allocated to it. Although the direct expenses will be removed, the indirect expenses that had been allocated to it will have to be reallocated to the remaining departments, and this will reduce their profits.

Standard Costing.   Another way to identify and control excessive costs is to use standard costing. Standard costs are predetermined costs for various expenses. They are used to determine whether or not a business is operating as efficiently as desired. Standard costs are based on a budget set at the beginning of the year. They represent goals. Differences between the actual costs and the standards can be used to evaluate performance. If the differences are unsatisfactory, you can take appropriate action to correct the situation.

Standard costing gives you a simple tool with which to evaluate your operation and monitor your performance. It enables you to detect problems quickly before they become serious. It is also useful in planning. With standard costing, you can estimate the cost of a job accurately.

Standard costs are usually expressed on a unit basis. The standard cost of labor, for example, is expressed as some fixed cost per hour. Even though there might be employees above and below this level, the standard cost is the average cost. Standards also reflect the amount of time or the quantity of material required for a job. If a particular job takes two hours to perform, then the standard cost for the job would be the standard cost of two hours of labor. The following example illustrates the application of standard costing:

A B Grimes Manufacturing Company	
Standard Cost of Labor	$6.75 per hour
Standard Time to Assemble Part #5478	2.75 hours
Standard Labor Cost for Part #5478	2.75 hrs. × $6.75/hr. = $18.5625

If a job called for sixteen units of part #5478, the cost of labor for the job would be:

$$16 \text{ units} \times \$18.5626 \text{ per unit} = \$297.00$$

Standard costs are useful for both planning and controlling costs. But where do the standards come from? There are three ways to set standards. The most accurate, and most expensive, way is to do an engineering study. Many large firms employ staffs to do standards studies. However, this kind of staff or outside consultants might be beyond the limits of a small business's budget. A second technique is to use your past experience as a standard. This has the advantage of being simple (if you have the records available). However, it has the disadvantage of continuing and reinforcing what might have been past inefficiencies. A third approach to the problem of setting standards is to make a "best guess." The usefulness and accuracy of your guess are limited by your own experience and knowledge. However, coupled with past experience, it could result in a useful standard.

The best rule of thumb for evaluating standards is to use two criteria. First, do the standards work? Are they useful in predicting and controlling costs? Second, are the standards achievable? A standard that is never reached because it is unreasonable or unattainable is not the useful tool you are looking for. Further, it could have negative effects on the morale and motivation of your employees. Standards should be looked upon as goals to be achieved.

Job Costing. Job costing is another technique of planning and controlling costs. It is used to determine the total costs of doing a particular job. These costs can then be compared with standards and your bid or estimate as a cost control and profit-planning technique. Job costing gives you an immediate measure of your performance without having to wait for monthly or quarterly financial statements.

Job costing begins with a job order cost form, such as the one illustrated in Figure 6.3. This form assists you in summarizing the various costs that go into filling an order for a customer. Each order for a customer is called a job and is assigned an appropriate number. The job order cost form follows the

NAME _____

ADDRESS _____

CITY/STATE/ZIP _____

DESCRIPTION:

ORDER NO. _____

DATE STARTED: _____

DATE COMPLETED: _____

BID PRICE: $ _____

QUANTITY: _____

MATERIALS			LABOR			OVERHEAD	
Date	Description	Cost	Date	Time	Cost	Labor Hours	_____
						Rate	_____
						O.H. Cost	_____
						SUMMARY	
						MATERIALS	_____
						LABOR	_____
						OVERHEAD	_____
						TOTAL COST	_____
TOTAL			TOTAL				

PROFIT: $ _____

Figure 6.3 Job Order Cost Form

job through your operation from start to finish. At each step of the process, appropriate costs are added to the form. For instance, when materials are requisitioned for use on the order, that cost is added to the materials column. In a similar manner, whenever someone works on the job, the date and amount of time spent on the project are added to the form. When the job is completed, the form is returned to the office for summarization. At that time, the costs of materials are totaled. The labor time is added and multiplied by the standard labor rate to determine the total cost of labor. The number of labor hours can also be used to determine the overhead cost applied to the job. All of these costs are then added to determine the total cost of the job. The price could also be added to the form and the cost subtracted from it to determine the profit on the job.

The overhead rate is an estimate of how much of a company's overhead costs should be charged against a particular order. Determining this rate is somewhat similar to the allocation process described earlier. As was mentioned, overhead costs are those costs of operating the company that do not directly contribute to the production of a product. The overhead rate is determined by dividing the total estimated overhead for the year by some base. The form illustrated in Figure 6.3 uses labor hours. The example in Figure 6.4 shows how the overhead rate can be estimated. This technique also allows

---

Estimated Total Overhead Expenses $220,000

Estimate of Labor time for the year:

Number of Employees:	6
Number of Hours worked per week:	40
Production hours per week	240
Number of weeks worked	50
Total of Labor hours for year	12,000

$$\text{Overhead Rate} = \frac{\text{Total Expenses}}{\text{Total Hours}} = \frac{\$220{,}000}{12{,}000} = \$18.33 \text{ per hour}$$

Figure 6.4 Calculation of Overhead Rate

---

the rate to be adjusted during the year if necessary. For instance, if the number of employees increases or decreases, the number of hours can be easily adjusted and a new rate calculated. In the same way, if there is a change in the overhead cost, the rate can be recalculated.

Inventory Control. For both retail and manufacturing businesses, the cost of inventory is a substantial expense in the operation of a business. There are several aspects to the cost of carrying inventory. If materials are not available for manufacture, the production line can be shut down. In the same way, if the retailer does not have an item in stock, there is a chance that a sale could be lost. These "opportunity" costs—lost sales resulting from a lack of inventory—must be balanced against the cost of carrying enough inventory to satisfy all demand immediately.

Carrying inventory involves two kinds of cost. One is the actual cost of storing the inventory. The rental of storage space or the allocation cost of existing space within the business will give you an estimate of the storage cost. The other aspect of carrying inventory is the financing cost. This is an estimate of what it costs a firm to have its funds tied up in inventory rather than invested elsewhere in the firm. One way to make this estimate is to use the current cost of borrowing. If the firm has $150,000 in inventory and needs $150,000 more for something else, it has to borrow the funds. If the current short-term interest rate at a bank is 11 percent, then the cost to keep and finance this amount of inventory is $16,500 ($150,000 at 11 percent for one year).

Figure 6.5 illustrates how the costs of storage and the order costs are related to the quantity of inventory carried. The total of these two costs is also shown. As illustrated, there is some ideal point where inventory costs are minimized.

One way to estimate the inventory required is to use the inventory turnover rate described in chapter 4. If your average industry turnover rate is eight and your annual sales are estimated to be $600,000, then you will need an inventory of $75,000.

Calculation:

$$\frac{\text{Sales}}{\text{Turnover Rate}} = \frac{\$600,000}{8} = \$75,000 \text{ Required Inventory}$$

One way to control inventories is to use the economic order quantity (EOQ), or the optimum size of each order of inventory. The EOQ is the point at which all of the costs associated with inventory are minimized. The formula for the EOQ is as follows:

$$EOQ = \sqrt{\frac{2\,DO}{S}}$$ where: EOQ = optimum order size   EQUATION

    D = annual demand (units)

    O = Cost to place 1 order

    S = Storage cost per unit

Annual Demand   = 50,000 units @ $12.00 per unit   EXAMPLE

    = $20.00 per order

    = $3.24 per unit

    a) Carrying Cost = $75,000 @ 11% = $ 8,250

    b) Warehousing Cost =   <u>12,000</u>

    $20,250

    c) Units Stored = $\dfrac{\$75,000}{\$12}$ = 6,250 units

    d) Unit Cost = $\dfrac{\$20,250}{6,250}$ = $3.25

$$EOQ = \sqrt{\frac{2 \times 50,000 \times \$20}{\$3.24}} = 785.67 \text{ units}$$ EXAMPLE

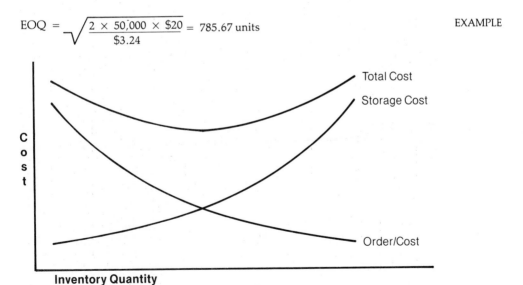

Figure 6.5 Inventory Holding Cost

Therefore, each order should be for 786 units. Orders should be placed about 64 times per year (Annual Demand divided by EOQ).

Inventory can also be controlled through the use of an inventory control ledger. In this ledger, a card is kept on each item in the inventory. Figure 6.6 illustrates a sample ledger card. Each time material is received or issued, a notation is made on the card. The card also provides for a running balance in the far right column. A quick glance at the ledger cards can then keep you advised as to the status of your inventory. Of course, this assumes that the cards are accurate and kept up to date.

What if you have an inventory that consists of thousands of items? Unless you have a computer, it would be logistically impossible to keep a card on each item. Therefore, you might resort to the ABC method of inventory control. In this method, you classify your inventory by the level of control needed. Items that you list as A items require detailed control. These might be high value or critical items that could shut down your company if they were not available. They could also be very expensive items, such as fur coats in a retail store. B items are important but require only periodic counts. You might want to use inventory ledger cards for A and B items. C items are those that you control through visual checks. These are low value and non-critical items. A hardware store's nail inventory might be a C level control item. This ABC system allows you to control your inventory with a minimum of cost and effort. Your effort and expense are focused on the areas of need.

Managerial Applications of Cost Information

Cost information is collected so that you, the manager, can make use of it to maximize the profit of your business. Cost control is the most obvious use of cost information. However, cost information can also be of help to you in pricing your product and planning for profit. It may also be useful for you in setting employee salaries.

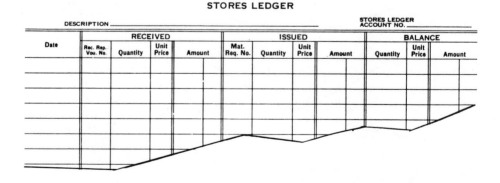

Figure 6.6 Balance of Stores Ledger Card

Cost Control. This chapter has included an extensive discussion of how cost information can be used to control costs. Cost control has three steps. First, costs must be classified. Second, they must be identified. After you have done this, you can start to control your costs. Control is achieved by assigning costs and profits to responsibility centers. Standard costing and job costing as well as cost allocations are ways to assign costs and to achieve control. Inventory costs can be controlled through the use of techniques like the economic order quantity and the ABC method.

Pricing. The discussion on breakeven points addressed the concept of the contribution margin. The contribution margin is the difference between the selling price and the variable cost of the product. Any change in the price of a product will have an immediate impact on the breakeven point. Once you know how a projected price change will affect the breakeven point, you can decide whether or not the proposed change will affect your total sales volume enough to justify the change. The following example will illustrate the effect of price changes on the breakeven point:

Effect of Price Changes on the Breakeven Point

Current Price: $15.00 per unit
Variable Cost: 12.00 per unit (80%)
Contribution Margin: 3.00 per unit (20%)
Fixed Costs: $60,000

Current Breakeven Point:

$$\frac{\text{Fixed Costs}}{\text{Contribution Margin}} = \frac{\$60,000}{\$3.00} = 20,000 \text{ units}$$

(or)

$$\frac{\$60,000}{20\%} = \$300,000$$

10% Increase in Price:
   Increased Sales Price: $16.50
   Revised Contribution Margin: 4.50
   Revised Breakeven Point:

$$\frac{\$60,000}{\$4.50} = 13,000 \text{ units } (\$220,000)$$

Decision Question:
   Will a 10% increase in the price of the product result in a drop in demand that will reduce profits below their current level?

10% Decrease in Price:
   Decreased Sales Price: $13.50
   Revised Contribution Margin: 1.50
   Revised Breakeven Point:

$$\frac{\$60,000}{\$1.50} = 40,000 \text{ units } (\$540,000)$$

Decision Question:
   Will a 10% decrease in the price increase my sales by 20,000 units?

Profit Planning. Breakeven analysis is also useful in planning profits. The earlier discussion of the breakeven formula showed how it could be used to determine the sales level required to reach a given profit. The contribution margin can also be used to estimate the profit from any given sales level. The following example will illustrate this:

Monthly Sales:	$30,000
Contribution Margin	20%
Monthly Contribution	$30,000 × 20% = $6,000
Monthly Fixed Costs:	$\dfrac{\$60,000}{12} =$ $5,000
Contribution − Fixed Costs = Monthly Profit = $1,000	

As can be seen from the example, the calculation of the contribution yielded by a given sales level will tell you how much is available to cover all of the costs for the period. The remainder is the profit that you can expect.

Salary Setting. The cost information provided by the techniques presented in this chapter can also help you determine the salaries that you should pay your workers. Although there are outside factors, such as the minimum wage laws and the general marketplace demands that you must consider, cost data can help you to determine the effect of a given wage structure on your company's overall profitability.

Labor costs are a variable expense. As such, they directly reduce the contribution margin available from every sales dollar. Therefore, a wage increase has the effect of immediately increasing your breakeven point. If you are able to measure this effect, you can better anticipate the effect on your business. You can also quickly calculate any price increases that are necessary to compensate for the increased wage expense. The following example illustrates how this can be done:

Current Selling Price:	$15.00
Current Variable Expenses:	12.00
Contribution Margin:	3.00
Fixed Expenses:	60,000.00

Breakeven Point: $\dfrac{\$60,000}{\$3.00} = 20,000$ units

Effect of a $.50 increase in labor cost per unit:

Selling Price:	$15.00
Variable Expenses (revised):	12.50
Contribution Margin (revised):	2.50

Revised Breakeven Point: $\dfrac{\$60,000}{\$2.50} = 24,000$ units

In this example it would be necessary to sell an additional 4,000 units to cover the cost of the salary increase if no adjustment were made to the selling price. However, if the selling price were increased by $.50, the contribution margin would gain by $3.00, and the breakeven point would return to 20,000 units.

The job cost form can also yield immediate information on the effect of a labor cost increase. The increased cost is reflected on the job cost form. This can be compared with the bid for the job. If the cost goes above the bid, you will have the necessary information for a bid renegotiation. You also have the data necessary to increase future bids to reflect the increase in labor rates.

John Washington can begin to control the costs in his company and to respond effectively to the bid requests that he receives by taking the following steps:

1. *Cost Classification.* He needs to identify his direct material, direct labor, and overhead costs. He should also classify these costs as fixed or variable.

2. *Common Size Statements.* Using common size statements, he should compare the current year's statements with those of past years. This will help him to identify excessive costs. He should also compare his data with that of other companies in his industry.

3. *Breakeven Analysis.* Once he has identified his fixed and variable costs, he should be able to determine the contribution margin and the breakeven point of his operation. This will give him a better idea of the amount of marketing that is required for his firm.

4. *Job Costing.* He should set up a job cost system employing a form similar to one in Figure 6.3. This will give him more control over his costs and give him a record of his performance on each contract. This kind of record will also help him to record the profitability of each of his major accounts. This data will give him accurate information on which to base his bids and will make his bids more profitable.

5. *Responsibility Centers.* He should consider setting up profit centers for his two major accounts. Since they account for 80 percent of his current business, it is very important that he closely monitor his performance with them.

CASE
SOLUTION

Washington Molding Company

The only way that costs can be managed effectively is through accurate information and control. This chapter has discussed a number of techniques that you can use to control costs.

Breakeven analysis is a good way to understand how costs behave. It shows the relationship between costs and sales volume and can help you to

CHAPTER
SUMMARY

determine the sales level necessary to achieve a profit. It can also be used to plan for profits, set prices, and make bids.

Cost control can be achieved through classifying costs and identifying those that are excessive or out of control. Costs are classified as materials, labor, or overhead. Excessive costs can be readily identified through the use of common size financial statements. They can also be identified through the use of control standards. Once costs have been identified, an effective way to control them is through the use of cost or responsibility centers.

Costs can also be identified and controlled through the use of a job cost system. This system accumulates costs for each project that you do. You can then determine whether or not the project has been profitable.

Inventory costs are controlled through close monitoring and control of related costs. One way to minimize total inventory costs is to use the economic order quantity. Another is to use the ABC method of inventory control.

Cost control is one of the fastest and surest ways to increase the profitability of your business and insure its future survival and prosperity.

DISCUSSION QUESTIONS

1. Identify five costs in your business that you think are fixed.
2. Identify five costs in your business that you think are variable.
3. Determine the breakeven point in dollars and units given the following situations:

   a. Variable Costs — $16.00 per unit
   Fixed Costs — $24.00 per year
   Selling Price — $17.50 per unit

   b. Variable Costs — $ 4.50 per unit
   Fixed Costs — $85,000 per year
   Selling Price — $ 5.00 per unit

   c. Variable Costs — $11.00 per unit
   Fixed Costs — $36,000 per year
   Selling Price — $14.00 per unit

4. The Johnson Toy Company manufactures a toy called Mr. Blogett. The following costs apply to this toy:

   Unit cost for material: $2.50
   Unit cost for labor: $1.25
   Fixed costs: $72,000 per year

   a. Determine the breakeven point if the selling price is $4.00.
   b. Determine the breakeven point if the selling price is $4.50.
   c. Assume that the Johnson Toy Company selected a selling price of $4.50. What would the effect of each of the following events be on the breakeven point? Consider each separately.

   A new mold machine was purchased. The annual depreciation on this machine increased the fixed costs by $6,000 per year.

A new labor contract with the company's employees added $.20 to the unit cost for labor.

The cost of raw materials for the toy increased by .75 per unit.

5. The Jameson Manufacturing Company supplies you with the following data:

Variable Manufacturing Cost:	$10.20 per unit
Variable Selling Costs:	$ 1.30 per unit
Fixed Costs:	$100,000 per year
Selling Price:	$13.50 per unit

a. What is the company's breakeven point?

b. What sales volume (in dollars and units) will the company need to achieve to reach a profit of $40,000 for the year?

c. What would the new breakeven point be if the following events occurred? Consider each separately.

The price decreased by $.20 per unit.

The variable costs increased by $.50 per unit.

The fixed costs increased by $25,000.

6. Western Sales Systems allocates its costs to its sales departments on the following basis:

Rent:	Departmental Floor Space
Heat:	Departmental Floor Space
Advertising:	Departmental Sales
Office Expense:	Departmental Salaries

The following information applies to the month of April:

Rent Expense:	$12,000
Heat:	2,400
Advertising:	6,000
Office Expense:	5,000

Department Information	Sales	Salaries	Area
Department 103	35,000	1,800	2,400
Department 107	40,000	1,600	2,800
Department 201	60,000	2,000	3,000
Department 205	15,000	600	400
Department 209	30,000	1,000	1,800
Totals	180,000	70,000	10,400

Allocate the rent, heat, advertising, and office expenses to each department.

7. The Harris Company uses a job cost system to determine the cost and profit for each job that it does. The standard costs for the company are as follows:

Labor Cost: ·	$7.50 per hour
Overhead Rate:	4.00 per labor hour
Materials Cost:	2.00 per unit used

Determine the cost and profit for each of the following jobs:

Job Number	Labor Hours	Materials	Selling Price
268	40	60 units	$ 620.00
275	20	35 units	375.00
276	80	200 units	1,200.00

8. The Blackwell Company uses 90,000 units of inventory item number 25984 per year. It has determined that its inventory carrying cost is $4.00 per unit and that it costs $16.00 to place an order. What is its economic order quantity?

9. Using the data in Quesion 8, what would the economic order quantity be if the inventory carrying cost were:
   a. $8.00 per unit?
   b. $2.00 per unit?

REFERENCES

Horngren, Charles T. *Cost Accounting, A Managerial Emphasis*, 3rd ed. Englewood Cliffs, N.J.: Prentice-Hall, 1972.

Matz, A.; Curry, O. J.; and Usry, M. F. *Cost Accounting, Planning and Control*, 5th ed. Cincinnati: South-Western Publishing, 1972.

FOOTNOTES

1. This case was prepared by one of the authors based on consulting work done for one of his clients. In order to maintain client confidentiality, the facts in this case differ somewhat from the actual case.

Financing Your Needs

7

□ **Where should you look for money for your firm, and when should you look for it?**

□ **Is debt good or bad or both?**

□ **When you need a loan, what should you know before you ask for it?**

CASE
PROBLEM

*Ski'in &
Swing'in*[1]

An avid snow skier and tennis buff, Tom Schmidt decided to start a store that would cater to the needs of his friends. He opened Ski'in and Swing'in in the fall of 1978. He stocks a wide variety of general and specialty merchandise for the tennis and ski trades. He concentrates his merchandise for each sport at different times of the year. Because the two product lines complement each other, his business is steady, with no drastic seasonal swings.

Tom has just found himself at a crossroads. His business has been growing at a steady rate since he opened. Over the past year his sales have increased 30 percent. Although the business made a profit of $25,000, he was able to draw out only $12,000. His rapidly expanding inventory is using up most of his cash. He takes particular pride in being able to meet any customer's needs. Therefore, when he receives a special order for an item, he generally orders an extra one so that he will be able to meet demand.

His strong sales growth has led Tom to consider opening a second store. He has just found a site in a city twenty-five miles from his present location. Two racketball facilities also just opened in town, and one is under construction near the site of the planned new store. Therefore, Tom wants to expand his product line to include racketball accessories and equipment.

Before taking the jump to open the new store, Tom has decided that a careful review of his financial statements is necessary in addition to the extensive market research that he has already done. The following conditions are causing Tom some concern:

1. His business is currently carrying a very high level of short-term debt. Most of this debt was incurred in acquiring inventory. He has a number of cash loans that will mature in about one month. In addition, his accounts payable level is 60 percent of his total current liabilities.

2. His liquidity ratios are marginal. His current ratio is 1.6:1 and his acid test is 0.9:1.

3. His inventory turnover rate is 1.3 times per year. The industry average for similar businesses is 2.6 times per year.

4. He is taking little cash out of the business. Although he is showing a good profit, there is little cash available to draw out. This has created a special burden around tax time.

If you were to survey businesses on their major problems, money would be bound to show up rather quickly. As Tom's case illustrates, even a profitable business can run into financial difficulties. Money can be the foundation of a business's success, but it can also lead to problems or failure. Although insufficient funds can stop a business, misuse or poor management of money can also contribute to problems. You may burden yourself with the wrong kind of money or get too much or too little. Another essential factor is to acquire your money at the right time—neither too early nor too late.

> **PROBLEM IDENTIFICATION**

To manage the finances of your business successfully, you need to do the following:

1. Recognize when you need funds.

2. Identify the different sources of funds.

3. Effectively manage your funds to take full advantage of the least expensive sources.

4. Establish an effective financial plan that will take full advantage of all sources without damaging your credit rating or endangering your sources.

The best financing package for your business is one that is well planned. Financial planning is a crucial key to success. An effective financial plan is based on these questions:

> **DIAGNOSIS**

Why do you need money?

How are you going to use your money?

How much money do you need?

What can you afford to pay for your funds?

If you borrow money, how and when will you pay it back?

These questions should be asked before you need money. By planning ahead you will not have to make a last-minute rush to get money. Last-minute money tends to be more expensive.

UNDER-
STANDING

There are several different ways to solve any financial problem that your business encounters. Running to the bank for a loan may be neither the easiest nor the best solution to your problem. In order to develop the best financial plan to help you to succeed, you need to know two things. First, what sources are available for the money that you need? Second, what is the best source for your needs?

There are three general categories of funding sources for your business. The first place that you should look is inside your business itself. These internal sources may be the cheapest and easiest to tap. If your internal sources are not adequate, however, you will need to look at external sources. There are two external sources of funds: the equity of the business and debt. Each of these sources has its own advantages and disadvantages:

1. Cost. How will the source of funds effect your profits?
2. Risk. How will the source expose your business to danger?
3. Flexibility. Will the source limit your ability to seek additional funds or your use of funds?
4. Control. Could you lose control of your business or have to share the decision making because of the source you use?
5. Availability. What can you get your hands on?

This chapter will explore the different sources of funds, evaluate them, and discuss how they can best be applied to typical financial problems.

Sources of Funds

Internal Sources.   Internal funding sources are those that come from within your business. Internal funds may be the easiest and cheapest money that you can find. Also, by using internal resources efficiently, you may make it easier to obtain money from external sources later. There are three sources of funding within your business: profits, customers, and suppliers.

Profit management and distribution is the first internal funding source. When a company makes a profit, the owners have two choices. They can either split up the money and take it out of the business or leave the money in the business. Money is taken out of a business through owner withdrawals of profits and through dividends. This action reduces the capital or equity of the business. However, if the owners choose to leave their profits in the business, the capital increases and can be used to finance the business. Profits are like the interest on a savings account. If you take the interest out of your savings account every year, the balance of the account will grow only if you add more money; but if you leave the interest in, then your interest starts to compound and your account balance grows faster.

You should watch your assets closely. If an item in your inventory is a slow mover, sell it at a discount and stop ordering it. You might also consider selling some of your fixed assets in favor of a less costly alternative. For instance, it might be cheaper to reimburse your employees for the use of their personal cars than to buy or lease vehicles for the company.

Another way to make it easier to keep more money in the business is to make more money. Tight-fisted management that increases profits is a good way to raise funds. Chapter 5 on financial analysis and chapter 6 on controlling costs discussed a number of ways to control expenses and increase profits.

Your customers are the second internal source of funding. You can raise money from them by expediting your collections from them. If you can get money moving into your business faster, you will have more available for your needs. For instance, if your customers pay you quickly, you will have the cash necessary to take advantage of cash discounts or quantity discounts. These discounts can reduce the cost of your merchandise and thereby increase your profits.

You can increase customer collections in two ways. First, you can encourage partial payments on long-term projects. For instance, you might request a down payment and periodic payments on lay-away sales. Second, you can put an aggressive credit collection policy into effect. This will reduce the number of bad debts that you might acquire as well as encourage your customers to pay their debts quickly. Both of these methods will increase your cash flow.

Trade credit granted by suppliers is the third internal source of funding. This is an excellent source of low- or no-cost cost money. Suppliers may be willing to extend interest-free credit on purchases of goods or services to well-established customers. A buyer might be granted thirty, sixty, or even ninety days to pay an invoice. This means that you may be able to order, obtain delivery, and sell an item before you have to pay for it. This is the same as an interest-free loan. To keep this source available to you, you must build and safeguard your relationships with your suppliers carefully.

A careful evaluation of internal sources in terms of the five factors listed earlier will help you to decide how you can best include them in your financial plan. Internal sources have a very low cost, and, in fact, in some cases they can actually save money. The risk involved in using internal sources is very low. However, you must be alert to some dangers. For example, you need to be careful that you do not alienate your customers with an overly aggressive credit policy. Also, you should not convert to cash those assets that are productive or necessary to the effective operation of your business. Your inventory has to be broad enough to satisfy normal customer demand. Internal sources give you maximum flexibility, as long as they are used carefully. These funds also insure that you retain control of the firm. The availability of internal funds depends on circumstances. Often they are somewhat limited and grow at a slow rate. Therefore, they may need to be supplemented with external funds. However, the firm that makes full use of its internal funds by carefully managing all of its assets and controlling its costs will find that it is much more attractive to external sources of funds. This should make it easier to raise money when it is needed.

Equity.   Equity is one of the two external funding sources available to you. Equity funds are those generated by the invested capital of a firm. The types of equity funds that can be generated depend on the organizational form of the business. From chapter 3 you know that there are three general forms of business organization: proprietorships, partnerships, and corporations. Each of these forms has unique ways to raise equity funds, with varying levels of ease and availability. Equity funding for each organizational form is discussed and evaluated below.

Sole Proprietorship.   In a sole proprietorship, the only source of equity funds is the owners's pocketbook. Other than internal sources of money, the only way that the sole proprietor can increase the invested capital in the business is to draw on personal assets. These include savings accounts, life insurance policies, and collateral loans on personal assets, such as a house. Therefore, equity funding is a very limited source of funds for most sole proprietors.

For a sole proprietor, the advantages and disadvantages of equity funding are similar to those of internal financing. The cost is relatively low. If the owner needs to borrow against personal assets, the cost might be personally high, but is still low for the business. The risk is also low. In addition, the proprietor is able to retain substantial flexibility and control with equity funding. The availability of equity funds is completely determined by the personal resources of the owner.

Partnership.   Partnerships find it easier than sole proprietorships to raise equity capital. In fact, many proprietorships become partnerships in an effort to raise additional funds. A partnership makes it easier to raise funds for two reasons. First, each of the partners can be tapped for additional funds. Second, additional partners and their money can be added to a partnership to increase its capital.

Equity funding needs to be evaluated separately for general and limited partnerships.

General Partnership: In a general partnership, each partner shares in the control and profits of the business. Taking on more general partners erodes the control of the original partners but adds capital and expertise to the business. General partners are a source of low-cost and low-risk equity funds. Although new partners add more funds, the original partners may experience a reduction in both their flexibility and control.

Limited Partnership: Limited partners are restricted to contributing capital and collecting on the distributed profits. The advantage of the limited partnership is that the general partner(s) can raise additional money at low cost and low risk while retaining control and flexibility. However, there is a danger that limited partners may want to get control of the business or withdraw if they see a danger to their investment.

Corporation.   A corporation is the most complex form of business organization. Although it has a much larger base from which it can raise equity funds, it is also subject to much more control than any other form of business organization. There are three general sources of equity funds available to the corporation: common stock sales, preferred stock sales, and special debt issues.

Common Stock: Common stock represents ownership in the corporation. When a business is incorporated, it is authorized to sell a maximum number of common shares. Once it has sold its initial stock offering, it can continue to sell common stock up to the authorized level. The existing stockholders are able to maintain their proportionate control of the business by exercising their pre-emptive right, which is their right of first refusal on all new stock issues. There is relatively little risk to a business if it issues additional stock, although there is some cost if the new stockholders demand more dividends than the existing stockholders. This may limit the firm's ability to raise funds internally and force it to resort to debt. There is also some limitation of control and flexibility if the new stockholders wish to exercise control over the policies and direction of the business.

Preferred Stock: Preferred stockholders have first call on any dividends distributed by the corporation. These dividends are often guaranteed. Therefore, the cost of issuing preferred stock is higher than that of common stock because there is a commitment to a constant outflow of funds. This outflow may also increase the risk of the business. However, because preferred stockholders do not normally have the right to vote, the control of the corporation remains with the common stockholders. The corporation can also retain a substantial amount of flexibility.

Special Debt Issues: There are two kinds of debt issued by corporations that are treated as equity fund sources—convertible debentures and debentures with warrants. Convertible debentures are debt issues that can be converted into shares of stock at the option of the holder. The advantage to the corporation is that it can borrow money by issuing the convertible debentures, but it may not have to pay that money back if the bonds are converted into stock. The cost and risk of convertible debentures are lower than for regular debt. However, they carry a potential loss of both flexibility and control. Debentures with warrants are bonds with coupons attached that allow the holders to cash them in for a specified number of shares of stock at a specified price. A warrant may reduce the cost of debt some, but the risk may remain relatively high because the debt continues. The potential loss of flexibility and control depends on how many of the warrants are used.

Special Sources.   There are also some special sources of equity funds. These include venture capitalists, risk capital investors, and state economic development programs.

Venture capitalists invest in new or expanding businesses in the hope of getting a return on their money as the businesses grow and prosper. Venture capital firms may be composed of banks and other financial institutions, insurance companies, large corporations, and private groups and individuals.

Often venture capital firms are interested in specific locations or types of businesses. When looking for potential investments, venture capitalists consider a business's management, its competitive advantage, and its potential for growth.

Venture capital is a high-risk investment. Therefore, investors are looking for opportunities for a high return. A venture capital firm may require a large portion of your business's equity, sometimes over 50 percent. It may also demand a seat on your board of directors or even control of your board as part of the price of its investment. This increases the risk to the entrepreneur because the investor could remove the entrepreneur if it were deemed necessary. One popular method used by venture capital firms is the leveraged buy-out. In this method, the investors buy out an existing company for the entrepreneur by borrowing against the assets to be acquired. Venture capital is frequently invested in new business start ups. A new development in the venture capital market is the business development company (BDC), which is a publicly traded venture capital firm.

Risk capital investors, such as small business investment companies (SBIC) and minority enterprise small business investment companies (MESBIC), are private venture capital firms chartered by the Small Business Administration. They are designed to make relatively small and limited investments in targeted small businesses. They tend to be conservative in their investments and are more interested in mature ongoing companies rather than those just starting out.

State business and development corporations are authorized by legislation and charters in some states. They make both equity and debt funds available to businesses that show the potential to grow and increase employment opportunities.

There may also be a number of other special programs that provide funds or services for special target groups of businesses, both existing and developing. To find out which ones are available to you, you should contact your local office of the Small Business Administration. You may also find out about local or state programs through your state's business development department or employment development department.

Debt.   Debt financing is the second external source of funding available to you. Debt is generally classified by the length of time that you have to pay it back. Short-term debt is usually paid off in less than one year. Intermediate loans last up to five years. Any debt with a maturity date beyond five years is called long-term debt. Another major difference between the types of debt is that short-term debt is often self-liquidating. This means that the loan is used for a purpose that will generate enough cash to repay it. For instance, if a loan is taken out to buy inventory, it will be paid back out of the funds generated when the inventory is sold. Intermediate and long-term debt, on the other hand, must be paid for out of the overall financial resources of a business.

As you start to develop your business, it is very important that you make contact with bankers. They can provide valuable advice as well as money. They will often have many contacts in the business community who can help you to solve the myriad problems that you will face. In developing a banking relationship, it is necessary to be totally honest. You should always provide the bank with accurate, complete, and detailed information. Bankers will want to know the answers to three questions:

1. Can you repay the loan?
2. Will you repay the loan?
3. If you don't repay the loan, how can the bank get its money back?

Your credit history and collateral can answer the last two questions. However, a well-thought-out business plan and financial projections are necessary to answer the first question. You should also keep your banker advised of the progress of your business. If there is a problem, it is better that you be the source of information about it. This helps to maintain a sound relationship between you and the bank. Also, the bank may be able to help you to solve the problem before it gets too serious.

Short-Term Debt.   Short-term debt is used to get a business through a shortage in its cash supply. Because the cash collections and payments of a business do not necessarily come at the same time, it may be necessary to borrow during a cash deficiency and pay back the loan during a cash surplus period. Short-term debt falls into several general categories.

Commercial Notes: Commercial notes are issued by banks and other lending institutions for short periods, generally thirty to ninety days, but even up to six months. These notes are usually repaid in one lump sum on the maturity date. Often there is no collateral on these loans, although some may be required depending on the borrower's credit standing. A compensating balance may also be required. This means that some portion of the loan must remain in one of the business's accounts at the bank.

Accounts Receivable Financing: Sometimes a business can arrange to get a percentage of its outstanding accounts receivable balance advanced to it. In return the firm will assign its customer accounts to the lender. These loans are essentially revolving lines of credit in that the funds are constantly being advanced, repaid, and readvanced. In this kind of arrangement, the lender can recover any bad accounts from the borrower.

Another type of accounts receivable financing is called factoring. A factor buys a business's accounts receivable and in return charges a fee plus interest. The factor also assumes responsibility for collecting on the accounts and must absorb any losses for bad debts. A factor relies on the honesty of the business, its willingness to stand behind its products, and the general credit policies followed by the firm.

Inventory Loans: An inventory loan is a special type of commercial loan used to buy inventory or raw materials. For instance, a retail store may need to borrow to acquire the inventory that it will need for the Christmas shopping rush. It will then pay the loan back after it has sold the goods.

Line of Credit: A line of credit is a prior arrangement with a lender to borrow money up to some maximum. The business can borrow against its line of credit any time during the duration of the agreement. However, interest is charged only against the amount actually borrowed. Therefore, a line of credit for a business is like a credit card at a department store for an individual. Lines of credit are given to businesses with well-established credit records.

Intermediate and Long-Term Debt. Intermediate and long-term debt is composed of loans and other credit arrangements that are paid off over a period longer than one year. Intermediate debt usually matures in less than five years. Long-term debt can last for as long as thirty years. Intermediate and long-term debt is used to acquire fixed assets and provide some of the basic financing of a company, such as working capital. It is paid off out of the general operating funds of the business rather than being self-liquidating like short-term debt. Intermediate and long-term debt falls into the general categories described below:

Unsecured Term Loans: An unsecured term loan is one issued to a company that can prove it has the financial strength and profitability to repay the loan. Ability to repay is usually demonstrated through the business's current and projected financial statements. An unsecured term loan is usually not issued to a new business unless the owners can contribute 40 to 50 percent of the required equity.

A contract for an unsecured term loan usually includes several clauses that restrict the operating and financial practices of the business. These might include restrictions on further debt, dividends and other profit distributions, and some salaries. The percentage of profits required to pay off the loan might also be specified. The contract might also require that a compensating balance be retained.

Equipment Loans: When you buy a car or truck, you probably put it on time, with the vehicle pledged as security on the loan. Equipment loans work the same way. Generally, they are secured by the equipment purchased and are paid off in regular installments over the term of the loan. The term of the loan will be the usable life of the piece of equipment, up to about five years. Equipment loans may be limited to 60 to 80 percent of the value of the equipment, depending on the policies of the lender and the type of equipment pledged as collateral.

Real Estate Loans: Real estate loans are mortgages secured by commercial and industrial property. They are made for a portion of the property's value and are amortized, or repaid, over a period of ten to twenty years.

Equipment Leasing: Leasing is becoming a more common method of financing. Instead of buying a piece of equipment, a business or individual will lease it from a financial institution, which actually owns the property. Because the business does not actually own the property, it does not necessarily need to declare the equipment as an asset or the lease obligation as a liability. This is like getting a loan without reporting the debt. Whether or not a lease obligation needs to be reported is best determined by an accountant. All lease payments are deductible business expenses.

Flooring: Flooring is a specialized debt vehicle used by certain retailers, such as car, boat, and furniture dealers. In a flooring arrangement, the lender retains a security interest in the merchandise. The business pays a monthly interest charge and pays off the principal as each item is sold. Generally, flooring arrangements are revolving and can be renewed periodically.

Evaluating Debt Financing.   All of the various kinds of debt yield similar results when evaluated. The cost of debt ranges from moderate to high. The actual cost depends on the type of debt, your individual credit rating, the credit rating of your business, and the general state of the economy. Debt also has a higher risk than either internal or equity financing, depending on the type of collateral pledged as security against the loan. A default on a loan can result in the loss of the collateral. The amount of flexibility with debt varies. Restrictive clauses in loan contracts and high compensating balances can significantly reduce management flexibility. Also, a lease can bind you to a piece of equipment or a facility that may not satisfactorily meet your needs. Debt does permit the owner to retain a moderate to high degree of control over the business.

Funding Problems and Suggested Financing Solutions

In deciding which funding source is most appropriate for your needs, you need to ask yourself not only how much money you need but also how long you need the money for. The answers to these questions will vary depending on what you are using your loan for. In the discussion below, the various reasons for borrowing are described and appropriate financing solutions suggested.

New Business Start Up.   When you buy an existing business or start one from scratch, you have two financing problems. First, you need funds to cover your start-up costs, such as the purchase price and the cost of inventory and equipment. Second, you need funds to cover the day-to-day operating expenses of the business until it becomes self-sufficient. Payrolls, rent, taxes, utility expenses, and your own personal needs will continue regardless of the success of the business. Therefore, your start-up funds need to take these expenses into account.

Your start-up funds should come from a long-range source, such as invested equity capital or intermediate or long-range debt. The best source of start-up funds is equity. Debt funds carry a pay-back provision that could strain the already limited resources of your business. If you do not have the funds available personally, you should look to other equity sources, such as partners or venture capitalists. Of course, if you want to "go it alone" or cannot find willing investors, you may need to resort to debt.

Short-term debt is the least desirable source of funds for starting out. First, its maturity date may arrive before you reach self-sufficiency. You could then find yourself in a cash crisis before you ever get going. Second, short-term funds may require higher monthly payments. These higher payments could strain the revolving cash needs of your business and force you into a continuing spiral of borrowing.

Working Capital.   Your initial working capital requirements should be met through your start-up funds. However, as your business expands, your need for working capital also increases. Because your working capital requirements are a relatively permanent part of your business, you should consider a long-range funding source. Some of your working capital can be arranged through internal sources. However, these may be exhausted quickly. Therefore, you may also need to look at increased equity investment or long-term debt. One source of equity financing is your business itself. Instead of taking all the profits out of the business as dividends or other withdrawals, you may find it more advantageous to allow your accumulated profits to increase your invested equity.

Seasonal Peaks.   Seasonal peaks, such as holiday inventory requirements, are short-term needs and are probably best met with short-term funds. A self-liquidating, short-term loan is a good method of financing seasonal peaks. The cost is relatively low, and the loan can be paid off with the revenue generated by the peak.

Capital Expenditures.   Capital equipment expenditures should be met with long-term financial resources. Long-term debt, such as an equipment loan for the life of the asset, or equity financing is a good way to pay for equipment. Capital expenditures may generate sufficient surplus cash to enable you to repay the loan. However, if the money to purchase equipment is unavailable to you, leasing is an attractive and feasible alternative.

Sustained Rapid Growth.   Sustained rapid growth is different from a seasonal peak in that it continues for several seasons. If it occurs rapidly, you may find yourself short of the necessary cash to expand your basic level of inventory, acquire needed equipment, or secure the expanded facilities needed. This kind of growth may require that several kinds of financial resources be used, including equity, long-term debt, and short-term debt. Before a particular mix of funding sources is decided on, you should prepare a careful financial plan. This plan should plot out your business's growth, with an estimate of its rate of increase and how long you expect it to last. Your plan should include a mix of available resources that contribute as much as possible to your profits.

When you are searching for solutions to the financial problems that confront your business, you need to keep in mind the entire spectrum of potential solutions available to you. Figure 7.1 summarizes the various funding sources and indicates how they rate in terms of the five evaluation factors.

Buying An Existing Business.   The purchase of an existing business is not really a unique financing problem. Rather it is a combination of the financing problems generally facing business. The purchase of an existing business is very much like starting a new business (acquiring capital assets), developing adequate working capital, providing for capital expenditures (for remodeling, renovation, and upgrading), and, if you can believe the present owner, providing for future growth.

When you are considering the purchase of an existing company, you need to answer two questions. First, what is the business worth? Second, how will you pay for it? This chapter has already addressed the second question. The various financial tools that have been discussed are the ones that you will want to use when buying the business. However, how will you determine how much you should pay for the business?

The bottom line on the cost of a business is an agreement between you and the present owner on what the value of the business is. The price will be set through negotiations. When you enter these negotiations, you need to be prepared. The existing owner will want as much as possible for the business. You should be willing to pay a fair price. However, you want to be certain that you do not pay more than the business is worth or more than is necessary. There are three factors used to determine the value of an existing business: the market value, the current net income, and the future growth prospects of the business.

The market value of the business is determined by two factors: the value of the assets and goodwill. The value of the assets is best determined by having an independent appraisal of the assets. This will insure that the value set on the assets is determined objectively. The goodwill of the business is harder to determine. Simply, goodwill is the difference between the price that is paid for the business and the value of the assets. Goodwill is attributed to the abil-

EVALUATION FACTORS	INTERNAL	Sole Proprietorship	EQUITY Partner	Corporation	DEBT
Cost	low	low	low	moderate	moderate—high
Risk	low-moderate	low	low	moderate	high
Flexibility	high	high	moderate	moderate-low	moderate—low
Control	high	high	moderate	moderate	moderate
Availability	?	?	?	?	?

Figure 7.1 Source of Funds

ity of a business to earn more than is normal because of its good reputation or prized location or some other factor. Goodwill is based on the net income of the business as well as the expected future net incomes. There are three ways to determine goodwill.

The first method is the *capitalization of the average earnings* of the company. The average annual earnings of the company are divided by an expected rate of return to yield the capitalized value of the business.

EXAMPLE

Average annual earnings:	$50,000
Expected rate of return:	8%
Capitalized value:	$\dfrac{\$50,000}{.08} = \$625,000$

Once the capitalized value of the business has been determined, the appraised value of the assets is subtracted. The difference is the goodwill. If the above example were expanded, the following would be the result:

EXAMPLE:

Capitalized value:	$625,000
Appraised asset value:	600,000
Goodwill:	$ 25,000

The second method of determining goodwill is the *capitalization of excess earnings.* This is done in two steps. First, the expected profits of the business are determined by multiplying the net assets of the business by the normal rate of return. Then these normal earnings are compared to the actual earnings and the excess are capitalized to yield the capitalized value of goodwill. The following example illustrates these steps:

EXAMPLE

Average Earnings:		$50,000
Net Value of Assets:	$600,000	
Normal return on Assets:	7%	
Normal Earnings: ($600,000 at .07)		42,000
Excess Earnings:		8,000

If we now assume that the excess earnings are capitalized at 16%, the goodwill would be calculated as follows:

Capitalized Goodwill: $\dfrac{\$\ 8,000}{.16} = \$50,000$

The capitalized value of this business would be:

Net Value of Assets:	$600,000
Goodwill:	50,000
Total Value:	$650,000

Present value analysis is the third technique used to determine the value of goodwill. This method has the advantage of limiting the amount of time that the earnings are capitalized. It is calculated by discounting the expected excess earnings at a capitalization rate for an agreed upon number of years.

Present value tables are used to get the discount factors for the capitalization rate. These factors are then multiplied by the excess profits to determine the amount of goodwill. There is a more detailed description of present value analysis in chapter 8. However, the following example illustrates how the calculation is done:

EXAMPLE

Discount factors at 16%	*Excess* × *Earnings*	*Goodwill* = *Contribution*
.862	$ 8,000	$ 6,896
.743	8,000	5,944
.641	8,000	5,128
.552	8,000	4,416
.476	8,000	3,808
	Capitalized Goodwill	$26,192

The above example uses five years at 16 percent to determine the capitalized goodwill. However, any number of years and any discount rate can be used.

The current net income, or the average net income, for any business is determined from the income statements of the business. However, if you are going to use the business's income statements as the source of the net income, you need to make certain that they are accurate and fair. The best way to guarantee accuracy and fairness is to have the statements audited by an independent public accountant.

The future growth prospects of the business can be predicted in two ways. First, you can do a trend analysis on the sales and net income (profits) of the business over a reasonable period of time. This time period should not be too long because outside economic forces can have a distorting effect. Your trend analysis should not be longer than five to eight years. Second, you can predict future growth with a market analysis. The business plan described in chapter 2 included a market analysis. Whether you are buying an existing business or starting from scratch, a market analysis should be done. It is a more valuable indicator of the future potential of a business than the past profit performance.

Ski'in and Swing'in has a number of problems common to many small businesses. There are several factors that contribute to these problems:

CASE
SOLUTION

Ski'in &

Swing'in

The business has experienced sustained rapid growth.

There is an opportunity to expand the business.

There is a serious cash flow problem.

Tom's management techniques are loose. His inventory turnover is much too low for his type of business. In addition, his liquidity ratios suggest that he may soon have a serious credit problem.

There are several steps that Tom Schmidt should take to address the financial problems of his business:

1. He should trim his inventory. Although his sales are increasing rapidly, his inventory is increasing even more rapidly. His turnover rate should be near the industry average, if not higher because of his sales growth. One of his problems may be his purchasing policies. By ordering extras of special order items, he may be carrying too many slow-moving items. By trimming his stock and ordering only those items actually requested, he should be able to improve his turnover ratio and reduce the funding level required to maintain his inventory.

2. He may have an inadequate level of working capital. Many rapidly increasing businesses find this is the case. He should consider a long-term financial solution that will reduce his current debt and increase his working capital. This should improve his liquidity position.

3. If his market research indicates that there is sufficient demand for both a new store and an expanded product line, he should seriously consider expanding his equity base. Because his personal situation limits the amount of funds that he can raise individually, he should consider the addition of a partner or look for some source of venture capital. The addition of more long-term debt would be of questionable value at this time. He may need to use his debt-carrying capacity to expand his working capital. More debt to finance the expansion of the business may aggravate his cash flow difficulties and limit his future flexibility.

CHAPTER SUMMARY

Because the financial structure of your business is crucial to your success, it needs to be well planned. To develop your financial plan, you need to answer the following questions:

Why do you need money?

How are you going to use your money?

How much do you need?

How much can you afford to pay for your funds?

How and when will you pay back any loans?

There are a number of reasons that your business may require funds. You may be starting a new business. Funds are also needed to establish and maintain working capital. Funds may be required for seasonal peaks or for new or replacement equipment. You may want to establish a firm financial base for sustained rapid growth.

Regardless of why you need funds, there are three principal sources of funding. You can turn to your own business and use internal sources. A second method is to expand your equity base by making an additional investment yourself or by adding partners or stockholders. Your last option is to use some type of debt.

All of your financial resources should be evaluated in terms of five factors. They include the cost of the resource, the risk involved, the impact that it will have on your flexibility to run your business, the effect it will have on your control of the business, and, perhaps the most important, the availability of the funding source.

To summarize, when you are considering the purchase of an existing business, you should consider the market value of the business, its current net income, and the future growth prospects of the business. The firm's market value is the net value of its assets plus the value of its goodwill. The net value of assets should be determined by appraisal. Goodwill can be determined by using capitalization of average earnings, capitalization of excess profits, or present value analysis. The business's current net income can be obtained from its income statements. Its future growth prospects can be predicted by either a trend analysis or a market study.

DISCUSSION
QUESTIONS

1. List five reasons a business may need money.

2. What are the major sources of money for a business?

3. What are the factors that you should consider when evaluating a source of funds for your business?

4. Name three sources of internal financing for a business.

5. What are the differences between a general and a limited partnership? What are the advantages and disadvantages of each in terms of financing a business?

6. What is the difference between preferred stock and common stock?

7. What is a venture capitalist?

8. List three kinds of short-term debt. Describe each.

9. What three questions will your banker want the answer to before you can get a loan?

10. Get a loan application from a bank for a commercial loan.

11. What advantages are there to leasing equipment as opposed to buying it?

12. Why should different financing tools be used for seasonal peaks and sustained rapid growth?

13. You are considering the purchase of an existing business. The following factors will provide the basis for your decision.

Appraised value of the net assets:	$800,000
Average annual net income (5 years)	55,000
Normal rate of return for similar firms:	6%
Expected rate of return:	10%
Excess earnings capitalization rate	14%

Determine the value for the business using the following methods:
a. Capitalization of average earnings
b. Capitalization of excess earnings
c. Present value of excess earnings

REFERENCES   Bank of America. *Cash Flow/Cash Management.* Small Business Reporter. San Francisco, 1977.

Bank of America. *Financing Small Business.* Small Business Reporter. San Francisco, 1976.

Small Business Administration. *The ABC's of Borrowing.* Management Aid No. 170. Washington, D.C., 1977.

Business Basics, The Profit Plan. Washington, D.C.

FOOTNOTES   1. This case was prepared by one of the authors based on consulting work done for one of his clients. In order to maintain client confidentiality, the facts given in this case differ somewhat from the actual case.

Appendix A

OUTLINE SAMPLE
LOAN PACKAGE

If you have decided that you need to borrow money, you might want to use this outline as a guide to preparing your loan application; however, there are no "standard" formats for a loan application. Also, much of what you have already prepared for your business plan can be used in your loan application.

  I. SUMMARY
      A. History or background of the business
      B. Amount and details of use for the loan
      C. Proposed repayment details
      D. Security or collateral for the loan
      E. Personal Data on Business Owner(s)
          1. Education and business experience
          2. Credit references
          3. Personal financial statement

 II. FIRM DATA
      A. Financial statements (last three years if available)
      B. Business plan
      C. Insurance details (life and casualty)
      D. Cash flow statements
      E. Sales agreements, contracts, leases, or other data relevant to the loan

III. PROJECTIONS
      A. Projected income statements or operating budgets
      B. Projected cash flow statements for period of the loan
      C. Pro forma balance sheet based on projections

NOTES: The loan will be between the bank or lending institution and the business (or business owner). The lender will need to have confidence in the security of the loan. Therefore, the loan request should be complete, accurate, and honest. These qualities are more important than a flashy presentation.

Venture Capitalists:

Western Association of Venture Capitalists
244 California Street, Room 500
San Francisco, CA 94111

National Venture Capitalist Association
10 South LaSalle Street
Chicago, IL 60603

Venture Capital (Periodical)
S.M. Rubel & Company
10 South LaSalle Street
Chicago, IL 60603

Small Business Administration
Washington, D.C. 20416

Office of Minority Business Enterprise
U.S. Department of Commerce
Washington, D.C. 20230

Appendix B

INFORMATION
SOURCES

Cash Management and Capital Budgeting

☐ Do you have enough cash or too much?

☐ How can you plan for the best, or most profitable, use of your cash?

☐ What are the best ways to control your cash flows, and what should you do with the excess cash?

☐ How can you evaluate alternative capital expenditures?

CASE
PROBLEM

Worldwide Printing[1]

Worldwide Printing was organized in 1972 by John Bernard. That year he acquired the rights to manufacture and market a daily diary for keeping track of business appointments. Worldwide's product line is currently carried by 135 independent distributors and 630 retail outlets, mostly stationery and office supply stores in the Midwest.

Although the company has enjoyed modest success during its life, there have been some changes in the last few years that have reduced the company's success. Although sales have continued to increase, the company has found that its cash position has steadily deteriorated. The company recently borrowed a significant amount of money, and the payments on this loan have further reduced its cash position. An examination of the company revealed the following information:

1. Accounts receivable show poor management. The average collection period for accounts has increased from 25.0 days in 1979 to 32.2 days in 1981. The business also carries many accounts that are over six months old. Accounts receivable make up 59.5 percent of the business's working capital.

2. The company carries a very high level of inventory. The finished goods inventory accounts for 78.3 percent of the company's total current assets. The current ratio is 1.4 and the acid test ratio is 0.3. The inventory is 2.5 times the working capital, a level about ten times the normal level for this industry.

3. The company's major product line, the daily diary, accounts for 86 percent of the total sales of the company. The profit rate on this product line is 1 percent of sales. The remaining product lines earn a 52 percent profit on their sales.

4. The company's production system is labor intensive. Labor costs account for 60 percent of all costs on the diary system. Most operations are done by hand with minimum machine assistance.

John is getting quite concerned about his business. Although his sales are increasing, he has found paying his bills more and more difficult. He has watched his profits slowly decrease. His current debt is straining the financial resources of the business.

In the previous chapter we explored the various sources that can be tapped to secure the money required to run your business. Just as important as knowing where to get money is knowing how to manage it effectively. For many businesses, including Worldwide Printing, problems arise not so much from a lack of funds as from poor management of funds.

PROBLEM IDENTIFICATION

There are two dimensions to effective financial management: the management of cash itself and the management of capital expenditures. Both of these factors can contribute to the success of your business if they are handled well.

Efficient cash management insures that your business has enough money to meet its continuing day-to-day needs. It also insures that you get the most out of the money that you have. Too little cash may mean that you will not be able to meet your obligations. Too much cash held in reserve may be an unprofitable use of one of your most valuable assets.

There are three factors that contribute to successful cash management:

1. Planning for an adequate cash supply

2. Controlling cash flows

3. Using excess cash profitably

If you can strike a good balance among these three factors, you will have made a big step toward the successful financial management of your business. This balance will not only help you to keep your head above water but also help you to increase your overall profitability.

The second aspect of financial management, capital budgeting, includes planning and evaluating expenditures for capital assets. Capital expenditures can use a substantial portion of your cash supply. You therefore must insure that you make the best decisions possible when purchasing capital assets. There are three dimensions to capital budgeting. First, you need to plan what capital expenditures your company needs to make. Second, you need to plan the initial outlay and the expected benefits, or cash returns. Third, you need to evaluate each expenditure carefully to insure that you are making the best decision.

Effective planning of your capital expenditures will insure that you have the equipment and facilities that you need when you need them. It will also help you to increase your profitability.

DIAGNOSIS   All businesses need to exercise tight control over their cash. Cash is the most liquid of all of your assets. As such, it can disappear much more quickly than you expect. It is also your most critical asset. Without cash you will be unable to pay your employees, purchase your inventory, or pay any of the other myriad expenses of your business. Therefore, it is essential that you have a clear picture of the flow of cash through your business and be able to determine your cash status quickly. In order to determine the quality of your business's cash control, you should ask yourself the following questions:

Can you predict when you will need to borrow funds?

Do you know the minimum level of cash needed to operate your business?

Do you know how to speed the flow of cash into your business?

Do you have a good record of collections on your accounts receivable?

Do you know how to pay your bills so that you maintain a credit rating and at the same time keep your profits at a good level?

These questions all have two answers. The first answer is a technique. If you know the technique, fine. If not, this chapter will teach it to you. More importantly, to answer these questions fully, you need to know how to use each technique to maximize the efficiency and profitability of your business.

Capital expenditures are the biggest single investments that you will make for your business. As such, they need to be carefully planned and evaluated. The following questions will help you to determine whether you have an effective capital management system:

Do you anticipate when you will need to make a purchase of a capital asset?

Do you know the techniques for evaluating which investment will be the most beneficial and profitable?

Is the amount of time required to recover the cost of an investment the best way to evaluate it?

How can you evaluate the relative benefit of different-sized projects?

This chapter will help you to answer these questions. As a result, you will be better able to make the capital decisions needed in your business.

UNDER-   In this chapter we will examine cash management and capital budgeting as
STANDING   two separate, but related, issues. Cash management is the day-to-day use of cash in a business. Capital budgeting is the analysis of the costs and benefits of major capital expenditures. Both of these issues are related to the use of cash. Cash management is more concerned with short-term issues, and capital budgeting is related to long-term issues.

Cash Management

There are three dimensions to cash management: cash budgeting, control of cash flows, and the use of surplus cash. A cash budget is a plan that details the circulation of cash into and out of a business. Cash flow management is a set of techniques used to speed the flow of cash into a business while carefully controlling the outflow of funds. The management of surplus funds involves using the extra cash that a business may have from time to time to increase the overall profitability of the business.

Before looking at these three dimensions of cash management, you need to understand how cash flows into and out of a business in the normal course of operations. The initial investment of cash is used to purchase inventory and to pay the normal operating expenses of the business. These expenditures provide the products or services that the business sells. These sales then generate cash, which is reinvested in the operation of the business. This circular flow of funds is illustrated in Figure 8.1.

The cash flowing into a business comes from two sources: the business itself and outside sources. Outside sources of funds include both investments by the owner(s) and loans. These funds are normally used to start the business or increase its size. The sale of goods or services is the main internal source of cash for the business. Those sales that are made for cash are direct sources. Credit sales flow through accounts receivable before becoming a source of cash.

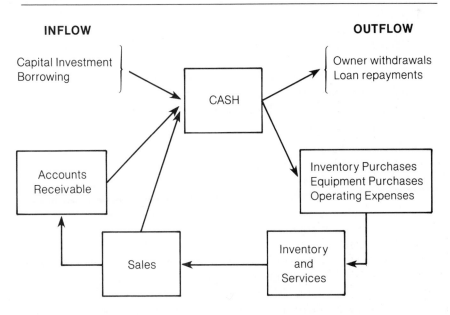

Figure 8.1 Circular Flow of Cash Through a Business

Once a business has a supply of cash, it can either remain in the business or be taken out. Cash is taken out of a business for loan repayments or for the owner's own use. These outflows reduce the cash supply available for company use. Those funds retained in the business can be recycled to purchase additional inventory or equipment or to pay the general operating expenses of the business. These payments result in additional goods or services, which are in turn sold by the company to generate more cash. Therefore, the circular flow of cash through the business becomes self-generating and continuous.

The purpose of cash management is to insure that the circular flow of funds is maintained. If too much cash flows out of the business, the profitability, or even the life, of the business could be hampered. Too much cash flowing into the cycle, however, could mean that your funds are not being used efficiently, which reduces your profitability. The following sections of this chapter describe the techniques used to manage and control the cash flow of your business.

Cash Budgeting.   A cash budget is a plan that outlines the expected cash receipts and disbursements of a business. It is used to determine when you will have a cash shortage so that you can plan for your needed borrowing. At the same time it can pinpoint periods of cash surplus to help you to plan for loan repayments or potential investment opportunities. A cash budget is developed by using a cash flow worksheet.

A cash flow worksheet is divided into three main sections: receipts, payments, and cash requirements. An example of a cash flow worksheet is presented in Figure 8.2. A cash flow can be developed for any length of time that is practical for your business. Since cash flow can change dramatically with the fortunes of your business, you should probably not prepare a worksheet for more than one year. It is also worthwhile to compare your estimated cash flow with your actual cash flow on a monthly basis. This will alert you to potential problems before they become serious. It will also make you more aware of potential surpluses that could be profitably invested.

Estimating Cash Receipts.   Cash flows into your business from three general sources: cash sales, collections on credit sales, and miscellaneous receipts from sources other than your normal operations. The sales forecast is the crucial ingredient in accurately determining your cash collections. Although an exact calculation is probably not possible, you should be able to make a fair approximation of your expected sales. If your business has been in operation for a while, your past experience should be a good guide to your future sales. You can also estimate sales based on your knowledge of your industry, the general market for your product, and the overall expected behavior of the economy in your area. The most important point to remember is that your forecast should be realistic. A forecast that is overly optimistic can result in an unexpected need for cash. Similarly, an overly pessimistic forecast can lead you to borrow money unnecessarily, thus reducing your company's profitability.

The recent experience of your company should tell you what proportion of your sales are cash sales. Generally, the proportion of your customers who pay in cash remains fairly constant. You may find that you have a surge in credit sales at certain times of the year. If this surge is significant, you should make an appropriate adjustment in your estimate of collections.

Your estimate of your collections on credit accounts depends on your business's general credit policy and your personal experience with collections. After you have made an estimate of the proportion of your total sales that are credit sales, you can then estimate when you will collect the cash. For instance, if you normally have a thirty-day collection period, you will probably collect a small percentage in the same month, the majority in the

	MONTH 1		MONTH 2		MONTH 3		MONTH 4	
	Budget	Actual	Budget	Actual	Budget	Actual	Budget	Actual
CASH RECEIPTS								
Cash Sales								
Collections on Account								
Other Cash Receipts								
TOTAL CASH RECEIPTS								
CASH PAYMENTS								
Inventory								
Salaries								
Taxes								
Rent								
Insurance								
Supplies								
Advertising								
Overhead								
Equipment								
Loan Payments								
Other Cash Payments								
TOTAL CASH PAYMENTS								
NET CASH FLOW								
Beginning Cash on Hand								
CASH BALANCE (SHORTAGE)								
LOAN REQUIREMENT								
ENDING CASH BALANCE								

Figure 8.2 Cash Flow Worksheet

next month, and the remainder in the next month or two. Each month you can add all of your collections together to determine the total collections on account for that month.

The other cash receipts that you receive come from various nonoperating sources. These include interest on savings accounts or certificates of deposit, dividend income from investments, and cash received for the sale of investments or other assets. Additional capital investments are another miscellaneous source of cash.

Estimating Cash Payments.   You probably have a pretty good idea of where your paycheck goes each month. When you have a business, you can also estimate what your monthly cash outflow will be. You will have two kinds of expenses—those that occur on a regular basis and those that occur somewhat randomly. Both kinds of payment should be considered when making a cash budget.

Random payments will be made for nonroutine purchases, such as equipment. These should be included in your estimate whenever you expect them. Regular cash payments are those that occur on a monthly basis. These include regular operating expenses and recurring loan repayments. You should make estimates of the following expenses if they are common to your business:

Inventory Purchases: Inventory purchases include those that you make on a regular basis as well as extra purchases for special promotions.

Salaries: All payments that you make to your employees are included under salaries. If you make regular withdrawals from the business for your personal use, they could also be included here.

Taxes: All taxes that your business pays should be estimated. These include rebates of sales taxes, employee withholding payments and Social Security payments, and property taxes.

Rent: All payments for rental of your facilities are included here.

Insurance: Fire, liability, business interruption, and any other kind of insurance your business has are included in this category.

Supplies: Regular supply purchases are listed here.

Advertising: Planned payments for any media advertising, such as newspaper ads and radio and TV spots, should be budgeted. The budget should follow your planned payment schedule.

Overhead: Overhead payments include those general expenses necessary for the continued operation of your business, including utilities, telephone, repairs and maintenance, and other recurring expenses.

Note Payments: Regular payments made to banks and other creditors should be included here. These include truck or car payments.

Determining Cash Requirements.   After you have estimated your cash receipts and payments, you will be able to determine a net cash flow for each month. If your receipts are greater, this flow will be positive. It will be negative if the payment total is greater.

Your monthly balance or shortage is determined by adding your beginning cash balance to the net cash flow for the month. Each business should have a minimum cash balance. If your cash balance is less than this minimum level, it may be necessary to borrow funds. If your cash balance is significantly above the minimum balance, you may have surplus funds that could be invested or used to pay off an existing loan.

After you have determined whether it is necessary to borrow any money, you can estimate your ending cash on hand for the month. This figure is carried forward to the next month, and the cash requirements are then calculated for that month.

Sample Cash Flow Worksheet.   A well-developed cash flow worksheet can help you to manage your business more efficiently and profitably. The following example demonstrates how to develop a worksheet for a six-month period. In this example, the Granmar Company is just starting operations. The following factors are used to develop the worksheet:

Sales Estimate

Month	*Amount*
September	$ 8,000
October	10,000
November	10,000
December	12,000
January	9,000
February	8,000

Collections Schedule

Cash Collections: 40% of total sales

Credit Collections: (Based on 60% of total sales)

Month of Sale	10%
First month after sale	50%
Second month after sale:	30%
Third month after sale:	10%

Other Planned Receipts

October: $1,500 for sale of equipment

December: $800 for collection of customer's note

Cash Payments

The estimated monthly cash payments for normally recurring expenditures are listed on the worksheet directly.

The calculations used to estimate expected cash sales are presented in Figure 8.3. This information is then used to complete Figure 8.4, which summarizes the expected cash collections for each month.

Once the information in Figure 8.4 has been compiled, it can be transferred to a cash flow worksheet. Figure 8.5 illustrates a completed cash flow worksheet. As you can see, there was sufficient cash available for the first month of operation. However, in the second month, the payments significantly exceeded the receipts, and it was necessary to borrow $2,200. Because of the detail provided by the worksheet, it was noted that it was necessary to borrow the funds for only a limited period of time. Four-hundred and forty dollars could be borrowed for one month, and $1,760 for two months. It can also be seen that there will be a surplus of cash in the months of December,

Month	Credit Sales	Collections on Account			
		Same Month (10%)	First Month (50%)	Second Month (30%)	Third Month (10%)
Sept	$4,800	$ 480	$2,400	$1,440	$ 480
Oct	6,000	600	3,000	1,800	600
Nov	6,000	600	3,000	1,800	600
Dec	7,200	720	3,600	2,160	720
Jan	5,400	540	2,700	1,620	540
Feb	4,800	480	2,400	1,440	480

Figure 8.3 Collection Schedule for Credit Sales

CASH SALES   (40% of total sales)

Month of Collection

Sept	Oct	Nov	Dec	Jan	Feb
$3,200	$4,000	$4,000	$4,800	$3,600	$3,200

CREDIT SALES

Month of Collection

Month of Sale	Sept	Oct	Nov	Dec	Jan	Feb
Sept	$480	$2,400	$1,440	$ 480		
Oct		600	3,000	1,800	600	
Nov			600	3,000	1,800	600
Dec				720	3,600	2,160
Jan					540	2,700
Feb						480
Monthly Total	$480	$3,000	$5,040	$6,000	$6,540	$5,940

Figure 8.4 Schedule of Collections From Sales

January, and February. Since the amount and duration of the surplus can be estimated, it might be possible to make profitable use of these funds.

Controlling Cash Flows.   You can use your cash budget to help you to plan your cash flow. It is a guide to the way in which money comes into and goes out of your business. Once you have an idea of where your money is going, you can start to control its flow. The flow can be controlled through the careful management of cash receipts, cash payments, and cash on hand.

Managing Cash Receipts.   Customers can pay for your goods and services at one of three times: before they receive them, when they receive them, or as soon as possible after they receive them. Prepayment for goods and services is the fastest way to get cash into your business. However, unless you have a product that is in exceptionally high demand, this is not a realistic expectation. Payment at the time of sale, or a cash sale, is somewhat dependent on your type of business. For instance, grocery stores do almost all of their busi-

	SEPT		OCT		NOV		DEC		JAN		FEB	
	Budget	Actual	Budget	Actual	Budget	Actual	Budget	Actual	Budget	Actual	Budget	Actual
RECEIPTS												
Cash Sales	3,200		4,000		4,000		4,800		3,600		3,200	
Collections on												
Account	480		3,000		5,040		6,000		6,540		5,940	
Other Receipts			1,500				800					
Total Receipts	3,680		8,500		9,040		11,600		10,140		9,140	
CASH PAYMENTS												
Inventory purch	6,000		7,200		5,400		4,800		4,500		4,500	
Salaries	400		500		800		900		600		400	
Taxes	100		600		700		750		800		650	
Rent	500		500		500		500		500		500	
Insurance			1,200								600	
Supplies	300		300		300		400		200		200	
Advertising	100		200		400		400		200		100	
Overhead	4,700								3,000			
Equipment												
Note Payments												
Other Cash Pmts					300							
Total Payments	7,600		10,700		8,600		7,950		10,800		7,150	
Net Cash Flow	(4,000)		(2,200)		440		3,650		(660)		1,990	
Beginning Cash	5,000		1,000		1,000		1,000		2,890		2,230	
Balance (Short)	1,000		(1,200)		1,440		4,650		2,230		4,220	
Loan Requirement	–0–		2,200		–0–		–0–		–0–		–0–	
Loan Repayment	–0–		–0–		440		1,760		–0–		–0–	
Ending Cash	1,000		1,000		1,000		2,890		2,230		4,220	
Potential Excess												
Cash	–0–		–0–		–0–		1,890		1,230		3,220	

Figure 8.5 Cash Flow Worksheet

ness through cash. However, 90 percent of a car dealer's business may be through some kind of credit. Therefore, for many businesses, collection on credit sales may be the most important aspect of controlling cash inflow.

Credit sales can be handled either through in-house credit systems or through credit card systems. In-house credit systems are those in which your business manages its own credit. You are responsible for your own billing and collecting of accounts. Credit card systems are usually run by a bank or other financial institution. Visa and MasterCard are two widely known systems. For a fixed fee, usually about 3 percent, they enable you to deposit sales drafts directly into your account without having to concern yourself with the collection of the credit sales.

In-house credit systems can be both profitable and expensive. They can be profitable because they can increase your sales volume and promote purchases by a clientele of steady customers. They are expensive because they require you to maintain a credit collection function. This function could entail the use of a subscription billing service. It requires that you maintain a bookkeeping department to handle the recording of sales and billings as well as collections. You also need to make provisions for bad debts. When considering an in-house credit system, you need to balance the cost of maintaining it against the benefits it can provide. You must also remember that you will need to tie up a portion of your working capital in the maintenance of a certain level of accounts receivable.

If and when you decide to have an in-house credit system, you will need to make provisions for both the granting and collecting of credit. You should never grant credit to anyone until you have conducted a careful investigation of that customer's credit worthiness. Local credit bureau's, merchants associations, and large credit-reporting agencies can help you to secure the necessary information.

Efficient and effective credit collection is necessary to prevent an excessive amount of your working capital from being tied up. There are three aspects to effective credit collection:

1. Prompt billing

2. Tight terms

3. Effective follow-up practices

Very few of your customers will pay before they receive an invoice. Therefore, the sooner you send out your bills, the sooner you will receive payment. You should use a billing system that is fast and tailored to your needs. You may find that a hand-generated system is fine for a small business with few credit customers. However, some type of automated operation may be necessary if you have a large volume of credit sales.

Your credit terms should be tight enough to encourage prompt payment. If your suppliers require that you pay within thirty days, then you cannot grant longer terms to your customers unless you are willing to pay to grant this privilege.

In order to follow up on collections, you need to know the payment status of each of your customers. If a customer drags out the payment on an account, your funds will be tied up for that period. One way of keeping track of your customers' payment behavior is with an aging schedule of accounts receivable. An aging schedule indicates the amount each of your customers owes and how long that amount has been owed. An aging schedule is illustrated in Figure 8.6.

This aging schedule indicates that the company has a slightly sloppy credit collection system. Only 60 percent of its accounts are current. Thirty percent are thirty days overdue. Account number 45678 has continued to receive credit even though there is a steady pattern of slow payment. If this company were to continue its credit collection program in this manner, its profits would soon suffer.

Managing Cash Payments.   While the effective management of cash receipts requires that you keep cash flowing into the business as fast as possible, the effective management of cash payments does not mean that you should slow down the outflow. Good cash management rather dictates that you use credit and control your payments to your best advantage. This means that you should make your payments on a schedule that considers the most relevant factors. These factors include the priority of the invoice, the credit terms or discounts offered by the vendor, and your own cash supply. If you make all of your payments on the same day, you are probably not managing your cash effectively. You could be missing out on the significant savings possible through cash discounts. You could also be alienating crucial vendors and other creditors by being consistently late in your payments.

One of the best ways to manage your cash payments is through the use of trade credit. As was mentioned in the previous chapter, trade credit is an excellent source of inexpensive short-term funds. Trade credit also offers other benefits. First, it can be used to develop and improve your overall cred-

Customer Account Number	Account Balance	Accounts Status			
		Current	Overdue		
			30 days	60 days	over 60 days
12345	$ 450	$ 400	$ 50	$	$
23456	300	300			
45678	250	50	50	100	50
70986	75		75		
TOTAL	8,600	5,160	2,580	700	160

Figure 8.6 Aging Schedule of Accounts Receivable

it rating. Second, the use of the cash discounts offered through trade credit can decrease your inventory costs.

Trade or cash discounts are usually stated in terms of a discount percentage, a discount period, and a net period. For example, the terms might be"2/10, net/30." This means that the seller will discount 2 percent off of the invoice price if the payment is made within ten days and that the full amount of the invoice is due within thirty days. The discount percentage, the discount period, and the net period are set by the seller.

A trade discount can yield significant savings. For instance, if you had an invoice for $1,500 with terms of 2/10, net/30, you could save thirty dollars on the invoice if you paid it within ten days of the invoice date. (2% × $1,500 = $30)

Another way to look at the savings offered by the trade discount is to calculate what it costs you in interest if you do not pay within the discount period. For example, if it costs you 2 percent in interest to wait an extra twenty days, then the annual interest rate would be 36.5 percent. (365 ÷ 20 days × 2% = 36.5%)

Leasing was mentioned in the previous chapter as a financing technique. It is also a way to manage your payments. Leasing permits you to spread the cash expenditures for an asset over the same period that the asset is generating funds. This creates a more balanced cash flow.

Personnel expenditures can be one of the largest recurring payments in a business. Therefore, they merit careful attention. Anything that can be done to keep down employee costs not only reduces expenses but also conserves cash. For example, you may find part-time employees or subcontractors less expensive than full-time employees. However, you should be aware that over reliance on these employees can reduce your effectiveness and efficiency. The timing of payrolls can also effect your cash flow. A biweekly or monthly payroll is less expensive than a weekly payroll. You should time the dates of your other regular payments, such as loan installments, so that they do not coincide with your payroll dates.

Previous chapters have addressed the questions of financing and cost control. The same advice given in those chapters relates to the control of cash payments. Any action that you take to minimize your expenses and reduce your financing costs not only increases your profits but also improves the cash management of your business. You should consider the following actions to further control your cash outflow:

Avoid large prepayments for expenses like insurance and rent.

Avoid large expenditures for frills like fancy offices and other nonessentials.

Don't jump at quantity purchase savings. You may end up paying a lot for more than you need.

Managing Cash on Hand.   The amount of cash that is readily available for your use in the business should be the minimum required to get by. However, you should have ready access to required funds. There are three ways in which you can control your cash, minimize the amount on hand, and improve your profitability.

1. Keep your business accounts separate and distinct from your personal accounts. You should never mix the two. If you need personal funds, transfer them from your business account to your personal account first.

2. Open and maintain a *checking account* for your business. A checking account is an easy and effective way to control and manage your business funds. As you know from your personal experience, cash has a bad habit of slipping away. If all of your business payments are made by check, you will have an ongoing and accurate record of where your cash is going.

3. Open and maintain a *savings account* for your business. If you do not need all of your cash, you can deposit it in your savings account until you do and you will earn some interest on it. You may not earn a lot of money, but it will be more than if you had stuffed your extra cash under a mattress or left it in your checking account.

Controlling Surplus Cash.   Surplus cash is money that you will not need in your business for a month or longer. For short periods of time, your savings account is a profitable investment, but what do you do if it appears that you may have surplus cash for an extended period? Figure 8.5 illustrates a situation where over $1,000 was going to be available for several months. There are several possible uses for these funds.

The first use of excess funds is to reduce short-term debt. In your cash-planning activities you will see periods of deficiency and surplus. An excellent cash management strategy is to borrow during the deficiency and plan to pay the funds back during the surplus. In this way you do not need to borrow funds any longer than necessary. This can both improve your credit rating and keep the cost of borrowing lower.

Another possible use of surplus cash is investment. When you consider your investment options, you should be especially concerned with liquidity and safety.

A liquid investment is one that you can convert into cash quickly if the need arises. Since an investment of excess cash is a short-term one, you should make certain that the funds will be accessible if you need them. Otherwise your profitable investment could be the source of a cash crisis.

It is also essential that your investment be a safe one. Because the money that you are using is only a temporary surplus, you need to insure that you will be able to get the cash back when you need it. Therefore, any investments that you make should carry a reasonable guarantee of solvency. This rules out any overly speculative investments.

There are a number of investment vehicles that you can use for your surplus cash. Many of these are both safe and liquid.

Certificates of Deposit: Many banks and other financial institutions issue certificates of deposit. These CDs carry interest rates substantially above those of savings accounts. However, they require larger investments and minimum deposit periods. The interest rates on CDs vary with the amount and timing of your investment. Therefore, you need to plan your investment to get the maximum benefit from it.

U.S. Treasury Bills: Treasury bills are short-term securities issued by the government. They are extremely safe and liquid. They are sold at a discount on a weekly basis and mature at their face value. Maturity is usually within three to six months. A broker or banker should be able to advise you on the availability of "T bills" and help you to purchase them.

U.S. Treasury Notes and Bonds: Treasury notes and bonds have a longer maturity period than treasury bills. Therefore, they may not be an attractive use of surplus cash.

Commerical Paper: Commercial paper investments are short-term unsecured notes issued by large, credit-worthy corporations.

Except for certificates of deposit, you may not find many of these investment vehicles readily accessible to you. Recently, however, there has been a significant expansion in the different kinds of money management systems available to you. Changes in the tax laws affecting Individual Retirement Accounts (IRAs) and All Saver certificates could yield significant benefits to you. You might also take advantage of money market accounts. Some of the major brokerage houses also offer special services such as cash management. All of these services may give you the opportunity to earn additional income for your business.

Therefore, you may find investment counselors or stock brokers useful. They have ready access to many of the investment vehicles mentioned above and may also know of alternative investments. They can provide you with a balanced portfolio that gives you a good rate of return while maintaining flexibility and liquidity.

Capital Budgeting

The second aspect of effective financial management is capital budgeting. Capital budgeting is the process of planning and evaluating expenditures for capital assets. It is important to you as a manager for several reasons. First, any capital expenditure decision that you make has to be lived with for a long time. Since you will be tied to the benefits and costs of your decision, it should be the best possible one. Second, purchases of capital assets need to be planned so that the assets are available when you need them. Third, prior planning assists you in getting the best possible assets when they are needed. By anticipating your needs, you can do the comparisons and bargaining necessary to get the best assets at the best price. Fourth, planning the timing of your purchases also assists you in planning your cash requirements and making the necessary financial arrangements.

There are three reasons for acquiring capital assets: replacement, expansion, and other purposes. Replacement decisions are generally the easiest to make. When an asset is too expensive to maintain or just does not work anymore, you need to replace it. However, your decision as to what to replace it with may be a little more complicated. Expansion purchases allow you to increase your existing capacity or facilities or to expand your business into new product lines or territories. The value judgments that need to be made with this type of decision are the most difficult.

Purchases of capital assets other than those for replacement or expansion fall into two categories: optional and mandatory asset purchases. Both can be very important, even critical, to the operation of your business. Mandatory purchases include pieces of equipment and alterations to your facilities required by an outside agency. Examples of these would be additional pollution control equipment, special modifications required to meet health and safety standards, equipment or modifications required for access or use by the disabled, or even a new sign to comply with a local ordinance. Although these expenditures may not improve your business, they may be as necessary to your continued survival as replacement decisions. Optional asset purchases are those that do not replace existing equipment, expand your business, or satisfy specific requirements. Examples would be the conversion of a hot water system to solar power or the installation of a heat reclaimer or water recycling system by a laundromat. These expenditures may not increase your business, but they do result in some savings in operating costs.

The purpose of capital budgeting is to help you to make decisions that will increase your business's profitability. The techniques to be discussed will help you to analyze various proposals for capital expenditures and determine which you should pursue.

Although there are several methods of analyzing capital expenditures, this chapter will address only three: cash payback, average rate of return, and net present value analysis. Profit and net cash flow will be used in the calculations in these methods. Profit is the net operating income expected from a project. Net cash flow is the profit plus depreciation.

In order to explain the calculations used in the three analysis methods, the same example will be used. Assume that there are two different machines that your company is considering purchasing. An analysis of the two machines yields the following information:

	Machine 1	Machine 2
Cost	$10,000	$12,000
Life	4 years	5 years
Annual Profit	$ 1,000	$ 1,500
Annual Depreciation	$ 2,500 (Straight-Line)	$ 2,400 (Straight-Line)
Annual Cash Flow	$ 3,500	$ 3,900

For the purpose of our analysis, assume that the two machines are equally desirable on all subjective and objective criteria other than cost, life, and expected profits.

Cash Payback Analysis. The cash payback period is the time required to recover the cost of an investment from the annual cash flow. The object of cash payback analysis is to determine which of your expenditure options has the shortest payback period, or, in other words, which will return your investment the soonest. A cash payback analysis of the two machines in the example yields the following information:

Year	Machine 1 Accumulated Cash Flow	Machine 2 Accumulated Cash Flow
1	$ 3,500	$ 3,900
2	7,000	7,800
3	10,500	11,700
4	14,000	15,600

As can be seen, the accumulated cash flow for machine 1 equals the cost of the machine sometime after the second year. For machine 2 the cash flow equals the cost after the third year. To calculate the fraction of a year required for payback, you divide the amount of cash flow needed in that year to complete payback by the total cash flow for the year:

	Machine 1	Machine 2
Amount needed in partial year	$10,000 − 7,000 (end of year 2) 3,000	$12,000 − 11,700 (end of year 3) 300

	Machine 1	Machine 2
Amount needed / Annual Cash Flow	$\frac{\$3,000}{\$3,500} = .857$	$\frac{\$\ 300}{\$3,900} = .077$

The total payback periods for the two machines would therefore be:

	Machine 1	Machine 2
Cash Payback Period	2.857 years	3.077 years

This analysis indicates that machine 1, with the shorter payback period, is the better investment.

The advantage of payback analysis is that it is easy to do. For this reason, it is one of the most frequently used methods. However, it has several disadvantages. It ignores the profit and cash flow performance of an asset after it has returned its original cost. It also fails to consider the value of money over time. Consequently, payback analysis may be a shortsighted way to evaluate an investment.

Average Rate of Return Analysis. The average rate of return is the rate of profit from an investment based on its average cost. It is calculated by dividing the average annual profit by the average cost of the asset. The average cost is one-half of the initial cost of the asset (cost /2).

$$\text{Average Rate of Return} = \frac{\text{Average Annual Profit}}{\text{Initial Cost}/2}$$

The average rate of return on the two machines would be:

Machine 1

$$\frac{\$1,000}{\$10,000/2} = \frac{\$1,000}{\$5,000} = 20\%$$

Machine 2

$$\frac{\$1,500}{\$12,000/2} = \frac{\$1,500}{\$6,000} = 25\%$$

Because machine 2 has a higher average rate of return, it would appear to be the stronger of the two alternatives.

The idea of a rate of return is common in business. In this case, the operating income from each asset is averaged out over its life to give a common base for comparison. The average rate of return also looks at the benefits received from the project over its entire life rather than just during the payback period. Therefore, it gives you a better perspective on the overall performance of the project. One of the major weaknesses of this evaluation method is that it is limited to a comparison of alternative projects. Its use as a standard for selection is therefore limited.

Net Present Value Analysis. The net present value (NPV) method of analyzing capital expenditures combines several aspects of both of the previous methods, as well as considering some additional factors. The most important aspect of the present value method is that it recognizes the *time value of money*. Stated simply, the concept of the time value of money is that a dollar today is worth more than a dollar one year from today. The obvious response is that this is true because inflation eats up the value of money. Even discounting inflation, however, present dollars are worth more. A present dollar can be invested. Even at the low rate of 6 percent, a dollar today becomes $1.06 in one year. When you add to this income gain the factors of uncertainty and possible alternative uses of your funds, it becomes even clearer that money has more value today than tomorrow.

An important component of the present value method is the hurdle, or acceptance, rate. The hurdle rate is the minimum level of return you expect or demand from your investments. It is usually the cost of capital. For instance, if you need to borrow funds at a rate of 10 percent, then that would be your minimum hurdle rate. Another way of looking at a hurdle rate is from the perspective of what your business should be earning. If you expect your business to return at least 12 percent for each dollar that you invest, then that rate could be your minimum acceptable rate of return.

The net present value is calculated as follows:

1. Select an appropriate hurdle rate.
2. Account for the time value of money by using a present value table (like Figure 8.7.) to select the discount factors for your hurdle rate.
3. Multiply the selected discount factors and the annual cash flow to get the discounted cash flow.
4. Add the discounted cash flows that you calculated in step 3 to determine the total present value of the cash flows.
5. Subtract the cost of the project from the total present value to determine the net present value.
6. Make your decision. If the net present value is 0 or less, the project should be rejected. The higher the NPV, the more attractive the project is.

The present value calculations for machines 1 and 2 are presented in Figure 8.8. As can be seen from the calculations, machine 2 has the higher net present value. Therefore, it would seem to be the more profitable option.

An alternative application of the present value method is the profitability index. The profitability index (PI) is useful when the alternatives that you are measuring have different costs, as is the case in the evaluation of the two machines. The profitability index is calculated by dividing the net present value by the cost of the project.

$$\text{Profitability Index} = \frac{\text{Net Present Value}}{\text{Cost}}$$

The PI is a useful tool because it eliminates the advantage that a larger project might have. A larger project might generate larger cash flows, and automatically yield a higher net present value. The PI eliminates this bias and allows for a comparison between different-sized projects.

N	8%	10%	12%	14%
1	.926	.909	.893	.877
2	.857	.826	.797	.769
3	.794	.751	.712	.675
4	.735	.683	.636	.592
5	.681	.621	.567	.519
6	.630	.564	.507	.456
7	.584	.513	.452	.400
8	.540	.467	.404	.351
9	.500	.424	.361	.308
10	.463	.386	.322	.270

Figure 8.7 Present Value of $1.00 Due at the End of N Years (selected)

When the profitability index is applied to the two machines, machine 1 has the higher PI and therefore appears to be the better investment.

The net present value method is a valuable tool for evaluating expenditures for three reasons. First, it considers the cash flow from a project. Second, by adding the factor of the time value of money, it considers the effect of the timing of the cash flows. Third, by using a hurdle rate, it provides a constant standard to measure a project by before making a decision.

Factor (12%)	Machine 1		Machine 2	
Year	Cash Flow	Discounted Cash Flow	Cash Flow	Discounted Cash Flow
1. .893	3500	3,125.50	3900	3,482.70
2. .797	3500	2,789.50	3900	3,108.30
3. .712	3500	2,492.00	3900	2,776.80
4. .636	3500	2,226.00	3900	2,480.40
5. .567	3500	1,984.50	3900	2,211.30
6. .507	3500	1,774.50	3900	1,977.30
7. .452	3500	1,582.00	3900	1,762.80
8. .404	3500	1,414.00	3900	1,575.60
9. .361	3500	1,263.50	3900	1,407.90
10. .322	3500	1,127.00	3900	1,255.80
Totals	35,000	$19,778.50	39,000	$22,038.90
Cost of Project		10,000.00		12,000.00
Net Present Value		$ 9,778.50		10,038.90

Figure 8.8 Net Present Value Analysis

$$PI = \frac{PV}{COST}$$

Machine 1
$$\frac{\$19,778.50}{\$10,000.00} = 1.978$$

Machine 2
$$\frac{\$22,038.90}{\$12,000.00} = 1.836$$

Figure 8.9 Profitability Index

John Bernard's cash shortage with Worldwide Printing is a symptom of several other problems. If John is able to get better control of his accounts receivable, improve his production efficiency, reduce his inventory levels, and diversify his product line, his business will become more profitable. The following specific actions could help improve the financial stability and profitability of Worldwide.

CASE
SOLUTION

Worldwide Printing

1. The effectiveness of the credit collection policy needs to be increased. Worldwide is dependent on a steady cash inflow to balance its outflow. This means that the collection time needs to be reduced.

2. The company should increase the mechanization level of its production process. Additional equipment would permit Worldwide to reduce its labor cost and increase its profitability. John should analyze the types of equipment that he needs and develop a capital budget to finance them.

3. Calendars have a very short life cycle. After the beginning of the year, there is little need to buy a calendar. Therefore, in order to stabilize his business over the year, John should diversify his product line. This would give him a broader base to absorb his overhead.

4. The finished goods inventory level should be reduced. If the production process is streamlined and the product line diversified, the company should find that it is less dependent on a high level of finished goods.

CHAPTER SUMMARY

This chapter has addressed the issue of effective management of your cash. Effective cash management insures that your business has the cash that it needs when it needs it. It is also a valuable tool for increasing your profits. Successful cash management consists of budgeting, controlling cash flows, and makiing profitable use of excess cash.

A cash budget is one of the best ways to manage your cash. It is a planning tool that helps you to determine when you will need to borrow operating funds. It can also predict when you will have surplus cash available to pay off loans or invest.

Control of cash flows involves speeding the flow of cash into your business while carefully managing the outflow to maintain your credit and maximize your profits. The best way to speed the flow of cash into your business is through the effective management of credit. This involves prompt billing, tight credit-granting policies, and effective follow-up procedures. Cash payments are best controlled through the use of the cost control methods mentioned in chapter 6. Trade credit, especially cash discounts, is another effective method of controlling cash outflow.

Surplus cash is cash above and beyond your business's immediate needs. When you determine you have excess cash, you can use it to pay off some of your debt or put it to profitable use in safe, liquid investments.

Capital budgeting is also a part of effective financial management. Capital assets are acquired for your business to replace worn or outdated equipment, expand your business, or for other uses, such as meeting legal requirements or taking advantage of cost-saving devices. Capital asset purchases are evaluated in two ways. First, you need to determine whether the new asset will meet your needs. Second, you need to evaluate the available options to insure that you get the most profitable piece of equipment. The common techniques for evaluating capital purchases involve calculating the cash payback, the average rate of return, the net present value, or the profitability index.

1. What are some uses for surplus cash that can increase the profits of your business?

2. List the advantages and disadvantages of an in-house credit system.

3. Determine how your business can use a bank credit card. Go to a bank and acquire appropriate applications.

4. How can you speed up the collection on your accounts receivable?

5. Your company is trying to determine which of two machines is the better investment. The following data has been submitted to assist you in your decision:

Machine #1:	Cost	$22,000
	Estimated life	4 years
	Annual profit	3,800
	Annual Deprec.	5,000

Machine #2:	Cost	$18,000
	Estimated life	5 years
	Annual profit	2,700
	Annual Deprec.	3,500

a. Determine the cash payback period for each machine.
b. Determine the average rate of return for each machine.
c. Which machine would make the better investment?

6. The Ames Company is trying to decide which of two machines to buy. The company uses a hurdle rate of 12 percent. Based on the following information, calculate the net present value and the profitability index of each of these machines.

	Machine #1	Machine #2
Cost	$25,000	$30,000
Cash Flows		
Year 1	10,000	10,000
Year 2	10,000	12,000
Year 3	8,000	18,000
Year 4	6,000	12,000
Year 5	6,000	12,000

7. Prepare an estimate of cash receipts for the months of April, May, June, July based on the following:

Sales Estimate: Feb: 25,000 March: 30,000 April: 20,000 May: 20,000 June: 35,000 July: 40,000

Collections Schedule: 60% cash sales, 40% credit sales

Credit Collections: 20% in month of sale, 50% in month after sale, and 30% in second month after sale.

Other Collections: June: $2,500 for equipment sale

REFERENCES   Anthony, R. N. *Management Accounting*, 4th ed. Homewood, Ill.: Richard D. Irwin, 1970.

Anthony, R. N.; and Welsch, G. A. *Fundamentals of Management Accounting*, 4th ed. Homewood, Ill.: Richard D. Irwin, 1974.

Bank of America. *Beating the Cash Crisis*. San Francisco: Bank of America, 1975.

Bank of America. *Cash Flow/Cash Management*. Small Business Reporter 13, no. 9. San Francisco, 1977.

Horngren, C. A. *Cost Accounting, A Managerial Emphasis*, 3rd ed. Englewood Cliffs, N.J.: Prentice-Hall, 1972.

Moyer, R. C.; McGuigan, J. R.; and Kretlow, W. J. *Contemporary Financial Management*. St. Paul: West Publishing, 1981.

FOOTNOTES   1. This case was prepared by one of the authors based on consulting work done for one of his clients. In order to maintain client confidentiality, the facts given in this case differ somewhat from the actual case.

Effective Marketing of Your Product

PART III

Finding Buyers for Your Product

☐ **What are you selling?**

☐ **Will people buy it?**

☐ **Why should they buy it from you instead of your competitors?**

CASE
PROBLEM

The Rocket Chemical Company[1]

In the 1950s an immigrant chemist in the United States noticed that the rocket industry had a need for a rust-preventing lubricant. Often stainless steel rocket nosecones developed hairline cracks under stress. The cracks eventually caused costly rust. The chemist persuaded three investors to put up capital and formed the Rocket Chemical Company.[1] In a short time he developed a petroleum-based, water-displacing lubricant that was an ideal rust preventer. It sold well to the rocket industry, and the company became profitable.

Despite the early success of the company, the product had two drawbacks. First, the rocket industry needed only a small amount of it. Even if the product were very profitable, sales would never be large enough to put Rocket Chemical on the map. Second, it was only a matter of time until several competitors would be able to develop similar products. When that happened, Rocket Chemical Company's product would just be one of many and would no longer be able to command a premium price. Profits would erode as the price was cut to try to save sales.

PROBLEM
IDENTIFICATION

No matter what your business is, you can anticipate having problems similar to those faced by Rocket Chemical Company. How you deal with these problems will determine whether or not your company experiences fast profit growth. Being aware of these problems and knowing what to do about them will give you a tremendous competitive advantage.

There are two basic problems:

1. How can you make your product distinctive so that it will offer more value to your customers than your competition's products?

2. What can you do to make sure your customers perceive the superior value of your product?

These two problems seem clear. Possible solutions come immediately to mind. Still, you can easily be misled. The danger lies in your definition of product value. If you believe that a well-built, high-quality product will sell itself, you are wrong. Making your product better is not enough to guarantee profits. Your customers must also perceive your product to be better.

Your customers are the ones who decide whether or not to buy your product. Their needs create the marketplace for your product, and the benefits they feel they get from your product determine what it is worth to them. You can spend an enormous amount of money improving the quality of your product only to have your customers reject it because it does not meet their needs. Your advertising dollars will be wasted unless you can show your customers that your product uniquely meets their needs and that its value to them exceeds its cost.

The answer to the two problems listed above is the marketing concept. This concept dictates that a business sell what customers want, at prices that produce profits. It is a way of focusing your attention on what really counts—increasing your net worth by serving your customers.

The founder of Rocket Chemical Company started out on the right track. He observed a strong need of potential customers. He developed a product that uniquely met this need. He brought the product to the attention of his potential customers. The customers saw that his product was particularly good at meeting their needs and that its value exceeded its cost. They bought it. Rocket Chemical Company made a profit.

In the jargon of marketing experts, the chemist followed a sound marketing strategy. He discovered a market, or a group of potential customers with similar needs, and developed a product targeted to meet their needs. He then developed a promotional campaign to demonstrate to customers in his target market how his product met their needs. The product was accepted by the target market and sold well.

For Rocket Chemical Company, the key to increasing future profits lies in continuing to apply the marketing concept. The company must first identify the potential benefits of its petroleum-based, water-displacing lubricant. Next, the company must identify groups of customers with a strong need for these benefits. These groups will be new target markets for the company's product. The company must then determine if these new target markets will be willing to pay enough for the product to produce a profit for the company. If the answer is yes, the company must devise means to reach these customers and demonstrate to them that its product has benefits that they value, benefits that are worth more than the price of the product, and benefits that surpass those of competitors' products.

If Rocket Chemical Company chooses to focus on improving the formula of its product rather than meeting the needs of its customers, it may spend a lot of money without increasing sales. If it chooses to advertise product quality rather than benefits to customers, it will lose sales to competitors who stress customer benefits in their ads.

DIAGNOSIS

Most of us feel we are doing a good job for our customers. How can you tell if you need to do better? How do you diagnose whether or not you can better employ the marketing concept and improve your marketing strategy?

Diagnosis begins with writing down your current marketing strategy. You need to determine what has worked and what has not and combine this with an understanding of your firm's strengths and weaknesses to get a clear idea of what future marketing opportunities you should pursue and how best to pursue them. The trouble is, even if you have been in business for a while, you may have been too busy trying to succeed to write all of this down in an organized manner. Assuming you have not written down your marketing strategy, this section shows you step by step how to do so.

Defining Your Mission

The best place to begin is with defining your company's mission, or reason for being. One way to tackle this is to consider a series of specific questions about your basic business philosophy, your business resources, and potential.

Perhaps the most important aspect of your business philosophy is whether or not you really believe in the usefulness of the marketing concept. Exhibit 9.1 presents a list of questions that will help you to determine whether or not you are currently using the marketing concept. Before reading further, mark the response scales as indicated and write down why you answered the way you did.

Exhibit 9.1   Your Marketing Concept Profile[2]

Instructions: Each question below is followed by a scale with a response statement at each end of the scale. For each question, mark the place on the scale that best describes your situation. For example, if the response statement at one end of a scale is totally true for your company and the other is totally untrue, mark the end of the scale under the true statement. Marking the middle of the scale indicates that each response statement is true about one-half of the time.

Example: Who makes the important decisions in your business?

I make all of the important decisions for my business.	I make none of the important decisions for my business.

Always	75–25	50–50	25–75	Always
/ _____ x /	_____ /	_____ /	_____ /

The example indicates that the respondent makes about 80 percent of the important decisions for his or her business. Presumably, the other 20 percent are made by partners or employees.

1. What is your attitude toward your customers?

Customer needs determine my business plans.	My customers should be glad I try to cut costs and bring out better products.

/ _____ / _____ / _____ / _____ /

2. How do you decide what products to offer?

I sell what I know how to make best or know most about.

I make (stock) what I can sell.

/ _____ / _____ / _____ / _____ /

3. Do you ever check with your customers first before you offer a new product?

Always

Never

/ _____ / _____ / _____ / _____ /

4. When you do talk to your customers, how do you approach them?

I try to see how they react to my ideas.

I try to determine their needs and how well my business is satisfying their needs.

/ _____ / _____ / _____ / _____ /

5. Why are you interested in something new?

Because it will allow me to cut costs and/ or produce more efficiently.

Because it is an opportunity to open up a new market.

/ _____ / _____ / _____ / _____ /

6. What is profit?

My number one objective.

What is left over after all my costs are covered.

/ _____ / _____ / _____ / _____ /

7. What do you think about selling to customers on credit?

It is a customer service.

It is a necessary evil.

/ _____ / _____ / _____ / _____ /

8. What is the most important use for the packages you put your product in? (Note: if you make or sell something like a TV set, the package may be the cabinet that encloses the working parts.)

Packages protect the product from damage.

Packages make the product more convenient for the customer and help to sell the product.

/ _____ / _____ / _____ / _____ /

9. How do you decide how much inventory to stock?

I stock enough to keep my production line flowing smoothly and/or I stock as little as possible to keep my costs to a minimum.

I try to stock enough to serve my customers quickly, while at the same time not letting costs get out of hand.

/ _____ / _____ / _____ / _____ /

10. What criteria do you use when making transportation arrangements?

I make them to get the product to the customer as cheaply as possible.

I make them to better serve my customers.

/ _____ / _____ / _____ / _____ /

11. What do you emphasize in your advertising?

How my products and/or services can
satisfy the customers' needs.

The features of my products and services,
how my products are made, and quality.

/ _____ / _____ / _____ / _____ /

12. When you or one of your sales people tries to sell your product, what is emphasized?

Helping the customer buy something that
best meets his/her needs.

Selling the product to the customer.

/ _____ / _____ / _____ / _____ /

Exhibit 9.2 shows the answers to the questions in Exhibit 9.1 for the ideal marketer, someone who subscribes to the marketing concept 100 percent. How do you compare? As you look over your written comments for each question, you will find that in many cases you have good reasons for differing from the ideal. Many times your reason will be cost. After all, the marketing concept says to sell what customers want, at a profit. In each case, the test to ascertain whether or not you should be doing more to follow the marketing concept is to ask yourself whether or not you will be able to add enough perceived value to your product in your customers' eyes. Will they be willing to pay a higher price that covers the extra cost of doing something more and adds to your profits?

You have only so much money to invest. You should spend it on the strategies that yield the most profit per dollar spent. If your basic business philosophy does not permit you to adhere to the marketing concept, you need to ask why. What other goals do you have that are more important than increasing your net worth? Can they be best served if you do not first serve your customers' needs?

Turning now to the basic questions of what your business is and what it should be, it is useful to ask several specific questions about 1) the expectations of those with a stake in your company, 2) your company's environment and 3) your company's distinctive competencies.[3] Answering these questions will help you further pinpoint your company's mission.

The people with a stake in your business include you and the other owners, your employees, people who loan you money, and finally, and particularly important, your customers. What does each group of stake holders expect? How well does your business satisfy the expectations of each group? How well should it?

The second category of questions deals with how your company fits into its environment. Environment is a vague word. In order to do a meaningful analysis, it is useful to view your company's environment as four interacting sets of forces: economic and technological; political, legal, and regulatory; cultural; and competitive.[4] Each suggests questions that can help you with your analysis of what your business is and what it should be. For example:

Economic and technological

1. How big is the economy your company exists in? Does it contain enough customers for your product or service to keep your company afloat?

2. How healthy is the economy your company exists in? Is it likely to grow steadily, or will it experience sharp ups and downs? Is it facing any current crises? Can it afford to pay for luxury items or for specialized services?

3. Is the technology that you need to take advantage of market opportunities available? Can you buy it at a reasonable cost?

4. Can you employ new technologies that have just been developed to better meet customer needs?

Exhibit 9.2   The Marketing Concept Profile for the Ideal Marketer

1. What is your attitude toward your customers?

   Customer needs determine my business plans.

   My customers should be glad I try to cut costs and bring out better products.

   ✓ _____ / _____ / _____ / _____ /

2. How do you decide what products to offer?

   I sell what I know how to make best or know most about.

   I make (stock) what I can sell.

   / _____ / _____ / _____ / _____ ✓

3. Do you ever check with your customers first before you offer a new product?

   Always   Never

   ✓ _____ / _____ / _____ / _____ /

4. When you do talk to your customers, how do you approach them?

   I try to see how they react to my ideas.

   I try to determine their needs and how well my business is satisfying their needs.

   / _____ / _____ / _____ / _____ ✓

5. Why are you interested in something new?

   Because it will allow me to cut costs and/ or product more efficiently.

   Because it is an opportunity to open up a new market.

   / _____ / _____ / _____ / _____ ✓

6. What is profit?

My number one objective.

What is left over after all my costs are covered.

✓ _____ / _____ / _____ / _____ /

7. What do you think about selling to customers on credit?

It is a customer service.

It is a necessary evil.

✓ _____ / _____ / _____ / _____ /

8. What is the most important use for the packages you put your product in? (Note: if you make or sell something like a TV set, the package may be the cabinet that encloses the working parts.)

Packages protect the product from damage.

Packages make the product more convenient for the customer and help to sell the product.

/ _____ / _____ / _____ / _____ ✓

9. How do you decide how much inventory to stock?

I stock enough and/or I stock as little as possible to keep my costs to the minimum.

I try to stock enough to serve my customers quickly, while at the same time not letting costs get out of hand.

/ _____ / _____ / _____ / _____ ✓

10. What criteria do you use when making transportation arrangements?

I make them to get the product to the customer as cheaply as possible.

I make them to better serve my customers.

/ _____ / _____ / _____ / _____ ✓

11. What do you emphasize in your advertising?

How my products and/or services can satisfy the customer's needs.

The features of my products and services, how my products are made, and quality.

✓ _____ / _____ / _____ / _____ /

12. When you or one of your sales people tries to sell your product, what is emphasized?

Helping the customer buy something that best meets his/her needs.

Selling the product to the customer.

✓ _____ / _____ / _____ / _____ /

Political, legal, and regulatory

1. Are there any laws or regulations blocking your company's attempt to succeed? Is there a trend toward more constraints?

2. Are there any laws or regulations that create opportunities for your company? Can you influence the enactment of such laws?

Cultural

1. Are there changes occuring in cultural beliefs or individual lifestyles?
2. Where are these trends heading? What do these trends imply about what people will want and where they will want to live?
3. Are you bucking one of these trends?
4. Are you riding on the crest of a trendy wave that is about to break?

Competitive

1. Are there any other firms that are trying to provide the same types of product or service to your present or potential customers as you are?
2. Whom do you have to compete with for the resources you need to get your product or service to your customers? Can you get the employees and materials you need? Can you get the components that you intend to sell built? Will wholesalers and retailers carry your product when they can carry whole lines of your competitors' products? Can you get sales representatives who will really try to sell your product, or will they be too busy selling their established lines?

The third category of questions addresses your company's distinctive competencies. Distinctive competencies are things your company does well. What does your company do well? Do you do them better than your competition? What do your customers think you do well? Your banker?

Recording Your Current Marketing Strategy

Once you have answered each of the specific questions listed so far, you should have a pretty good idea of what your basic business philosophy is, what your business is, and what it should be, or, in other words, what your business's mission is. The next step is to take a systematic look at the strategy you are currently using to accomplish your business's mission.

Exhibit 9.3 lists a series of questions that will help you write down your current marketing strategy. These questions cover all of the major components of a comprehensive marketing strategy. You will note that many of the questions restate in action terms questions you have already tackled in defining your company mission. The work you have done earlier will help you to answer these questions. Your answers will suggest refinements to your statement of your company's mission.

Identifying Your Marketing Gaps

Once you have answered the questions in Exhibit 9.3, your analysis of your firm's current and potential performance is complete. The final phase of your diagnosis is to review Exhibits 9.1 and 9.3 and write down any strategic marketing gaps you find between the results you can expect from continuing to do things the way you are now and the results you want. Gaps may exist due to invalid strategies or unexploited strengths. An invalid strategy is one that does not contribute to your mission. An unexploited strength is a distinctive competency that is not being exploited by your present strategy.

All companies have strategic marketing gaps. Certain gaps are commonplace for smaller companies. As a small business owner, you need to understand why these common gaps exist and how to close them. In the "Understanding" section of this chapter we will first identify and analyze the reasons for the strategic marketing gaps common to small businesses. Next, we will show you how to close the strategic marketing gaps your company faces, given your financial resources.

Exhibit 9.3 Recording Your Current Marketing Strategy[5]

1. What specific groups of customers, or target markets, should you serve in order to accomplish your mission?

2. What have you done to date to serve these target markets?

3. In particular, what has been done to date for each target market that appears to have contributed positively to your mission?

4. What has been done to date for each target market that has not contributed to your mission?

5. What have you done about the environmental trends that are affecting the needs of your targeted customers?
   a. Economic?
   b. Technological?
   c. Political, legal, and regulatory?
   d. Cultural?

6. What are you doing to combat your competition?

7. How do you define your products?
   a. How do you come up with new product ideas?
   b. How do you decide what products you should offer? (Describe products you have added or dropped recently.)
   c. How do you decide what your product should look like and do?
   d. How do you decide what services you should offer with your product to make it complete?
   e. How does your product's package help your product?

8. How do you decide where to sell your product?

9. How do you decide who should sell your product?

10. How do you get your product to your customers?

11. Are your customers getting your product when they need it?

12. How do you set your prices?
    a. How do you determine how much to charge?
    b. What payment terms do you require?
    c. Do you offer specials at certain times of the year? Why?
    d. Do you give better deals to big buyers?

13. How do you promote your product?
    a. Do you advertise? How and where?
    b. Do you use sales people?
       i. Do they work only for you?
       ii. How are they trained to sell your product?
       iii. Do you have sales drives at particular times of the year.
    c. Do you ever go after free publicity?
    d. Do you consciously try to tie all your promotional activities together to support your company mission?

The Marketing Advantages and Disadvantages of a Small Business

UNDER-STANDING

Many of the strategic marketing gaps you listed after reading the previous section reflect the basic disadvantages and advantages you face as a small businessperson trying to market your product or service in an economy dominated by big businesses. Some of your gaps are due to invalid strategies that fail to avoid the basic pitfalls all small businesses face when marketing products or services. Other gaps are due to unexploited strengths, or not capitalizing on marketing advantages common in small businesses and hard to duplicate in large businesses. If you understand what your disadvantages and advantages are as a small business marketer, you will be able to redesign your marketing strategy to close both types of gap and greatly strengthen your marketing strategy. Exhibit 9.4 summarizes the special marketing advantages and disadvantages of being a small business. How many of your marketing gaps are due to an invalid strategy you have used to deal with one of the disadvantages listed in Exhibit 9.4? How many are due to not exploiting one of the advantages listed in Exhibit 9.4?

Some comments should be made about certain of the disadvantages and advantages listed in Exhibit 9.4 to clarify their nature and help you to determine how they relate to your marketing strategy.

The first disadvantage listed—competing in big markets—is self-explanatory. However, the second disadvantage—offering too much choice—needs clarification. If you offer a full line of clothing, from infants to senior citizens, it will cost you a lot just to offer a small selection for each age group. Customers will have a hard time finding what they want in your store since your selection is not wide enough. By trying to satisfy everyone, you will end up satisfying very few. Even worse, your customers will be confused about whom you are aiming to please. If you are a manufacturer, too full a line will cause your production and selling costs to go up since you will be making less of each item and having to sell to different markets. You will tie up a lot of money and have less to carry you through emergencies or to invest in new opportunities.

Skip now to the fourth disadvantage—being small. This disadvantage reflects a basic economic reality that is dangerous to ignore. What it boils down to is that big companies can make and sell products for less than you can. They can get better service. The market system is biased in their favor. You have to recognize this bias and devise means to work around it. One thing is clear. You will almost always lose a price war with a big company unless you have figured out a way around the problem of being small.

The first advantage listed in Exhibit 9.4—making profits, not politics, your top priority—can be clarified with an example. Suppose a plant manager in a large company has been producing a particular product for a long time. He has accumulated the right machinery, everyone is trained, and things are running efficiently. He looks good to the big brass. The same company has a marketing manager who gets paid for coming up with innovative products. She wants to make changes in the product so that it is new and improved. She will look good to the big brass if the new, improved product sells well. Of course, the changes will require the plant manager to buy new machinery, retrain his workers, and incur larger expenses until the assembly line is fine tuned to accommodate the new product. The plant manager and the marketing manager are in basic conflict. One of them looks best if things stay the same. The other looks best if things change. Even more basic, neither is primarily concerned about profits. Enter politics. Each manager will try to influence others to win this conflict. Political coalitions will form, compromises will be made, and the resulting decision may be based more on political expediency than on making the most profit.

In contrast, as a small business owner, you can provide a unity of direction to your business that is hard to duplicate in a large business. You can concentrate on your bottom line. You can focus on the essentials that must be taken care of to insure that your profits grow fast. You can avoid the political infighting that in big business often clouds profit objectives and leads to products that do not meet customer needs. Indeed, it is one of the ironies of big business that, even though it can afford to spend large sums of money to research carefully what its customers want, it often cannot produce exactly what its customers want because of internal politics.

Concerning the second advantage listed in Exhibit 9.4—being more flexible—it is important to remember that flexibility can be a disadvantage if carried to the extreme. Selectivity is the key for two reasons. First, if you select the right opportunities you can continue to dominate the marketplace even when the big company finally responds. The trick is to be selective and to exploit only the most profitable opportunities. Second, you have only limited resources. Taking advantage of too many opportunities can cause you financial problems.

It is interesting to note the kinds of products that give the small businessman the edge suggested by the fourth advantage listed in Exhibit 9-4—offering the right product. Good products for you to consider are those that must be custom-made, or at least individualized, for each customer. Also good are products that require a lot of skilled labor to set them up and keep them going. In other words, you should be especially interested in products that are really combinations of products and services where personal service is what

Exhibit 9.4   Typical Small Business Marketing Disadvantages and Advantages

Small Business Marketing Disadvantages You Must Avoid:

1. Competing in big markets

While it is nice to dream of every household using your product or service, it is risky for a small business to try to make such a dream a reality. Satisfying the needs of big markets requires big resources—resources you do not have. If you enter into a big market with a good product that is well received by consumers, you can bet it will not be long before you find yourself in direct competition with a big company that has the resources necessary for mass production and national advertising. The large size of the market works to the advantage of the big company. Conversely, you have a fighting chance in a small market, where mass production and large advertising budgets are less important than the ability to uniquely meet the needs of customers.

2. Offering too much choice

Often small businessowners can identify sales that have been lost because they did not offer an item a customer wanted. If only they had had what the customer wanted, they could have made a sale. The trouble is that a small business cannot afford to offer too wide a choice of products.

3. Doing it all yourself

You need help to design the best marketing strategy for your firm. You can do a lot; but, depending on your business, you need the perspective of years of experience in such areas as location analysis, package design, displays, merchandising, advertising, selecting distribution channels, personal selling, and marketing research. You simply cannot be an expert on everything.

4. Being small

You must recognize the disadvantages of being a relatively small account. Small accounts do not get as much service, and they pay more. It will cost you more for each advertisement because you do not do as much advertising as a large firm. It will cost you more to get your product distributed because your product is less well known. It will be hard to get good service from suppliers. Small orders wait until the big ones are filled. You may not be able to purchase on credit. It will be hard to get good service from distributors because your products are not proven sellers. They will promote established brands they know will sell. It may be difficult for you to get display space for your products in retail stores for the same reason.

Small Business Marketing Advantages You Must Exploit:

1. Making profits, not politics, your top priority

By now it should be clear that profits are the name of the game and that the source of profits is responsiveness to the needs of your customers. Since you own your own business and want to make a profit, it is obvious that your marketing strategy should focus on creating in your customers' minds a perception that your product best meets their needs. Because it is worth more, they will pay more. All your marketing efforts, then, are aimed directly at your goal of building a successful, profitable business. Big companies often do not work this way. In larger companies the focus on profits through consumer satisfaction often becomes a secondary issue simply because most of the managers in the company do not see the big picture. These managers are assigned specific jobs and are evaluated on how well they do these jobs, not on their contribution to company profits. They gain their goals through politics, not profits.

2. Being more flexible

One side benefit to you from the political infighting that goes on in big business is that the infighting slows the big business down. The big business may be slow to recognize new marketing opportunities. Once the opportunity is finally recognized, it can take a surprisingly long time to act. You can make a lot of money in the meantime by seizing the opportunity and responding to it quickly. The key to flexibility is the willingness to act.

3. Thinking small

Big businesses are geared for big markets. They think big. As a practical matter, the top management of a big business cannot profitably handle a lot of little projects. No matter how profitable the little projects are per dollar spent, the profits will not add up to enough to pay for the big company's tremendous amount of overhead. The big company needs a few large projects that fully utilize its plant, equipment, and people. It needs large sales to cover big costs, even if the profit per dollar spent is less.
On the other hand, you, as a small businessperson, can think small. There are many groups of customers, or markets, that are small in size, have a strong need for a product or service, and are willing to pay top dollar to get it. Examples include minorities with strong ethnic identification, the very rich, the very poor, retired elementary school teachers, and Southerners in a northern city, just to name a few. Is there a product or service one of these groups needs that you can provide profitably without making a big investment?

4. Offering the right product

Generally speaking, big businesses are better at making standardized products that can be mass produced and require little personalized follow-up service. They prefer products that are going to be around awhile. They tend to miss the boat on fad items. By picking the right product or service to offer, the small business can compete effectively with larger companies, if the large company competes at all.

5. Getting to know your customers

One advantage of being small is that it is possible for you to get to know your customers. You can keep in personal touch with them and you can learn about what they really need and want. What you find out through informal conversations with your most important customers can easily be of more value to you than an expensive consumer survey is to a big business.

gives the combination unique value. Lastly, if you are willing to take a higher risk, perishable items or fad items are good possibilities.

Finally, the importance of the fifth advantage—getting to know your customers—cannot be stressed too much. You have a unique opportunity to learn firsthand what your customers value and how to help them get added value from your company's products or services. If you can get to know your customers, you will learn what your marketing strategy should be. You will be able to quickly test any strategy change for effectiveness before you commit a lot of time and money to it. Remember that you become successful by helping your customers successfully meet their needs. A small business owner is in a unique position to learn what will make his or her customers successful and how to contribute to this success.

After reviewing the disadvantages and advantages you face as a small businessperson, it should be apparent that you can easily fall victim to big business competition if you pretend you are a big business. You must recognize the pitfalls of being small and the strategic marketing gaps these pitfalls create. Fortunately, big businesses do not have things all their way. Being small also has unique advantages. If you remember these advantages and exploit them, your small business can be extremely profitable.

Now that you understand the basic marketing disadvantages and advantages you face as a small businessperson, the next steps are to analyze your marketing gaps and to redesign your marketing strategy. It is time to discuss solutions.

Analyzing Your Marketing Gaps

To redesign your marketing strategy, you first need to analyze your strategic marketing gaps in light of the two basic marketing problems discussed earlier in this chapter:

1. How can you make your product distinctive so that it will offer more value to your customers than your competition's?

2. What can you do to make sure your customers perceive the superior value of your product?

As you review your list of strategic gaps, you will find that some relate to the first marketing problem and some to the second. At this point, you should divide your list accordingly. Remember that some of the gaps you listed may be symptoms of a poor existing solution to either of the two basic marketing problems.

As you review the gaps you have linked to the first marketing problem, you will find it either relatively easy to close the gaps and solve this problem or very difficult and frustrating. The more you know about your customers, the easier your review will be and the more effective your solution will be. In order to make any real progress toward solving the first marketing problem, you must clearly define who your potential customers are and determine what they want. Then you must decide whether you can satisfy their needs profitably by manipulating the limited resources you have at your command.

As you develop a good solution to the first problem, you will create strategies for price setting, distribution, and promotion that also close the gaps linked to the second problem and solve that problem. Analyzing your marketing gaps in this way is the essence of good marketing strategy.

Good marketing strategy consists of two intertwined parts:

1. Selecting target markets—Identifying relatively homogeneous groups of customers who you feel can get exceptional value from your product and will be willing to pay top dollar for it so you can make a good profit.

2. Selecting the marketing mix—Developing the mix of product features, price, advertising, and distribution that will best serve your target customers, reinforce the exceptional value they get from your product, and provide you with a good profit.

The two parts of a good marketing strategy roughly parallel the two basic marketing problems we have discussed in this chapter.

It is important to recognize that both basic marketing problems are closely intertwined. In terms of the two parts listed above, you really cannot say which target market will be the most profitable for you unless you consider the cost of the marketing mix necessary to sell to that market. Conversely, a target market that is inexpensive to reach from a marketing mix standpoint is of little value to you unless there are enough potential customers in that target market who can be convinced to pay you enough for your product so that you will earn a profit. Keeping this in mind, let us now focus on how good marketing strategy, as defined by marketing professionals, can help you solve the first basic marketing problem, and at the same time help you formulate your solution to the second.

The best way to start to solve the first basic marketing problem from a marketing strategy standpoint is to divide all possible customers into subgroups and to focus your attention on those subgroups, or "target markets" that are likely to have a strong need for your product. You then study these target markets carefully to make sure you can serve their needs at a profit.

Since you have only limited resources, you must focus on those target markets that have the most profit potential. The trick to the selection is to divide up your potential customers based on similarities they possess in three areas: their needs and preferences; their probable response to adjustments in your marketing mix; and their buying behavior. Analysis of each target market will suggest solutions to the second basic marketing problem. You can attach price tags to these solutions to determine whether or not you can profitably serve the target markets in question. For example:

Suppose you are thinking of opening a shop that will sell inexpensive curios. One target market you might consider is tourists. Obviously there are many kinds of tourists. You can divide up the tourist market further according to age, income, social values, where they typically tour, and the type of curios they prefer. For instance, you may define a possible target market as tourists who are retired, have a strong religious background, have low to medium income, and who visit a particular tourist destination because of its religious significance.

As you become more specific about the target market, you will get an idea of approximately how many customers there are in the target market. You will also begin to get ideas about where your shop should be located, what curios you must stock, what your prices should be, how to advertise, and even what time of year you will get the most business. In other words, as a target comes into focus, it suggests a workable marketing mix. Next, you analyze the target market for profitability. Several things could disqualify a target market. For example, rents may be too high for shop space visible to tourists visiting the religious monument to allow you to make a profit, given the prices you must charge and the number of customers you anticipate. There may be several stores in the area selling the same products, which would take customers away from you. However, if your study of a target market and the marketing mix necessary to best serve it indicates you can make a good profit, there is a good chance your business could be successful. The more you know about your customers, the easier it will be for you to develop a good marketing strategy.

There is more to being a good marketing strategist than picking a profitable target market. You must consider alternatives, and you must follow them through to make sure that you get the most profit, given your personal objectives and resources.

The successful marketer does not jump into the first marketing opportunity that looks like it has a good chance of being profitable. He or she takes a hard, clear look at the entire marketplace, searching for all the possible target markets to appeal to and which can yield a good profit. The successful marketer explores different ways to serve the target markets that look sound, and formulates the most profitable approach to satisfy the needs of each target market. Only then does the marketer decide on the most promising target markets and the marketing mix for each chosen target market that he or she feels will yield the most profits without causing undue financial strain. Only then, after considering all the alternatives, will the successful marketer commit to his or her marketing strategy and start planning the who, what, how, when, where, and why for putting that marketing strategy into effect. By considering alternatives, the successful marketer avoids tunnel vision.

Tunnel vision can cause you to make decision too quickly. Remember, One major cost of each opportunity you pursue is your time. Accepting one opportunity often precludes you from accepting the next, possibly even bigger opportunity that comes along. This is not to say that you should be overly cautious and fall into the trap of paralysis of analysis. However, you need to weight your alternatives sufficiently to allow you to be reasonably sure that the opportunities you do accept will satisfy your needs.

Successful marketing strategists do one other thing that you can and should do. They *follow through.* When they plan their strategy they set goals. When they implement their strategy they follow through to make sure they accomplish their goals. After all, how else will they know if they are succeeding? Successful marketing strategy is good planning, but it is also good doing. Successful strategists set up yardsticks to measure progress toward their goals. They use these yardsticks frequently to monitor their progress, and they take corrective action if things are not working out the way they planned. They control their success. They make it happen. You can too.

Key Marketing Strategy Steps

At this point you know what you need to be a successful small business marketing strategist. In the coming chapters we will focus on how to map out your strategy. Exhibit 9.5 highlights the key marketing strategy steps we have discussed in this chapter so that you can refer to them easily as you need them.

Exhibit 9.5   Key Marketing Strategy Steps

---

1. Record your present marketing strategy.

2. Search for strategic marketing gaps.

3. Divide your gaps into those which apply to appropriate target markets and those which apply to appropriate marketing mix given your target market.

4. Consider your alternatives. Are there other target markets you can aim for? What are the feasible marketing mixes for each of the markets you are presently in? For each new market you might enter?

5. Analyze your alternatives. Do your strategic gaps suggest your present target markets are appropriate if your mix is improved? Or do they suggest new target markets will be more profitable?

6. Make your choice. Decide which target markets and what marketing mixed you are going to use.

7. Work out the details and implement the plan. Specify the who, what, how, when, where, and why for putting your marketing strategy into effect.

8. Follow through. Translate your goals into measurable objectives. Develop yardsticks to measure your progress. Decide on milestone dates for applying the yardsticks to check on progress. Be prepared to take corrective action if things are not working out the way you want.

CASE
SOLUTION

The Rocket Chemical Company

The Rocket Chemical Company accidentally stumbled across the target market that led to its success. Workers at one of the plants where Rocket Chemical's petroleum-based, water-displacing lubricant was used were "borrowing" jars of the lubricant and taking it home for their own use. The executives at Rocket Chemical heard about this and, to their credit, they recognized a strong potential market for their product. They studied this new target market and considered the marketing mix necessary to exploit it. They decided they could enter this market profitably and implemented their marketing strategy. They packaged their product in spray cans for consumer convenience. They established an easily remembered brand name, WD-40 Company. By 1969 they were selling $2 million per year to 1200 wholesalers who, in turn, sold to hardware, sporting goods, and automobile-supply retailers. After John Barry became president of the company in 1969, the company's marketing strategy became even more focused. Capitalizing on the fact that WD-40 had unique value to consumers as a product that could be easily used to stop squeaks and unfreeze rusty fasteners, Barry improved the packaging, advertised it to consumers as a product that uniquely met their lubricant needs, and pushed for distribution. Today WD-40 Company has over 14,000 wholesalers distributing their product. In 1979 WD-40's sales were over $35,000,000. *Over half* of the company's earnings were paid out to the stockholders as dividends.

Large competitors such as 3M and DuPont have recognized WD-40's success, but have found it difficult to compete, since the name WD-40 is uniquely recognized by consumers as a product that meets their lubrication needs. There is no one word that the competitors can use that says as much to consumers about lubrication needs as WD-40 does. As Barry explains, "Competitors can't shoot you off the fence if they can't get you in their sights."

Barry also points out, "We appear to be a manufacturing company, but in fact we are a marketing company." Indeed, the company has only 30 employees, most of whom are clerical. A few employees mix the WD-40 concentrate, which is shipped to five independent suppliers who package it into cans and ship it to the wholesalers. The main push is on marketing—establishing and maintaining WD-40's standing in consumers' eyes as *the* product which can meet their needs at a premium price.

If the WD-40 company is a success story, it is a success story about effective small business marketing strategy.

CHAPTER
SUMMARY

This chapter emphasizes that finding buyers for your product is a common concern of small business people but that it is actually not the primary concern. The critical question is really: "What do my customers need?" Once this question is answered you can custom-tailor your product to be a superior value to your customers by making sure it does an exceptional job of meeting their needs. This approach is called the *marketing concept.* The marketing concept can solve two very difficult marketing problems for you: how to make your product distinctive; and how to demonstrate your product's superior value to your customers.

In this chapter, matters of marketing strategy are discussed. The idea of marketing strategy is defined. You are shown how to analyze your present marketing strategy and improve it by defining your company's purpose and overcoming ineffective strategies to exploit your company's strengths. This process requires an understanding of the special advantages and disadvantages of being a small business.

DISCUSSION
QUESTIONS

1. **Short Case: Frances's Fantastic Fabric Cutters I**

   Frances Chapman is a professional seamstress with an electronic bent. She has invented a pair of electric shears for her own use which she likes better than anything she has seen on the market. Frances is considering taking a second mortgage on her house to finance the manufacture of these shears. Based on what you have read in this chapter, what would you suggest she do first?

2. Which of the small business marketing disadvantages and advantages described in Exhibit 9.4 seem particularly applicable to a small:
   a. Retail store
   b. Construction firm
   c. Manufacturer
   Explain why in each case.

3. Sinclair Peters is licensed to sell real estate. He has been in business ten years working for other companies. He would like to open an office in your neighborhood. Analyze the various environmental forces that would impact Sinclair's small business. Specifically, what will he experience in your neighborhood, city, and state in regard to:
   a. Economic and technological forces
   b. Political, legal and regulatory forces
   c. Cultural and life-style forces
   d. Competitive forces

4. Justin Abrams, like Sinclair Peters in question 3, wants to start his own business in your neighborhood, but he wants to open a computer-electronic game parlor next to your local junior high school. Analyze how the environmental forces would impact Abrams's business.

5. Based on your observations about the needs of the people in your community, what is the greatest existing unfulfilled need that a small business could meet profitably? Defend your answer.

REFERENCES

Brennen, William H. *Successful Marketing for Your Small Business.* Englewood Cliffs, N.J.: Prentice-Hall, Inc. 1978.

Gilmore, Frank G. "Formulating Strategy in Smaller Companies," *Harvard Business Review,* Vol. 49 (May–June, 1971) pp. 71–81.

Kollat, David T.; Blackwell, Roger D.; and Robeson, James K., *Strategic Marketing.* New York: Holt, Rinehart and Winston, Inc., 1972.

McCarthy, E. Jerome. *Basic Marketing,* 6th ed. Homewood, Ill.: Richard D. Irwin, Inc., 1978.

St. Thomas, Charles E. "A Basic Guide to Marketing for the Smaller Company," *Industrial Marketing,* Vol. 44, Part 2 (June, 1959) pp. 3–14.

_____. "Business Basics—Marketing Strategy." Washington D.C.: Government Printing Office, undated. A self-instructional booklet published by the U.S. Small Business Administration.

FOOTNOTES

1. This case is adapted from Thomas R. Murphy's description of the company in his article, "What is WD-40?" *Forbes* 125, no. 2 (January 21, 1980): 102–3. Quotations used were selected from those cited by Mr. Murphy.

2. Adapted from E. Jerome McCarthy, *Basic Marketing,* 6th ed. (Homewood, Ill.: Richard D. Irwin, Inc., 1978), p. 32 and Robert F. Vizz; Thomas E. Chambers; and Edward J. Cook, *Adoption of the Marketing Concept—Fact or Fiction?* (New York: Sales Executive Club of New York, 1967), pp. 6–15. Reprinted with permission of Richard D. Irwin, Inc., Homewood, IL, and The Sales Executives Club of New York, 122 E. 42nd St., New York, NY, 10017.

3. David T. Kollat; Roger D. Blackwell; and James K. Robeson, *Strategic Marketing* (New York: Holt, Rinehart and Winston, Inc., 1972), pp. 14–15. © 1972 by Holt, Rinehart and Winston, Inc. Reprinted by permission of Holt, Rinehart and Winston. These authors suggested two questions and the three-step approach that follows.

4. Kollat, Blackwell, and Robeson, *Strategic Marketing,* pp. 4–6. The following outline of the four interacting sets of forces is adapted from their discussion.

5. Two useful sources which influenced the list of questions given in this exhibit were Frank G. Gilmore, "Formulating Strategy in Smaller Companies," *Harvard Business Review* 49 (May-June 1971), pp. 71–81 (especially his list of questions to use in formulating strategy on page 80) and Charles E. St. Thomas, "A Basic Guide to Marketing for the Smaller Company," *Industrial Marketing* 44, part 2 (June 1959), pp. 3–14. Reprinted by permission of the Harvard Business Review, and *Industrial Marketing,* June 1959, © 1959 by Crain Communications, Inc.

Estimating Sales and Profits

10

☐ **What do your customers really want?**

☐ **Can you sell them enough to make any money?**

☐ **How can you find out?**

CASE
PROBLEM

*Cole
National
Corpora-
tion*[1]

About forty years ago, Joseph Cole was working for a Cleveland key firm. He observed that the making of replacement keys was inconsistent with the trend toward self-service, which was emerging in retailing at that time. Firms like Kresge and F. W. Woolworth were beginning to move away from the mainstream of retailing to become mass merchandisers. Instead of emphasizing service and selection for local customers and charging high prices to cover the costs of these extras, the new approach was to offer lower prices on popular merchandise to appeal to larger markets. No attempt was made to stock a complete assortment of goods. Lower profits per item sold were partially made up for by faster sales and a larger sales volume. Savings were also achieved by emphasizing self-service to save on labor costs. Instead of having sales counters and cash registers located throughout the store, check-out counters were placed in the front of the store, with little or no sales help available on the floor.

Keys do not fit well into the mass merchandiser's self-service approach to retailing. Keys are small-ticket items that require special attention. They have to be made to order. As Cole explained recently:

> "A big general store has neither the time, the ability, nor the talent to pay special attention to small-ticket items . . . The handling of keys involves an intricate assortment of maybe 1,000 types. The regular personnel can't handle it without specialized training."

Cole got the idea of leasing small spaces in big stores to make replacement keys for the large volume of customers the mass merchandisers attracted. His key-cutting machines first appeared at Woolworth, Grant, and Kresge stores. By 1959 Cole had expanded his basic idea of providing services shunned by the big retailers. He had entered the prescription eyeglasses market and was operating optical shops in several Sears stores. His company was profitable. He began buying retailing companies specializing in watchbands, keys, engraving, and shoe repair.

However, by 1970 Cole National Corporation was in trouble. Its profits were down by half. The basic problem appeared to be that Cole National's host stores were moving out of downtown areas into smaller stores in the suburbs. These new stores were too small to support a key or optical vendor. In order to survive, Cole National had to reassess its position. Were there still consumers who wanted special services? Could Cole National get access to enough of them to sell its services and prosper? How could Joseph Cole find out?

A quick review of Exhibit 9.5 makes it clear that Joseph Cole created an effective marketing strategy for his fledgling company. Cole recorded the emerging self-service strategy of the mass merchandisers and recognized two strategic marketing gaps in their strategy. First, their strategy focused on high volume and self-service to save money for their customers but failed to offer the special services these same customers sometimes needed and were willing to pay extra for. Second, their strategy did not take full advantage of the large number of customers they attracted to one store. The odds were that at any given time the large crowd shopping for discount items in a store would include several customers who also needed a special service like having a key made. Both gaps indicated an unserved target market.

PROBLEM IDENTIFICATION

Accordingly, Cole initially defined his target market as consumers who wanted to save money by buying from mass merchandisers but still had a need for certain specialized services like having keys made. His analysis of the strategic gaps also suggested a viable alternative marketing strategy to reach this target market with an appropriate marketing mix. His product, keys, would be offered with a high personal service element that added value in the eyes of the consumer. The keys would be sold within stores patronized by the target market to provide the convenience of one-stop shopping. Because of these added values, a premium price would be charged. Cole also realized that big stores would not steal his business because they could not be bothered with training personnel to operate relatively small personal service shops within their stores. They were too big. Because Cole was small, his marketing strategy proved successful for several years.

Cole National ran into problems, however, when its target market changed and Cole National did not change with it. The changes in the target market were not sudden. They could have been anticipated if Cole National had followed through over the years to make sure it was still meeting the needs of its target market. Cole National should have reassessed its marketing strategy. It should have studied its target market and determined if there were a way to continue to serve it profitably.

The problems faced by Cole National are by no means unique. As a small business owner, you face the same two problems:

1. How can you select the right target market(s) for your business without spending a lot of money?
2. How can you keep up to date on your target market(s) to make sure you anticipate the trends that will affect the profitability of your marketing strategy?

Both of these problems have practical solutions that you can afford. Indeed, the history of Cole National Corporation clearly indicates that you cannot afford to leave either of these problems unsolved. This chapter will show you how to deal with the above two problems step by step. It will also answer the three questions at the beginning of this chapter by showing you how to find out what a target market really wants and how to find out if you can sell enough to this target market to make your business profitable.

DIAGNOSIS   Diagnosis of your marketing strengths and weaknesses involves a study of three things:

1. How you find your target markets and determine what each target market really wants,

2. How you count the number of buyers for your product or service in each market, and

3. How you determine whether or not you can serve each market profitably.

Exhibit 10.1 presents a list of questions that address the three areas you need to study to do your self-diagnosis. Before reading further, mark the response scales as indicated and write down a brief account of what happened the last time you did what is described in each question. (Hint: If you have already answered the questions listed in Exhibit 9.3, refer back to your answers for ideas.)

How do you measure up? The exhibit provides a scoring guide. If you scored between 72 and 96, you are an excellent small business marketing strategist. You are both shrewd and disciplined. You will get some good ideas from this chapter that you will be able to use immediately. If you scored between 48 and 71, you have a basic idea of what needs to be done to find the right target markets for your business, but there are some rough edges and inconsistencies in your approach. This chapter will show you where you can improve your chances for profitability. If you scored less than 48, beware! You are missing major profit opportunities and taking unnecessary, large risks in your approach to marketing your company's products and services.

In the "Understanding" section of this chapter we will discuss why a high score on the questionnaire is important to you as a small business marketer. As you will see, each question presents a strategy that can be used to solve the two basic marketing problems discussed in this chapter. We will demonstrate how to employ these strategies in a systematic, economical manner to select the right target markets for your business and to keep up to date on these target markets. Like the real life private detective who relies more on thoroughness and attention to detail to solve a case than on exploits like those dramatized on TV, you will find the path to solution suggested in this chapter routine and not particularly exciting. However, following our approach can lead to some exciting payoffs.

Exhibit 10.1 How Good Are You at Finding Profitable Target Markets?[2]

Instructions: Each question has five responses listed after it. Choose the one that best describes your marketing strategy.

PART I: How do you find your target markets and determine what each target market really wants?

1. I start by looking for markets that have needs for products or services that I am capable of providing.
    a. Always
    b. Almost always
    c. Sometimes
    d. Not too often
    e. Never
2. I look for markets that need products or services that are closely related to products or services I already provide.
    a. Always
    b. Almost always
    c. Sometimes
    d. Not too often
    e. Never
3. When I find a market that may be of interest, I list all the needs that I can think of that the customers in this market might have.
    a. Always
    b. Almost always
    c. Sometimes
    d. Not too often
    e. Never
4. When I consider a new market, I make it a practice to study the products and services already being offered to this market by the competition. I try to determine what needs my competitors are serving and how well they are doing.
    a. Always
    b. Almost always
    c. Sometimes
    d. Not too often
    e. Never
5. I routinely subdivide the markets I study into three or more submarkets, or target markets, based on differences I perceive concerning who buys what and why.
    a. Always
    b. Almost always
    c. Sometimes
    d. Not too often
    e. Never
6. I double-check my own perceptions about my target markets by asking representative individuals from each target market what they buy and why.
    a. Always
    b. Almost always
    c. Sometimes
    d. Not too often
    e. Never

7. When I study the different target markets, I find their differences more interesting than what they have in common.
   a. Always
   b. Almost always
   c. Sometimes
   d. Not too often
   e. Never

8. I try to name each target market based on the needs it has that set it apart from other target markets.
   a. Always
   b. Almost always
   c. Sometimes
   d. Not too often
   e. Never

PART II: How do you count the number of buyers for your product or service in each market?

9. Once I have identified target markets of potential interest, I try to determine the size of each target market.
   a. Always
   b. Almost always
   c. Sometimes
   d. Not too often
   e. Never

10. In order to determine the size of each target market, I try to tie each with demographic facts, such as geographical location, age, sex, income, education, and occupation.
    a. Always
    b. Almost always
    c. Sometimes
    d. Not too often
    e. Never

11. I use published demographic data from private and public sources to estimate target market size.
    a. Always
    b. Almost always
    c. Sometimes
    d. Not too often
    e. Never

12. I use my company sales records for products I have sold to each target market in the past to predict my sales for new products.
    a. Always
    b. Almost always
    c. Sometimes
    d. Not too often
    e. Never

13. I use estimates by experienced salespersons to help to predict how well my new product or service will sell.
    a. Always
    b. Almost always
    c. Sometimes
    d. Not too often
    e. Never

14. I survey my wholesalers and distributors to determine how well they think my new product will sell.
    a. Always
    b. Almost always
    c. Sometimes
    d. Not too often
    e. Never

15. I try my new product idea out on a limited number of potential customers to get their reaction and estimate sales based on their response.
    a. Always
    b. Almost always
    c. Sometimes
    d. Not too often
    e. Never

16. I compare target market size (total number of sales possible) with the number of sales being made by my competition (as estimated by my suppliers and salespersons). This gives me an idea of what my share of sales to the target market can be if I do a good job serving the needs of the targeted customers.
    a. Always
    b. Almost always
    c. Sometimes
    d. Not too often
    e. Never

PART III: How do you determine whether or not you can serve each target market profitably?

17. I begin with the needs expressed by the target market. I poll my target customers to try to determine what product or service characteristics are necessary to meet their needs uniquely so that my product or service will have an advantage over the competition.
    a. Always
    b. Almost always
    c. Sometimes
    d. Not too often
    e. Never

18. I calculate what it will cost to produce my product or service, given the characteristics it must have to compete. I double-check my cost figures with equipment suppliers and others to insure that they are reasonably accurate.
    a. Always
    b. Almost always
    c. Sometimes
    d. Not too often
    e. Never

19. I try to determine ways to make my target customers aware of my product or service, and, after checking with representatives of the media, I estimate the costs of promoting my product to create awareness and convert awareness into the number of sales I have forecast.
    a. Always
    b. Almost always
    c. Sometimes
    d. Not too often
    e. Never

20. I analyze ways to get my product or service to my customers, and I estimate the cost of doing so based on information from available distributors.
    a. Always
    b. Almost always
    c. Sometimes
    d. Not too often
    e. Never

21. Based on my poll of my target customers, I try to determine the maximum price I can charge and still achieve my sales forecast.
    a. Always
    b. Almost always
    c. Sometimes
    d. Not too often
    e. Never

22. I compare the price my target customers will be willing to pay for my product with the costs implied by the product characteristics they want, the promotion that appears necessary, and the required means of distribution. This gives me a rough idea of my profits if I am able to sell what I expect to sell.
    a. Always
    b. Almost always
    c. Sometimes
    d. Not too often
    e. Never

23. I consider options. Based on my knowledge of my target cuistomers and the costs of serving them, I try to predict the impact on my costs, sales, and profits of changing product characteristics, price, promotion, or means of distribution.
    a. Always
    b. Almost always
    c. Sometimes
    d. Not too often
    e. Never

24. I keep up to date. I constantly watch what my target customers are buying and what my competitors are doing. I double-check what I think I see by collecting the views and opinions of my customers, my suppliers, my distributors, and my employees.
    a. Always
    b. Almost always
    c. Sometimes
    d. Not too often
    e. Never

Give yourself 4 points for each *a* response, 3 points for each *b* response, 2 points for each *c* response, 1 point for each *d* response, and no points for each *e* response.

UNDER-STANDING As we have just discussed, the twenty-four questions in Exhibit 10.1 share a common theme. This theme is the core of an effective marketing strategy. It is the essence of what distinguishes a realistic marketing strategy based on hard fact from a hopes-and-dreams marketing strategy based on conjecture. The theme is simple: in order to select the right target markets for your business and to make sure they will be profitable, you must check things out thoroughly and systematically.

Checking things out involves more than being a bookworm who bores through old statistical manuals in the library. It involves talking to a lot of people. Further, it involves talking to the right people and asking the right questions.

Checking things out is absolutely necessary if you are going to select the right target market(s) and keep up to date on your target market(s). Good product ideas are worth nothing unless they check out. Yesterday's view of your target customers is of little value unless it checks out today.

Our assertion that you must check things out thoroughly and systematically to be an effective small business marketing strategists tells you *what* you must do. It does not, however, tell you *how* to do it. Further, since you have a limited amount of time and money, you will naturally want to know how to do it as quickly and as cheaply as possible. We will now address these issues.

Eighteen Steps to Efficient Marketing Research

The procedure recommended in this section for checking things out economically dictates that you check out cheap, readily available information first. If satisfactory answers are not found, the procedure then progresses to more expensive, time-consuming checks. At each step you decide whether or not you know enough to solve your problem intelligently. This procedure allows you to eliminate quickly and economically ideas that have little merit. Better ideas require more study but at the same time are worth more study. If you follow our procedure, you will always be in control of the amount of time and money you spend checking things out for any given idea.

Exhibit 10.2 summarizes the procedure. As you move from the top to the bottom of the exhibit, the steps become more time consuming and expensive. You proceed down the exhibit with a target market for one of your existing products or services or with a new product or service. You can stop at any time. When you stop, you will have decided either that the prospects for your new idea are so dismal that you have to discard it or that the evidence is favorable enough to persuade you to adopt your new idea. Either way, you will not have spent a dime more than necessary to make your decision. This procedure is the essence of efficient marketing research.

We will now analyze the steps in Exhibit 10.2 and explain in detail how to carry out each one. We will also give you an idea of what each step costs and what you get for your money in terms of usable information. One last observation about following our procedure is needed before we go over each step. Depending on the nature of your business and the experience of your employees, you may find it valuable to ask selected salespersons and other employees for their views. Their observations are readily available, cost you

Exhibit 10.2   A Step-by-Step Procedure for Checking Out New Products/Services and New Markets[3]

Step 1:   List your company's distinctive competencies (things your company does/makes well).

Step 2:   Select a new product/service idea or a new market that fits your distinctive competencies and that you intuitively feel is worth checking out.

Step 3:   List consumer needs in the market. If you have a new product/service idea do Steps 3A, B, and C. If you are looking at a new market do Step C only.

Step 3A: Ask yourself if this new product/service idea is really new. Is anything else like it available that you are aware of? Have you sold something like it in the past? Have your competitors? How is it sold and who buys it? These questions will suggest possible markets for your product/service.

Step 3B: Select a market that you intuitively feel is worth checking out.

Step 3C: List all the needs that you can think of that the consumers in this market might have that could be addressed by the kinds of product/service you provide. Hints: (1) Don't be too specific about your product/service characteristics. You may have to redesign your product or service to meet the needs of this new market. (2) Include all the needs that might conceivably apply to your product/ service area. Write all of them down. No ideas should be tossed out at this point.

Step 4:   Analyze competitive offerings in detail. What competitive offerings are selling well? Where are they sold? Who buys them? Why? Which of all the needs in Step 3 appear unmet? For whom?

Step 5:   Divide the market into submarkets, or target markets, based on your perceptions concerning differences in needs. Are there significant differences in who buys what and why in this market?

Step 6:   Separate the needs you think your target markets have in common from the needs that appear to apply uniquely to one or a few target markets. Ask yourself if you can satisfy the common needs. Then ask yourself if you can also satisfy the unique needs of one or more target markets better than your competition. Can you do this at a reasonable cost and for a reasonable price? Note the target markets where you think your chances for success are good.

Step 7:   Based on the unique needs you perceive for each target market, give a name to each target market in which you think your chances of success are good. Briefly describe the type of people in this target market with words that characterize their unique needs. Ask yourself how you would recognize someone in a particular target market if you met the person and could ask him/her questions.

Step 8:   Repeat Steps 6 and 7 to make sure you have not overlooked any needs that effectively separate two target markets.

Step 9:   Make an initial estimate of the size of each target market. Are there demographic characteristics, such as geographical location, age, sex, income, education, and occupation, that tend to separate the target markets you are interested in from everyone else? What percentage of consumers in each target market is already served by your competitors? What does this imply about your potential sales and profits?

Step 10:   Determine whether you can reach your target markets. How would you find your target consumers if you wanted to talk to them or sell to them? Do they come together at certain places and times? Can you get your product or service to them at a reasonable cost?

Step 11:   Summarize your beliefs about your target market: common needs, unique needs, needs currently inadequately met, demographic characteristics, size, and degree of competition.

Step 12: Your basic concern is whether or not a target market will be profitable. Restate your beliefs about the target market as questions that you can investigate to see if the target market will be profitable.

Step 13: Specify how you will seek the answer to each question. Always seek answers from existing data (secondary data) before spending time or money gathering new data (primary data).

Step 14: When you decide to seek answers by collecting new, or primary, data, establish a sampling plan. Whom will you talk to? How many will you talk to? For example, will you question every customer in the target market (a 100 percent sample) or will you talk to 1 in 1,000? How will you pick your sample consumers to make sure they are representative of all the customers in your target market? As a general rule, collect information about your target markets from your suppliers, your industry associations, and your salespersons and distributors before you decide whether or not to interview consumers in your target market.

Step 15: Before you spend a lot of time and money collecting primary data by using a particular technique such as a questionnaire, try the technique out on a small sample to debug it.

Step 16: Prepare a time and cost budget. Estimate how much time and money it will take to accomplish Steps 12–15. Compare these costs with the benefits you expect. How much information do you need to make a good decision?

Step 17: Proceed with the collection of secondary and primary data.

Step 18: Tabulate and interpret results. How confident are you that what you now know about your target market is correct? What do your results suggest you should do?

---

nothing extra, and can be helpful to your analysis. This is particularly important at Step 13, but it can also be helpful in Steps 1 through 10.

List Competencies. Step 1 relates back to the analysis of your company's mission you did in the last chapter. Care should be taken not to be overly specific about your company's distinctive competencies. For example, don't list making rainbow-colored suspenders as a distinctive competency. Rather, list more general product- or service-related skills that could give you a competitive edge if they were brought to bear on the needs of some market.

Select A Product or Service or Market. Step 2 focuses your attention on a particular product or service or market for review. Of course, since you have limited time and money, you should at least intuitively suspect that your focus will be worthwhile.

List Consumer Needs in the Market. Steps 3A and B are performed for new products or services only. Step 3C is performed both for new product or service ideas and for new markets. Steps 3A and B are based on the premise that you may be exposed from time to time to a new product or service idea before you have given much thought to who might buy it. A salesperson, for example, might bring a new product to your attention and try to persuade you to sell it in your store. Your bottom line is profits; so you have to ask yourself if this new product will uniquely meet any of your customers needs. A good way to determine the market for a new product or service is to use what marketing experts call the substitute method. Using this approach, you ask yourself what old product the new product is likely to compete with successfully. This allows you to pick out the potential uses for the new product and suggests potential markets for it.

Step 3C is to list all the possible needs the consumers in the market might have that could be satisfied by your kind of product or service. Some needs might be pretty basic, like the need for food. Others might be subtle, like the need for status. It takes creativity to come up with a complete list of needs. Empathy also helps. If you can empathize with the consumers in this market by looking at your product or service from their point of view, you will do a better job of identifying why they might need your product or service.

Exhibit 10.3 will help you with Step 3C. It lists selected needs for two kinds of buyer. The top part of the exhibit lists the needs of the consumer—someone buying for oneself. Gift buyers and parents buying for their children also are included in this part of the chart. The bottom part of the chart suggests the special needs of a different kind of buyer—the intermediate buyer. This buyer purchases a product or service with the intention of (1) selling it to someone else, (2) using it to make something to sell to someone else, or (3) using it to provide a service that can be sold to someone else. Farmers, retailers, and manufacturers are examples of this type of buyer. The government is too, even though it may give away some of its products and services. You might expect intermediate buyers to be more rational and cost conscious than consumers when they buy because they are in business. However, they are people too. Therefore, many of the needs listed in the top part of Exhibit 10.3 apply to intermediate buyers also.

Up to this point, all you have invested in our procedure for checking out new products or services and new markets is one or two hours of free time and some creative energy. Even so, it is surprising how many times one realizes a potential bonanza has become fool's gold by the time Step 3C is completed.

Analyze the Competition.   Step 4 may require some window-shopping, depending on how well you know what your competitors are up to. As a result, it can consume a significant amount of time and money, although perhaps not as much as what you might think. What is selling well need only be estimated at this point. If your competitor is a fast food restaurant, for example, is it packed at lunch time; or does the fancy French restaurant down the street get all the business?

You should view your competitors as a free testing ground for your ideas. Far from being disappointed when you find out that one of your competitors is doing exactly what you have in mind, you should be happy. If the

Exhibit 10.3   Selected Needs That Your Product Or Service Might Satisfy[4]

CONSUMER NEEDS

PHYSIOLOGICAL NEEDS
(For the body to survive and/or be comfortable.)

Self-survival	Sleep/Rest	Freedom from pain	Acquired needs:
Air	Health	a. Physical	a. Mobility
Water	Comfort/Warmth	b. Mental	b. Cigarettes
Food	a. Clothing	Sex	c. Liquor
Waste elimination	b. Shelter		d. Drugs

SAFETY NEEDS

The Consumer	*The Consumer's Job*	*The Consumer's Money*	*The Consumer's Community*
Security, Order, and Protection as provided by:	Security and Protection is provided by:	Security and Protection as provided by:	Order, Stability, and Protection as provided by:
God (Faith)	Job position	Insurance	Organized world
Mental attitude	Meaningful work	Liquid savings	Economy of country
Peace of mind	Supervisory attitude	Home investment	Politics of country
Goals	Recognition	Investments	Armed forces
Abilities	Location stability	Fringe benefits	Laws & courts
Skills	Seniority and Unions	Part-time work	Police & fire
Education	Retirement	Spouse's work	protection
Experience	programs	Credit rating	Medical progress
Health	Routine	Budget	Scientific progress
Appearance		Rich parents	Educational
Social groups			progress
Racial groups			Religious progress
Family ties			Charities
Physical location			
Sex (Identity)			

SOCIAL NEEDS
(Belonging—Need for warm, satisfying, and fulfilling human interactions.)

Love	*Groups*	*Recreation*	*Work*	*Miscellaneous*
Affection from:	Affiliation with:	Affiliation with:		
Family	Social	Sports	Work groups	Contributing to society
Friends	Civic	Parties	Conversation	Helping other people
Sweetheart	Business	Dancing	Telephone	Doing volunteer work
Spouse	Professional	Drinking	Coffee break	
Children	Educational	Theater	Lunch	Being alone at times (Solitude)
Pets	Political	Card playing	Meetings	
	Church	Hobbies	Training	
	Labor			

SELF-ESTEEM NEEDS
(Self-confidence—Self-worth)

Self-Respect			*Respect From Others*	
Liking yourself	Acceptance	Honor	Reputation
Achievement	Appreciation	Kindness	Respect
Expertise in your field	Attention	Recognition	Seeking our advice
Skills and talents	Consideration	Patience	Status
Positive qualities and	Confidence	Praise	Support
characteristics	Courtesy	Prestige	Tolerance
Being yourself	Fair dealings	Promotion	Understanding
	Friendship	Raise in pay	

SELF-ACTUALIZATION NEEDS
(Self-fulfillment—Self-realization—Need to become all that one is capable of becoming.)

Fulfilling one's potential
Using one's capabilities
Self-improvement
Challenge
Competition

Striving to achieve
Seeking new knowledge
Striving toward meaningful goals
Using creativity

INTERMEDIATE BUYER NEEDS

SAFETY NEEDS

Security and Protection As Provided By:

Company profits
  (particularly if buyer owns company)
Job position (if buyer is employee)
Company stability
Company new business
Company reputation

Company politics (Will buying from you make the buyer
  look good?)
Job performance (reputation for getting good deals)
Supervisor attitude (if buyer is employee)
Promotions & raises (if buyer is employee)
Routine (following the book, or policies and
  procedures)

SOCIAL NEEDS

Work groups (Members of the buying committee)
Suppliers

SELF-ESTEEM NEEDS

Increasing company profits
Increasing personal empire
Expertise (knowing how a product will help the
  company)
Sense of achievement (getting a good buy)
Consideration (by you!)

Fair dealings
Reputation
Prestige
(See consumer list above for more ideas.)

SELF-ACTUALIZATION NEEDS

Learning how to make more money
Learning more about a product/service
Developing creative solutions to buying problems

The challenge of getting the best deal
Competing with others for the best deal

competitor is successful, this shows you have a good idea. You might be able to copy this success in a different geographical area with similar needs. If the competitor is having problems, figuring out how to solve these problems will help you debug your idea so that you can serve the market's needs better.

Competitors who are selling their business offer a unique source of information you might want to tap at this stage. They will provide a lot of information to interested buyers. You can count on such information to paint an optimistic picture; but, taken with a grain of salt, it can reveal a lot.

The time and expense required to analyze your competitors if you know nothing about them already depends on the nature of the market. It might only take one or two days to do an analysis when the market is local and has constant year-round needs. It might take a couple of years, however, when needs vary greatly from month to month or from year to year. For example, how do you know which retail store merchandises well? Is the Christmas promotion more successful than the back-to-school promotion? A high vacancy rate at a competitor's ski lodge may mean one thing in July and another in January. If it is July, can you get a reservation for next January? If you have experienced salespersons or other employees who have had direct contact with your competition, asking them for their observations will speed completion of Step 4.

Divide the Market into Target Markets.   Step 5 is a creative step. You have several choices concerning how to accomplish this step. Three approaches are particularly useful. We suggest you try all three.[5]

The first approach is to view the marketplace as a heterogeneous group of customers that can be divided into smaller groups of customers, each group having similar, relatively strong needs. The logic is that if you can isolate and serve the needs of one of these smaller groups, you will make a good profit. This approach is similar to what Joseph Cole did at Cole National.

The second approach is to view each customer as an individual with unique needs and to aggregate people with similar needs in one market. For example, you may speculate on how your needs are different from someone who is richer. If your needs and the rich person's are the same in regard to a particular product or service, you are both part of the same market and are indistinguishable from the standpoint of the seller of that product or service. On the other hand, if your needs are different, the seller would gain by directing his or her sales presentation either to the special needs of richer people or to the needs of people like you. The first and second approaches lead you to the same end. They are heads and tails of the same coin. When you use either approach, it is important to remember that many of the buyers for your products and services may not be buying for themselves.

The third approach is to define target markets according to the special needs of consumers regarding market mix variables, such as product characteristics, price, sales location, and promotion. For example, do some consumers in the market need a lot of service? What kind? Is friendly service needed more than expert service by some consumers? Do some need a specialized product? Do some need a perishable product? Do a significant number of consumers need a high quality product? What about price? Do some consumers need economical prices? Is price not an issue to some? Do some need the status of paying more? Do certain consumers need a new place to shop? Do some need a more convenient place to shop? Do a good number of consumers need information, or promotional literature, about product advantages? Do some need the help of a salesperson to choose?

One of the factors you should consider if you use the third approach is how people buy. Some buying decisions are made by individuals. Others are made by groups. Some purchases are made frequently to meet daily needs. Other purchases are made once a year. Understanding how your product or service is purchased will suggest needs that separate consumers into different target markets. Pencils, for example, are sold in packages of five or six at drugstores most of the year. They are bought by a wide variety of people. At the beginning of the school year, things change. Then, students and mothers purchase the most, and they buy in larger average quantities. In contrast, businesses and governments buy larger quantities less frenquently, and they buy about the same quantity each time, no matter what the time of year.

Whichever approach you choose to accomplish Step 5, it is important to remember the distinction between consumers and intermediate buyers when selecting target markets. Generally, it is logical to place consumers and intermediate buyers in separate target markets. Intermediate buyers have different needs, are fewer in number, buy in larger quantities, and tend to be more geographically concentrated than consumers. As with earlier steps, Step 5 is primarily a conceptual process through which you develop a hypothesis about what the marketplace for your product is like. All the steps so far can be accomplished without a lot of research.

Look for Common Needs and Unique Needs.   Steps 6, 7, and 8 continue the process of developing hypotheses. The purpose of Step 6 is to distinguish among the various target markets you have identified within the marketplace. Also, you will consider whether or not you can adequately serve the needs of each target market. In distinguishing among target markets, the relevant differences are differences in needs. However, common needs are also of interest since you may not be able to fulfill an important need common to all the target markets. For example, all of your target markets may have a strong need for the cheap wood siding that you produce, but none will be able to use it unless it meets building code requirements. You have to satisfy their common need of conforming to code.

Name Target Markets.   Step 7 translates the target markets you have identified into the types of consumer you will be serving if you enter into these target markets. It puts your target markets into human terms. This translation simplifies your thinking process and helps you to visualize how to serve the market. The object is to pick a name that fits each target market and reminds you of the needs that set it apart from the others.

Estimate the Size of Each Target Market.   The purpose of Steps 9 and 10 is to test your thinking about the feasibility of serving the target markets you have identified in earlier steps. As a practical matter, many target markets may be too small even for a small business. Your costs for custom tailoring your product to meet the needs of such a target market might easily exceed the dollar sales you could hope to achieve. Step 9 deals with the size problem.

Determine If Target Markets are Reachable.   Step 10 deals with the related, but more subtle, issue of your ability to reach your target markets. If you consider the whole world to be your marketplace, you can almost always convince yourself that there are enough people in any target market to justify launching a product to meet their needs. The trouble is that it may cost you a fortune to find these people, to verify that they really want a product like yours, to let them know your product exists, and to get your product to them. What you should be looking for are target markets that can be reached at reasonable cost.

The best way to deal with Steps 9 and 10 is to link your target markets to demographic characteristics, such as geographical location, age, sex, income, education, and occupation. For example, if in Step 7 you characterize one of your target markets as affluent, retired senior citizens, the relevant demographic characteristics probably are geographic location, age, and income. Assume that you are interested in consumers who have incomes over $25,000 per year, who do not work, who are over sixty-five, and who live in Arizona. An hour or two in the reference section of your local library will provide you with good estimates of the number of people who meet these demographic criteria. You will find statistics published by the U.S. Bureau of the Census and updated periodically concerning age, employment, and income for each state. These data are even available for counties, Standard Metropolitan Statistical Areas (SMSA), and towns with populations over twenty-five hundred. Government data can be crosschecked with private sources, which are also available at your local library.. The two major sources applicable to the example above are *Sales Management* magazine's "Survey of Consumer Buying Power" and *The Editor and Publisher Market Guide*. Both provide figures on population by age, effective buying power (retail sales), and income for states, counties, metropolitan areas, and most cities with populations of ten thousand or more.

The information you need to do a good job handling Steps 9 and 10 is readily available and, in most cases, free. Because of this, we cannot overemphasize the importance of augmenting your intuitive estimates in Steps 9 and 10 with hard data. Appendix A at the end of this chapter provides a list of selected reference materials for small business marketers. The section of Appendix A entitled "Demographic Data for Target Market Analysis" goes into more detail about where to find demographic data.

Summarize Your Beliefs about Each Target Market. Once you complete Step 10, you should have a pretty good idea of which target markets are worth looking into further. Even if you are satisfied that you have found the target markets that are right for you and do not intend to do further research, you will find it worthwhile to summarize your thinking as described in Step 11. Such a summary for each target market clarifies what you believe about each market and is a convenient reference when you plan your marketing mix.

Check Target Market Profitability. Once you complete Step 11, you may notice some gaps in what you know, or you may be uncomfortable with certain assumptions you are making about a target market. If this is the case, you may want to do further research. Step 12 is to state the questions to be answered or double-checked by this research. For example, you may feel that your target market of retail stores values quick delivery from suppliers and that the competition is not meeting this need. You can meet the target market's need by stocking a big inventory so that items can be delivered the same day ordered. You have determined that carrying this inventory will cost you money and that you will therefore have to charge a bit more than the competition. You do not know whether the need of the target market is strong enough to support the extra cost. Three questions are suggested by this example:

1. Do my target retailers value quick delivery from my type of supplier?

2. Is my competition delivering quickly enough to satisfy my target retailers?

3. How much extra would my target retailers be willing to pay to insure quick delivery?

The questions you develop in Step 12 should be specific. They should each focus on one topic.

Specify How to Answer Marketing Questions. Once you have determined the specific questions you need answered, the next step is to specify in Step 13 how you will seek the answer to each question. Continuing the example used in Step 12, you might do the following:

1. Interview each of your salespersons who currently call on your target retailers to determine if the retailers have emphasized a need for quick delivery, if the retailers are satisfied with competitors' delivery time, and if they have ever offered to pay more for quick delivery.

2. Inspect a cross section of retailers to determine which supplies are in stock and the estimated delivery times of items out of stock. This is to be done by a shopping study.

3. Interview a sample of retailers about their quick delivery preferences, their attitudes about the competition's delivery, and the extra value they attach to quick delivery.

In seeking answers, you should use information that is already available before going to the expense of gathering new data. Gathering new data is expensive if you do it right. It is also surprisingly time consuming. Also, the results you get may be hard to interpret. Your limited resources may prevent you from obtaining valid and reliable results. Therefore, for most small businesses, it will pay to avoid the formal collection of new data unless absolutely necessary. This does not mean that you should not ask appropriate people a lot of questions as you go along to double-check your opinions.

Existing data are available in a variety of forms. If you have been in business for a while or have just bought an established business, your company's existing sales records can be very useful. Invoices can tell you who your best customers are, where they live, what they buy, when they buy, and which one of your salespersons they buy from. Another form of existing data that can be very valuable is the opinions of your experienced salespersons or other employees. Their opinions about a new product or market should be collected and carefully analyzed before you proceed with the collection of new data. Still another source is the vast pool of statistical data gathered by governmental and private sources. Appendix A at the end of this chapter provides a list of selected reference materials for small business marketers, which is subdivided according to how you can use the data to find out more about your customers.

Design Sampling Plans for New Data Needed.   If you do decide to collect primary data, you must establish a sampling plan, as described in Step 14. Sampling means selecting a relatively small number of potential customers from your target market study, rather than studying all target market customers. This saves time and money if you have a large number of customers. In order for what you find out to be useful, what you find out about the sample must be an accurate reflection of what is true for the target market as a whole. Marketing experts refer to good samples as representative. They represent well the true character of the entire target market. Selecting a representative sample is not easy. If you don't, however, you have no way of knowing whether the answers you get from the sample you select are truly representative of what your target market thinks. If you are selling a product or service to intermediate buyers, it is sometimes economical to talk to every intermediate buyer in your target market. If you are able to do this or are able to come close with a reasonable effort, sampling is not a major problem for you. If you sell to consumers, however, sampling is a big problem whenever you need primary data. Appendix B to this chapter shows you how to select a good representative sample.

One of the strategies used most frequently to gather data from samples is soliciting answers to a list of prepared questions. Whether you ask your sample customers questions on the telephone, talk to them in person, or mail them a questionnaire, correct wording of questions is critical. Writing good questions is an art. Appendix C to this chapter presents a discussion of the basic issues and demonstrates how to write good questions.

Debug Questions.   Step 15 emphasizes an important point about the use of questionnaires or any other research technique you intend to use. You should try them out on small samples first to get the bugs out before you begin the full-scale study. Appendix C notes several reasons for this.

Tabulate and Interpret Results.   Steps 16 and 17 are self-explanatory, but the word "confidence" in Step 18 bears careful analysis. At one extreme, your confidence in your knowledge of your target market can be a gut feeling that cannot be quantified. At the other extreme, if you have collected good primary data about your target market, your confidence can be defined precisely in terms such as, "The odds are nine to one that I am right when I say that my target retailers value quick delivery from my type of supplier." Appendix B to this chapter discusses the issue of confidence and how to figure the odds that your primary data are accurate.

In general, even if you do not try to collect primary data systematically, it pays to express your conclusions about your target market in terms of odds. Comparison of your odds of success for products or services and new markets will enable you to choose the most profitable, given the risk you are willing to take.

The purpose of the eighteen-step procedure for checking out new products or services and new markets is to avoid catastrophic failure and to focus your attention on a few special opportunities for growth. For each opportunity you check out, you should estimate the best outcome, the most likely outcome, and the worst outcome. For example, you may feel you have one chance in 10 of selling $1,000,000 to a target market, 7 in 10 of selling $500,000, and 2 in 10 of selling as little as $200,000. Your expected payoff would then be 1/10 ($1,000,000) + 7/10 ($500,000) + 2/10 (200,000), or $490,000. If your costs are $400,000, your expected profit would be a $90,000. However, if the $400,000 is all you have in this world, a 2 in 10 chance of losing one-half of it may be intolerable. In this case, perhaps it would be better to take a second option, where your odds of selling $550,000 would be 2 in 10; of selling $500,000, 4 in 10; and of selling $450,000, 4 in 10. Your expected payoff is the same, 2/10 ($550,000) + 4/10 ($500,000) + 4/10 ($450,000), or $490,000. Your chance of making a big killing is less, but your chances of a big loss is also eliminated.

One last point to remember when comparing your risks in Step 18 is to remember that a decision to proceed is not all or nothing. Big risks can be divided into a series of smaller steps. If the first one works, the odds that subsequent steps will succeed can be revised upward. For example, you may consider investing $500,000 to introduce an unproven new product into a region too risky, with only a fifty-fifty chance of making more than the $500,000 invested. However, it may cost you only $10,000 to try selling the product on a limited basis in one small town in the region. If it sells well in the test town and you earn $20,000 on your $10,000 investment, you can be quite confident that investing the rest of the $500,000 will pay off big.

Joseph Cole recognized he had a problem and brought in help to deal with Cole National's lagging profits. He hired several M.B.A.s. One of them, Boake Sells, is now president of Cole National. What did the M.B.A.s do? They followed the procedures outlined in this chapter. They recognized that the company's distinctive competency was special service. As Sells says, "We are an oasis of service in a sea of self-service." They focused on target markets that would permit them to exploit their competency to uniquely meet customer needs. "We add value," Sells explains. "If we can't we don't go in. We looked into other leased shops in Sears stores, like health food, but we turned them down because there was no way we could add value."

This approach kept Cole National in optical products (40 percent of sales). You can still get your eyes tested in twenty minutes at a Cole booth and get your glasses in ten days. Keys are now 20 percent of sales, and personalized gifts are also 20 percent.

The same approach has also led to new ventures and new directions. Cole National's Craft Showcase chain (13.5 percent of sales) runs forty-one shopping mall stores that offer art and craft supplies along with instructions on how to use them. Most recently the company has started a baked-while-you-wait cookie chain (5 percent of sales). The company is working hard to get floor space in large shopping malls with the traffic necessary to support its special services.

How successful has Cole National been since 1970? Last year the company sold $160 million and earned a topnotch 24 percent on stockholders' equity. Cole National has gotten back in touch with what its target customers really want and is keeping up to date on where its customers shop. As long as it continues to do so, Cole National will be an excellent example of a company that makes its marketing strategy work.

CASE SOLUTION

Cole National Corpora-tion

CHAPTER
SUMMARY

This chapter has presented an eighteen-step procedure for selecting the right target markets for your business without spending a lot of money. This same procedure can be used to keep up to date on your target markets to make sure you anticipate the trends that will affect the profitability of your marketing strategy. The eighteen-step procedure shows you step by step how to determine what your customers really want and how to find out if you can sell them enough to make any money.

The next three chapters focus on questions about your marketing mix: how to advertise, where to sell your products, and what price to charge. The eighteen-step procedure developed in this chapter can answer these questions. In fact, you will save time and money if you are aware of the questions you must ask about marketing mix prior to proceeding with your analysis of your first market. The eighteen-step procedure is really a step-by-step procedure for profitable marketing strategy. Asking questions simultaneously about the two major components of marketing strategy—target markets and marketing mix—is logical and necessary to give you a complete picture of your prospects for success.

DISCUSSION
QUESTIONS

1. **Short Case: Frances's Fantastic Fabric Cutters II**
   Question 1 at the end of the last chapter presented a short case concerning Frances Chapman's electric shears. Using the eighteen-step strategy (Exhibit 10.2) given in this chapter, analyze the prospects for Frances's shears. (Hint: Review your analysis of this case done for chapter 9.)

2. Exhibit 10.3 distinguishes between consumer needs and intermediate buyer needs. How valid do you think this distinction is? Why?

3. Why is Step 15 of the eighteen-step marketing strategy, debug questions, necessary?

4. Select one need from each of the five categories of consumer needs listed in Exhibit 10.3, and describe a product or service idea that can serve the need well at a reasonable cost.

5. Step 10 of the eighteen-step marketing strategy, determine if target markets are reachable, refers to a critical concern. Name three businesses in your area or three products or services being sold in your area that do not appear to be reaching their intended customers. Why aren't they reaching their intended customers?

REFERENCES

Brennen, William H. *Successful Marketing for Your Small Business*. Englewood Cliffs, N.J.: Prentice-Hall, Inc., 1978.

Emory, C. William. *Business Research Methods*. Homewood, Ill.: Richard D. Irwin, Inc., 1980.

Justis, Robert T. and Jackson, Bill. "Marketing Research for Dynamic Small Business," *Journal of Small Business Management* 16: 4 (October, 1978), 10–20.

McCarthy, E. Jerome. *Basic Marketing*, 6th ed. Homewood, Ill.: Richard D. Irwin, Inc., 1978.

Trombetta, William L. "An Empirical Approach to Marketing Strategy for the Small Retailer," *Journal of Small Business Management* 14: 4 (October, 1976), 55–58.

Tull, Donald S. and Albaum, Gerald S. *Survey Research: A Decisional Approach.* New York: Intext Educational Publishers, 1973.

1. This case is adapted from the information provided in "Service at A (Stiff) Price," *Forbes* 125, no. 3 (February 1980): 84. Quotations used were selected from those cited in this article. **FOOTNOTES**

2. Questions 1 through 8 of this questionnaire are based on the seven-step approach to market gridding suggested by Jerome E. McCarthy, *Basic Marketing: A Managerial Approach* (Homewood, Ill.: Richard D. Irwin, Inc., 1975), pp. 118–23.

3. *Ibid.* The first nine steps of this procedure owe much to McCarthy's seven-step approach to market gridding.

4. The general classifications shown in this chart follow those suggested in Abraham H. Maslow's influential work, *Motivation and Personality* (New York: Harper and Row, 1954). See especially pp. 80–107.

5. These three approaches are discussed in detail by William H. Brannen, *Successful Marketing for Your Small Business* (Englewood Cliffs, N.J.: Prentice-Hall, Inc., 1978), pp. 56–63.

Appendix A

FINDING OUT ABOUT YOUR CUSTOMERS AND COMPETITORS CHEAPLY AND QUICKLY

The purpose of this appendix is to describe the most important sources of existing information that you can use to check out new products or services and new markets. All the sources described in this appendix are readily available to you. In most cases it will cost you nothing but your time to collect the information you need about your customers and your competitors from these sources.

Most of the sources listed in this appendix can be found at the reference desk in your local library. A well-trained reference librarian can be extremely helpful to you in your search for information. Once you define specifically the information you need, your reference librarian will help you to find the reference source that contains the information. Even if the material is not available at your local library, your reference librarian can track down a library that does have what you need and obtain it through regional or national interlibrary loan networks. Since it is impossible to cover all information sources in an appendix such as this, your reference librarian will also prove useful in helping you find additional references that apply to your particular marketing problem. This is particularly true for information from local rather than national sources.

Basic Reference Sources

There is a variety of basic reference sources available that will help you to find likely sources of the marketing information you need:

> *Bibliographic Index: A Cumulative Bibliography of Bibliographies.* New York: H. W. Wilson Company, quarterly.
> Lists bibliographies on specific topics.

Business Periodicals Index. New York: H. W. Wilson Company, monthly except July.
Indexes over 150 business periodicals; cites many practical articles concerning specific produccts, industries, trades, and companies.

Daniells, Lorna M. *Business Information Sources*. Berkeley: University of California Press, 1976.
Provides an exhaustive list of business-related reference material.

Encyclopedia of Business Information Sources: A Detailed Listing of Primary Subjects of Interest to Managerial Personnel, With a Record of Sourcebooks, Periodicals, Organizations, Directories, Handbooks, Bibliographies, and Other Sources of Information on Each Topic. 3rd ed. Detroit: Gale Research Company, 1976.
Provides an extensive listing of information sources by general topic and by geographic source.

Guide to U.S. Government Publications. McLean, Vir.: Documents Index, 1973–.
Lists U.S. government serials and periodicals by issuing agency, title, or documents number.

Johnson, Herbert Webster. *How to Use the Business Library, With Sources Of Business Information*. 4th ed. Cincinnati: South-Western Publishing Company, 1972.
Provides basic guide to the use of a business library; notes special types of materials useful to your research, such as handbooks, yearbooks, and government publications.

Sheehy, Eugene P. *Guide to Reference Books*. 9th ed. Chicago: American Library Association, 1976.
Includes data sources for a wide range of business topics.

U.S. Department of Commerce. *Publications: A Catalog and Index*. Washington, D.C.: Government Printing Office.
Details the many publications of the department's offices, administrations, and bureaus, including the data published by the Bureau of the Census.

U.S. Superintendent of Documents. *Monthly Catalog of United States Government Publications*. Washington, D.C.: Government Printing Office, monthly.
Lists publications by all branches of the federal government; includes monthly and annual subject index.

Basic Marketing References

American Marketing Association. *A.M.A. Bibliography Series*. Chicago: American Marketing Association.
Lists sources devoted to marketing topics.

Marketing Information Guide. Garden City, N.Y.: The Trade Marketing Information Guide, Inc., monthly.

Sources of Data About Your Competition

Data about your competition are available in a wide variety of forms. Often the same sources that provide demographic data about your customers also provide similar data about your competitors. Sometimes the data available do not identify specific competitors. However, even when this is the case, you can get a good idea of how many competitors you have and how well they are doing.

Many of the data about your competitors are found in business directories. Directories for specific industries or associations can contain far more than just organized lists of companies. They often include a wealth of comparative data.

Another major source of data about your competitors may be your trade association. Trade associations compile detailed information on the location and economic health of their members. The two publications on associations listed below will help you find the associations closely tied to your product or service. Also, the Small Business Administration currently contracts with an extensive list of associations to provide advice to small businesses. You can find out if an association applicable to your product or service is on the list by contacting your SBA field office.

A final important source of information about your competition is the data provided by credit-checking services. The data provided to you when you run a credit check often go beyond finances and payment record. Dun and Bradstreet's credit reports, for example, are much more detailed than the information provided in their *Million Dollar Directory* or *Middle Market Directory*. Further, they can often provide information on small companies or sole proprietors not listed in either directory. Often, if you have an established banking relationship, your banker will order the credit checks you want. Normally, this information will not be released to you. However, you can read it once it arrives at the bank.

If your customers are intermediate buyers, the sources listed in this section can also be used to gather specific information about your target markets. Useful data on your intermediate buyers that can be found in these sources include size in dollar sales, number of employees, nature of business, who their customers are, geographic location, and their purchasing procedures.

Many of the publications listed in this section use Standard Industrial Classification (SIC) numbers as cross-references. See *The Standard Industrial Classification Manual* prepared by the Office of Management and Budget to determine the SIC numbers of interest to you.

Dun and Bradstreet, Inc. *Middle Market Directory*. New York: Dun and Bradstreet, annually.
Similar to *Million Dollar Directory*; provides data for about thirty thousand firms with a net worth of $500 thousand to $1 million. Dun and Bradstreet maintains data on about three million businesses and publishes a variety of more detailed, specialized directories, such as *Metalworking Marketing Directory*.

Dun and Bradstreet, Inc. *Million Dollar Directory*. New York: Dun and Bradstreet, annually.
Lists alphabetically, geographically, and by product classification over thirty thousand businesses with a net worth of $1 million or more.

Encyclopedia of Associations. Detroit: Gale Research Co., annually.
Volume 1 gives brief description of national organizations in the United States and notes addresses and publications.

Funk and Scott Index of Corporations and Industries. Cleveland: Predicasts, weekly.
Indexes articles of current interest by type of product and company name.

Klein, Bernard. *Guide To American Directories: A Guide to the Major Business Directories of the United States, Covering All Industrial, Professional, and Mer-*

cantile Categories. 9th ed. Coral Springs, Fla.: B. Klein Publications, Inc., 1975.
Lists the wide variety of directories available through publishers, associations, chambers of commerce, and government offices.

MacRae's Blue Book. Hinsdale, Ill.: MacRae's Blue Book Co., annually.
Lists companies by forty thousand product classifications and alphabetically; includes company catalogues.

National Trade and Professional Associations of the United States and Canada. Washington, D.C.: Columbia Books, Inc., annually
Lists national trade and professional organizations.

Robert Morris Associates. *Annual Statement Studies*. Philadelphia: Robert Morris Associates, annually.
Provides financial and operating ratios and profit and loss data for about three hundred lines of business.

Sources of State Information and State Industrial Directories. Washington D.C.: Chamber of Commerce of the United States, 1977.
Lists, by state and other classifications, industrial directories and directories of manufacturers published by state and private organizations.

Thomas Register of American Manufacturers and Thomas Register Catalogue File. New York: Thomas Publishing Company, annually.
Lists by state and by city about seventy-five thousand products and services and the companies that supply each; also contains catalogues of companies.

Troy, Leo. *Almanac of Business and Industrial Financial Ratios*. Englewood Cliffs, N.J.: Prentice-Hall, annually.
Contains financial and operating ratios, etc. for about 160 lines of business.

U.S. Bureau of the Census. The following titles are available from the U.S. Government Printing Office in Washington, D.C.: *County Business Patterns, Census of Selected Service Industries, Census of Manufacturers and Census of Retail Trade*.
Each provides financial data and statistics on number of businesses and size by geographical location and industry.

Demographic Data for Target Market Analysis

The sources described in this section will provide you with a variety of demographic data about the consumers in your target markets. In addition to the sources listed here, much valuable information can be obtained from local banks, chambers of commerce, newspaper research departments, employment development departments, industrial development agencies, and city-planning departments.

Exhibit 10–A.1 provides you with a list of demographic categories for which data are readily available. Most data from national sources are for towns of ten thousand or more.

Editor and Publisher Market Guide. New York: Editor and Publisher Company, annually.
Tabulates current estimates of population, incomes, households, and retail sales for nine major sales classifications; sorts data by state, county, SMSA, and fifteen hundred daily newspaper markets.

Exhibit 10–A.1   Demographic Classifications Of Consumer Data[1]

FOR HOUSEHOLDS

Size of County, Geographic Area:	Location in SMSA and size or Urban—Central City Urban—Fringe Places over 10,000 population Places 2,500–10,000 population Rural
Geographic Region:	New England Metro New York Mid-Atlantic, etc.
Ages of Children:	No children Age of youngest child
Family Size:	1 or 2, 3 or 4, 4 or more
Family Income:	Number of people receiving $5,000–10,000; 10,000–15,000, etc.
Home Ownership:	Own or Rent, Time in one place
Dwelling Characteristic:	Single Family; Multiple Family

FOR INDIVIDUALS

Age:	Under 6, 6–11, 12–17, 18–34, 35–49, 50–64, 65 or over.
Sex:	Male, Female
Education:	Grades 1–8, Some High School, Graduated High School, Some College, Graduated College
Marital Status:	Married, Widowed, Divorced or Separated, Single (never married)
Occupation:	Unemployed, Retired, Student, Employed: Professional/technical, Manager, Clerical, Sales, Craftsman, Foreman, Operator, Armed Services, Housewife, etc.
Race:	White, Black, etc.

FOR HOUSEHOLD HEADS

Sex:	Male, Female
Age:	24 or younger, 25–34, 35–49, 50–64, 65 or older
Education:	Same as for individuals above.
Occupation:	Same as for individuals above.
Race:	Same as for individuals above.

FOR HOUSEWIVES	
Age:	Same as for household heads above.
Education:	Same as for household heads above.
Employment:	Employed outside the home, employed full time (30 + hour per week), employed part time (less than 30 hours per week), not employed outside home, unemployed—looking for work.

Rand McNally Commercial Atlas and Marketing Guide. Chicago: Rand McNally and Company, annually.
Presents marketing data and area statistics in atlas form.

Statistics Sources: A Subject Guide to Data on Industrial, Business, Social, Educational, Financial, and Other Topics for the United States and Internationally. 5th ed. Detroit: Gale Research Company, 1977.
Locates useful demographic data published by all types of government and private organizations; arranged in dictionary style.

"Survey of Buying Power." In *Sales and Marketing Management*. New York: Sales Management, Inc., July and October issues each year.
Provides demographic data and buying-power information for states, counties, and cities.

U.S. Bureau of the Census. *Census of Population*. Washington, D.C.: Government Printing Office, every ten years.
This is the basic government source concerning population. Provides population statistics by sex, age, education, occupation, income, and race.

U.S. Bureau of the Census. *County and City Data Book*. Washington, D.C.: Government Printing Office, annually.
Contains data for states, counties, Standard Metropolitan Statistical Areas (SMAs), and many cities.

U.S. Bureau of the Census. *Current Population Reports: Population Estimates*. Series P–25. Washington, D.C.: Government Printing Office, monthly.
Updates the census statistics between census dates.

U.S. Bureau of the Census. *Directory of Federal Statistics for Local Areas: A Guide to Sources*. Washington, D.C.: Government Printing Office, 1978.
Provides guidance on where to find local demographic data contained in over 180 publications of thirty-three federal agencies. A similar guide is available for states.

U.S. Bureau of the Census. *Directory of Nonfederal Statistics for States and Local Areas*. Washington D.C.: Government Printing Office, 1968.
Lists nonfederal sources of current demographic statistics.

If you decide to go directly to your potential customers to find out what they need, you must decide whom to talk to. Normally, you will have sufficient resources to talk to only a relatively small number of your customers. It simply would be too time-consuming and expensive to talk to all of them. Deciding whom to talk to is critical because you need to make sure that the sample of consumers you interview is representative of all the consumers in your target market. In other words, you have to be confident that your sample has the same needs and the same intensity of need as the entire target market. Obviously, there will never be a perfect match. There will always be some difference between what your sample says and what the target market really wants. The object is to get results you can be fairly confident in at a reasonable cost.

The process of picking whom to talk to is called sample design. There are three steps to sample design:

Step 1: Listing your customers

Step 2: Selecting your sample

Step 3: Deciding how to contact your sample.

We will discuss each of these steps in detail.

Step 1: Listing Your Customers

Before you can choose a sample, you need a list of people from which to choose. Since you want to study the consumers in your target market, the first step in sample design is to get a list of the names and/or addresses of the consumers in your target market.

Sometimes getting this list is relatively easy. For example, if you plan to operate a twenty-four-hour grocery store, your target market may be all the adults in the immediate neighborhood. Assuming all the adults have listed telephone numbers, your neighborhood telephone directory can give you the list you need. If many adults do not have listed telephones, you can settle for a list of the addresses of all the dwelling units in the neighborhood.

Sometimes getting the list of your target market customers is more complex. If you plan to open your store on a state highway, for example, your target market will include many people who are just passing through. It will be impossible to come up with a list of such transients. Further, you cannot be sure what percentage of your business will come from such people, as opposed to local residents. A little creativity will suggest some solutions. Sampling the customers of a competitor's twenty-four-hour store in a similar location down the highway as they leave the store may give you an idea of why they stopped, what they needed, how much they spent, and the number of local customers versus transients. If there is not another twenty-four-hour store, interviewing customers at the nearest twenty-four-hour gas station on the highway may be enlightening. Would they have stopped at a twenty-four-hour store if one had been open?

Whether you list the consumers in your target market by finding out their names or by figuring out where they are, problems of accuracy will occur. Your list of names may be incomplete or may not be exactly what you want. A list of local manufacturers from the Chamber of Commerce, for example, will include members only. The companies not on the list may turn out to be your most important customers. If you

Appendix B

FINDING OUT
WHAT YOUR
CUSTOMERS
WANT—HOW TO
PICK WHOM TO
TALK TO

select samples based on location, you may have to settle for locations that only approximate your ideal location, as in the example described above. It is often quite difficult to estimate the magnitude of inaccuracy that will result from picking your sample incomplete lists or approximate locations. You must decide for yourself whether or not your list is a good enough approximation of all the people actually in your target market.

It is important to remember that your list of target market consumers and the real list are bound to be different. Statisticians have developed elaborate means for determining how many people on your list you need to talk to in order to draw conclusions about your target market that have, for example, a 95 percent chance of being accurate. However, these calculations are based on the assumption that your list and the ideal list are identical. If your list is suspect, you will have to build an extra fudge factor into the possible error in your conclusions.

Step 2: Selecting Your Sample

The second step in sample design is to specify how you will pick whom to talk to from among all those on your list of your target market. Also involved in this step is deciding how many people you will select for your sample.

The most critical thing that must be done to insure that your sample is truly representative of your whole target market is to devise a random means of selection. For selection to be random, two conditions must apply. First, each person on your list must have an equal chance of being selected for your sample. Second, the fact that you select one individual for your sample should not make it any more or less likely that any other individual will be the next one chosen.

The twenty-four-hour grocercy store example given above can be used to illustrate the various ways of selecting a random sample. Consider first the situation where you feel the neighborhood telephone book is a good list of the people who make up your target market. The alphabetical listings may have 100 pages with an average of 320 listings per page, or 32,000 names. You could number each name from 1 to 32,000 and use a random number table to select your sample. Any basic statistics book will include such a table and explain how to use it. Basically, such tables are long lists of numbers that have been selected in a manner to insure randomness. Table 10-B.1 is an excerpt from one such table.[2] One way to read numbers off this table is to use the first five digits in the first row, then the first five digits in the second row, etc. Five digits are used because our target population is a five-digit number (32,000). For example, the first three numbers from the table are 44178, 88671, 53181. All three exceed 32,000. However, if we set up a consistent scheme to reduce these numbers, they can still be used. In this case, we will subtract multiples of 32,000 (the population's total size) from each number until the remainder falls between 1 and 32,000. Thus, we end up with 12,178, 24,671, and 21,181. The first person you select for your sample is the person whose telephone directory listing you have numbered 12,178, the second is the person with the listing number 24,671, and the third is the person with the listing number 21,181. You continue in this manner until you have selected the number of people you need for your sample. If you have to work from a list of addresses instead of names, you simply number the addresses, use a random number table to select a random sample from these addresses, and interview the household heads living at the selected addresses.

In the example where you do not have a list of addresses or names, you need to insure that the people you interview outside the competitor's store are representative of those who shop there. This is usually done by choosing a study period considered representative, dividing the hours the store is open during that period into a large number of time slots, and then selecting a random sample of these time slots. You then interview everyone who comes out of the store during each selected time slot. For example, 100 five-minute time slots might be selected through the use of a random number table from the 4,232 five-minute time slots available in a two-week period. This two-week period includes peak and slack hours, weekdays and weekends. Because the 100 time slots are chosen randomly, your sample will be representative of the two-week period.

Sometimes, if your target market is made up of two or more nonoverlapping subgroups of consumers, you may want to make sure you interview a representative sample of each subgroup so that you can determine the special needs of each. To do this, you need to select a separate random sample from each nonoverlapping group. This procedure is called stratified random sampling. It enables you to combine what you learn from each subgroup into aggregate estimates for your whole target market. For example, in the case of your twenty-four-hour grocery store, you may decide to interview local residents at their homes and transients at your competitor's store. You may randomly select the local residents from telephone directory listings and randomly select the transients based on time slots. The results from both surveys would then be combined to give you an overall sales forecast and a rough idea of how precise and reliable your forecast is. If you do use stratified random sampling, the important thing to remember is that your sample from each subgroup needs to be large enough to achieve the desired level of confidence in your results.

How large should your sample be? Generally speaking, the answer to this question depends on four factors: 1) how confident you want to be in your results, 2) how

Table 10–B.1   Example of Random Number Table

44	17	81	63	93	91	52	43	50	74	61	99	02	19	94	26	77	28	14	95	39	22	25	30	53
88	67	13	65	42	16	55	42	78	81	12	66	58	07	30	20	59	47	14	96	78	59	58	69	07
53	18	13	47	12	81	71	93	43	14	45	90	39	29	77	47	92	81	23	69	70	56	79	90	60
88	57	56	97	96	24	63	95	32	41	90	43	48	61	52	05	74	80	89	89	12	76	37	73	88
49	37	69	38	27	16	62	64	95	32	63	31	18	12	21	68	08	84	16	48	33	93	67	46	98
66	00	15	15	06	86	14	07	76	69	84	86	58	40	08	58	63	87	36	88	19	90	93	66	23
17	07	89	49	45	65	08	01	23	92	30	67	99	66	81	88	60	41	47	47	28	53	64	08	12
73	99	60	72	28	09	19	34	62	10	49	62	95	68	60	91	13	06	88	83	46	64	87	59	24
11	33	21	44	43	15	91	22	07	59	28	42	12	76	76	20	27	24	24	70	78	93	67	51	61
43	08	41	21	85	32	51	09	47	54	45	23	51	66	66	50	44	27	63	67	16	08	28	32	25
57	56	85	67	62	97	61	49	23	51	35	95	77	49	03	10	42	91	43	94	50	57	03	49	38
62	38	42	48	72	35	81	64	85	19	29	39	03	71	60	19	86	80	21	92	34	33	81	80	35
21	73	14	67	12	30	23	68	19	78	55	90	37	25	71	03	99	59	12	51	47	82	45	25	58
75	65	33	81	82	13	23	96	76	82	86	23	82	51	50	64	17	55	28	41	95	03	63	62	95
61	13	17	91	71	77	05	72	82	73	67	52	45	97	77	51	16	78	93	01	91	17	66	61	26
72	56	13	65	11	38	13	00	50	56	82	68	31	33	12	41	61	84	23	92	13	13	55	38	14
97	53	14	68	19	44	44	70	74	30	71	09	35	63	80	55	10	31	95	97	17	11	39	44	32
35	79	16	21	57	81	75	53	33	60	94	77	79	29	49	07	85	47	83	12	22	55	88	46	13
22	64	20	80	44	28	22	09	90	58	41	06	16	23	35	36	38	02	23	49	46	95	65	00	07
87	88	39	37	23	99	34	19	32	45	33	73	30	66	95	80	65	92	68	67	31	91	29	79	83
50	76	04	65	30	15	56	76	70	61	88	39	27	70	46	09	46	73	04	97	55	24	55	10	12
02	76	80	86	96	52	36	34	74	80	76	33	60	20	92	29	77	41	81	94	05	73	64	28	13
34	36	90	26	29	39	20	76	95	42	67	34	58	69	47	56	81	35	65	86	23	82	53	24	47

precise you want your results to be, 3) the variation, or dispersion, that exists within your target market, and 4) the number of people in your target market.

Lets look at the first two factors together. The first factor, confidence, indicates how valid you want your estimated results to be. For example, you may desire the odds to be nineteen to one (a 95 percent chance, or a 95 percent level of confidence) that your actual result will be within a given percentage of the result you estimate from your sample. The second factor, precision, refers to how close you want the actual result to be to your estimated result. Consider the example of the twenty-four-hour grocery store again. Suppose you want the odds to be nineteen to one that your actual average sale per transient customer will be within plus or minus two percent of the average sale you estimate from your sample. The nineteen to one odds or 95 percent level of confidence, is the degree of confidence you desire. The plus or minus 2 percent is the degree of precision you desire. Specifically, you want a big enough sample to insure that if the average sale per sampled transient were $5.00, then the odds would be nineteen to one that your actual average sale per transient when your store opens would be between $4.90 and $5.10. If you were willing to accept odds of nine to one (a 90 percent level of confidence) and a degree of precision of plus or minus 10 percent, you could get satisfactory results with a much smaller sample. Remember that the level of confidence and degree of precision are your choices. The more demanding you are, the bigger, and therefore more costly, your sample has to be.

The third factor relevant to sample size is the variation, or dispersion, that exists within your target market. You must guess this from what you know about your target market. For example, you might estimate that the purchases made by the vast majority (95 percent) of transient customers at the twenty-four-hour grocery store will fall between $0.00 and $10.00. The probable dispersion of purchases, then, is $10.00. This dispersion implies that a certain sample size will be necessary to estimate with a given degree of confidence and precision the average purchases transients will make at your store. As dispersion increases, the necessary sample size also increases. For example, if you estimated that the dispersion in purchases was $25.00, you would need a larger sample to obtain your desired levels of confidence and precision.

Since you estimate dispersion before you calculate sample size and therefore before you choose a sample or do any interviewing, it should be obvious that your dispersion estimate is only an educated guess. Statisticians use a statistic called the sample standard deviation to measure dispersion. A rough rule of thumb is to divide the range you anticipate by four to estimate the sample standard deviation, "s". Then your estimate of s is used to determine sample size by using the sample size equation described below.[3] Thus, if you anticipate the average transient purchase described to be between $0.00 and $10.00, s = $2.50. For a range of $0.00 to $25.00, s = $6.25.

The fourth factor relevant to sample size is the size of your target market. Usually the size of the target market makes a big difference in required sample size only when you wish a high degree of confidence and precision and when the sample size suggested by the calculations below is larger than 5 percent of the size of your target market.

Now that you have been introduced to all four factors affecting sample size, we will show you how to calculate sample size. The basic equation for the kind of problem we have been discussing is:

EQUATION 10-B.1

$$\sigma_{\bar{x}} = \frac{s}{\sqrt{n-1}}$$

where:

n = the sample size you should use.
(We will be solving for this.)

s = the sample standard deviation.

(Our estimate is the dispersion divided by 4 or $2.50 for the dispersion of $10.00 and $6.25 for the dispersion of $25.00.)

$\sigma_{\overline{x}}$ = the standard error of the mean.

(The mean in this case is the average purchase made by transients. The standard error of the mean is the precision you desire divided by the standard error associated with the degree of confidence you desire. For example, suppose you want to have a 95% level of confidence that the average transient will purchase within + 50¢ of the average purchase made by your sample of transients. 50¢, or .50, is the precision you desire, but what do you divide by? What is the standard error associated with a 95% level of confidence? The statistical theory involved is complex, but Table 10-B.2 summarizes the results you need.[4] Drawing from this table, the standard error for the 95% level of confidence is 1.96. Therefore,

$$\sigma_{\overline{x}} = \frac{.50}{1.96} = .2551.)$$

Substituting s and $\sigma_{\overline{x}}$ into equation 10-B.1, we get:

$$.2551 = \frac{2.50}{\sqrt{n-1}} \text{ or } n = 97$$

for the $10.00 dispersion in average purchases, and:

$$.2551 = \frac{6.25}{\sqrt{n-1}} \text{ or } n = 601$$

for the $25.00 dispersion in average purchases.

As you can see, the sample you must select is much larger for the larger dispersion.

If you are willing to settle for less precision, plus or minus $1.00, for example, the sample size you need will be reduced. In this case, if we keep the 95 percent level of confidence, $\sigma_{\overline{x}} = \frac{1.0}{1.96} = .5102$; and $.5102 = \frac{2.50}{\sqrt{n-1}}$ or n = 25 for the $10.00 in dispersion in average purchases.

Similarly, if you are willing to settle for a lower level of confidence, the sample size you need goes down. Assume you decide you need only an 80 percent chance that the actual average purchase by transients will fall within plus or minus $.50 of the average purchase by the sample of transients. In this case, $\sigma_{\overline{x}} = \frac{.50}{1.28} = .3906$; and $.3906 = \frac{2.50}{\sqrt{n-1}}$ or n = 42 for the $10.00 dispersion in average purchases.

If your calculation of sample size using equation 10–B.1 results in a sample larger than about 5 percent of the total number of people in your target market, we recommend you use Equation 10–B.2 to calculate your required sample size instead.

$$\sigma_{\overline{x}} = \frac{s}{\sqrt{n-1}} \times \sqrt{\frac{N-n}{N-1}} \qquad \text{EQUATION 10-B.2}$$

where: N = the total number of people in your target market. In the 24-hour grocery store example, N = 32,000.

$\sqrt{\dfrac{N-n}{N-1}}$ will always be less than one. It is a correction factor to be used when the sample size indicated by Equation 10–B.1 is really larger than needed. This correction fac-

Table 10–B.2

Odds that you desire that the actual average will fall with the range you set:		The standard error to use in the calculation of $\sigma_{\bar{x}}$ in Equation 10–B.1 (nearest. 01):
2 to 1	(67% chance)	.97
3 to 1	(75% chance)	1.15
4 to 1	(80% chance)	1.28
9 to 1	(90% chance)	1.65
19 to 1	(95% chance)	1.96
48 to 1	(98% chance)	2.33

tor will not significantly reduce sample size unless the sample size calculated with Equation 10–B.1 is relatively large in comparison to the total number of people from which the sample is to be drawn (larger than 5 percent of the total target market).

The equations for sample size change somewhat if the type of question to be researched changes. In the above example, we wanted to know the average dollar purchase made by transients. We might also want to know what percentage of transients would shop at the store. How large a sample is needed to have a 90 percent chance that the percentage of sampled transients who would shop at the store is within 5 percent of the percentage of all transients who would? In this case, the object is to estimate the percentage of people in the target market with the attribute of willingness to shop at your store. By definition, the percentage with the attribute plus the percentage without it equals 100 percent. These percentages are usually stated as decimal fractions. If 1 represents everybody in the target market, then .30 might represent the 30 percent of transients who would shop at your store and .70 would represent those who would not. The proportion of people with the attribute you are studying is symbolized by p. The proportion of people without the attribute is symbolized by q. Here, p = .30, q = .70, and p + q = 1. The equation to calculate sample size for questions about attributes is:

EQUATION 10–B.3

$$\sigma_p = \sqrt{\frac{pq}{n-1}}$$

where: σ_p = standard error of the proportion = desired precision divided by the standard error associated with the degree of confidence you desire.

The calculation of sample size using equation 10–B.3 is similar to those done above. For example, if your desired level of precision is plus or minus 5 percent (± .05) and your desired level of confidence if 90 percent, $\sigma_p = \dfrac{.05}{1.65} = .0303$. You can either estimate the value of p based on your experience or, if you have no basis for estimating, set it at .5. A p value of .5 gives a conservative estimate of sample size because if p equals .5, q will also equal .5 and pq will equal .25, the maximum possible. Assuming that p = .5 and σ_p = .0303, Equation 10–B.3 becomes:

$$.0303 = \sqrt{\frac{.25}{n-1}} \text{ or } n = 273.$$

When the sample size is 5 percent or more of the total target market, a correction factor can be applied to Equation 10–B.3 in the same manner as it is applied to Equation 10–B.1. The correction factor is once again $\sqrt{\dfrac{N-n}{N-1}}$ You would then use Equation 10–B.4 to calculate the sample size instead of equation 10–B.3:

$$\sigma_p = \sqrt{\frac{pq}{n-1}}\ \sqrt{\frac{N-n}{N-1}}$$

EQUATION 10–B.4

At this point, you know how to calculate how large your sample should be and how to select your sample. We will now discuss the third step of sample design—setting effective procedures for contacting your sample.

Step 3: Deciding How to Contact Your Sample

It is one thing to select a sample of potential customers. It is another thing to contact them and get them to respond. What do you do if one of the people in your sample is not home when you call? If you are using time slots to sample transients at the twenty-four-hour grocery store, what do you do when six transients leave the store almost simultaneously? If you mail your sample questionnaire, what do you do when some of the sample customers do not respond?

All of the above questions relate to the problem of retaining the randomness of your sample. Sample consumers who cannot be found, who do not respond, or who refuse to respond are not taken into account in the equations shown in Step 2 above. The sample sizes calculated in Step 2 do not include allowances for the errors created by not being able to contact the selected sample or not getting them to respond. Ideally, the solution is to keep after your sample until you can find each selected consumer and get the answers you need.[5] This is often not economically feasible. You have to make a real effort to contact the entire sample; but if you cannot reach some people after repeated tries, you will have to give up. Statistical procedures are available to estimate and measure the amount of error introduced into your results when you cannot contact or get responses from your whole sample.[6] We recommend that you do not simply ignore such errors, but rather at least try to estimate their magnitude subjectively when reviewing the results of your research.

The basic point to remember when deciding how your sample will be contacted is that you need to make a real effort to contact each member of the sample. Contacting only those who are easy to reach will introduce an unknown amount of error into your results. You should keep track of those you cannot reach so that you can estimate whether or not their lack of response will make the responses you did gather unrepresentative of the consumers in your target market. For example, if you interview neighborhood residents only during normal working hours, you may consistently miss working adults. In the case of the twenty-four-hour grocery store, these may be the very people who would be your best customers. It is obvious that you should try contacting these people in the evening to avoid a major error in the conclusions you draw from your survey.

This appendix has shown you step by step how to pick whom to talk to when surveying consumers in your target market. You now know how to develop customer lists, how to select your customer sample, how to decide how big your customer sample should be, and how to contact your sample. Deciding what to ask your customers when you contact them is the next step. Appendix 10–C discusses how to ask the right questions.

Appendix C

FINDING OUT
WHAT YOUR
CUSTOMERS
WANT—HOW TO
ASK THE RIGHT
QUESTIONS

Once you have decided to go directly to your potential customers to find out what they need, you must decide what questions to ask. This decision is relatively easy as long as you remember a few simple rules:

1. In order to be able to compare the answers you get from various customers, you need to make sure you ask them all exactly the same questions. Therefore, you must write down the questions you plan to ask and ask them in the same sequence each time. If you use a questionnaire, you will to do this automatically. If you conduct interviews, you still need to do it. The best interviews are done using standard lists of questions that have spaces for responses. One copy of the standard list is used for each interview. The interviewer fills in the answers the respondent gives to each question.

2. Your questions should stick to what you need to know. You will not be able to ask about everything. Respondents tend to run out of patience with long, drawn-out interviews and questionnaires. Remember, a short list of questions that focuses on what you really need to know is best.

3. When you write a question, be sure that it is unambiguous and that it does not lead the customer to a particular answer. You want to know what the customer really thinks. It will be hard for the customer to answer accurately if he or she does not understand the question. Even worse is a question that guides the customer to answer in a certain way. For example, a good question is: "What is most important to you when you purchase XYZ kind of product—price, quality, speed of delivery, or other (please explain)?" A bad question is: "Low price is very important to you when you purchase XYZ kind of product, is it not?" The best way to make sure your questions are sound is to try them out on a small pilot sample of customers before you begin your full-fledged market survey. This will help you to debug your questions.

4. When using interviews as a survey device, how questions are asked is just as important as how they are worded. The expert interviewer asks questions in an *impersonal* manner that does not reveal his or her biases. Some people try to answer questions with what they think the interviewer wants to hear. Others will lie when they feel a question is too personal.

5. People are more likely to answer truthfully when they think that questions are being asked by an independent research firm and that the results will be kept confidential. Confidentiality should always be promised.

6. Some of your questions should solicit demographic data, such as sex, age, whether the head of the household works full time, the number of children living at home, and income level of the family. You should ask only for demographic data that will be useful to you. You should ask for it at the end of your list of questions. If you do not wait you will appear to be prying into personal matters for no good reason.

    Demographic data can tell you a lot about the probable needs of your customers. It also can be used to check whether or not your sample is representative. For example, you may find that the average family in your sample is larger and less affluent than the averages indicated by secondary data sources.

7. Your questions should cover the following topics concerning buying behavior: where, what, when , how, who, and why. In addition, your questions should probe marketing strategy options, including products or services the company should provide, advertising the company should use, places the company's product should be offered, and prices that should be charged. Table 10–C.1 lists sample

Table 10-C.1 Sample Questions[7]

TOPIC	SAMPLE QUESTIONS
Where	• Which store do you shop at most often?
	• Where else do you shop for the type of product you find at this store?
What	• What are your two main reasons for shopping at the store you shop at most often?
When	• What time of day do you normally shop for this product?
	• When do you normally buy this product?
How	• How often do you purchase this kind of product?
	• Within the last month, how many times have you bought this kind of product?
	• How did you find out about this product?
	• How much is X amount of this product worth to you?
	Increasing _____ to _____ $
	$ Amounts _____ to _____ $
Who	• Who in your family decides on this kind of purchase?
	• Whom in your family do you buy this kind of product for?
Why	• Why do you prefer the product you buy most often?

questions that touch on these important topics and conform well with the rules discussed in this appendix.

8. Your questions should offer choices among specific responses. Typically, it is preferable that you list probable alternative answers to your questions so that your respondents have a choice of specific answers as opposed to having to respond off the top of their heads. For example, the question:

> Where do you buy greeting cards most often?
> A. Grocery store
> B. Drugstore
> C. Stationery store
> D. Gift shop
> E. Other (please explain)

is better than the same question asked without giving possible responses. Note that part E gives the respondent an opportunity to suggest other sources. Open-ended questions such as "Why?" may yield interesting answers, but these answers can be hard to interpret since respondents may not know exactly what you are looking for. If you do use open-ended questions, you should try to categorize the answers you get to facilitate analysis.

APPENDIX FOOTNOTES

1. Summarized from William H. Weilbacher, "Standard Classification of Consumer Characteristics," *Journal of Marketing* 31, no. 1 (January 1967): 27–31, published by the American Marketing Association.

2. Donald S. Tull, and Gerald S. Albaum, *Survey Research: A Decisional Approach* (New York: Intext Educational Publishers, 1973), pp. 225–226. Reprinted by permission of Harper and Row Publishers, Inc., © 1973.

3. This assumes that your range estimate will include about 95.45 percent of the possible occurences under a normal approximation. See C. William Emory, *Business Research Methods* (Homewood, Ill.: Richard D. Irwin, Inc., 1980), chapter 6 for a more technical discussion of the derivation of s. Suffice it to say here that following our short cut for calculating s will give you a conservatively large sample size.

4. *Ibid.* See chapter 6 for the theory.

5. *Ibid.* See chapter 10 for ideas on how to do this.

6. See Tull and Albaum, *Survey Research: A Decisional Approach*, chapter 4 for suggestions on how to calculate sampling error due to nonresponse.

7. These questions were adapted for illustrative purposes from several sources. Particularly helpful were Robert T. Justis, and Bill Jackson, "Marketing Research for Dynamic Small Businesses," *Journal of Small Business Management* 16, no. 4 (October 1978): 10–20; William L. Trombetta, "An Empirical Approach to Marketing Strategy for the Small Retailer," *Journal of Small Business Management* 14, no. 4 (October 1976): 55–58; and Tull and Albaum, *Survey Research: A Decisional Approach.* An excellent discussion of the issues involved in survey instrument design can be found in Emory, *Business Research Methods.*

Promotional Strategy

11

□ **Where should you spend your advertising dollar?**

□ **What kinds of sales promotion will work for you?**

□ **How can you build your company's image?**

CASE
PROBLEM

Katzmar Jewellers[1]

Frank and Helen Katz opened Katzmar Jewellers, a retail jewelry store, on December 22, 1978. The store was located in a suburban shopping center. A grocery store was the key tenant in this center, and there were several other small retailers selling a variety of merchandise. Lease provisions prohibited any other store in the center from selling jewelry.

Frank had learned how to manufacture and repair jewelry from his father, who was a jewelry manufacturer in New York. Helen had retail sales experience at several major department stores. Neither had operated a retail jewelry store before.

The Katzes entered the retail jewelry business because it seemed easy to get into. They had originally looked into purchasing an existing store; but it was too run down, and they were afraid it did not have a good reputation as a result. Therefore, they opened Katzmar in a new shopping center still in the process of leasing to tenants.

The Katzes wanted to convey a luxury image in their store and spent considerable money on elegant wall decorations, carpet, and display cases. The store was well designed and impressive. However, setbacks in the construction schedule delayed their opening until late in the 1978 Christmas season. Because of this, they missed the Christmas business, which they had been told by their suppliers amounted to about half of annual sales for stores like theirs.

The Katzes persevered and were able to make a small profit during the slow months. They looked forward to the 1979 Christmas season to provide them with a nice profit for their first year of business. Sales during the 1979 Christmas season, however, did not meet their expectations. They ended the year with a respectable, but not outstanding, profit picture.

Although several established retailers in the area had remarked that 1979 was a slower than normal year, Frank and Helen began to suspect they were doing something wrong. It appeared they had a good store location. The neighborhood was new and affluent. The nearest competing jewelry store was over a mile away. Their store layout was topflight. Their merchandise was a mix of elegant name brands and Frank's custom designs. Frank and Helen waited on customers personally and made every effort to be friendly and helpful. What, then, were they doing wrong?

Frank and Helen Katz seemed to be doing everything right; yet something was wrong. Their sales success indicated they had done a fairly good job, albeit by trial and error, in checking out their market. In terms of the eighteen-step procedure for checking out new markets presented in chapter 10, Frank and Helen had picked a business that fit their distinctive competencies. They had analyzed the needs of their customers. They had picked an affluent target market with no near competitors. They were centrally located in a market area that should have been able to provide them with more than enough business. What was missing?

PROBLEM IDENTIFICATION

The answer centers around Step 10 of the eighteen-step procedure—determining if your target market is reachable. If Frank and Helen did consider this step and develop conclusions about it, they did not sufficiently exploit their knowledge. Step 10 involves developing answers to questions like:

How would you find your target customers if you wanted to talk to them?

How would you find your target customers if you wanted to sell to them?

Do your target customers come together at certain places and times?

What do your target customers read and watch?

What organizations or trade associations do your target customers belong to?

The answers to these questions are vital because they tell you how to reach your customers with promotional appeals catering to their needs. Knowing who your customers are, what their needs are, and how best to meet these needs is not enough. You need to reach them with the message that your business exists. Your message has to convince them that you can meet their needs better than your competition.

This chapter focuses on how to turn your knowledge about your customers into effective promotional strategies. We will show you how to capitalize on the knowledge you gain from the eighteen-step procedure presented in chapter 10 to sell more through advertising and other promotional techniques. In particular, we will discuss where you should spend your advertising dollar, how to determine if a particular sales promotion is likely to work for you, and how to build your company's image.

Your company has a story to tell. It is a happy story about how you have worked long and hard and have devised a way to meet the needs of certain fortunate consumers. How good are you at telling this story? Are you doing

DIAGNOSIS

a good job getting your message to your potential customers and convincing them that they should buy from you?

Exhibit 11.1 presents a marketer's barometer, designed to help you to analyze how you are spending you marketing dollar. Take the time now to write down your answer to each question. The implications of your answers will be discussed below.

If you had a tough time answering Questions 1, 2, and 3, you are probably wasting a lot of the money you spend on promotion. There is no precise answer to Question 3, but you should have some sort of scheme to determine if what you are buying with your promotion dollar is working.

Questions 5, 6, and 7 test your knowledge of what you want out of your advertising. They also get at the issue of whether or not you know if the media you are using reach your customers efficiently.

If you can't answer yes to Questions 9 and 10, you know far less about your customers than you should. An outdated list makes direct mail contact less efficient. Lack of a mapping of customer location makes it harder to visualize who your customers are and which media cover areas where new customers might be found.

Questions 11 and 12 are designed to see if you use outside help to plan your promotions. Underutilization of help from advertising agencies, media, and suppliers is a common mistake made by small businesses.

Free publicity, referred to in Questions 13 and 14, is a major form of promotion and should be used regularly to complement paid advertising. You are missing out if you do not reinforce your paid advertising with periodic press releases about important developments in your company.

Many small businesspersons do not understand Question 15. They simply do not know what cooperative advertising and joint advertising are. Yet these two forms of advertising can give you much more advertising for your advertising dollar. Cooperative advertising alone pays for about 15–20 percent of the savvy retailer's advertising budget. We will explain how these two forms of advertising work later in this chapter.

Question 16 tests your knowledge of your image and of how to project your image to your customers. We will discuss which image factors are important and how to exploit them below.

Your answer to Question 17 should be compared with your answer to Question 20 about the timing of your advertising. Is your advertising indeed timely? Does it address why customers are purchasing when they do?

The last question in Exhibit 11.1 is somewhat of a trick question. All fourteen items listed are types of promotion. How many should you use? Definitely more than one, but as we shall see, it does not pay to spread your marketing budget too thinly over too many promotional options.

At this point, you have your completed Marketer's Barometer in front of you and have some initial ideas about where your strengths and weaknesses are. It is now time to analyze these strengths and weaknesses so that you can redirect your promotional strategy and get more results for your marketing dollar.

Exhibit 11.1 Marketer's Barometer

The questions below will help you evaluate how well you are promoting your business. Answer each carefully. Don't just answer yes or no. Write down your reasons as well. If you are planning a new business, read the following questions in the future tense. For example, Question 1 can be read, "How much do you plan to spend on promotion during your first year?" All of the questions except 6 and 14 are relevant to the start up of a new business if restated in the future tense. When answering Question 3, consider how you will keep track of responses.

1. How much did you spend on promotion last year?

2. What did this include?
   A. Which media did you use?
   B. How much did you spend on each?
   C. How many times did you use each last year?
   D. When did you use each last year?
   E. Exactly what did you do each time?
      (e.g., September 15, Sunday local newspaper X, one-quarter page display ad in sports section, cost $XYZ)

3. What kind of response did you get each time, and how do you know? Were certain times better than others?

4. Did it take you a long time to answer the first three questions, or did you already have the answers written down?

5. If you had $10,000 available that had to be spent on promotion, how would you spend it?

6. Do you have a promotional budget for each of the next twelve months?

7. How do you decide where to spend your promotional dollars?

8. How often do you revise your promotional budget? Describe why you made the last revision.

9. Do you keep an up-to-date list of your customers' names and addresses?

10. Have you ever prepared a map pinpointing where your customers come from?

11. Do you use the services of an advertising agency?

12. Do you use services provided by the media you advertise in?

13. Do you make press releases and seek free publicity?

14. Describe the last time you received free publicity. Where did it appear? Was it likely to be noticed by your customers?

15. Have you ever used cooperative advertising? Joint advertising?

16. What is the image you wish to convey to your customers? Describe how each of your promotional activities reinforces this image.

17. When do most of your customers buy from you? Why?

18. Which of the following do you consider to be types of promotion? Which do you use?

A. Advertising	H. Letterheads/Logos
B. Demonstrations	I. Store signs
C. Direct mail	J. Sales
D. Free publicity	K. Offering credit
E. In-store displays	L. Offering free delivery
F. Product packaging	M. Policy for handling merchandise returned by customers
G. Window displays	N. Contributions to memberships in community organizations

---

The Elements of Promotional Strategy: Paid Advertising,
Sales Promotions, and Free Publicity

When you think about how to make potential customers aware of your product or service, one of the first things that comes to mind is advertising—a newspaper advertisement, a TV commercial, or a mass mailing of a sales brochure, for example. We are all familiar with advertising; yet few realize how complex it really is. As a result, many small businesspersons make serious advertising mistakes that stunt their companys' profit potential and waste their money.[2]

Actually, a paid advertisement such as a newspaper ad is only one aspect of an overall promotional strategy. Promotion is a general term that includes not only all forms of paid advertising but also sales promotions and free publicity. Therefore, while our primary focus in this chapter is on the various kinds of paid advertising, we will also discuss how to mix elements of sales promotion and publicity with your paid advertising to increase the effectiveness of your promotional strategy. For example, a contest where customers guess how many jelly beans are in a jar is a sales promotion. The contest can also be used as a theme for your paid advertising, making sure that customers know there is a possibility they will win a prize if they visit your store while the contest is being conducted. The contest entry blanks will provide you with a mailing list for follow-up direct mail advertising. Finally, the awarding of prizes is a newsworthy item which will probably interest your local paper thereby giving you free publicity.

The Objective of Promotion

The objective of promotion, be it paid or free, is to communicate clearly to potential customers how your business can meet their needs. A successful promotion is one that attracts buyers and loyal customers. In dollar terms, a successful promotion is one that increases your firm's profits. As we will see, analyzing the success of one particular promotional tactic, such as a paid advertisement in your local paper, is tricky. This is because it is hard to isolate the impact of just one part of your promotional strategy.

Successful promotion begins with the eighteen-step procedure discussed in chapter 10. Following these steps, you have defined your target markets. You know who your customers are and what their needs are. You know how your company can meet their needs, and you have a plan for meeting their needs better than the competition. The objective of successful promotion can be restated as that of showing your target customers how appealing your company really is, thereby convincing them to try you out. Further, once they do try you out, your objective is to have them come back and give you more business and also to have them recommend you to friends with similar needs. A number of factors that you might not initially think of as forms of promotion encourage repeat or referral business: for example, store layout, your product's shipping carton, the directions on the back of your product's container, or the fact that you sponsor a local junior soccer team. What works depends on the needs of your target customers.

Image Building Through Effective Promotional Strategy

Generally speaking, an effective promotional strategy creates and reinforces an image of your company as the one best able to meet certain needs of your customers. While all companies have an image whether or not they deliberately set out to create one, the savvy small business marketer does not leave image to chance.[3] Rather, he or she determines the desired image before the company opens its doors and uses promotion as a major tool to convey that image to the customer. Promotion builds upon factors such as price, quality, assortment, fashion, location, convenience, and service to create the desired image.[4]

Three concepts are central to building an image and promoting your business successfully. They are branding, continuity, and repetition. Branding refers to the process of creating in your customers' minds the perception that your product or service offers a premium value.[5] Continuity refers to the consistent projection of the company's selected image in all promotions. Repetition refers to the repeating of promotions. Each of these three concepts merits your careful consideration.

Branding.   Branding is another name for what was advocated in chapter 9. It is the selling of exceptional customer benefits. If you offer exceptional benefits, your customers will perceive your product as having a value to them that exceeds its price and also exceeds the value of your competitor's product. As a result, they will buy your brand.

Branding does not just increase your sales volume. It also increases your profit on each sale. This is because the perceived premium value of your product opens the door to charging a premium price. Because you are giving something extra, people are willing to pay extra for it.

Once you have developed a product with superior value for its users, promotion emphasizes the superior benefits your customer will receive from your product and makes it clear that the product's benefits exceed its price. Promotion also makes it clear that dollar for dollar your product gives more value than the competition's product. An effective promotional strategy focused on branding will make your product the product category's standard of value. At this point, your company symbol or logo can also be used to brand related products, thus permitting premium prices to be charged for your whole line. Designer clothes, Tiffany jewelry, Barbie doll clothing, and name brand oils selling for 60 to 100 percent more at their service stations than at independents are all examples of the branding phenomenon. You do not have to be large to take advantage of the branding concept. Famous-Amos chocolate chip cookies and Maui potato chips are just two examples of successful small business brands.

Continuity. The second term you must keep in mind as you plan your promotional strategy is continuity or the consistent projection of your image. Once you have decided how you will respond to such image factors as quality and convenience, you need to build an image platform.[6] Like the platform of a political party, an image platform states how you plan to handle each image factor. Each promotional activity follows your image platform, thereby consistently representing your company in the same light. Your platform will determine the kinds of promotion and advertising you select. Continuity of an appropriate image will make your company and its products immediately recognizable and distinguish them from your competition.

Repetition. Repetition of a consistent brand message, particularly if done with an artful mix of paid advertising and free publicity, keeps you on your customer's mind. An ad appearing only once does not create a brand. Indeed an ad that appears only once may not even be noticed by most of your potential customers reached by the medium the ad is in. A properly conducted promotional campaign builds momentum through repetition of the brand message.

To summarize the discussion so far, in order to use promotion effectively to build your image you must:

1. Brand your products based on the needs of your target customers;
2. Maintain the continuity of your image in all of your promotions;
3. Take every opportunity to tell your customers about your image platform, as long as the media used reach your customers efficiently and are appropriate for your image.

Selecting Efficient and Appropriate Media for Promotion

What do we mean when we say, "as long as the media used reach your customers efficiently and are appropriate for your image"? The two key words in this proviso are "efficiently" and "appropriate."

Efficiency refers to a number of questions concerning the media: (1) Do the media reach only your target customers, or are you paying to reach a lot of people who really are not your target customers? (2) Do your target customers know and respect the media you are using? (3) When they buy, do they use these media as a guide? (4) Are the media relatively inexpensive in terms of dollars of cost versus dollars of profit from additional sales? The ideal medium in terms of efficiency is a very selective media that reaches only your target customers, one that is viewed as an authority on your kind of product, and one that costs relatively little compared to the profits it can generate for you.

A medium is appropriate for your image when it reflects your image, or in other words, when your target customers expect a company like yours to use that medium. For example, consumers expect a luxury-oriented product to be advertised in a luxury context. This means the media used must be recognized as oriented to the buyer of luxury goods and that the messages placed in these media must speak of luxury—in the words, type-set, layout, and images projected. While a discount clothing store might find small display ads stressing low price very effective in a pennysaver tabloid, a quality clothing store might find ads stressing quality in the same tabloid worse than useless. Not only might these ads fail to draw new customers but their presence in the tabloid might give potential customers the impression that the store carried cheap merchandise.

Which media will be efficient and appropriate for you depends on the nature of your image platform. Regardless of whether you are considering paid advertising or seeking free publicity, your efforts should be guided by the efficiency and appropriateness of the media.

Exhibit 11.2 presents a listing of many of the media available to you and notes the characteristics of each. Although the chart is necessarily general, it should give you some idea of where to start as you plan which media to use to implement your promotional strategy. We will refer to this chart as we discuss how to build your company's image with efficient and appropriate advertising, sales promotion, and publicity.

Exhibit 11.2 can be used as follows: The first two columns list the types of media and describe each briefly. The third column, campaign cost, gives you an appropriate idea of the amount of money it takes to mount an effective campaign in each medium relative to the others. Both the direct costs of purchasing media space and the indirect costs of producing an advertising message are included for the purposes of this comparison. The fourth column, efficiency, refers to how efficient each medium can be in adding to your profits. Unfortunately, you may not be able to afford the campaign cost of certain media that would be efficient for you. We will discuss some ways around this problem later in the chapter. The entries in the efficiency column are based on the assumption that the medium is appropriate for you. If it is not, its efficiency could be much lower. The last three columns can be used to help you determine appropriateness.

The fifth column, best use, refers to the best way to use each medium to obtain its maximum level of efficiency. The sixth column, what you can expect, indicates the kind of customer response you can expect from each medium. Finally, the seventh column indicates the kinds of company each medium will work best for. The legend at the top of the exhibit explains the abbreviations used in this column. Remember when reviewing this column that the most common media error made by small business is to select media with an inappropriate audience—either one that is too broad or one made up of the wrong type of consumer. It bears repeating that the most appropriate medium is a very selective one that reaches only your target customers, is viewed as an authority on your kind of product, and costs relatively little compared to the profits it can stimulate for you.

Exhibit 11.2 The Efficiency of Major Forms of Media: A Small Business Perspective[7]

MEDIA Type	Description	CAMPAIGN COST 5 = High 4 = Fairly High 3 = Moderate 2 = Modest 1 = Low	EFFICIENCY A = Excellent B = Very Good C = Average D = Below Average F = Poor	BEST USE	WHAT YOU CAN EXPECT	WORKS BEST FOR (See Legend*)
Regional Newspapers	Cover an entire metropolitan area; general readership; may have special sections for your area.	4	C+	Regular campaign stressing price & product; occasional coupons.	Increased store traffic.	1, B, P, C, R
		3	B+			1, B, P, C, L
Local Newspapers	Cover a specific neighborhood; general readership.	2	A–	Regular campaign stressing price & product; occasional coupons.	Increased store traffic.	1, B, P, C, L
Specialty Newspapers	Cater to specific groups of people (Spanish-speaking, single, sports enthusiasts, etc.).	1–2	A	Regular campaign stressing price & product; occasional coupons.	Increased store traffic.	1, B, P, C, L
Shopping Sheets	Unsolicited junk mail in newspaper format but light on editorial content.	2	D	Sale of product or service of general interest in localized area; price deals & coupons essential.	Increased store traffic.	1, P, C, L
Tabloids	Pennysaver advertising media with no editorial content; similar to shopping sheets except that people read them.	2–3	B	Regular campaign stressing price of product. Classified ad may work as well as display ad. Occasional coupons.	Increased store traffic.	1, P, C, L
National Consumer Magazines	Nationally distributed; general audience; may have regional editions for your area.	5	F	Image building or product information.	Very little unless you distribute directly to the consumer.	1, B, C, N
		4	C–			1, B, C, R
Local Consumer Magazines	Regionally distributed; general audience.	4	C+	Image building or product information.	Product information inquiries if ad well designed.	1, B, C, R

Medium	Description	Grade	Number	Purpose	Results	Best for
Business Magazines	Nationally distributed; general business audience; may have regional editions.	D C+	5 4	Image building or product information.	Product information inquiries if ad well designed.	1, 2, 3, 4, B, M, N 1, 2, 3, 4, B, M, R
Business Papers	Newspaper or magazine aimed at a particular industry; can have national or regional appeal.	A− A−	4 3	Image building or product information.	Product information inquiries if ad well designed.	1, 2, 3, 4, B, M, N 1, 2, 3, 4, B, M, R
Farm Publications	Newspaper or magazine aimed at a farming specialty; typically regional distribution.	A−	4	Image building or product information	Product information inquiries if ad well designed.	1, 2, 3, 4, B, M, R
Signs	Advertiser-owned permanent displays, typically at or near business location.	B	4	Display company name, identify type of business, locate business.	Passers-by will know where you are located.	1, B, C, L, but *all* companies benefit.
Outdoor Advertising	Billboards, posters, etc., temporarily erected on leased space.	C−	5	Attract business from travelers passing through your area.	Increased traffic from one-time, out-of-town customers.	1, B, C, L
Direct Mail	Advertiser-prepared materials mailed to mailing list or to occupants in a specific geographical area.	B − (if addressed to occupant) A (if personalized)	3–4	Make personalized appeals to narrow target markets (regular campaigns work well).	A proportionately small response, but largely composed of serious buyers.	All companies, but especially small ones.
Direct Advertising	Advertiser-prepared materials distributed by the advertiser.	C+	2–3	Distribution by your salespersons at your store or to obvious users of your product.	Small percentage response by serious buyers.	L, or companies using salespersons.
Yellow Pages	Classified section of public utility telephone books (neighborhood directories often available in larger metropolitan areas).	A− A	3–4 3	Well-organized ads and *ad locations* that make it easy for buyers to see that you can supply what they need. *Cross index!*	Reach consumers who have already decided to buy; also reach many business buyers.	All companies

Type	MEDIA Description	CAMPAIGN COST 5 = High 4 = Fairly High 3 = Moderate 2 = Modest 1 = Low	EFFICIENCY A = Excellent B = Very Good C = Average D = Below Average F = Poor	BEST USE	WHAT YOU CAN EXPECT	WORKS BEST FOR (See Legend*)
Directories	Proprietory directories of all kinds; range from neighborhood telephone books to specialized buying guides for a particular industry.	3	A	Well-organized ads and *ad locations* that make it easy for buyers to see that you can supply what they need. *Cross index!*	Reach business buyers who have already decided to buy.	2, 3, 4, B, M, R, N
Specialties	Advertising messages printed on useful giveaway items such as pens, matchbooks, note pads and calendars.	3–4	B (if unique and clever)	Display brief message on long-life items used by your customers.	Repeated exposure of your ad message during the item's life.	All companies except those with limited ad budgets.
Product Packaging	Special form of direct advertising, including imprinted messages, quality of container, displayability of container, etc.	3	B +	Enhance salability of product by assisting in its display, making it easier to recognize, etc.	Increased probability of brand recognition.	All companies
Letterheads/ Logos	Company symbols used on all correspondence, bids, billings, business cards, etc.	2	B	Repetition of company symbol, which identifies your business and leaves positive impression.	Build positive image; reinforce brand.	All companies
Point-of- Purchase Displays	Displays set up in the store where the customer buys that spotlight your product.	2–3	C + (B + if product is small with wide assortment)	Draw attention to your product in positive manner; display complete line well.	Remind people of your brand while in store; push slow-moving or sale items.	1, 3, B, C, M, L, R, N
Trade shows	Specialized events that show your product and cater to your target industries.	3–4	A −	Get a large number of trade contacts in a short time.	Increased distribution to a larger geographical area.	2, 3, 4, B, P, M, R, N

Media	Description	Code	Type	Objective	Results	Legend
Local Radio	am or fm broadcasting in your market area, network or independent.	4–5	B	Reach specific target markets (teenagers, cooks, etc.)	Good response if specific offer is made.	1, P, C, R
Local TV	Network or independent.	5	C	Advertise special sales to an entire metropolitan area.	Increased store traffic, but not all buyers.	1, P, C, R
School Newspapers	High school or college student publications.	1	A	Regular campaign stressing price and product for items used by students; coupons effective.	Increased store traffic.	1, P, C, L
School Annuals	High school or college yearbooks.	1	F	Identify company and student-oriented products.	Good will.	1, B, C, L
Local Transportation	Advertising panels on trains, buses, taxis, etc.	3–4	D	Exposure of company name in large area.	Very little unless your product has many local outlets.	1, B, C, R
Movie Theaters	Appeals shown on the screen during intermission.	3–4	D –	Specialized appeals to teenagers or other frequent attenders.	After-movie business if you are conveniently located.	1, P, C, L

*Legend:

1 – Retail Business
2 – Wholesale Business
3 – Manufacturer

4 – Technical Service Company
B – Brand Oriented Company
P – Price Oriented Company

C – Company Selling Directly to Consumers
M – Company Selling to Other Businesses
L – Local Sales Oriented Company

R – Regional Sales Oriented Co.
N – National Sales Oriented Company

Building Your Company's Image with Advertising, Sales Promotion, and Publicity

Now that you have been introduced to promotional strategy and media characteristics, it is time to discuss how to use what you have learned. How can you build your company's image? As we noted above, there are three things you must do: (1) Brand, (2) Maintain continuity, (3) Repeat your brand message using efficient and appropriate media. If these are done effectively, your company's image will be under your control and will evolve as you desire. Image is not built overnight, nor is there any guarantee that once you have a positive image, you will keep it. It takes careful planning and continued effort to develop and maintain the image you desire. Image building, then, is a lot of work. Still, the rewards are great. Once you have successfully developed your brand image in the minds of your customers, you will have opened the door to superior profit growth.

You have already begun solving the problem of how to build your company's image if you have applied the recommendations made in chapters 9 and 10 to your business. In essence, what you have done so far is to develop a sound foundation for branding your products. You have determined who your customers are, what their needs are, and how you can meet their needs better than the competition. Having done this allows you to base your brand on exceptional customer benefits that are real and not just promotional hot air.

Before reading further, see if you clearly understand the philosophy of branding. Assume you manufacture wrist watches, and answer the following two questions: Is it necessary for your watches to have technical superiority over those of the competition in order for you to be able to brand them? Can your watches be technically superior and still not be branded, that is, still be unable to command a premium price?

The answer to the first question is no. The answer to the second question is yes. Both answers are based on the fact that, *the essence of branding is creating exceptional value for your customers, not just adding value to your product*.[8] The technical superiority of low price digital watches is causing serious problems for Timex, which sells low price conventional watches. Other brands of conventionally made watches remain untouched by the onslaught of the digitals, even though they are vastly more expensive. The reason is that they are branded based on quality rather than on price. The owner of a Rolex watch, for example, perceives it as a piece of jewelry, a work of art, a status symbol. In other words, a Rolex watch has exceptional value to its wearer.

As a small business you really have little choice. You must brand based upon superior user value if you want to obtain rapid profit growth.

Developing an Image Platform: Ten Key Image Factors.   How do you go about branding your business? Once you have the exceptional user values that will permit you to brand in mind, the next step is to build an image platform on which to base the consistent projection of your brand image. To be specific, you must decide how you will address each of the following image factors, given your desired brand image:[9]

1. Price
2. Quality (Usefulness)
3. Assortment
4. Fashion (Status)
5. Sales personnel
6. Location
7. Convenience
8. Service
9. Store atmosphere
10. Reputation as adjustable

1. Price. The first factor, price , can mean a number of things to a customer. A low price can imply either a great bargain or shoddy merchandise; a high price can imply either an elite status or a bad deal. The price factor is a good example of the interdependence of the ten image factors. The competitive edge provided by a good price can be defeated by poor quality or surly salesclerks. A good store atmosphere and fashion merchandise create an expectation that prices will be high and a willingness to pay them.

Your prices can range from so low that you will lose money on each sale to so high that you will sell nothing. The whole purpose of branding is to allow you to charge a premium price. Reinforce your right to do so by emphasizing to the buyer the extra value that brands the product. For example, users expect to pay more when a product is custom-made, when it is specially designed for a small target market, when it is a high fashion or fad item, when it involves a lot of hand labor, when it has many uses, when many of support services are provided with it, or when it will have a long, useful life.

The only exception to the general rule of charging a premium price occurs when a low price for the product can boost your profitability by increasing sales of other profitable items. This exception works best when the other items are high markup accessories for the product being discounted. This concept will be reviewed in more detail in chapter 13.

2. Quality. The second of the ten image factors is quality. For quality to be used to maximum advantage as an image factor, care must be taken to stress those aspects of quality that are relevant to the consumer, or those the consumer perceives as adding extra benefit. For example, many durable toy trucks are available at your local toy store. Two makes, however, dominate in terms of perceived quality—Tonka and Creative Playthings. Tonka trucks are made of metal and give an impression of durability. The trucks by Creative Playthings are made of wood and are probably less expensive to make; yet they command an even higher price because they are perceived as handcrafted, durable, and educational. There is a very close link between product quality and premium price as long as the consumer perceives the quality as contributing to the product's usefulness. Many of the product characteristics that cause a consumer to expect to pay more have to do with perceived usefulness.

3. Assortment. The third factor, assortment, affects perceived benefit in two ways. First, it allows the consumer to pick something just right. Second, an assortment of related accessories makes the basic product more versatile and valuable. For example, the Villager clothing line for women markets wool jackets and skirts in a number of sizes and in coordinated colors. It also offers blouses in colors that complement the jackets and skirts. Because the blouses are of good quality and match so nicely, they command a premium price. Is it possible the availability of the blouses also makes the jackets and skirts more salable? Yes. Simply marketing a large variety of wool jackets is not nearly as effective as marketing a smaller number of well-coordinated separates. Not incidently, the Villager line makes buying easier for department stores since the department store buyer does not have to search for separates from other manufacturers to match the Villager line. The Villager line is an assortment of complementary products that better meets the needs of the professional buyer and thereby increases the manufacturer's sales. You can be sure the maker of the Villager line stresses this point in its promotions.

4. Fashion. The fourth image factor, fashion, is based on the appeal of what is new, in vogue, and exclusive. Fashion is desirable because of the status it lends to the buyer. Because the need for status is widespread, cultivation of the fashion image factor is worthwhile for a surprising variety of businesses. One life insurance company, for example, sells one-million-dollar policies partly based on status of having such a large amount of coverage. Computers are often sold to businesspersons based on the status of being computerized or being a leader in industry. One very expensive restaurant has even made a status symbol out of its matchbooks by limiting distribution to one per table. Strategic placement of these matchbooks in ashtrays around the home is an indisputable sign of wealth.

5. Personnel. The fifth image factor is sales personnel. Employees contribute to image not only by what they do and how they do it but also by how they look and what they know. Personal selling will be discussed in more detail in chapter 12. For now, remember that if you have good salespersons, make sure your customers know it. The way to do this is to stress what makes the salespersons good. What makes them good is the way they satisfy customer needs. For example, one construction firm uses in-house engineers to bid on construction jobs. These engineers are responsible for selling bids to clients. They are salespersons. Because the fact that they are engineers lends a lot of credibility to what they say, the company never misses an opportunity to stress to clients that unlike competing construction firms, it has salespersons who know what they are doing and have the degrees to prove it.

6. Location.   Location is another important image factor. Your location can either reinforce or refute your claims about the kind of business you are. The type of neighborhood you are in and you proximity to competitors and transportation networks are all elements that you can stress. People expect to find certain businesses in certain places. It is possible to go against these expectations, but it is better to go along with them and then base your promotions on having done so. One lighting company did a careful study of where its suppliers and customers were before renting its store location. It discovered that if the store were very close to its two principal suppliers, it could guarantee same-day delivery on any order made before 1:00 P.M. in its market area. Anything out of stock could be picked up quickly from suppliers. None of the competitors could do this. The company exploited its location advantage by advertising, "All orders in by 1:00 P.M. delivered the same day, or we will give you the order for free." Of course, there were some fine print exceptions to this claim, but it did apply to most merchandise. So far the company has not had to give away an order, but it still gets a lot of big orders between noon and 1:00 P.M.

7. Convenience.   The seventh image factor is convenience. Convenience has a broad appeal to people. Often your customer's perception of convenience is indistinguishable from the location of your store, its orderliness, or the length of your check-out lines. Convenience encompasses a wide variety of little things that make your goods easy to buy or easy to use. Have you made it easy for people to find you and buy from you? Have you made your product easy to assemble and use by everyday people? Or have you inadvertently created obstacles between your product and customers? One major aspect of the personal touch is to make it easy for your customers to buy and use your products. Since small businesses can typically exploit the personal touch better than big businesses, you should make a real effort to provide convenience, and your promotions should emphasize the convenience you provide.

8. Service.   Service is the eighth image factor. It is another major aspect of the personal touch. Attentive, helpful service impresses prospective buyers. Prompt attention to the problems of those who already own and use your products keeps customers happy and leads to repeat business. A customer who is served well will probably come back to buy again even if your product is only average. Surly service can negate the virtues of an outstanding product. Quality service is a major image builder. It also builds your business because the word gets around.

Quality service is an inseparable part of your product. Nine times out of ten the person who buys from a small business is buying a service as well as a product. Build service in, and make sure your promotions emphasize it.

One successful print shop provides free pickup and delivery with large orders. Aggressive promotion of this service has attracted business from several architectural and engineering firms, who provide a constant stream of lucrative large copy and blueprint business. The print shop charges top prices, but its customers are willing to pay more because the service saves them valuable time.

Another small business specializes in auto, boat, and plane care. The company's vans come to the customer's vehicles and wash, wax, clean chrome, treat vinyl roofs, paint stripes, etc. Each van even has its own generator to provide the electric power to run the cleaning equipment. This company uses an artful mix of status, convenience, and service appeals in its advertising.

9. *Atmosphere.*   The ninth image factor is store atmosphere. Store atmosphere has to do with the layout and decoration of your shop. The way your store is decorated reinforces your image or destroys it in the eyes of the buyer. Your store is a promotional vehicle, in and of itself. It can also be used in your promotions.

Big orders always seemed to elude one manufacturer of machine parts. The owner couldn't understand it. Buyers from big companies always seemed to like the quality of samples sent to them. They also liked the price. After they visited the little manufacturing company, however, orders never came. The wife of a friend who dropped by the shop one day solved the mystery with five words. When she walked in she said, "This place is a mess." It was. The owner's office was stacked with piles of yellowing papers. Employee work clothes were unkempt. The shop floor was cluttered with raw materials, barrels of scrap, and boxes of half-finished parts. The general impression was one of chaos—hardly an atmosphere to instill confidence in a major buyer. Of course, a messy shop may get the work out as fast and as well as a clean one, but it gives the impression that the work will be shoddy and delivered late. What does your store say about you?

In this case, the owner cleaned up and got organized. A uniform service was employed to provide work clothes and keep them clean. The shop and office were straightened up and cleaned. The walls were repainted. The restrooms, long neglected, were now kept spotless. The machinery had always been well maintained; but now nonessential parts were cleaned and repainted, and a maintenance schedule was posted in a prominent location near each machine. Photographs were taken of the shop and incorporated into promotional materials. Soon the big orders began to come in.

10. *Adjustability.*   The last of the ten image factors is the company's reputation as being adjustable. This reputation is built by two words: "satisfaction guaranteed." These two words reduce the customer's risk when purchasing a new product. They also say something more subtle: "Our business is not just to sell you our product. Our business is to meet your needs." Customers may not always be right, but it helps your reputation to act as though they are. Your promotions should emphasize your adjustability. For example, one small automobile tire manufacturer stresses its "no-strings" warranty. Another small manufacturer doesn't go this far because it doesn't want to add the extra cost of a full warranty to its price, but it does offer road hazard

insurance to cover exceptions in its basic warranty. If you want it, you pay a little extra; if not, you get your tires a little cheaper. Both companies advertise their warranties heavily. By living up to them, they have built reputations for adjustability (and quality) that allow them to compete with the major tire companies.

How do you think each of the ten image factors described above applies to you? Take the time now to write down your company's image platform. Based on how you plan to brand your company, describe in writing how you will handle each image factor. Remember, when you do this you are creating the planks of your image platform. These planks will be used to guide each promotional activity you engage in, thereby consistently reinforcing your brand image. Your image platform will determine the kinds of promotion you select and the advertising media you use.

Designing Promotions: A Systematic Procedure

Once your image platform is complete, you are ready to begin designing your promotions. Your image platform will help you to maintain the continuity of your image in all your promotions and to repeat your brand message as often as possible using efficient and appropriate media. By referring to your image platform, you will be better able to tell if a promotion is appropriate. Having a well-defined image platform will also help you to assess the relative efficiency of alternative promotional tactics.

Even with the guidance of a well-built image platform, promotional design is much more complicated than it first appears. As Exhibit 11.2 clearly illustrates, the number of paid advertising media you can choose from is large. The best way to transmit your brand message varies from medium to medium. It is not easy to learn from scratch how to make correct decisions about what to say and the way to say it. Expensive trial and error can be involved. Then, too, there is the question of how to blend sales promotion and publicity with your paid advertising. Money is also important. How much should you spend on promotion? Finally, how do you know if you are getting your money's worth?

Step 1: Listing Promotional Options. The best way to clear a path through the promotional jungle is to follow a systematic procedure. We suggest you begin by listing as many promotional options as you can and then thinking about how you might use each. Exhibit 11.2 gives you a good list of paid media to think about. Exhibit 11.3 provides a list of possible sales promotion and publicity items. Exhibit 11.3 is only a starting point. The possible variations custom tailored to your business are many.[10]

Step 2: Scanning for Efficiency. Once you have developed your list, the next step is to give each promotional option on it an initial scan for efficiency. Will this promotional option reach your target customers? Do they know

Exhibit 11.3 Sales Promotion and Publicity Ideas

Sales Promotions are really themes for your advertising. They often include price breaks and/or giveaways and should be coordinated closely with your advertising. Some ideas for sales promotions include:

- Seasonal sales, presales, early bird sales, moonlight specials, etc.
- Arrival of new shipments of merchandise
- Store visits by celebrities (movie stars, Santa Claus, etc.)
- In-store giveaways of specialty items (Never give away live animals!)
- Contests
- Special merchandise exhibits tied to demonstrations
- Store decorations and employee costumes tied to a theme (can be combined with a rollback to prices of the theme era)
- Displays of collections, artwork by local residents, etc.
- Store/plant tours (best if tied to giveaways)
- Charity fundraisers: "For each XYZ purchased, I will donate one dollar to ABC charity."
- Store mascots (that can't reach the customers to bite them)

Publicity is generally free and is generated by making the news media aware of what you are doing that is newsworthy. Unusual sales promotions can be newsworthy and earn publicity, thereby pyramiding the results of your paid promotional efforts. Some newsworthy ideas include:

- Unusual or historical displays at your store
- Introduction of new product or service
- Opening of a new department, expansion, remodeling
- Sponsorship of a local organization or a recreational event
- Hirings, promotions, retirements of employees
- Success stories, such as closing a big sale, landing a big contract, achieving a record sales volume
- Community service by you or employees
- Unusual company practices tied to social issues (like a four-day work week, government job-training programs, etc.)
- Use or availability of your facilities for community activities
- Use of your facilities or personnel to teach classes, availability of class schedules, etc.
- Special events of community interest (art fairs, flea markets, etc.)

---

and respect this option? When they buy, will they use it as a guide? Is this promotional option relatively inexpensive in terms of cost versus profit from additional sales?

When you have doubts about the efficiency of a medium, discuss your questions with its local representatives. They can often provide you with demographic data about their audience, which they have collected themselves or have hired independent services to collect.[11] They can also provide you with cost information and point out special sections or time slots in their medium that they feel are particularly appropriate for your kind of business.

If a promotional option is very good at reaching your target customers but seems expensive, we suggest you keep it on your list of possibilities at this early stage. There are two reasons for doing so. First, the extra cost of a promotional option that very effectively reaches your target market may be more than offset by the profits it generates. For small businesses catering to industrial clients, for example, personalized direct mail can be very profitable. Second, an expensive promotional option may not need to be repeated very often if it is followed up with less expensive promotional options. Balancing expensive and inexpensive promotional options may prove more efficient than spending the same amount of money solely on less expensive options. For example, you cannot rely solely on free publicity to support your business, but announcements of appointments of key people or new products in a magazine can combine nicely with your ads. Although you cannot control exactly what the magazine says about your company, readers may consider it a more credible source of information than the sales pitch in your ad.

Step 3: Determining What You Can Afford to Spend.   After you have screened your promotional options for efficiency, the next step is to decide approximately how much you can spend. This budget figure will guide your selection of a promotional mix and may eliminate certain media outright. Almost invariably, what you could spend on promotion exceeds your budget. The trick is to set priorities among your promotional options to maximize efficiency and get the most for your advertising dollar. To do this, you need to ask yourself how much extra profit you can expect by spending your promotional dollars on one mix of options as compared with other mixes. Budgeting is a juggling act aimed at getting the most profit per dollar spent. As a practical matter, you will probably never achieve an ideal budget, but you can get close. Here are a few guidelines to help you to decide how much to spend on what:

1. Don't budget the same amount for promotion each month. Most new small businesses do not spend enough on advertising. The bulk of your first year's advertising budget should be spent in the first two or three months. Established businesses typically have busy seasons. Focus your spending to exploit seasonal ups and downs.

2. Prepare a promotional budget for at least a year in advance. Do this by setting up worksheets for each month of the year detailing how much you plan to spend that month, which media you will use, and how much you will spend on each. To fill in the dollar figures on the worksheets, begin with your promotional objectives, or what you expect your promotion to contribute. Perhaps you want to increase sales in a particular department, or maybe you want to sell more of a particular product. Next, spell out what tasks have to be accomplished to reach your objectives. Which customers do you have to reach? Where are they? How will you reach them? Which media will you use? Which image factors will be stressed? Once you decide what advertising you need, figure out how much it will cost. If the total for a month is too much, cut back on less promising options.

3. Prepare a promotional diary. As you carry out each month's promotional strategy, keep track in writing of the following for each promotional objective: the media used, the size of the ad or the specific details, when the promotion ran, and the apparent results. Did your sales really go up because of that Easter promotion? Why or why not?

4. Review your promotional diary frequently, and revise your budget, spending more on specific promotional options that appear to be contributing to your objectives and dropping those that don't appear to be paying their way. Don't cut out options after only one or two tries. With repetition, effectiveness may snowball.

5. Focus your promotional dollars on a relatively small number of promotional options so that your results can snowball with repetition. Never, however, invest all your promotional dollars in one option. There has to be more than one efficient promotional option for reaching your customers.

6. Focus your advertising geographically if you are a retailer. The vast majority of your customers will live or work or visit within a mile or two of your store. Investing in advertisements that reach outside this geographical circle will do little good.

7. Get help in preparing your promotional material. If you plan to spend more than $10,000 per year on advertising, consider using an advertising agency. A significant number of major agencies will seriously consider your account.[12] The help of a good agency could be invaluable to you. Even if your advertising budget is small, don't be afraid to ask for free advice from the media that will run your ads about how to produce the copy or broadcast message. Making good decisions about what to say and how to say it is a lot harder than you think.[13]

8. Form promotional joint ventures. Cooperative advertising and joint advertising are two versions of promotional joint ventures. Cooperative advertising occurs when a manufacturer advertising brand name products nationally enters into an agreement with local retailers to share the cost of advertising where to buy the products locally. Joint advertising occurs when several noncompeting, but related, retailers or manufacturers combine resources to advertise. A full page display ad in a newspaper for a local shopping center, for example, may include inserts for each of the participating stores in the center. Promotional joint ventures can effectively stretch the small business advertising dollar.

Step 4: Monitoring Your Promotional Program.   One more difficult question remains. How do you know if you are getting your money's worth from your promotional expenditures? Finding this out after the money has been spent or predicting what will work in advance remains one of the more mystifying and difficult challenges you face as a marketer. Marketing is an imprecise art form. After all,

> . . . can the subtleties of the consumer's mind, his fickleness, foibles and unpredictability ever be trapped to where they can be confined within the bounds of a computer, formula, equation or other scientific approach?[14]

We think not. If you follow some basic recommendations made by Elizabeth Sorbet, formerly Associate Professor of Marketing at the University of Southern Mississippi, we believe you will get about as close to measuring the effectiveness of your advertising as the corporate giants do. Here are some of her recommendations:[15]

What Results Do You Expect?

Essentially, measuring results means comparing sales with advertising. In order to do it you have to start early in the process—before you even make up the advertisement. The question to answer is: What do you expect the advertising to do for your store?

In thinking about the kinds of results to expect, it is helpful to divide advertising into two basic kinds: immediate response advertising and attitude advertising.

Immediate response advertising is designed to cause the potential customer to buy a particular product from you within a short time—today, tomorrow, the weekend, or next week. An example of such decision-triggering ads is one that promotes regular price merchandise with immediate appeal. Other examples are ads which use price appeals in combination with clearence sales, special purchases, seasonal items (for example, white sales, Easter sales, etc.), and "family of items" purchases.

Such advertising should be checked for results daily or at the end of 1 week from appearance. Because all advertising has some carry-over effect, it is a good idea to check also at the end of 2 weeks from appearances, 3 weeks from appearances, and so on to insure that no opportunity for using profit-making messages is lost.

Attitude advertising is the type you use to keep your store's name and merchandise before the public. Some people think of this type as "image-building" advertising. With it, you remind people week after week about your regular merchandise or services or tell them about new or special services or policies. Such advertising should create in the minds of your customers the attitude you want them to have about your store, its merchandise, its services, and its policies.

It is your reputation builder. To some degree, all advertising should be attitude advertising.

Attitude (or image-building) advertising is harder to measure than immediate response advertising because you cannot always attribute a specific sale to it. Its sales are usually created long after the ad has appeared and are triggered by the customer some time after having seen the ad. However, you should keep in mind that there is a lead time relationship in such advertising. For example, an ad or a series of ads that announces you have the exclusive franchise for a particular brand probably starts to pay off when you begin to get customers who want that brand only and ask no questions about competing brands.

In short, attitude advertising messages linger in the minds of those who have some contact with the ad. These messages sooner or later are used by people when they decide that they will make a certain purchase.

Because the purpose of attitude advertising is spread out over an extended period of time, the measurement of results can be more leisurely. Some attitude advertising—such as a series of ads about the brands which the store carries—can be measured at the end of 1 month from the appearance of the ads or at the end of a campaign.

Tests for Immediate Response Ads

In weighing the results of your *immediate* response advertisements the following devices should be helpful:

Coupons brought in. Usually these coupons represent sales of the product. When the coupons represent requests for additional information or contact with a salesman, were enough leads obtained to pay for the ad? If the coupon is dated, you can determine the number of returns for the first, second, and third weeks.

Requests by phone or letter referring to the ad. A "hidden offer' can cause people to call or write. Include—for example, in the middle of a paragraph—a statement that on request the product or additional information will be supplied. Results should be checked over a 1-week through 6-months or 12-months period because this type ad may have considerable carry-over effect.

Split runs by newspapers. Prepare two ads (different in some way you would like to test) and run them on the same day. Identify the ads—in the message or with a coded coupon—so you can tell them apart. Ask customers to bring in the ad or coupon. When you place the ad, ask the newspaper to give you a split run—that is: to print "ad A" in part of its press run and "ad B" in the rest of the run. Count the responses to each ad.

Sales made of particular item. If the ad is on a bargain or limited-time offer, you can consider that sales at the end of 1 week, 2 weeks, 3 weeks, and 4 weeks came from the ad. You may need to make a judgment as to how many sales came from display and personal selling.

Check store traffic. An important function of advertising is to build store traffic which results in purchases of items that are not advertised. Pilot studies show, for example, that many customers who are brought to the store by an ad for a blouse also bought a handbag. Some bought the bag in addition to the blouse, others instead of the blouse.

You may be able to use a local college or high school distributive education class to check store traffic. Class members could interview customers as they leave the store to determine: (1) which advertised items they bought, (2) what other items they bought, and (3) what they shopped for but did not buy.

Testing Attitude Advertising

When advertising is spread out over a selling season or several seasons, part of the measurement job is keeping records. Your aim is comparing records of ads and sales for an extended time.

An easy way to set up a file is by marking the date of appearance on tear sheets of newspapers ads, log reports of radio and television ads, and copies of direct mail ads. The file may be broken down into monthly, quarterly, or semi-annual blocks. By recording the sales of the advertised items on each ad or log, you can make comparisons.

In attitude (or image-building) advertising, the individual ads are building blocks, so to speak, which make up your advertising over a selling season. The problem is trying to measure each ad and the effects of all the ads taken together.

One approach is making your comparisons on a weekly basis. If you run an ad, for example, each week, at the end of the first week after the ad appears, compare that week's sales with sales for the same week a year ago. At the end of the *second* week, compare your sales with those of the end of the first week as well as year-ago figures.

At the end of the *third* week, 1 month, 3 months, 6 months, and 12 months from the appearance of the ad, repeat the process even though additional ads may have appeared in the meantime. For each of these ads, you will also make the same type of comparisons. You will, of course, be measuring the "momentum" of all of your ads as well as the results of a single ad.

After a time, you probably will be able to estimate how much of the results are due to the individual ad and how much to the momentum of all of your advertising. You may then make changes in specific details of the ad to increase response.

When comparing sales increases over some preceding period, allowances must be made for situations that are not normal. For example, your experience may be that rain on the day an ad appears cuts its pulling power by 50 percent. Similarly, advertising response will be affected by the fact that your customers work in a factory that is out on strike.

Some of the techniques which you can use for keeping on top of and improving attitude advertising follow:

When You Use Several Media

When your ads appear simultaneously in different media—such as the newspaper, on radio and television, in direct mail pieces, and as handbills—you should try to evaluate the relative effectiveness of each. You can check one printed medium against the other by using companion (the same or almost identical) ads in the newspaper, direct mail, and handbills.

You can make the job of analyzing and comparing results from among the media easier by varying your copy—the message. Your ad copy, thus, becomes the means of identifying your ad response.

You can check broadcast media—radio and TV—by slanting your message. Suppose, for example, that you advertise an item at 20 percent reduction. Your radio or TV ad might say something like this. "Come in and tell us you want this product at 20 percent off."

You can compare these responses with results from your "20 percent off" newspaper ad. Require the customer to bring in the newspaper ad— or a coupon from it.

Some of the ways to vary the copy are: a combination of the brand name with a word or some words indicating the product type; picture variations; size variations; and color variations. You might use the last three to check your printed ads against each other as well as against your radio and TV ads.

Be careful that the copy variation is not so great that a different impression is received from each medium. Here you would, in effect, have two different ads.

Frank and Helen Katz began solving their promotion problem by preparing their own version of the marketer's barometer presented in this chapter. Their review turned up some interesting facts. They discovered that 85 percent of their clientele came from two neighborhoods directly north and south of their store. Fifty-five percent came from the rapidly expanding north neighborhood and 30 percent from the more established south neighborhood. They also discovered that while several new jewelry stores had opened recently to the south, Katzmar was the only such store within or immediately adjacent to the north neighborhood.

The next thing they noticed was that even though they had been spending five hundred dollars per month on advertising, only a relatively small percentage of this had been used to purchase space in media that reached the two neighborhoods where most of their customers were. Most expenditures had been for yellow page ads in the county telephone directory and several neighborhood directories, ads in a small, county-wide consumer magazine, ads in the *Christian Science Monitor,* and joint mailings to a list put together by Katzmar and two other stores in the shopping center. Katzmar had never sought and never received free publicity of any kind.

From a survey of existing customers, Frank and Helen concluded that they should brand based on an image platform of a broad assortment of quality merchandise and honest, competent service. Those surveyed felt Katzmar needed to round out its assortment of high-priced, quality merchandise with good quality, but less expensive, merchandise, such as Citizen watches and charms that parents could buy as graduation gifts. The survey also showed that customers were impressed by Frank's jewelry experience and considered honesty and personalized service very important. Katzmar's promotions had not stressed these factors.

Frank and Helen completed their analysis of Katzmar's marketing by reviewing customer files. Comparing invoices against the mailing list indicated the mailing list was out of date. The Katzes also noticed that they knew very little about their customers except their names and addresses.

Based on their analysis, the Katzes decided to eliminate advertising in neighborhood telephone directories except for the directory covering the two neighborhoods from which most of their customers came. The size of the ads in the county directory was reduced. Ads in both directories emphasized Katzmar's street address and the name of the shopping center, which would be readily recognized by local residents. Cross-references were added in each directory under jewelry repair. Advertising in the *Christian Science Monitor* was discontinued.

The Katzes also reviewed eight newspapers circulating in the local area as options for their advertising. They eliminated the regional paper and two county-wide papers because they didn't want to pay for coverage they didn't need. Three local weeklies were of good quality, but only one of these served the neighborhoods the Katzes wanted to reach. A fourth local newspaper and a tabloid were eliminated because their bargain-oriented advertising was inconsistent with Katzmar's desired image. Interestingly, the cost of running a nice-sized display ad for one year in the one weekly that met Katzmar's needs was less than the cost of running a similar ad in the regional paper for a single Sunday!

The Katzes like the idea of advertising in a local consumer magazine. However, they discovered that the one they were using did not have good local circulation. They therefore switched to a more prestigious local magazine that had better local circulation and comparable advertising rates.

While the above media changes had merit, the redirection in promotional strategy that made the most sense was for Frank and Helen to personalize their service and design their promotions and direct mail to reinforce this service image. Frank and Helen were catering to an elite market that responded well to personal service. Since they sold big-ticket merchandise, they could affort to spend time to deal with each sale on a personal level.

To help them do this, Frank and Helen set up a customer file system. With such a system, each time a new customer made a purchase, a card would be filled out noting how the customer had heard about Katzmar, customer name, names of family members, addresses, birthdays, anniversaries, and other key dates. The card also had space to note purchases made, date of purchase, dollar amount of sale, and comments about preferences and tastes. The idea was for Frank and Helen to make an extra effort to memorize the names of their customers so that they could acknowledge them by name when they entered the store. When a customer entered the store, his or her card was used to give the Katzes a quick refresher on what the customer had purchased in the past, how much had been spent, general preferences, and any approaching special dates, such as birthdays. This total recall is very flattering. It makes customers feel special.

Frank and Helen had always conducted the usual promotions for Christmas and Valentine's Day, but their customer cards also permitted them to mail personalized birthday and anniversary promotions to their clients, send thank yous for purchases, mail birthday, anniversary, and Christmas cards, and inform customers of the arrival of items they thought the customers would like. If a customer didn't come in for a while, they could send a personal note to find out why.

As the system developed, introductory coupons for free jewerly repairs were given to customers. Customers could distribute these to friends who have not tried Katzmar before. New customers were also attracted by a series of exhibitions of unusual jewerly promoted through direct mail and to existing customers, ads in the local paper, and publicity releases to the local papers. The jewerly on display in the exhibitions were loaned free of charge to Katzmar by its suppliers.

The net result of this promotional strategy for Katzmar was and will be an expanding circle of loyal customers. The new mix of media expenditures is so efficient that Frank and Helen can afford a good level of continuity in their newspaper ad and direct mail appeals. Their ads and company logo will be recognized in the two neighborhoods and associated with quality and good service. Their repetition of their image platform and their follow-through on their promotions, as noted on the customer cards, will keep their promotions both appropriate and efficient. This is the essence of effective promotional strategy.

CHAPTER SUMMARY

This chapter has explained how to build an effective promotional strategy systematically. The use of paid advertising, sales promotion, and free publicity has been discussed, with examples to demonstrate how these three elements of promotional strategy can enhance your company's image. Three concepts central to building an image, discussed in this chapter are branding, continuity, and repetition. Ten key image factors that can be used to develop an image platform for your company were listed. They include price, quality, assortment, fashion, sales personnel, location, convenience, service, store atmosphere, and reputation as adjustable. Each of these factors was explained in detail. Also discussed was a four-step procedure for systematically designing promotions so that you can get maximum benefit from what you spend on promotion. The steps are: listing promotional options, scanning for efficiency, determining what you can afford to spend, and monitoring your promotional program. The last step is particularly difficult so detailed suggestions are given on how to deal with it.

DISCUSSION QUESTIONS

1. **Short Case: McFerris's Trains, Ltd.**
   Doug McFerris has collected model trains most of his adult life. Five years ago he opened a small specialty shop dedicated to the hobby in New York City. After a slow start, business has developed to the point where McFerris has a few extra dollars he would like to use for promotion in hopes of turning a so-so business into a great business. What would you recommend he do? Relate your answer to the concepts discussed in this chapter.

2. Can you name a small business in your neighborhood that has been successful at branding its product or service? How did it brand its product or service? Why did its approach work?

3. Review the advertising media described in Exhibit 11-2. Which would be best for:
   a. A pharmacy?
   b. A construction firm specializing in room additions?
   c. A small office-supply retailer?

4. How would you determine if it were worth the cost for a twenty-four-hour plumbing service to run a quarter-page display ad in the yellow pages?

5. Of the ten image factors suggested by Berry and Kunkel (see page 20), which could be a key part of an image platform for:
   a. A tennis shop?
   b. A bookkeeping service?
   c. A pet store?

REFERENCES

Cook, Harvey R. *Selecting Advertising Media: A Guide for Small Business.* Washington D.C.: U.S. Small Business Administration, 1977.

Gomperts, Rolf. *Promotion and Publicity Handbook for Broadcasters.* Blue Ridge Summit, Penn.: Tab Books, 1977.

Hanan, Mack. *Fast Growth Management.* New York: AMACOM, 1979.

Lewis, H. Gordon. *How to Handle Your Own Public Relations.* Chicago: Nelson-Hall Publishers, Inc., 1976.

Malickson, David L. and Nason, John W. *Advertising: How to Write the Kind that Works.* New York: Scribner's, 1977.

Siegel, Connie McClung. *How to Advertise and Promote Your Small Business.* New York: John Wiley & Sons, Inc., 1978.

Stevans, Mark. *36 Small Business Mistakes and How to Avoid Them.* West Nyack, N.Y.: Parker Publishing Co., 1978.

FOOTNOTES

1. This case was reported by one of the authors based upon a Small Business Institute report completed under his supervision. In order to maintain client confidentiality, the facts given in here differ somewhat from the actual case.

2. Mark Stevens, *36 Small Business Mistakes and How to Avoid Them* (West Nyack, N.Y.: Parker Publishing, © 1978), pp. 67–70. He argues that this occurs because far too many owner-managers confuse familiarity with advertisements with expertise in advertising. They are not the same.

3. L. Lee Manzer, et al., "Image Creation in Small Business Retailing: Applications of Newspaper Advertising," *Journal of Small Business Management* 18, no. 2 (April 1980): 18–19.

4. Leonard L. Berry and John H. Kunkel, "A Behavioral Conception of Retail Image," *Journal of Marketing* 32, #4 (October 1968): 26.

5. This definition and the discussion of branding presented below are based on an insightful analysis presented in Mack Hanan, *Fast Growth Management: How to Improve Profits with Entrepreneurial Strategies* (New York: AMACOM, a division of American Management Associations, 1979), pp. 91–103.

6. Manzer et al., "Image Creation," p. 19.

7. This chart is adapted from two charts prepared by Mark Stevans, *36 Small Business Mistakes and How to Avoid Them*, pp. 71–72. Additional media entries and evaluative remarks were suggested by Connie McClung Siegel, *How to Advertise and Promote Your Small Business* (New York: John Wiley & Sons, Inc., 1978), pp. 73–84 and 99–106; Harvey R. Cook, *Selecting Advertising Media: A Guide for Small Business* (Washington, D.C.: U.S. Small Business Administration, 1977), pp. 17–74; and William H. Brannen, *Successful Marketing for Your Small Business* (Englewood Cliffs, N.J.: Prentice-Hall, Inc., 1978), pp. 298–302.

8. Hanan, *Fast Growth Management*, p. 93.

9. Berry and Kunkel, "A Behavioral Conception," p. 26.

10. Three excellent sources for sales promotion and publicity ideas, which we referred to when developing Exhibit 11.3, are Siegel, *How to Advertise and Promote Your Small Business*; H Gordon Lewis, *How to Handle Your Own Public Relations* (Chicago: Nelson-Hall, Inc. Publishers, 1976); and Rolf Gompertz, *Promotion and Publicity Handbook for Broadcasters* (Blue Ridge Summit, Penn.: Tab Books, 1977). These sources also provide guidance on how to write press releases for various media.

11. To illustrate, larger newspapers can provide audited circulation statements. Smaller ones usually have sworn circulation statements. Services such as the Starch Readership Service provide data on magaziine readers. Audited audience statistics are also available for radio and television. In the case of radio, for example, broadcast-measuring services audited by the Broadcast Rating Council regularly sample audiences to detemine a station's share of audience, the sex and age of listeners, etc.

12. Jack Dart, "The Advertising Agency Selection Process for Small Business: Tips from the Agencies," *Journal of Small Business Management* 18, no. 2 (April 1980): 3.

13. You should understand enough about how to create advertising to be able to evaluate the advice you receive. Some good advice on the preparation of advertising copy and broadcast messages is provided by Siegel, *How to Advertise and Promote Your Small Business*, pp. 85–98; Elizabeth M. Sorbet, *Measuring the Results of Advertising*, Small Marketers Aid, No. 121 (Washington, D.C.: U.S. Small Business Administration, 1978), p. 2; and David L. Malickson and John W. Nason. *Advertising: How to Write the Kind that Works* (New York: Scribner's 1977).

14. "And Whose Little Marketing Dollar Are You?" Reprinted from the September 1971 issue of *Business Management*, in *Annual Editions Readings in Marketing '75–'76*, ed. Richard Wendall (Guilford, Conn.: Dushkin Publishing Group, Inc., 1974), p. 246.

15. Sorbet, *Measuring the Results of Advertising*.

Selling Your Product or Service

12

□   **Where should your product or service be sold?**

□   **When should it be sold?**

□   **Who should do the selling?**

CASE
PROBLEM

*Mary's
Gardens*[1]

Mary Kempton owned a retail nursery in a medium-sized Sun Belt city. She wanted to expand her sales and profits, but her location did not appear to offer much opportunity for this. It was limited in size and in an older neighborhood. Although she did a good business at this location, her sales had leveled off. They had been about the same for each of the last three years.

Mary was becoming restive. The sales promotions she had tried in the last two years had brought in the public, but they had not changed the total sales picture very much. She was not meeting her company growth goals. She speculated that the lackluster sales performance might be the result of her store's location or maybe inadequate selling techniques, but she did not know where to begin to figure out exactly what was wrong.

**PROBLEM
IDENTIFICATION**

Mary's problem is common to small retailers and can have many causes. For example, her store's location might have been less than ideal to begin with. This would have doomed the store to a limited sales potential no matter what she tried. It may be nothing short of a retailing miracle that her management expertise has overcome the location she has saddled herself with enough for her to be doing fairly well. Perhaps Mary's initial choice of location was fine; but in the last two years the neighborhood may have declined, or several new competitors may have opened their doors. This would make each sale harder to get now than it once was, and extraordinary steps would be required to keep old customers and attract new ones.

It could be that Mary's salesclerks are surly and/or lack knowledge about the store's products. This might explain why advertising increased store traffic but not sales. Customers may put up with grumpy experts or friendly incompetents, but they will rarely put up with someone both surly and ignorant.

It may even be that Mary's suppliers are not giving her good advice on what to stock or are unreliable in delivery so that what customers want is not on the shelves when they come into the store. Perhaps her suppliers are charging her too much, thereby making the prices she has to charge her customers too high to permit an adequate number of sales.

All of these potential causes of Mary's problem have one thing in common—selling. Selling involves having your product in the right place at the right time. It involves deciding who should do your selling, how they should sell for you, how they should be trained to sell, and what you should pay them. It also involves being selective about whom you allow to sell to you. Careful attention to these factors can dramatically increase your company's sales and profits.

How good are you at selling? Do you know how to manipulate the selling factors that affect your business? Is your selling strategy working as well as it should? Exhibit 12.1 contains questions for you to answer to help you to detect your selling strengths and weaknesses. Each question is related to a major issue to be discussed in this chapter. Comparison of your answers with the discussions that follow will give you ideas for dealing more effectively with each issue.

    Before reading further, answer each of the questions in Exhibit 12.1. Be sure you write notes to yourself on why you answered each question the way you did. Check your answers against those we think are best for each question. How do your answers compare?

DIAGNOSIS

Your answers to the questions of where, how and when to sell and who should do the selling have a major impact on the success of your firm. In this section we will first review each question and explain why your answers to it affects your probability of success. After that, we will discuss how to tackle certain problems related to each question. This will enable you to develop sound answers and effective selling strategies.

UNDER-STANDING

Where to Sell?

The first question is: Where should your product or service be sold? The answer to this question must be based on knowledge about your target market. Where would your target customers like to buy your product or service? Where do they shop for it? The buying habits of your customers tell you where to sell.

    Many people shop without leaving their home or business. They read ads and product reports, respond to direct mail, or check directory listings and make telephone calls. This shopping process may lead them to you. The places you sell to them are in the media and on the telephone. Media selection was discussed in chapter 11. We will discuss how to handle customers who shop by phone later in this chapter. For now, it is important to recognize their telephone calls for what they are—opportunities to make sales. During these conversations you have to convince the callers that you can meet their needs better than the competition.

Exhibit 12.1   Is Your Selling Effort Truly Effective?

Instructions: Each question has five responses. Circle the response you think is best for each.

1. Selling is best done—
   a. in your store.
   b. at the customer's home or business.
   c. where the customer wants to buy.
   d. by advertising.
   e. by your middlemen. (A middleman is someone who distributes your product for you, such as a wholesaler.)

2. Effective personal selling relies most heavily on—
   a. product knowledge of the salesperson.
   b. a good product that is competitively priced.
   c. good commissions for the salesperson.
   d. the salesperson's ability to create exceptional value for the buyer.
   e. friendship between buyer and salesperson.

3. If you are a manufacturer but do not sell directly to those who use your products, you must select middlemen to help you sell your product. The important thing to remember when doing this is that—
   a. a good product sells itself both to the middleman and to the ultimate user.
   b. middlemen must be shown how selling your product will create exceptional value for them as well as for the ultimate users.
   c. there are many middlemen to choose from in each market area; so you should pick the one tailor-made for your product.
   d. the best way to sell to each market area is pretty much the same for each product, i.e., the same type of middleman should be used in each market area.
   e. it is actually easier to sell your product to middlemen than to ultimate users because middlemen are profit oriented, while ultimate users buy based on emotion.

4. Selling is best done—
   a. on weekends.
   b. just before Christmas.
   c. just before the start of the school year.
   d. on weekday mornings.
   e. when the buyer is receptive.

5. When deciding whether to hire your own sales people or to contract with a middleman to sell for your new business, your main economic concern should be—
   a. the percentage commission you will have to pay one as opposed to the other.
   b. the total sales cost for each sale.
   c. the relative amount of money you will have to invest in the selling effort before a profit is realized.
   d. the relative number of sales that will be made.
   e. the price you will be able to charge.

6. When deciding whether to hire your own sales people or to contract with a middleman to sell for your business, your main management concern should be—
   a. the relative degree of control you will have over how your product is sold.
   b. the relative ease in coordinating shipping of your product.
   c. the relative ease of providing training about product benefits.
   d. the relative ease in recruiting good sales people.
   e. the relative quality of follow-up service that can be provided.

7. A good business location for a small business—
   a. is only important for retailers.
   b. is generally not a prime location (due to high rents, etc.).
   c. is one where there is a lot of traffic (people in cars or on foot) going by.
   d. is no substitute for good business sense.
   e. is one of the most important selling decisions made by the owners since a good location can overcome a lot of management mistakes.

8. The secrets of effective personal selling—
   a. are not really secrets and can be learned with practice.
   b. are difficult, if not impossible, to learn, which means only experienced sales people should be hired.
   c. boil down to strategies for duping hapless consumers into buying things they really do not want or need.
   d. are pretty much the same for all types of selling jobs.
   e. center on selling specific product features.

9. An effective salesperson—
   a. focuses on a single function—selling.
   b. is a persuader, an information gatherer, and a customer ego builder.
   c. is all the things in "b" and has the flexibility and interpersonal skills to juggle these roles.
   d. must represent both the company and the customer.
   e. needs little or no training.

10. Selecting sales people—
   a. requires an extensive, careful search.
   b. can be relatively easy or a major problem, depending on the type of sales job.
   c. should be based on product knowledge.
   d. should be based on whether or not the applicant is affable.
   e. is not that hard because it is easy to train people to sell.

Recommended Answers

1. c	6. a
2. d	7. e
3. b	8. a
4. e	9. d
5. c	10. b

Some people buy your product at their homes or businesses but need personal contact with you or your salespersons before they buy. Their interest can be turned into sales only by calling on them at home or work.

Other people prefer to come to you to buy. You sell to these people at a location that is convenient for them and meets their expectations about where to find what they are looking for. This may be your store, or it may be a chain store that carries your products. Catering to this type of buyer requires an analysis of store types and locations. Guidelines for selection of store locations are given in Appendix A to this chapter.

Your answer to the question of where to sell may be selection of a site for your store, or it may involve selection of middlemen to distribute your product to the right sales outlets. This latter choice involves still more questions about where to sell because middlemen also have to be reached and convinced that your products can provide exceptional value for them. Guidelines for selection of middlemen will be discussed later in this chapter.

We will also discuss two related topics: how to train others to sell and how to manage those who sell for you. As you will see, effective personal selling, like effective promotion, relies heavily on the concept of branding—the ability to create exceptional value for the buyer. Your sales force helps your customers to gain this exceptional value through the use of your products or service.

How to Sell?

Person-to-person selling techniques are often required to close a sale. This is true whether you go to your customers for the personal contact or they come to your store. These techniques will be discussed later. We will also discuss two related topics: how to train others to sell and how to manage those who sell for you. As you will see, effective personal selling, like effective promotion, relies heavily on the concept of branding—the ability to create exceptional value for the buyer. Your sales force helps your customers to gain this exceptional value through the use of your product or service. They show your customers how to get the most out of your product or service. As a result, they are selling a package of superior benefits rather than just a product. Interestingly, in order to get your sales people to work hard for you, you have to do the same thing for them. You have to brand your product or service in their eyes. You have to show them how selling your product creates exceptional value for them. This is especially true if your sales people are not employees of your company.

When to Sell?

The next question is: When should your product or service be sold? Knowing the answer to this question is often the key to successful selling. The answer is simple in theory: your product or service should be sold when your customers want to buy. How to put this answer into practice is sometimes obvious; for example, when a retailer advertises heavily just before Christmas. At other times, however, the practical application is more worrisome. Should you keep your store open in the evenings? Should your restaurant offer a Sunday brunch? When will the business buyers of your product be most receptive? The important thing to remember is that each product or service has its moment—a point in time when buyers are particularly receptive. The art of selling includes the ability to perceive when this moment has arrived and the capability to deliver exceptional customer benefits before the moment is lost. Exhibit 12.2 provides a list of key moments for you to refer to. Which of these apply to your product or service? Can you think of others that are more important for you? How can you find out when your customers will experience one of these moments?

Exhibit 12.2   When to Sell Your Product: Key Moments That Affect Buyers' Receptivity

Human Events
- Births
- Hunger
- Illnesses
- Relocation
- Aging (Passages that lead to desire for self-improvement, education, etc.)
- Death

Social Events
- Holidays
- Vacations
- Religious events (Christenings, bar mitzvahs, etc.)
- Marriages
- Anniversaries
- Divorces
- Graduations
- Fads

Job Events
- New Job
- Transfer
- Promotion
- Loss of Job
- Established Schedule (hours worked, break times, days of week worked, etc.)
- Closing of a Big Deal
- New Product Introduction
- Tax Time

News Events
- Heroism
- Casualty Losses
- Dramatic Crimes
- Elections
- War
- Peace
- Depression
- Inflation

Who Should Sell?

The final question to consider is: Who should do your selling? Should you? Should one of your employees do it? Or should it be done by someone else? We will review criteria for selecting salespersons in more detail later in this section. Our present discussion focuses on how cost and control relate to your choice.

Generally, it requires a greater investment of time and money to maintain your own sales force than it does to hire an independent contractor to do personal selling for you. With some businesses, of course, doing it yourself is the only way. When you own and operate a restaurant, for example, you and your employees are the logical choice to do the selling. However, if you begin to bottle your secret salad dressing for sale to the general public, you will probably find it much more effective to use an independent middleman to sell your product. You can't afford to abandon your restaurant to go on the road to sell your product. Hiring an employee to do the same thing means you have to pay all the employee's expenses. The independent middleman, however, typically sells several related products in one sales call. This divides the selling cost among several products. Your share of the cost is a lot less after paying commissions.

In deciding who will do your selling, you cannot simply look at the total amount of sales expenditures. The effectiveness of each sales dollar must also be considered. In many cases, particularly for a new company, efficiency will dictate that you select an experienced middleman to sell your salad dressing rather than selling it yourself. This is because a middleman with a good track record for your type of product knows where to sell your product and when to sell it. Such a middleman is already branded with the retailers you hope will carry your product. The middleman's reputation for delivering exceptional benefits will cause retailers to accept your product more readily, thereby quickly increasing your distribution.

There is always a tradeoff between cost and control when you delegate selling to others. Good or bad, when you sell your product yourself, you can control exactly what you say. You know how often your customers are being called upon because you are doing it yourself. You may not always make the sale, but at least you know you did your best. When you delegate selling tasks to others, however, you lose some control. You no longer know for sure if your product is being sold right, although there are some ways to check up on your employees' selling efforts.

You have the least control over selling your product when independent middlemen sell it for you. It is even harder to check up on outsiders than it is to check up on your employees who sell in the field. Even if you keep close track of the number of sales calls, you will find it difficult to know how hard your independent middlemen are pushing your product.

The very thing that makes middlemen efficient sellers may work against you. Middlemen gain efficiency by selling a number of related products. How hard are they going to work to sell your product when it is only one of many they have to offer? If your product is new and untested or requires a demonstration to prove it is effective, you may be disappointed in your initial sales results. The salesperson may be reluctant to push your product when it is easier to sell a well-proven product to the customer instead.

What can be done about the control problem? The best solution is to brand your product or service both in the eyes of your customers and in the eyes of your salesperson.

Determining Where to Sell Your Product or Service

As noted above, the answer to where your product or service should be sold is found by analyzing your target market. The techniques presented in chapter 10 can be used to deal with this issue. Observation of customer purchasing habits, surveys of customers, and surveys of those who buy your type of product for retail outlets will lead to the answers you need. Questions you might ask consumers include:

Where would you expect to be able to purchase a product like this? Why?

Where would you prefer to be able to purchase a product like this? Why?

Questions you might ask retailers include:

Who does your buying for you?

Where would you expect to be able to purchase a product like this? Why?

Do you have a choice of whom to buy this type of product from? Why?

If you do have a choice, how do you choose whom to buy from?

If you do not have a choice, would you like one?

What services would have to be offered to cause you to switch to a new supplier?

Appendixes B and C to chapter 10 will give you more ideas about how to select people to talk to and what questions to ask. There are two important things to remember as you do this. First, once you decide where your product should be sold, there may not be a lot of choice about how to get it to the marketplace. There may be only one middleman who distributes your kind of product in a particular market area. If you want efficient distribution, you will have to deal with this middleman. It pays to know this before you open negotiations since you are not in a strong bargaining position. You will have to make a special effort to get the distribution terms you want. The second thing to remember is that each market area is somewhat different in terms of distribution. As you introduce your product or service into each new market area, you will have to find out the best way to distribute it. The national market is composed of myriad local markets, each with its own set of marketing customs. If you fail to recognize this, you can make serious blunders in your choice of middlemen as you expand into new locales. Each new marketplace has to be methodically researched.

The two observations made in the previous paragraph apply to you only if you are a small manufacturer that sells through middlemen. If you sell directly to the ultimate user of your product, your location and personal selling skills become critical. Although they are important for a small manufacturer, they are absolutely essential for the retailer. How to pick the location for your business is discussed in Appendix A to this chapter.

Effective Personal Selling Techniques

The art of effective personal selling is no secret. It has been studied in great depth by numerous authors, and they have identified several tried-and-true sales strategies that you can use effectively if you practice diligently. We do not pretend that these few paragraphs will tell you all that you need to know to master this art form. We can, however, provide you with an invaluable guiding philosophy for your personal selling efforts. We can also provide you with a short list of readings that contain a wealth of proven personal selling tactics. This list is found in the References at the end of this chapter.

One of the things that is remarkable about good personal selling is that it is so hard to find today. Big businesses selling consumer products rarely use the personal touch. They stress self-service, merchandise assortment, pricing, and advertising rather than the more expensive personal selling effort. If you know what you want and are looking for an inexpensive price, the chains are hard to beat. If you are uncertain about what is best for you and want that magical thing called service, chain stores leave a lot to be desired.

One would expect small businesses to fill this service gap since they emphasize the personal touch, and service is certainly very personal. A suprising number of small businesses, however, miss this point completely. We suspect this is because personal selling has an undeserved bad name. The small business owner does not provide the service the customer really needs and wants because doing so is selling, which they consider distasteful.

Good personal selling is not a strategem for duping hapless consumers into buying things they really do not want or need. Still, the common stereotype of a salesperson includes a strong dose of rapacity. It is this stereotype that makes us shy away from salespersons in used car lots and furniture stores.

What good personal selling really is, is service. Bert Rosenbloom explains this nicely for retail establishments:

> Personal selling in retailing is essentially a matching of the customer's needs with the retailer's merchandise and services. In general, the more skillfully this match is made the better the personal selling. If salespeople

make a good match, not only is a sale made but a satisfied customer is created (or maintained). Thus a long-term profitable relationship can be established . . .

There are three basic skills needed to make this match effectively:
1. Salespeople must be skilled in learning the needs of the customer.
2. They must have a thorough knowledge of the merchandise and service offered by the retailer.
3. They must have the ability to convince customers that the merchandise and service offered by their store can satisfy the customer's needs better than that of their competitors.[2]

Rosenbloom's words can be applied to all personal selling endeavors. They are more than just a definition. They are a guiding philosophy for your personal selling efforts that can lead to big profits for you.

Five Strategies that Make Your Salesperson a Valuable Part of Your Product. Concepts discussed in earlier chapters clarify the importance of personal selling. In chapter 9 we saw that the essence of the marketing concept is to identify consumer needs and meet them, thereby making a profit. When the customer profits, you profit. In chapter 11 we saw that branding entailed doing this particularly well—delivering perceived premium value to your customers so that they demand your products or services rather than those of your competitors. Personal selling should be viewed as an integral part of the branding process because it adds to the perceived value of your goods or services in your customers' eyes. A good salesperson becomes a valued part of the product or service you offer. Mark Hanon suggests five strategies that your salespersons can use to increase the value of your product:[3]

1. *Positioning as profit improvers.* The effective salesperson takes a position with a customer of being an improver of the customer's benefits. "Don't think of me as a salesperson," this person says. "Consider me someone who is here to help you, without charge, to better meet your needs, increase your benefits, or improve your profits."

2. *Interacting as a consultant.* The effective salesperson assumes the role of a consultant helping the customer better meet needs, increase benefits, or improve profits. This person gives advice on how to lower customer costs and increase customer sales. This person collects enough information from the customer to enable him or her to give sound advice. This person follows through to keep up to date on the customer's situation so that his or her counsel will remain informed and valid.

3. *Ruling out debate on product merits.* Effective salespersons do not sell specific product features and benefits that might be compared to competing brands. Instead, they create acceptance for what their product or service can do to meet the consumer's needs, increase the consumer's benefits, or improve the consumer's profits. The emphasis is on end results, not on what the product is made of or what it does specifically.

4. *Appropriating the industry standard of value.* The effective salesperson sets his or her company's ability to meet needs, yield extra benefits, or increase profits for the customer as the standard for the industry. "You must do business with us," this salesperson aruges, "because we are the industry standard. Until our competitors can match our ability to meet your needs, they must be measured against us unfavorably."

5. *Selling systems.* The effective salesperson packages several products and product-related services into a single unit called a "system." Systems are designed to deal more thoroughly and comprehensively with customer problems than single products or services, thereby synergistically increasing need satisfaction, benefit yield, or profits. The ability of a salesperson to sell systems gives concrete proof to the customer that the salesperson's company understands the customer's needs and can custom tailor realistic solutions to them.

Proven Personal Selling Tactics.   These five strategies should make it clear that effective personal selling sells what your products or services can contribute to satisfying customer needs rather than the product or service itself. The effective salesperson focuses on creating added value for the customer out of the products or services you offer. This is the essence of branding. If it is successfully accomplished, it will increase both your sales and your profits per sale. The personal touch as applied to personal selling means that the salesperson finds out what the consumer really needs and devises a unique system of products and services to meet these needs. This should be the guiding philosophy for your personal selling efforts. (The books listed in the Reference section at the end of this chapter cover all aspects of effective personal selling including selling, techniques, selection of sales personnel, and training and managing salespeople.)

Before discussing how to deal with those who will do your selling for you, we would like to comment on one area of personal selling where glaring violations of our guiding philosophy occur frequently—answering telephone calls. Detailed inspection of this one area should give you some general insights into what transpires when a customer talks to an effective salesperson.

As we noted earlier, many of the calls a small business receives are from people who do their shopping by phone. These shopping telephone calls provide opportunities to win customers and make sales. However, improper handling of such inquiries can lose customers before you even see them. The investment in advertising to get the prospective customer to call in the first place can easily be lost in a few seconds.

What can you do to insure that your telephone is answered effectively? The key is to remember that everything said should make it clear that your company is willing to take the time to determine what the caller really needs and to devise a system of products and services to meet these needs. If this message can be conveyed over the telephone, it is unlikely the caller will be able to resist coming to your store. Good service, after all, is hard to find.

There is no standard script that details word for word how to handle a shopping telephone call. However, the following conversations illustrate the type of things that should be said.

Illustrative Conversation 1—Knowledgeable Answerer

Answerer: Hello, this is ABC Company, how may we serve you?

Caller: I am looking for XYZ product. Do you carry it?

Answerer: Yes we do. We also carry several similar products that, depending on your needs, may work better for you. I will be glad to help you select what will meet your needs best. Just come on by, and when you get here ask for _____. That's me!

Caller: O.K. How late are you open?

Answerer: Until 5:00 P.M. However, if you can't make it by then, I will be glad to assist you after hours if you want to make an appointment, Mr. _____?

Caller: I'm John Smith. Thanks, but that won't be necessary, I can make it before five.

Answerer: Great! I will look forward to serving you, Mr. Smith. Before you hang up, tell me what you want to do with XYZ product so I can think about how best to tackle your problem. That way I will be able to serve you more efficiently when you arrive.

Illustrative Conversation 2—Unknowledgeable Answerer

Answerer: Hello, this is ABC Company, how may we serve you?

Caller: I'm looking for XYZ product. Do you carry it?

Answerer: I am not sure. We have divided our company into departments so that the personnel in each can specialize and become experts on how their products can benefit you. If you will please describe briefly what you intend to use XYZ product for, I will be able to transfer your call to the expert who can help you.

Caller: Well, I want to use it for . . .

Answerer: I see. _____ in Department X will be able to serve you. I will transfer your call. Whom shall I say is calling?

Caller: My name is John Smith.

Answerer: Thank you, Mr. Smith. I will transfer your call now. If you are cut off, please call right back collect. We do want to serve you!

In both conversations the answerers stress the willingness to serve. In the case of the unknowledgeable answerer, the answerer still collects sufficient information to make a referral to the right expert and stresses that the know-how to meet the caller's needs exists in the company. Receptionists do not have to be product experts, but they should be given a list of the company's experts and told what each is an expert in. Knowledgeable or not, the answerer should be friendly and emphasize a willingness to make a special effort to meet the customer's needs.

It pays to train your people how to answer your telephone. Whether they are knowledgeable or not about your product—and it is preferable that they are—they should be taught that a telephone call is an opportunity to make a sale and not just an interruption of their work. The people who answer your telephone are an important part of what you are selling to your customers.

Selecting Sales Employees

The job of selecting good sales people to work for you can vary markedly in difficulty, depending on the nature of the selling jobs you need to fill. Some types of selling are easy, with a pleasant personality and a willingness to provide good service being all that is required. You can hire almost anyone who is reasonably articulate and has a positive attitude for these jobs. Other selling jobs are so complex and emotionally demanding that only a few special people have the ability to learn to do the job really well.

Successful selection of sales employees requires that you first take a close look at the nature of the selling job you are seeking to fill. Then, you must devise means to see if prospective employees have the knowledge and emotional qualifications to handle the job. Chapter 14 will outline the general procedure for selecting new employees, including salespersons. We will give you some ideas here about what you must consider when defining the sales positions you need to fill.

To varying degrees, a salesperson must walk a tightrope when dealing with a customer. On the one hand, the salesperson must represent the company. The sale must be made for the company to survive. On the other hand, the salesperson must empathize with the customer and understand the customer's needs. To develop a sale, the salesperson must represent the customer and provide the customer with the best benefits. Sometimes it is extremely difficult to maintain a balance between these conflicting musts. While walking the tightrope, the salesperson may have to change roles several times to make one sale. James Belasco suggests, for example, that the salesperson might have to be a persuader, a service person, an information gatherer, an expediter, a coordinator, a problem definer, and a customer ego builder.[4] Juggling these roles, while at the same time walking the tightrope of musts, can be emotionally draining. It requires flexibility and well-refined interpersonal skills. Still this is not the whole story.

Belasco points out that in addition to walking a tightrope and juggling roles, the salesperson may have to perform without an audience. There is no applause or booing to indicate how things are going. Particularly in the case of field salespersons, there is no boss available to respond at the appropriate moment. To a large extent, the whole performance must be given before the salesperson finds out what the home office really thinks of it. The salesperson must therefore be able to function independently—physically, socially, and psychologically.

The type of selling job largely determines just how skillful and self-reliant the salesperson has to be to succeed. This, in turn, determines the selection process you have to go through to fill the job. The more skill and self reliance required, the more it will pay you to search carefully for the right salesperson for your company and the more methodical you will have to be in your selection process to avoid hiring the wrong person. Exhibit 12.3 presents one scheme for classifying sales jobs that should prove useful to you.[5]

Generally speaking, the seven sales jobs described in this exhibit can be viewed as a continuum from the very simple to the very complex. If your company needs salespersons for jobs at the first or second level, your search

Exhibit 12.3   Types of Sales Jobs

1. Positions in which the salesman's job is primarily to deliver the product—e.g., driver sales for soft drinks, milk, or fuel oil. His selling responsibilities are secondary. Good service and a pleasant personality may lead to more sales, but few of these men originate many sales.

2. Positions in which the salesman is primarily an *inside* order taker—e.g., the retail clerk standing behind a counter. The customer comes to the salesman. Most of the customers have already decided to buy; the salesman only serves them. He may use suggestion selling, but ordinarily he cannot do much more.

3. Positions in which the saleman is primarily an *outside* order taker, going to the customer in the field—e.g., a packinghouse, soap or spice salesman who calls on retail food stores. In his contacts with chain store personnel, he actually may be discouraged from doing any hard selling; that task is left to executives higher in the organization. Although good service and a pleasant personality may help him, he does little creative selling.

4. Positions in which the salesman is not expected or permitted to solicit an order; his job is to build goodwill, perform promotional activities, or provide services for the customers. This is the missionary salesman for a distiller or the detail salesman for an ethical pharmaceutical manufacturer.

5. Positions in which the major emphasis is placed on technical product knowledge—e.g., the sales engineer.

6. Positions that demand creative selling of tangible products, such as vacuum cleaners, airplanes, encyclopedias, or oil well drilling equipment. Here, the salesman's job often is more difficult because the customer may not be aware of his need for the product, or he may not realize how the new product can satisfy his wants better than the product he is now using. When the product is of a technical nature, this category may overlap that of the sales engineer.

7. Positions that require creative selling of intangibles, such as insurance, advertising services, consulting services, or communications systems. Intangibles typically are more difficult to sell because they are less readily demonstrated or dramatized.

need not be exhaustive. A positive attitude, pleasant appearance, and some prior experience may be all that is required. If your company needs salespersons for jobs at the seventh level, however, you have a major selection problem. In chapter 14, we explain why, as a small business owner, you should consider only highly trained, experienced applicants with a proven track record for this kind of job.

Training Your Salespeople

Because of the nature of the salesperson's job, training is critical. Even a very simple sales job requires training in areas such as how to be pleasant, what to say when answering the telephone, and how to provide good service. The salesperson needs sufficient knowledge of your company's products and services to be able to locate them or refer customers to one of your company's experts. A complex sales job requires a big investment in training time. Even if you hire a well-qualified salesperson, you will have to provide careful training concerning the unique customer benefits your product or service systems offer. You will have to show the salesperson how to brand your product or service and how to become a part of your brand.

An effective sales training program, like any other training program, serves several purposes:

1. It increases productivity by establishing specific objectives and demonstrating how to achieve them efficiently.
2. It reduces employee turnover by reducing failures.
3. It increases morale since the employees know their purpose in the company and feel well prepared to deal with any challenge.
4. It helps control employees by explaining how management will monitor their job performance.
5. It shows the employee how to render service to customers and how to deal effectively with complaints.
6. It reduces supervision costs since employees know what to do, and less supervision is required.
7. It gives the salesperson a sufficient knowledge base to permit flexibility and innovation in the face of changing customer preferences and encroaching competition.[6]

Sales training is essential. No salesperson should begin selling on his or her own before being fully trained in the techniques required to sell your products or services well. It is important for your salespersons to gain sales experience, but trainees should first observe more experienced personnel.

If you plan to do your own selling, you should also follow the advise given in this section. Seek experienced salespeople to train you to sell. Don't expect to be able to learn everything you need to know about selling on your own, especially if you will be selling at the sixth or seventh level of the sales job.

Managing the Sales Effort

An effective sales effort must be well managed. You must provide the branding plan to be used by your sales people and make sure they follow it. You must determine sales territories. You must determine sales compensation. In other words, even though you may be relatively inexperienced in sales, you still have to make sure your company's sales effort is well planned, carefully organized, and kept under control. You have to provide the incentives for your work force to work harder. How should you go about this? One recent survey of seventy-three top sales people from thirty-seven small businesses across the United States led to seven key findings that will help you to manage your sales force:[7]

Finding #1. Low salary combined with high commission was perceived as the strongest compensation arrangement to encourage above average sales personnel to produce more. They were motivated by incentives over which they had control.

Finding #2. "Fairness" was the most important expectation sales people had of a financial incentive plan followed by "reward for meeting present goals," and "reward for performing good customer service." Length of service definitely was not considered an expectation of an incentive plan by better-than-average sales people.

Finding #3. The two most important "demotivators" for better-than-average sales people were (a) a "better" job offered by another company, and (b) dislike of the job.

Finding #4. Generally, high-producing sales people liked sales contests. The observation most frequently made was that "prizes should be merchandise, not money."

Finding #5. The consensus among the respondents was that fringe benefits are necessary to attract sales people but, presumably since they are now widely used, are not really important as motivators. High-achieving sales people take them for granted, and do not work harder because of them.

Finding #6. Among nonfinancial incentives, "enjoyment of work" and the "challenge of achievement" were the most important as viewed by better-than-average sales people. Recognition and personal encouragement were not considered important motivational factors.

Finding #7. "Is unable to communicate effectively" and "doesn't include sales personnel in the decision making process" were considered the two largest motivational errors committed by management.

The profile of top sales personnel sketched by the above seven findings is an interesting one. Top sales persons are self-reliant and like the big payoff potential of commission selling, but they want to know in advance what they can make if they do well. They want to be paid fairly, with differences in sales potential from territory to territory and other relevant factors taken into account. They want challenge, but they want to sell a product system that will make customers reasonably agreeable. They want to advance in responsibility and expertise through training, education, and their own initiative. Finally, they want to be included in decisions about sales goals and other performance requirements. To sum up, good sales people are self-starters and can cope with a great deal of autonomy once the game plan has been carefully laid out and mutually agreed upon. If you neglect to build a game plan with their help, you will not keep good sales people long. Chapters 15 and 16 review how small business owners can get the most out of their employees. Many of the observations made in those chapters apply to sales people.

Selecting Middlemen to Sell for You

What are the differences between the middlemen available to you? How can you determine which will be best for you? Exhibit 12.4 lists the two major types of middlemen and describes how each can help you. Each has strong and weak points as far as you are concerned. These are also noted in Exhibit 12.4. The specific services provided by a middleman of either type vary widely. Also, the image of middlemen ranges from luxury to cut-rate. We recommend, therefore, that you discuss services provided and consider the match between your image and the middleman's image carefully before making a commitment. Even if you have little choice about which middleman to use in a given market area, a middleman may be willing to offer you a surprising number of services if you ask for them. Keep in mind that the selection process works both ways. The middlemen are selecting you every bit as much as you are selecting them.

How do you find the middlemen you need in the first place? The answer is to work backward from the ultimate consumer or industrial user in each market area. Where is your type of product purchased? Where does the retailer buy this type of product? Which middlemen do the retailers consider reliable and trustworthy? The key thing to remember is that the means of distribution you choose must provide the information, convenience, variety, and service desired by your target customers.

Exhibit 12.4   Types of Middlemen[8]

	I. MERCHANT WHOLESALERS	II. AGENTS AND BROKERS
Type	Common names: Service Limited service General merchandise Specialty Cash-and-carry Drop shipper Truck Mail order Rack jobber	Common names: "Reps" Auction companies Brokers Commission merchants Manufacturers' agents Manufacturers' representatives Food brokers Selling agents
Description	These middlemen take title to the goods they handle. They may provide a full service to the consumer by carrying stocks, delivering goods, granting credit, and giving advice, or they may provide limited service. They may carry a broad line of merchandise or specialize in a narrow range of products.	These middlemen do not take title to the goods they handle. They sell for a commission. Typically, they specialize by customer type and by product or product line. Their services to customers are limited in most cases to product information and advice concerning reliable sources of supply.
What They Will and Will Not Do For You	1. They know their markets and are in a good position to tell you whether or not your product will do well. 2. They may buy from you and put your product in their inventory, thereby reducing your need for working capital. 3. They carry inventories of your merchandise, thus reducing your storage costs. 4. They sell for you, offering your products to many customers it would be costly for you to reach. 5. They provide the credit to final consumers. If someone doesn't pay, it's their problem, not yours.	1. They know their markets and are in a good position to tell you whether or not your product will do well. 2. They will sell for you; and since reps tend to be experienced, highly motivated sales people, they may sell for you better than you could for yourself. 3. They may save you substantial selling costs and improve your cash flow since, unlike your own sales people, they pay their own expenses and are not paid by you until you are paid by the customer. 4. Unlike your sales people, an established rep will not quit after you have spent considerable time and money to train them.

I. MERCHANT WHOLESALERS	II. AGENTS AND BROKERS
However,	*However,*
1. Typically they carry many products and will not take the time to push yours too hard. You have little or no control over how they sell your product.	1. Typically reps are very independent and will handle the selling of your products their way. This means you lose a degree of control over how your products are sold. It also means that you may have to deal with a different set of administrative procedures for each rep used.
2. Because of the risks involved, they may not take your unproven product.	2. Reps typically represent several firms. You cannot expect to have the rep's full attention.
3. You will still need sales people to sell to the wholesalers.	

When working backward from the ultimate consumer, trade publication ads and directories may also lead you to the middleman you want. For example, manufacturers' agents may be found by consulting:

Manufacturers' Agents National Association (MANA)
2021 Business Center Drive
P.O. Box 16878
Irvine, CA 92713
(714) 752–5231

Manufacturers' Agent Publishing Company, Inc.
663 Fifth Avenue
New York, N.Y. 10022
(212) 682–0326

The selection of a middleman should be culminated with a written contract specifying boundaries of sales territories, commissions, terms of payment, and the duties of each party to the contract. If you are a retailer, your exclusive rights to sell certain product lines is an important consideration. Organizations like MANA will supply sample contracts for a small fee. All such contracts should be reviewed by your legal counsel.

Use of middlemen does not relieve you of certain key sales management responsibilities. Even though middlemen are experienced salespersons, they need to be shown how to brand your product in the eyes of the buyer. Someone in your organization must provide this training and back up the middlemen with expert product advice when needed. You should make every attempt to support the sales effort of the middlemen by providing requested promotional materials promptly and by expediting orders. If you do this, you will sell more because your product will become branded both in the eyes of the ultimate consumer and in the eyes of the middleman. Your product will become branded to the middleman because you do everything you can to increase the middleman's profitability by making their sales job easier.

When considering how to control sales efforts by middlemen, remember they are professionals. Goals and progress yardsticks set mutually by you and the middlemen will work best. If they are able to work out a sales plan with you and see that you listen and respond to their advice, they will work harder for you. If they know they can rely on you for sales support and prompt service to customers, they will work harder for you. If you treat them like servants or embarrass them by not delivering as promised, they will desert you. Treat them well. Let your competitors make the mistake of treating them badly.

CASE
SOLUTION

*Mary's
Gardens*

Mary Kempton decided that she needed outside help to solve her selling problem. She hired a consultant to help her analyze why her sales performance was lagging. She wanted to know if anything could be done to improve sales at her present location. If not, she wanted to move.

The consultant began by developing a list of competitors in the area. Each was visited and analyzed concerning store location, layout, and selling techniques.

Next, the consultant solicited the opinions of Mary's suppliers concerning her location and product line. Particular attention was paid to products that seemed to sell well in the area but moved more slowly in Mary's store.

The suppliers were also asked to name outstanding gardening retailers in the region and to explain why they considered them outstanding. These outstanding retailers were visited and their sales practices analyzed.

Sales practices at Mary's Gardens were then observed and compared with the practices of these outstanding retailers.

Once this comparison had been made, the techniques described in Appendixes B and C to chapter 10 were employed to select a sample of Mary's customers. This sample was interviewed concerning their likes and dislikes. An effort was made to interview, at selected times, a sampling of both those who left the store with purchases and those who did not buy anything. Specific competitors were mentioned in the survey, and respondents were asked to rate Mary's Gardens relative to the competition. Similar samples were drawn from customers leaving competitors' stores when permission was granted to do so.

The above research uncovered much useful information. For example, it was discovered that Mary tended to understock certain plant materials and chemical additives and to overstock others. Suppliers pinpointed which products were selling well in other local stores. Also, both customers who made puchases and those who did not complained that Mary's salesclerks lacked gardening knowledge. Although the young people working for Mary were friendly and courteous, they could give little guidance to customers. Mary was an expert, but she had to spend most of her time managing the company.

The research also showed that Mary had little choice among suppliers for name brands but that the suppliers would provide private label merchandise e.g., Mary's Plant Food. They also were willing to provide expert advice on displays and promotions and to help Mary take advantage of cooperative advertising opportunities offered by their manufacturers.

Finally, it was found that no new competitors had opened in Mary's market area in the last few years and that all of the gardening retailers in her area operated in about the same fashion as Mary's Gardens from similar locations. However, marked differences were noted at two of the outstanding nursery retailers mentioned by suppliers located in similar cities outside Mary's market area. These retailers stressed expert service in their selling approach.

Drawing on what had been discovered, Mary revised her selling strategy. Recognizing now that many of her customers had very limited gardening knowledge and sought expert help, she began a service program for customers. The two major aspects of this program are an information booth and gardening classes. The information booth is in the center of the nursery and is identified with a big sign reading, "Plant Doctor." The person selected to staff the booth is very knowledgeable about horticulture. This individual diagnoses customers' plant problems and prescribes soil conditioners, fertilizers, insecticides, and the like to solve them. The booth is well stocked with samples of what is needed. The Mary's Gardens brand name items are prominently displayed in the booth and prescribed when appropriate. For larger quantities, a prescription form is filled out, and a salesclerk is called to fill the order for the customer.

The nursery's plant doctor also teaches gardening classes in a small open area next to the booth. The classes draw well, and many customers walking through the store stop to listen as the plant doctor explains how to use the products the nursery sells to make plants happy and healthy. The nursery's private label merchandise is prominently displayed at each lesson, and lessons often feature daily specials.

Mary is also experimenting with display areas to show finished landscaping. This allows customers to shop for a look without having to know the names of the plants used in the display. Mary believes the carefully maintained landscape displays have been a real boost for her landscaping service. People like what they see and want their yard landscaped by an expert.

Another concept Mary is trying is living flower arrangements. Plants are arranged in clay pots with properly conditioned soil, and the pots and arrangements are sold as colorful, instant mini-gardens for gift givers and people who don't want to get their hands dirty. The arrangements are sold complete with a humorous, but thorough, set of instructions about how to care for the plants.

Mary's sales have increased markedly during the past year, even though her markups are higher than some of her competitors. As Mary puts it, "I receive top dollar for my merchandise. My private label items and the living flower arrangements are particularly profitable. My unit sales are up, but my profits are up even more."

Mary's Gardens is doing well because the nursery is actually selling a system of products and services that does an admirable job of meeting its customers' gardening needs. Mary's approach is by no means original or unique. Most of her selling strategy was suggested by suppliers or borrowed from the pioneering work of other outstanding nurseries. However, her approach does uniquely meet the needs of the customers in her target market, and they are willing to pay for the exceptional value Mary's selling efforts have created. Mary's Gardens has become a branded selling system.

CHAPTER SUMMARY

This chapter has explored four central questions about your product or service: where to sell it, how to sell it, when to sell it, and who should sell it. In theory these questions have simple answers. In practice the answers become complicated.

The answer to the question of where to sell is to sell where your customers shop. However, determining where your customers shop may be no simple task. They may shop by reading ads, watching TV, reading directory listings, calling various companies on the telephone, or visiting your business. They may expect you to visit them to sell your product.

The answer to the question of how to sell your goods and services can be found in the adoption of effective personal selling techniques. The basic skills involved are discussed as well as strategies for making your salespersons a valuable part of your product. The special requirements for selling on the telephone are then discussed.

The answer to the question of when to sell also seems simple. All you have to do is to sell when your customers want to buy. However, deciding what time of year, what time of day, and what time in their lives this is may be difficult. Each product or service has its moment—a point in time when buyers are particularly receptive. Several of these moments are described in this chapter.

Finally, the question of who should sell your product or service must be answered. The choices include yourself, your employees, or middlemen. What you need in a salesperson depends on the nature of the sales job. The skills required for different kinds of sales jobs were discussed. The objectives and advantages of sales training programs were also reviewed, as well as how to manage the sales effort effectively.

Finally, selecting middlemen to sell for you is discussed. The two major types of middlemen, merchant wholesalers and agents and brokers, are defined as well as what they will or will not do for you.

DISCUSSION QUESTIONS

1. **Short Case: The Kloset Kleaners**

   The Kloset Kleaners was founded a few years ago by Ted Andrews. Ted was a carpenter by trade. He had noticed that many people needed extra storage space in their houses and also had messy closets that held far less than they could because they were unorganized. Ted could design a shelf/rack system for the typical closet that doubled or tripled usable storage space and also made items stored more visible and easier to find. Ted founded Kloset Kleaners as a company specializing in the design and construction of closet organizing systems. So far, he has been selling his product/service by running ads in the local throwaway paper. When calls come in, he goes to the caller's house and explains what his company does. Although sales have been fair, Ted is wondering if there is a better way to sell his product.

   a. Based on what you have read in this chapter, where should Ted sell, how should he sell, when should he sell, and who should sell his product/service?

   b. Based on the discussion of advertising media in the last chapter, what do you think about Ted's advertising choice?

2. Ray Carter, who lives in Oregon, has invented a fluid that can be used to white out errors on photocopies without smudging the print. His fluid costs less, covers better, and lasts longer by volume than the nearest competition. Ray knows that his competitor's product is sold to offices all over the country and believes there is also a national market for his product. How can he get his product to market? Where should it be sold, and who should sell it? Be sure to discuss the economic and control implications of your answer.

3. We have noted in this chapter that each product or service has its moment, when buyers are most receptive to it. What do you think are the best moments for the following products/services?

   a. Life insurance
   b. Car insurance
   c. Medical office equipment
   d. Diamonds
   e. House and/or carpet cleaning.

4. Given the moments you selected for the five products/services listed in Question 3, how would you find out when these moments occurred or will occur for the target customers? Explain for each.

5. As noted in this chapter, Mark Hanon has suggested five strategies for making your sales people a valued part of the product or service you offer. Describe how these strategies could be employed to sell the following:
   a. Men's clothing
   b. Art
   c. Auto parts

REFERENCES

Gorman, Walter. *Selling: Personality, Persuasion, Strategy*. New York: Random House, 1979.

Lawyer, Kenneth. *Training Salesmen to Serve Industrial Markets*. Small Business Management Series No. 36. Washington, D.C.: U.S. Small Business Administration, 1975.

Pederson, Carlton A., and Wright, Milburn D. *Selling: Principles and Methods*, 6th ed. Homewood, Ill.: Richard D. Irwin, Inc., 1976.

Rosenbloom, Bert. *Improving Personal Selling*. Small Marketer's Aid No. 159. Washington D.C.: U.S. Small Business Administration, 1976.

Russell, Frederic A., and Beach, Frank H. *Textbook of Salesmanship*, 10th ed. New York: McGraw Hill Book Co., 1978.

Stanton, William J., and Buskirk, Richard H. *Management of the Salesforce*, 4th ed. Homewood, Ill.: Richard D. Irwin, Inc., 1974.

FOOTNOTES

1. This case was prepared by one of the authors based upon information collected during a small-business consulting project. In order to maintain client confidentiality, the facts given here are somewhat different from the actual case.

2. Bert Rosenbloom, *Improving Personal Selling*, Small Marketers Aid No. 159 (Washington, D.C.: U.S. Small Business Administration, 1976), pp. 2–3.

3. This list is adapted from Mark Hanon, *Fast Growth Management: How to Improve Profits with Entrepreneurial Strategies* (New York: AMACOM, a division of American Management Associations, 1979), pp. 97–98.

4. Adapted from James A. Belasco, "The Salesman's Role Revisited," *Journal of Marketing*, 30: 3 (April 1966): 6–11.

5. William J. Stanton and Richard H. Buskirk, *Management of the Salesforce*, (Homewood, Ill.: Richard D. Irwin, Inc., 1974), p. 141. This classification system, as noted by Stanton and Buskirk, was adapted from Robert N. McMurray, "The Mystique of Super-Salesmanship," *Harvard Business Review* (March-April 1971): 114. Reprinted by permission of the *Harvard Business Review.*

6. See chapter 16, "Keeping Good Employees," for more details.

7. Eleanor Brantley Schwartz, "Motivating Superior Outside Sales Personnel," *Journal of Small Business Management* 16, no. 1 (January 1978): 19–26.

8. Adapted from E. Jerome McCarthy, *Basic Marketing: A Managerial Approach*. 6th ed. (Homewood, Ill.: Richard D. Irwin, Inc., 1978), pp. 357–371; and Robert H. Collins, "Manufacturers' Representatives for Small Firms," *Journal of Small Business Management* 16, no. 1 (January 1978): 13–18.

Appendix A

HOW TO FIND A GOOD LOCATION FOR YOUR BUSINESS

No matter what kind of small business you operate, selecting the right business location is important.[1] If you are a retailer, choosing your location may be the most important decision you make.

How good a location is, is determined by its profitability. The best location is the one that promises to be most profitable. There are two sides to profits: costs and revenues. Small business owners often give too much attention to costs at the expense of revenues. Costs include lease payments, energy costs, transportation costs, local labor costs, local taxes, etc. Many cost factors vary considerably from neighborhood to neighborhood. Lease rates for retail space in particular can vary markedly from storefront to storefront within the same small neighborhood.

The temptation for the business owner opening a new retail location on a limited budget is to rent the cheapest space available in a target market area. "After all," the argument goes, "since I have what my target customers want, they will be willing to go a little out of their way to find me." While this may be true for certain types of wholesale-open-to-the-public retailers, it is generally not true. Choice of an inexpensive location may be false economy. High lease rents often indicate a proven heavy flow of consumer traffic. The lifeblood of any retail business is consumer traffic. This traffic generates sales revenues. Sales revenues pay for your costs and provide your profits. A poor location can bring even the most competent small business retailer to grief since it simply will not generate enough sales revenue to be profitable. A good location may save your neck since the high volume of customer traffic will continue to generate sales even if you make some serious mistakes while you learn your business. Not any kind of consumer traffic will do, however. The following steps offer specific suggestions for evaluating a retail store location.[2]

Step 1—Describe your target customers. What are their needs? Where do they live? Where do they work? Where do they play? How much do they earn? The strategy described in chapter 10 should help you with the demographic profile of your target customers.

Step 2—Based on what you know about your customers describe a perfect location for your business. This is a mythical place you can use as a yardstick to see how the actual locations available measure up.

Step 3—Select a market area likely to contain a large number of your target customers. The potential for heavy customer traffic is based on a market area that contains a large number of people with demographic characteristics similar to your target customers. While not all of these people will buy from you, the more there are, the more likely some will become your customers. You are looking for things like:
  a. The number of households in your market area
  b. The median income of these households
  c. The proportion of the typical household's annual income spent on the types of goods and services you plan to sell

You can obtain most, if not all, of this information from secondary sources such as those described in Appendix A to chapter 10.

Step 4—Analyze the competition. How many competitors are there? Where are they located? Sources such as those described in Appendix A to chapter 10 will help you in this analysis. The data available will give you not only an idea of how many competitors you have but also an estimate of their sales volume and sales per merchandise line.

Step 5—Calculate your sales potential in the market area. Using the information you have collected in Steps 1 through 3, you can estimate how much of your kind of product can be sold in this market area: (number of households) × (median income) × (proportion of income spent on your kind of product). From this you can subtract the sales of your competition. This leaves an estimate of the sales left for you. If you think you can draw customers away from existing competitors, take this into account in calculating your sales potential. Remember, however, old habits die hard. If you are planning to enter a market with established competitors who appear to have absorbed all the sales potential in the area, be very conservative in your estimate of your ability to lure customers away from them. Also, if you plan to open a store in a new area, remember that today's sales potential can be seriously eroded as new competitors open stores in your area. Check with your local planning agency to see where your type of store would be permitted. Check with the landowners to see if potential competitors have preleased retail space yet to be constructed. Many new planned communities limit the amount of retail development. This fact, plus a restrictive covenant in your store lease prohibiting the landlord from leasing other space in your shopping center to competitive businesses, can virtually assure you a good sales potential. Keep this in mind.

Step 6—Select a site for your store. Once you determine a market area has good sales potential, the next question is whether or not there is a specific site in the market area that will permit this sales potential to be realized. Site selection and market potential calculations are of course interdependent. If a particularly good site remains in the target area, opening your store on this site may permit you to attract many of your competitors' customers. This will allow you to increase your sales potential estimate. On the other hand, if all the good sites have been taken by your competitors, revise your sales potential estimate downward. Your competitors have a major advantage that is not easily overcome. Questions to consider when analyzing a particular site include:

1. Will people in this market area be willing to buy your type of product at this site?

2. Is this site accessible to the people in the market area? Can it be easily seen and gotten to from the street, especially at the time of day when your customers are likely to buy? Is it easy to find? Is there sufficient parking? Is this store conveniently located next to other stores often used by your customers, such as a grocery store or the only shoe repair shop in town? Does this site allow you to cater to passers-by who might drop in due to your convenience?

3. Does the site have a future, or does it have a history of failure?

4. Does the customer have to pass by this site to get to other stores selling similar products? Can you intercept these potential customers with signs and displays? It is no accident that most of the major entrances to regional shopping malls are also doorways to department stores. Will people buy there before they come to your store in the mall and never see what you have to offer?

5. Does the site offer one-stop shopping by clustering a number of competitive and complementary stores together in one area? Automobile dealers and car leasing companies can often be found grouped together since a large number of serious car buyers are likely to come to an area that permits ready comparison between makes and models.

Step 7—Calculate the site's profitability. Given the costs of operating the store at this site, such as lease payments, utilities, common area maintenance expense, etc., and given your sales potential, what are your estimated net profits before taxes?

Step 8—Compare the profitability of several alternative sites, and choose the one that appears to yield the most. When you do this consider both today and tomorrow, but do not give up too much profit in either to obtain good profits in the other. Also weigh risks. A site with a large, but risky, profit potential may be less (or more) desirable to you than a site with a smaller, but more certain, profit future.

Step 9—Take a closer look at the lease. What are the terms? Is the lease net or gross? A gross lease means you just pay your monthly rental, and the landlord provides everything—building maintenance, utilities, etc. A net lease means you pay for some things in addition to the space you rent, such as utilities, a proportionate share of the property taxes on the building, or a share of the cost of maintenance of the common area. What appears to be an attractive rental rate for your store can easily be more than doubled by these extra costs. Another lease term to pay attention to is the cost-of-living clause. This type of clause adjusts your monthly rent (usually upward) based on changes in the cost of living. Certain landlords will pay all or part of the expense of making your store ready for you. Others will provide only four bare walls. What are you going to get? If prestige is important to you and you will be sharing the building with other tenants, what assurances do you have that the building will be maintained? Is there a clause in your lease that prevents the landlord from leasing the space next door to yours to another company that will compete with you? These questions should make it clear that you need to study any lease carefully before signing it. A lease is a long-term commitment. Read it word for word. Then take it to an attorney, and have the attorney explain each clause to you. Leases are negotiable—once you figure out what changes you need to negotiate.

APPENDIX FOOTNOTES

1. Although the following discussion focuses on the location of a retail business, other small businesses must also consider location carefully. Location guidelines useful to you if you are a small manufacturer or wholesaler may be found in Fred I. Weber, *Locating or Relocating Your Business*, Management Aid No. 201. (Washington, D.C.: U.S. Small Business Administration, May 1979 reprint).

2. These steps are a composite of those suggested for evaluating retail locations. We found the following sources particularly helpful: Roger A. Kerin and Michael Harvey, "Evaluation of Retail Store Locations Through Profitability Analysis," *Journal of Small Business Management* 13, #1 (January 1975): 41–45; Richard L. Nelson, "Principles of Retail Location," in *Management Perspectives in Retailing*, 2nd ed., ed. Ronald R. Gist (New York: John Wiley and Sons, Inc., 1971), pp. 204–208. Lyn Taetzsch, *Opening Your Own Retail Store* (Chicago: Contemporary Books, Inc., 1977), chapter 2; Ross McKeever, *Factors in Considering a Shopping Center Location*, Small Marketer's Aid No. 143 (Washington D.C.: U.S. Small Business Administration, 1970; James R. Lowry, *Using a Traffic Study to Select a Retail Site* Small Marketer's Aid No. 152 (Washington D.C.: U.S. Small Business Administration, 1979).

Pricing 13

☐ **Is your price too high, or is it too low?**

☐ **How do you tell?**

☐ **Will loss leaders increase your profits?**

*Minnetonka,
Inc.*[1]

In 1964 Robert R. Taylor founded Minnetonka, Inc. with $3,000. He was twenty-six. Taylor was a bath products manufacturers' representative in the Midwest when he came up with the initial product for his company, brightly colored, hand-rolled soap balls. Taylor had noticed that his gift shop clients liked unusual, attractively packaged gifts. Some fancy European soaps filled this bill, but gift shops had a hard time getting a reliable source of supply. There were no domestic manufacturers. He surmised that consumers would like soap balls that were color coordinated to match bath towels. Sure enough, Minnetonka sold $38,000 worth of soap balls to gift shops in Minneapolis the first year, using the Village Bath Products brand name. His initial success allowed Taylor to enlist a team of manufacturer's reps to sell to department stores for their bath sections.

By 1968 Minnetonka was selling to all major department stores in every state. It had added several products to the Village Bath Products line, such as bath oils, body lotions, fruit shampoos, and fancy bar soaps. The company now offered 125 innovative products in bright, eye-catching packages and had sales of $650,000. As Taylor noted, "The only way to survive in the gift business is to come up with new, creative concepts and devise exciting packaging."

Taylor took the company public in 1968 and set his sights for really big revenues. Initially, company sales benefited from Taylor's expanded distribution—increasing to $5.7 million in 1971 and to almost $9 million in 1972.

By the end of 1972, however, it was clear something was very wrong. Even though sales were up for the year—due in part to the acquisition of Claire Burke, Inc., a maker of toiletries and scented sachets—net income leveled off in 1972 and turned to a loss in the first quarter of 1973. Taylor had predicted $20 million in sales and a good profit for Minnetonka in 1973. Instead, the loss grew to $1.1 million dollars for 1973, and sales turned out to be only $9.3 million for the year.

To be sure, rapid growth and entry into many unrelated markets were real problems for Minnetonka. They are for many small companies that experience early success and grow rapidly.

Taylor recognized these problems and took corrective action. Sophisticated physical and financial control systems were implemented to allow him to keep track of his products and their costs. He cut costs wherever he could and dropped unprofitable products. Still, sales fell in 1974 to $8 million. The company's loss increased to $1.6 million. By 1975 losses totaled $3.2 million. Obviously, more was needed than just cost cutting and good physical and financial control procedures. The question was, what?

Profitable pricing requires a good understanding of both your customers and your costs. When Taylor founded Minnetonka, he understood his customers and costs quite well for the line of soap he introduced. His product/service system of brightly colored, hand-rolled soap balls attractively packaged and color coordinated to match bath towels turned ordinary soap into a brand for Minnetonka. It uniquely met the gift shop owner's need for an attractive, high markup soap product to sell and the consumer's need for a product that was both a hand cleanser and a bath accessory. This uniqueness made the product more valuable to Minnetonka's customers. As a result, Minnetonka received top dollar for its soap, and its sales grew. As a matter of fact, Taylor was able to charge extremely profitable prices during this period.

PROBLEM IDENTIFICATION

It was when Taylor lost his clear understanding of his customers that he lost his ability to price profitably. His lack of close attention to the market caused him to lose sales to the competition. As Taylor put it, referring to the declining sales of Village Bath Products in 1973, "Our lead in continually introducing new products and new fashion trends was slipping away. We were no longer unique."

How good are you at pricing? Do you have a way to find out if your prices are too high or too low? Do you take full advantage of your opportunity as a small businessperson to get top dollar for your products or services by branding them? Are you missing out on profits unnecessarily by charging the wrong price?

DIAGNOSIS

Exhibit 13.1 is a list of questions that will help you to diagnose your pricing strategy. Before reading further, answer the questions in this exhibit. We also suggest you write down how you determine the price for two of your products. Pick one that appears to sell well and one that does not. Do you set the price for each in the same way?

Check the answer key for the questions in Exhibit 13.1. How well did you do? If your answer differs from ours on Question 3, 6, 7, 8, 10, or 11, you may be letting some extra profits slip away that you could capture by making minor adjustments in the way you price. If your answer differs from ours on Question 1, 2, 4, 5, 9, or 12, you should be particularly concerned. These questions deal with major pricing pitfalls that can not only erode your profitability but also turn profits into losses. The next section should make it clear why we answered each of the twelve questions in Exhibit 13.1 as we did.

Exhibit 13.1   Price Strategy Analyzer

Instructions: Describe each of the following statements as either true or false. Answer "true" if you believe the statement says something that should guide your pricing strategy. Answer "false" if you feel the statement gives pricing advice that is misleading or incorrect.

1. If you can increase your sales volume by reducing price, profits will soar.

2. A small business can be assured of long-term success by producing efficiently and charging markedly less for its products than its big competitors charge for theirs.

3. Each product or service you sell must stand on its own. Each must make a good profit.

4. If a customer perceives all products as about the same in terms of quality, availability, convenience, etc., then the customer will focus on price and buy the cheapest.

5. Your costs should determine your price.

6. It rarely pays to increase your price since you lose customers by doing so.

7. If you experiment with a price increase and lose customers, you can't always get them back by reducing your prices to previous levels.

8. If you have a product that meets the needs of a certain type of customer very nicely but is not very useful to anyone else and sales of the product have stopped growing, you stand to gain little by cutting its price.

9. If you can brand your products in the eyes of your customers, you will be able to increase both your prices and your unit sales.

10. If you can brand your products in the eyes of your customers, you may not increase your unit sales unless you increase your price.

11. All of your customers for a given product are pretty much the same in terms of the nature of their need for the product.

12. The prices you charge need be a serious concern only if you are losing money.

Answer Key

1.	False	5.	False	9.	True
2.	False	6.	False	10.	True
3.	False	7.	True	11.	False
4.	True	8.	True	12.	False

UNDER-STANDING

The Goal of Pricing

All of your efforts to find buyers for your product, to advertise, and to sell must lead to profits for your business to succeed. Sales are not enough. You must also profit from your sales. Profits are needed to finance the growth of your company and put food on the table. The prices you set for your products or services will determine your profitability.

The Role of Customers in Pricing

A properly branded small business can demand and get top dollar for its products. Once your customers accept your product/service system as one that uniquely meets their needs, they will perceive that it has extra value and be willing to pay more for it. In short, when you give more, you can get more.

Remember, though, it is the customer who determines whether or not what you are giving is really more or not. The customer also determines when your price is too high. Prices, then, must be set high enough to cover your costs and provide a reasonable profit but low enough to insure enough sales to turn markups into company profits.

The Role of Costs in Pricing

Your costs set a floor for the prices you can charge. How high above this floor should your prices be? Are your prices too high or too low? How do you tell? One way to understand what is involved in answering these questions is to consider what economists have said about pricing.

What Economists Have Said About Pricing

Traditionally, economists have described two basic competitive situations: (1) Customers perceive all products or services similar to yours to be about the same as yours. In other words, no competitor has done a good job of branding its products. (2) Customers perceive significant value differences among the products or services available from various competitors. In other words, at least one competitor has done a good job of branding its products.[2]

The former situation can be very detrimental to you. If the customer perceives all products as about the same in terms of quality, availability, convenience, etc., then the customer will focus on price and buy the cheapest. The only way you can compete in this situation is to sell for less. This is fine as long as you are markedly more efficient than your competitors. If it costs you less to provide your product or service, what are costs for your competitors are profits for you. You can charge a price that would barely allow your competitors to break even, make a lot of sales, and build up big profits.

Unfortunately, as noted in chapter 9, a small business usually ends up as the profit loser rather than the profit gainer in this type of situation. Usually it is the large business that has the efficiency advantage due to mass production, better service from suppliers, and better credit terms. You will be the one barely breaking even while the larger competitor makes a reasonable profit at the prevailing market price.

"But wait a minute," you say. "My Uncle Harry runs a small discount appliance store, and he is doing very well. He works out of an old storefront and makes a good living on a much lower markup than is charged by the big department stores." This may very well be true, but Harry's situation is an example of the second type of competitive situation rather than the first. Harry is focusing on selling to the relatively small number of people in his area who want name brand products cheap and are willing to forgo all the frills to get a good price. If you know what you want and don't need or care about credit, a big assortment, or follow-up service, you go to Harry. Economy-minded customers perceive that Harry is offering a significantly different product system that uniquely meets their needs. Harry has created a brand for himself and can charge extra for it. Although Harry's prices are lower than those in the department store, they are still higher than they have to be to keep Harry in business. They are extremely profitable because Harry has low overhead and a good sales volume.

It is worthwhile to take a closer look at the above appliance store example. As long as the big department stores do not consider the economy-minded market big enough to warrant their attention, Harry really has no competition in his market. To a certain degree, he has what economists call a "monopoly." If the big stores decide to compete by opening discount outlets of their own, they will be able to use their buying power to beat Harry's prices, thus wiping out his monopoly and profits. The result is the first type of competitive situation described above, which economists call "pure competition." Until that time, Harry's low prices—which are actually premium prices, given the cost of the product/service system he supplies—will continue to earn him good profits. Monopoly pays. Pure competition doesn't. In other words, according to the economists, you really have little choice as a small business. Either you brand your company in some manner, thereby becoming a monopolist, or you go out of business.

Practical Pricing Advice

Economists also have some suggestions about pricing once you have branded your company. They urge you to remember that as you increase your price, you will generally lose some of your buyers. Some will no longer buy your product/service system because it is too expensive. Of these dropouts, a few will simply not buy anything at all like your product. They will wait to see if your price goes down in the future. Most dropouts, however, will probably switch to other product/service systems to meet their needs. Now that your price is so high, these other product/service systems become more desirable. On the other hand, as you lower your price, you will probably pick up some new business. Some of these new customers will be new to the marketplace, but most will have switched from other product/service systems that have lost their attraction.

The better you have done the job of branding your company, economists argue, the higher you will be able to raise your prices relative to the competition without losing a significant number of customers. The weaker your brand, the more sensitive your customers will be to even slight price increases. Similarly, you stand to gain little by cutting prices if you have a strong brand; but if you and your competitors have weak brands, you might gain a lot by cutting your prices slightly, provided your competitors do not respond with their own price cuts.

Economists suggest that you can often charge a lot more for your product and increase the number of buyers for it by strengthening your brand position. This is done by making your new, higher price seem like a bargain due to improvement in the product/service system you provide your customers. If, in your customers' eyes, you radically improve your system's unique ability to meet their needs, you strengthen your brand. A radical jump in price may actually attract customers as long as the perceived value of the improvement in meeting customer needs exceeds the increase in price. The whole nature of customer demand for your product/service system shifts in your favor. In fact, you may hurt yourself if you do not increase price. The consumer may wonder how you can provide higher value at so low a price and assume that your new offer is overstated. "At that price," the consumer may reason, "there is no way this company can provide the service I need"; or, "they are selling this product so cheap, there must be something wrong with it."

Economists also point out that the strength of your brand varies greatly from product to product in your product line. They argue that strengthening your brand position for certain products with relatively high branding potential can be successfully accomplished by selling products that cannot so easily be branded at a loss. By manipulating prices of the products for which you have little brand leverage, you reinforce your brand for related items. Some examples can clarify how this is done:

1. A grocery store offers two or three really terrific specials each week. The store actually sells the specials for prices below their cost. Still, the store comes out ahead. Why? Because the people who buy the specials also buy the rest of their week's groceries at the store, and the other items the people buy are priced to be very profitable.

2. A toy manufacturer sells its basic train set for a price very near cost. However, the accessories available to expand the train set into a model railroad, such as extra track, extra railroad cars, and scenery designed to scale, all carry a healthy markup.

3. A computer firm sells its laser print for a very reasonable price, but the printer is designed to work only as part of a word-processing system designed by the company. The markup on the rest of the equipment is significant. The markup is also significant on the print-out paper used by the computer system.

In each of the examples, the business offers the price-minded consumer a good deal for the basic item. The sale of this item then opens the way for future sales of related items at a less advantageous price for the consumer. The basic item is known as a loss leader. It usually is a relatively durable item that is well known to the consumer and for which he or she has a good idea of value. The consumer therefore recognizes the deal right away. The follow-up items are usually nondurable, small-ticket items. They are used up quickly, ideally to make something with the basic item.

Of the three examples of loss leaders given above, the grocery store example is the toughest to make work because the individual who buys strawberries, for example, on sale will not necessarily buy anything else in the store. There are ways around this problem, however. For example, how many buyers could resist boxes of shortcake displayed next to the strawberries? Of the examples above, the laser printer example offers the most promise because the printer will not work without the related items.

A General Theory for Setting Prices

Economists have developed a general theory of pricing, which will add to your understanding of pricing. Briefly stated, this theory proposes that both sales potential and costs must be considered in order to determine the best price. According to the economists, the best way to compare these two factors is to estimate the impact of a price change on each.

Exhibit 13.2 gives an example. Say your selling price for the pocket calendars you manufacture is $1.95 per unit. You now sell 5,000 units per week, which pays the rent and production costs and leaves you with a profit of $.50 per calendar, or $2,500.00 per week. Not bad! However, you are operating at only two-thirds of capacity; so much of the time your equipment is idle. If you could operate at full capacity, your extra cost to make the extra 2,500 calendars would be only the cost of materials and labor, or about $.40 per extra calendar. Would it pay you to lower your price to $1.45 per calendar, which is equal to your present average unit cost, if it appeared you could easily sell 7,500 per week at that price? To answer this pricing question, economists suggest you compare your extra costs with your extra revenues. If the extra money you bring in exceeds your extra costs to get that revenue, you will come out ahead.

In the step-by-step analysis of the proposed price cut to $1.45 shown in Exhibit 13.2, it turns out that if you cut your price to $1.45, you will make an extra $125 per week. Not too bad, but maybe not good enough if there is a significant risk that the extra sales will not materialize at the lower price.

The reason the above example works out to a profit is that the business has a lot of money tied up in its building and equipment that is currently not working as hard as it could. The rent and the payments on the equipment have to be paid whether or not the extra sales are made. Thus the extra cost for the extra sales is only $.40 × 2,500 = $1,000, not $1.45 × 2,500 = $3,650. Although the average cost per unit at 5,000 units is $1.45, the extra cost per unit for the extra 2,500 units drops radically to $.40 per unit. The average cost per unit is of course also reduced. In this case the average cost per unit drops to: $\dfrac{(\$1.45 \times 5,000) + (\$.40 \times 2,500)}{5,000 + 2,500} = \dfrac{\$8,250}{7,500} = \$1.10,$

Exhibit 13.2   Pricing Example—Pocket Calendar

The Present

Present selling price	$1.95
× Present sales in units per week	× 5,000 calendars
= Dollar sales per week	$9,750.
− Rent, Production Costs, etc., per week	− 7,250. ($1.45 per calendar)
Profit	$2,500. ($.50 per calendar)

What We Know

1. 5,000 calendars represents two thirds of our weekly production capacity. Capacity must therefore be $\frac{5000}{2/3}$ = 7,500 calendars per week, or 2,500 per week more than we are making now.

2. The extra cost of making calendar 5,001 is only the cost of extra labor and materials since we are already paying for the rent and production equipment. In this case, the extra cost of labor and materials per calendar if we increase production is $.40.

3. If you lower your price to $1.45, you could easily sell all the calendars you can make (i.e., 7,500 per week).

Analysis of a Proposed Price Cut to $1.45

Calculating Extra Revenues
Your sales now are $1.95 × 5,000 = $9,750.
If you cut your price, you expect your sales to be $1.45 × 7,500 = $10,875.
Your *extra revenues* will be $1,125 ($10,875 − 9,750).

Calculating Extra Costs
Your extra costs to produce the 2,500 additional calendars will be $.40 × 2,500 = $1,000.
extra revenues minus extra costs yields
1,125 − 1,000 = $125. *Extra Profits.*

---

where ($1.45 × 5,000) is the cost for the first 5,000 units and ($.40 × 2,500) is the extra cost for the additional 2,500 units. Spreading these costs over all 7,500 units gives less the average cost per unit of $1.10. Also, the profit per unit is less:

Present Situation: $1.95 Price − $1.45 Cost = 50¢ Profit per unit
After Price Cut to $1.45: $1.45 Price − $1.10 Cost = 35¢ Profit per unit

However, overall profit is greater, as comparison of your extra costs with your extra revenues will tell you.

Comparison of extra costs with extra revenues is useful whether you are calculating the impact of a price increase or a price decrease. One thing to remember, however, is that you need to consider the impact on your total product line. Thus a loss leader will look bad if you just calculate the extra revenues versus the extra costs for the loss leader alone. If you add in extra revenues and extra costs, if any, generated from sales of other related products resulting from the drawing power of the loss leader, the picture should look much better.

Four Pricing Rules

You now should understand the critical elements of pricing strategy. Our pricing advice and the advice of economists can be summarized with four pricing rules:

1. Seek markets where you can create a brand for your company. You will be able to charge a higher price for your product relative to its costs if your customers see your product as being worth more to them because of its unique ability to meet their needs.

2. Design product/service systems that have superior value to the consumer. The profits made on such systems can be more than the profits made on the individual items that compose them. Creating systems allows you to introduce big price hikes for basic products that have long been sold for a lot less because no one has branded them.

3. Loss leaders are really profit leaders. Selling carefully selected items at cost or even at a loss can increase your overall profits since these items help brand other items for you.

4. When pricing, compare the extra costs and extra revenues that will result from a price change. If the extra revenues exceed the extra costs, the price change will add to your profits. *This holds true even if your new price is equal to or less than your present average unit cost of production.*

Four Types of Pricing Strategy

The pricing rules given above suggest that certain pricing strategies will be effective and others will not. Unfortunately, some simple pricing strategies may be very costly in terms of profits, while it takes considerable time, money, and effort to use pricing strategies that are effective at squeezing out every last dollar of profit from each sale.

As a matter of fact, most small businesspersons do not invest enough time and effort in pricing. As long as their profits are good enough, not much thought is given to prices. As a result, profits are needlessly lost.

What is the best solution for most small businesses? The answer is a compromise between quick and easy pricing strategies that are relatively costly profit-wise and more complex pricing strategies that have greater profit potential. Just exactly what kind of compromise will work best for you depends on your particular business and the nature of your customers. We can, however, review four commonly used pricing strategies and show you the strengths and weaknesses of each. Once you understand how each strategy works, you will be able to combine the different types in whatever way works best for you.

The four types of pricing strategy are:

Type I—The Cost-Plus, or Markup Pricing Method

Type II—The Economists' Pricing Method

Type III—The Intuitive Pricing Method

Type IV—The Market Experiment Pricing Method.

Our experience has been that the simplest pricing strategy (Type I) can be very costly in terms of lost profits because it ignores the intensity of customer needs. On the other hand, the most complex pricing strategy (Type II) requires information that is simply not available to the small business at a reasonable price. Still, Type II pricing strategy is so much better than Type I that even an educated guess concerning the information needed for Type II can lead to markedly better profits than the deceptively precise Type I strategy. Type III and Type IV are compromise pricing strategies that employ Type I strategy to develop an initial price, which is then modified by applying Type II pricing concepts.

Type I: The Cost-Plus, or Markup Pricing Method.   Type I strategy is widely used by small businesses. Its methodology boils down to determining price by adding a fixed markup of some kind to cost. Referring back to the pocket calendar example given in Exhibit 13.3, you would use this pricing method as follows:

You are presently producing 5,000 calendars per week at an average cost per calendar of $1.45. Of this $1.45, assume that $.40 is for labor and materials—the actual costs of producing the calendars. Assume also that the balance of your costs, $1.05, is for building rent, equipment payments, front office wages, and the like—bills you have to pay each month no matter what, or your overhead. In this example, overhead totals $5,000 per week. Your accountant has rightfully stressed the necessity of adding an allowance for overhead to your prices. Otherwise, your prices will not bring in enough to pay the rent, and you will go broke. Charging $1.35 each for a production run of 5,000 calendars per week, for example, would cause a loss of $500 per week (5,000 × $.10), even though $1.35 is more than enough to pay your $.40-per-calendar production costs. You certainly do not want to make this kind of mistake. Not only do you not want to lose money, you want to make a good profit. This leads you to follow pricing strategy based on what you know about your costs:[3]

Step 1: Estimate the job's direct cost—mainly the cost of materials and labor time used to do the job.

Step 2: Add a standard charge to cover the job's fair share of your overhead—rent, equipment payments, and indirect costs, such as the wages of your accounts receivable clerk.

Step 3: Add in a profit percentage.

In dollars and cents, the above three-step strategy would be carried out as follows for 5,000 units per week of production if you are satisfied with profits of 34.5%:

Step 1: $.40

Step 2: $.40 + $1.05 = $1.45

Step 3: $1.45 + (.345)(1.45) = $1.95

If you get a new order for an additional fifty calendars per week, it seems reasonable to assume that your direct costs for the new order will be about $.40 and your overhead costs about $1.05. Rather than recalculating all your costs for the new order, you may just apply a lump sum standard cost of $1.45 to each new calendar and charge your usual profit percentage (34.5%) to give the price of $1.95 each for the new calendars.

A lot of companies price like this. They apply their lump sum standard cost to each new order and add to their reasonable profit percentage. Other companies estimate direct costs for each new job and then add in a standard overhead charge in the form of a flat fee or percentage per unit sold, a specific amount per hour of labor time spent on the job, or a specific amount per hour of machine time to be used to do the job. Then, the reasonable profit percentage is added to determine the price to be charged.

Returning to the pocket calendar example in Exhibit 13.3 once again, let's see how well cost-plus pricing works. Assume that someone approaches you with an offer to buy 2,500 calendars per week. What price will you bid? Following the three steps, you would first estimate your direct costs—the cost of labor time and materials used to make the extra 2,500 calendars. In Exhibit 13.3, this was estimated at $.40 per calendar. Next, you add in your standard overhead charge of $1.05 per calendar. Finally, you apply your profit percentage of 34.5 percent. This means you end up with a price bid of $1.95 per calendar for the extra business i.e.:

$$\$.40 + \$1.05 + .345 (\$.40 + \$1.05) = \$1.95$$

If the buyer accepts your price, you will do very well indeed—possibly far better than you suspect.

If you think that the $1.95 price assures you a 34.5 percent profit, you are wrong. The actual profit percentage is 370 percent! The reason for this is simple: the standard overhead charge used to calculate the $1.95 price is wrong.

Actually, there is no extra overhead incurred as a result of accepting this new job since we are using excess capacity. Therefore, the extra cost per unit for doing this job is $.40, not $1.45. To provide a 34.5 percent profit on this

$.40, you need to charge only $.54 per calendar. By charging $1.95, you give yourself a 370 percent profit.

The above example dramatically illustrates the three-fold problem with the cost-plus pricing method:

1. It gives you inaccurate cost estimates if your current sales volume differs significantly from the historical sales volume on which you based your standard overhead cost calculation. In many cases, this can cause you to overprice your product and lose business. The right costs to consider are your extra costs, which may or may not be the same as the lump sum standard costs calculated from your financial statements.

2. It assumes the customer wants to pay you a reasonable markup when the customer may be willing to pay much more (or less). If the customer really wants the calendars, you may be able to charge $2.10 or even $2.25. If not, you may be able to get only $1.25. Certainly, limiting yourself to a 34.5 percent markup can be patently ridiculous if your other customers are paying $1.95 each. The new customer would probably be shocked if you charged only $.54. This works the other way too. Would you turn down a 30 percent profit on a deal that doubles your sales?

3. It assumes you have no competitors. Will the buyer who wants the 2,500 calendars go somewhere else to buy if your price is too high? Should you trim your prices as your sales volume increases to reflect your own improved operating efficiency and to forestall new competitors from opening their doors in pursuit of easy profits?

Why then do so many firms use the cost-plus pricing method? There are four main reasons:[4]

1. It is relatively easy to calculate, which is important if you have to price a lot of items—for a retail shoe store, for example.

2. It helps you make sure you will get at least reasonable profits on each sale, which may be good enough if your overall sales volume seems adequate.

3. It reflects the reality that you often can't change your price to match the intensity of need of each new customer. Customers may expect prices to be marked on your merchandise, or your advertising may be based on a fixed price for basic services regardless of who walks in the door.

4. It is easier to justify price increases to the public if they are based on cost increases than if they are based on your desire to squeeze extra profits out of someone who really needs your product badly.

As we mentioned above, it is possible to achieve satisfactory pricing results by modifying the simple Type I pricing method with elements of the complex Type II pricing method. Before looking at these compromise pricing strategies, we will discuss Type II—the theoretically ideal economist's pricing method.

Type II: The Economist's Pricing Method. The economist's pricing method is based on the general theory of pricing discussed earlier in this section. This method requires you to estimate both sales potential and costs each time you analyze a price change. As long as the extra sales revenues exceed the extra costs of achieving the higher sales revenues, you will add to your profits, and the price switch is desirable. For the economist's pricing method to work, you must have good estimates of the extra sales revenues that will be generated and the extra costs that will be incurred. Unfortunately, in practice it is almost impossible to use pure Type II strategy because these extra costs and revenues can only be guessed. This is particularly true if you sell several closely related products in a competitive situation where your competitors may or may not match your price change.

In the pocket calendar example, we wanted to know whether a cut in price to $1.45 would be profitable. It was demonstrated that given the estimated extra sales of 2,500 calendars per week and the estimated extra costs of $.40 per calendar, you would come out ahead to the tune of an extra $125 per week. This is not too bad if the extra sales actually materialize at the lower price. If they don't, however, you will have thrown away your existing profits of $2,500 a week in an attempt to make an extra $125 per week. This is why the accuracy of the sales forecast is critical to the efficacy of Type II pricing method.

One example of Type II pricing that can be very profitable for you even if your estimates of extra costs and benefits are only approximate is known as "price stepping."

Price stepping can get dramatically better profit results than an across-the-board price cut and, at the same time, can greatly reduce the risk involved in an across-the-board price cut. There are two variations of the price-stepping strategy: differential pricing and quantity discounts. Both are based on dividing the total market for your product into submarkets based on intensity of need. In the pocket calendar example, instead of charging everyone the new price of $1.45, you charge those who want the product the most $1.95 and groups with less intense needs progressively less until the relatively few people with a lukewarm need for your product pay only $1.45.

Differential pricing applies the price-stepping strategy, exactly as described above, to more than one buyer. Submarkets with differing intensity of need are separated from each other, and higher prices are charged to submarkets with stronger needs.

Quantity discounts apply the stepping strategy to a single buyer, who pays the regular price for normal purchases but is given a discount on extra purchases over a certain quantity. Instead of getting a lower price on every item bought, which may be less on average than the buyer is willing to pay, the buyer pays prices that ideally step down along with the buyer's lessening interest in buying more and more merchandise. These steps squeeze out the extra amount the buyer is willing to pay, which would be lost if the lowest price were charged from the beginning.

Two examples will illustrate how price stepping works. Continuing the pocket calendar example, let's assume that you anticipate that your price reduction to $1.45 will sell extra pocket calendars largely because it will open up the student bookstore market. Your pocket calendars, which have always sold well to regular stationery stores for $1.95, will now be priced low enough so that, after normal markups by student bookstores, students will be willing to buy them. Therefore, you expect student bookstores to buy big quantities. If you are satisfied that the bulk of students buy pocket calendars at student bookstores and that the bulk of other people buy pocket calendars at regular stationery stores, you can view the two markets as separate and try differential pricing. To do this, you simple charge $1.95 to regular stationery stores and $1.45 to student bookstores.[5] Figure 13.1 shows the results.

Part (A) of Figure 13.1 depicts the across-the-board price cut from $1.95 to $1.45. As shown in Exhibit 13.2, total sales revenue after the price cut ($1.45 x 7,500 = $10,875) is larger than total sales revenue before the price cut ($1.95 x 5,000 = $9,750). This is represented in the figure by the area in the rectangles; i.e., the sales revenue rectangle with corners a-c-d-h is larger than the sales revenue rectangle with corners a-b-f-g. Taking a closer look at Part (A), you can see what happens as the price is cut to make extra sales. You gain the sales revenue rectangle b-c-d-e, but you lose the sales revenue rectangle h-e-f-g.

In Part (B) of Figure 13.1, the impact of the price-stepping strategy is shown. In our example, the two-step price structure earns the company the extra profit represented by the rectangle h-e-f-g ($.50 x 5,000 = $2,500). Since it is anticipated the stationery stores will still buy 5,000 calendars per week at $1,95, while the college bookstores will now buy 2,500 additional calendars per week at $1.45, the company has its cake and gets to eat it too. It is able to operate at its full capacity of 7,500 units per week, which is more efficient, and its price-stepping strategy preserves the sales revenue rectangle h-e-f-g, which would otherwise have been lost in a general price cut.

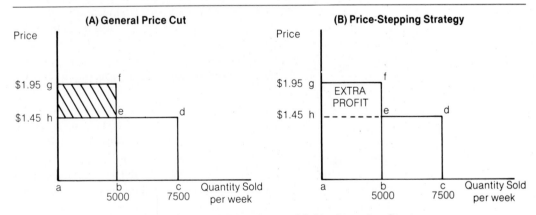

Figure 13.1 General Price Cut and Price-Stepping Strategy

Figure 13.1 can also be used to illustrate the quantity discount price-stepping strategy. Assume now that the 5,000 units sold per week are sold to one buyer who might be induced to buy 7,500 units if the price were lower. Assume further that the product being sold is perishable so that you don't have to worry about the buyer taking a low price today and stocking up so that your sales will fall next week. As with the last example, you can either offer a general price cut or employ a price-stepping strategy. In this case, the price-stepping strategy involves offering a quantity discount to the buyer along these lines: "If you buy in larger quantities, we give a discount. For example, you pay $1.95 for the first 5,000 units purchased. For each unit purchased above 5,000, you only pay $1.45." Once again, the general price cut causes a loss of the sales revenue rectangle h-e-f-g, while the price-stepping strategy turns this rectangle into extra profit.

Price stepping unlocks extra profits and can be employed in a surprising number of cases. If you are a clothing store, differing lines of clothing can have different markups based on differing intensity of need. Children's clothes, for example, may have a higher markup than clothes for adults. If you are a typing service you may charge a different hourly fee to students than you do to attorneys. If you repair TVs, you may charge a premium for house calls that more than offsets the extra cost involved.

Type III: The Intuitive Pricing Method. The intuitive pricing method begins with a Type I price calculation. The resulting price is then modified up or down based on intuition in an attempt to charge what the market will bear. The intuition of able business owners presumably takes into account such factors as the perceived intensity of consumer demand, suggestions by suppliers, what the competition is doing, and upcoming changes in economic conditions that will affect sales.

The strong point of this approach is that it does incorporate elements of the Type II method into the pricing decision. The Type I method is used only to set initial guidelines. The weakness of this approach is that it is very subjective, and the pricing is often based more on vague premonitions than on solid facts. Still, if solid facts are not obtainable at a reasonable price in terms of your time and money, the intuitive approach can work out pretty well. The trick to using the Type III method is to write down why you are pricing the way you are—what criteria you have established and how much relative weight or priority you give to certain factors. If this is done, you will at least be able to see after the fact where your price strategy broke down. Most likely, you will be able to see how current pricing situations differ from historical ones, which in turn will suggest whether your markups should be higher or lower. If you plan to use the intuitive pricing method, we also recommend that you explain your pricing logic to one or two other good business people. Their comments and suggestions will probably point out flaws in your thinking.

Type IV: The Market Experiment Pricing Method.   The market experiment pricing method tests your intuition. When planning a price change using this method, you come to your conclusion as to what the price change should be but before introducing the new price to all your customers, you try it out on a selected few. If they buy as you expected, your experiment tells you your price change is workable. If they do not buy as you expected, you learn the hard truth without losing everything. The efficacy of the Type IV method relative to the Type III method depends on the care used in selecting those the new price is tried on. If those selected are representative of all your customers and the number of people selected is large enough, your price experiment may give you a very good idea indeed about what the impact of a price change will be on your sales. In the pocket calendar illustration, offering the calendars to a representative sample of twenty or so bookstores for $1.45 will tell you if the new price works or not.

The strength of the market experiment pricing method is that it verifies the intensity of customer need for the product in a pragmatic matter—trying out the new price on a small scale and seeing if the customers buy as predicted. Some would argue that it is as close as you can get to Type II pricing in the real world. The problem with this method is that it takes time and is hard to control. It can also be expensive to administer if the sampling procedures that should be used, described in Appendices 10–B and 10–C, are followed conscientiously. The time spent represents lost market opportunities. Also, your experiment may tip off competitors, and they may beat you to the price punch. Finally, your sales figures may be overly optimistic if your customers flock into the store where you are offering your special price, abandoning other stores where your product is carried but your special is not offered (or vice versa in the case of a price increase). This last problem can be partially overcome by keeping track of your sales levels at stores where you offer no change in price and where no switching will be likely to occur and using the sales levels for these stores as a control. Control sales levels can be compared with sales levels at stores near the store used in the test to see if there is a difference in the pattern of sales. Such a difference would indicate switching had taken place. Any such comparisons, of course, are only as good as the representativeness of the stores involved.

One last comment concerning Type IV experimental pricing may be helpful to you. Quantity discounts and specials can be used experimentally. For example, a limited time offer may give you a good idea of how responsive customers are to a price change. As another example, retailing a special collection of more expensive items will often indicate whether or not your customers are willing to pay more for certain lines of merchandise.

When conducting such experiments, be sure to consider how many sales were made during the experiment at the expense of future sales. If your customers tend to stock up when you offer specials but use about the same amount of your product during the year no matter what your prices, a price cut during an experiment may lead to a big jump in sales; but making the price cut permanent will not increase your unit sales all that much over the course of a year. Therefore, a business like a restaurant can learn more from experimental pricing than a business like a washing machine manufacturer.

To summarize, there are four types of pricing. The first, the cost-plus, or markup, pricing method, can set an initial benchmark price for you as long as your present sales volume is close enough to your historical sales volume to make your cost per unit estimates realistic. The second type of pricing, the economist's pricing method, is rarely found in practice due to the complexity of real-world pricing situations and to uncertainty about the exact impact of a change in price on demand. It is simply too costly to conduct a complete Type II price analysis for every price change. However, the basic idea of the Type II pricing method—comparing extra costs to extra benefits—is a good one. As a result, you will probably find either the intuitive (Type III) or the market experiment (Type IV) pricing method profitable since both methods improve the Type I approach by blending in elements of the Type II approach. Just how sophisticated you choose to be should be based on a comparison of the probable benefits you can expect to gain from a closer look at a pricing decision with the probable costs of collecting the needed data to make a more precise decision.

The benefits of careful market research spill over into your pricing decisions. If you have carefully researched your market and have successfully identified a branded product/service system you can offer to your customers, you will have a good idea of the price you can charge. This price will be surprisingly high and profitable given the costs of the various components that make up the product/service system.

CASE
SOLUTION

Minnetonka, Inc.

Robert Taylor had gotten out of touch with his markets. As a result, he had lost his brand advantage. At the same time, competition had increased and was seriously threatening the sales of the Village Bath Products line. For example, two large competitors, Gillette and Clairol, introduced fruit shampoos similar to Minnetonka's products in drugstores and food stores. This caused sales of Minnetonka's shampoo line in gift stores and department stores to wither.

To reverse the downward trend, Taylor began to concentrate on what he knew best—the branded bath product business. He once again sought products that could be branded—unusual products that could be placed in appealing packaging and sold with high markups. For example, in 1976 he introduced Lip Lickers lip balm in eight flavors packaged in tiny tin cases. Lip Lickers sold $1.5 million in the first year. Other products were introduced—beer shampoo and luxury bar soaps in a variety of scents. In 1978 alone Minnetonka introduced 150 new products, and sales rose to $16.1 million. His improved physical and financial controls could now cope with his product line, and net income was $1.3 million. Sales climbed further to $25 million in 1979.

Has Robert Taylor learned his lesson? A review of the development of one of his major products reveals the answer. After Taylor began to concentrate again on branding his product line, he revived a product from a discontinued subsidiary. It was a liquid soap in a skin lotion pump dispenser. Although it had not sold well originally, several consumers had written the company indicating they liked the product because it was convenient and eliminated messy soap dishes. Taylor reasoned that a colorful, attractive container might get people to try the product and that once they did, they would like it. The product in its bright new container was dubbed the Incredible Soap Machine, and priced at $4.95, sold more than $400,000 its first year. This was despite the fact that this kind of product was three to four times as expensive per hand washing as a conventional bar soap such as Dial. Taylor reasoned that this product might sell well nationally and put the product before focus groups, which were samples of shoppers selected and interviewed by marketing experts. The focus groups liked the Incredible Soap Machine but thought it was too expensive. The interviews also indicated people expected to buy such a product in grocery stores.

In mid-1978 Taylor came out with an inexpensive version of his pump-dispensed liquid soap. It was called Softsoap and, priced at $1.50 for nine ounces, was to be mass marketed through supermarkets and other food stores. Taylor proceeded cautiously in this new distribution channel. He took Softsoap back to focus groups. The sampled consumers liked it. Softsoap was tested in Minneapolis and Milwaukee in September 1978 and was distributed through food brokers to ten additional midwestern cities in 1979. It sold an estimated $3.5 million in 1979, capturing a 2 to 6 percent share of the hand soap market in the test areas despite the fact that its price per nine-ounce container was almost five times that of a personal-sized bar of Dial soap. (*Consumer Reports* estimates the container of Softsoap delivers about the same number of hand washings as 1 ½ bars of personal-sized Dial.) Softsoap was easy to brand because it was innovative, and its package was well designed. Because it was branded, it sold for a premium price. It was, of course, only a matter of time until the big soap makers introduced their own versions of Softsoap; but in the meantime, Minnetonka enjoyed the premium price and profits that a good brand creates for a well-managed company.

CHAPTER
SUMMARY

This chapter has reviewed several important pricing concepts. A properly branded small business can demand and get top dollar for its product/service systems. The actual cost for your product or service actually has less to do with your pricing decisions than you might think. You must cover your costs to stay in business, but your prices do not have to be locked to your cost by, for example, a fixed markup percentage. If you develop a branded product service system you can become what economists call a monopolist and demand premium prices for your offerings without losing too many customers to your unbranded competitors. This general theory of setting prices is discussed in this chapter. Four pricing rules are recommended:

1. Seek markets where you can create a brand for your company.

2. Design product/service systems that have superior value to the customer.

3. Understand that loss leaders are really profit leaders.

4. When pricing, compare the extra costs and extra revenues that will result from the price change.

The chapter concludes with a discussion of four types of pricing strategy:

Type I—The Cost-Plus or Mark-up Pricing Method

Type II—The Economist's Pricing Method

Type III—The Intuitive Pricing Method

Type IV—The Market Experiment Pricing Method

For small businesses either a Type III or Type IV strategy usually proves to be a good compromise between ease of implementation and profitability.

DISCUSSION
QUESTIONS

1. **Short Case: Plant Management, Inc.**
   Gary Stein was a botany major in college. Gary wanted to start a business dealing with plants. He noticed that plant boutiques were a dime a dozen: even grocery stores sold plants. He also noticed that the nursery business was highly competitive. As a result, Gary decided to sell and lease plants for use in offices and model home complexes at new housing subdivisions. Gary planned to provide maintenance contracts and guarantees for the plants he serviced.

   In terms of the concepts discussed in this chapter, has Gary picked a good small business? Will he be able to get top dollar for his product/service system? Explain.

2. Explain the economist's general theory of pricing in your own words.

3. What is the basic problem with the Cost-Plus, or Markup pricing method?

4. Explain in your own words how a loss leader works.

5. Erhart Enterprises is a small company specializing in framing pictures for art galleries. Mr. Erhart, the owner, typically bids on framing 50 to 100 paintings or lithographs at one time. He could easily frame 3,000 pictures

a month. He is currently framing pictures at the rate of 1,500 per month. Lately Mr. Erhart has lost some large bids (1,000–1,500 frames), and he is wondering if his price is too high. What do you think? Here are the facts:

a. Mr. Erhart and his wife are the company: they have no employees.

b. Mr. Erhart's rent, equipment payments, utility bills, and other overhead total $2,500 per month; his average monthly sales volume for the last two years has been 1,000 frames per month. Thus he estimates he must allocate $2.50 from each frame sold to cover his overhead.

c. Mr. Erhart wants to draw $24,000 per year from his business, which amounts to $2.00 per frame if he frames 1,000 pictures per month.

d. Mr. Erhart has invested $25,000 in his business, which he feels should earn a 24 percent return (2 percent per month), or $500 per month.

e. The cost of materials for a frame has averaged $20.00 over the past year. (This average is for all types of material—metal, wood, etc.)

f. Based on the above numbers, Mr. Erhart figures his bids as follows:

    i. Estimate material cost per frame.

    ii. Add $2.00 labor cost per frame.

    iii. Add $2.50 overhead per frame.

    iv. Add $.50 profit per frame.

REFERENCES

Brigham, Eugene F., and Pappas, James L. *Managerial Economics*. Hillsdale, Ill. The Dryden Press, 1972.

Henry, William R. and Haynes, W. Warren. *Managerial Economics: Analysis and Cases*, 4th ed. Dallas: Business Publications, Inc., 1978.

Lennon, Victor A. *What is the Best Selling Price?* Management Aid No. 193. Washington, D.C.: Small Business Administration, 1978.

Spencer, Milton H. *Managerial Economics: Text, Problems and Short Cases*, 3rd ed. Homewood, Ill.: Richard D. Irwin, Inc., 1968.

Truett, Lila J. and Truett, Dale B. *Managerial Economic Analysis, Problems, Cases*. Cincinnati: South-Western Publishing Co., 1980.

Walker, Bruce J. *A Pricing Checklist for Small Retailers*. Small Marketers Aid No. 158. Washington, D.C.: Small Business Administration, 1976.

Wilsted, William D. *Pricing for Small Manufacturers*. Management Aid No. 226. Washington D.C.: Small Business Administration, 1978.

FOOTNOTES

1. This case problem was condensed from Bill Hendrickson, "They Cleaned Up Their Act," *Inc.* 2, no. 4 (April 1980): 72–78; and from Geoffrey Smith, "Softsoaping P & G," *Forbes*, 125, no. 4, February 18, 1980 pp. 97–99. Quotations from statements of Minnetonka officials used in this chapter were taken from the Hendrickson article and reprinted with permission of *Inc.* Magazine, April 1980. © 1980 by United Marine Publishers, Inc. The comparative attribute and price data regarding liquid hand soaps were found in "Toilet Soaps," *Consumer Reports* 46, no. 3 (March 1981):160–163.

2. The analysis of what economists have said about pricing reviewed in this section and the discussion of the four types of pricing introduced in the solutions section re-

flect what we deem to be a consensus of opinion among economists who have written about the pricing decision in business. Unfortunately, many of the discussions of pricing that we found helpful when writing this chapter may prove frustrating to study if you are unfamiliar with the jargon and models popular with economists. Still, the following sources are quite good and will broaden your understanding of effective pricing if you can invest the time to break the jargon-model barrier:Bringham, Eugene F., and Pappas, James L. *Managerial Economics*. Hillsdale Ill.: The Dryden Press, 1972, Chapters 10 and 11; Henry William R., and Haynes, W. Warren. *Managerial Economics: Analysis and Cases*. 4th ed. Dallas: Business Publications, Inc., 1978, Chapters 11 and 12; Palda, Kristan S. *Economic Analysis for Marketing Conditions*. Englewood Cliffs, N.J.: Prentice-Hall, Inc., 1969, Chapter 7; Spencer, Milton H. *Managerial Economics: Text, Problems and Short Cases*. 3rd ed. Homewood, Ill.: Richard D. Irwin, Inc., 1968, Chapter 9; Truett, Lila J., and Truett, Dale B. *Managerial Economics Analysis, Problems, Cases*. Cincinnati: South-Western Publishing Co., 1980, Chapters 5, 7, 8, and 10.

Three practical discussions about pricing are available free from the U.S. Small Business Administration, Washington, D.C. They are:

Lennon, Victor A. *What is the Best Selling Price*, Management Aid No. 193 for Small Manufacturers, 1978; Walker, Bruce J. *A Pricing Checklist for Small Retailers*. Small Marketers Aid No. 158, 1976; Wilsted, William D. *Pricing for Small Manufacturers*. Management Aid No. 226 for Small Manufacturers, 1978.

3. This summary of the three-step cost-plus pricing strategy is adapted from Milton H. Spencer, *Managerial Economics*, 3rd ed. (Homewood, Ill.: Richard D. Irwin, Inc., 1968), p. 295.

4. *Ibid.*, p. 296. These four reasons are adapted from the reasons given by Spencer.

5. This example assumes stationery store buyers will not find out what price student bookstores are getting and demand similar prices. It also assumes that the student bookstores will pass the savings on to the students. One way to minimize such problems is to make superficial alterations in the product. For example, imprint the cover of the calendar sold to stationery stores with gold letters, "Executive Planning Calendar," and imprint the front of the student version with, "Student Study Scheduling Calendar." If this is done, the two products can be advertised side by side in the company's sales catalog with the different prices shown, and stationery stores will buy one and college bookstores the other with no problems.

Personnel Management Strategies That Work

PART IV

Hiring 14

☐ **What kinds of people do you need**

☐ **How do you find job applicants?**

☐ **How do you tell which applicant is the best for the job?**

CASE
PROBLEM

Paragon Injection Molders, Inc. [1]

After receiving a college degree in industrial engineering from a local university, Paul Green went to work for Quality Injectors. This firm specialized in the production of plastic injection molded parts to exacting specifications for the aerospace industry. Aerospace firms used the plastic parts in the products they assembled.

During his four years with Quality Injectors, Paul developed an expert knowledge of all aspects of the production process. He also became convinced that although the company's product quality was acceptable, prices were too high. Further, the company lost business because it had a deservedly bad reputation for late deliveries.

After doing his best to talk the owners of the company into correcting these defects and getting nowhere, Paul decided to quit and to open his own business to compete with Quality Injectors. Paul called his business Paragon Injection Molders, Inc. Paul was confident that acceptable product quality combined with reasonable prices and on-time deliveries would be very attractive to aerospace buyers and would insure a profitable sales volume for his company.

The injection molding business requires expensive equipment. Although molds are typically custom-made by subcontractors for each job, the cost of the molding equipment required to produce quality parts can quickly add up to well over $100,000. Further, unless the machines are operated and maintained expertly, they can wear out quickly, necessitating costly overhauls or replacement.

Because of his expertise and experience, Paul was able to obtain loans to purchase the equipment he needed. He was soon set up to handle a profitable volume of business but found himself in a dilemma. On the one hand, he was the only one in his company who knew how to operate and maintain the machines properly. On the other hand, if he didn't get out more and sell his company's services to aerospace buyers, he would not have enough orders to be profitable. He would have to more than double his present sales volume to break even. Clearly, he could not handle all the machine work and sales himself. He had to hire help, but what kind, how much, and who?

Paul Green identified a potentially profitable target market for his company based primarily on the shortcomings of the existing competition (his former employer). He raised the money he needed and purchased the right equipment. Now he is at a critical point. He needs to hire help. In order to avoid some serious mistakes, he needs to have a hiring plan. You might argue that what Paul needs is a reasonably qualified warm body either to operate his machines or to do his selling. This is true, but in order to obtain one efficiently, Paul needs a plan. He needs to define the work that has to be done. He has to decide what he should do himself and what he should assign to others. He has to take into account how his manpower needs will change as his company grows. If he plans to grow rapidly, for example, it may benefit him to pay extra for experienced machine operators now rather than trying to save a few dollars initially by hiring and training a novice. Paul has to translate his sales forecasts into the people he needs to meet his sales goals and make his company a success. If this is not complicated enough, he has to define job openings so that he has a chance of finding good people interested in filling them at wages he can afford. After all, the bottom line is profits.

Once Paul has defined the kind of employee he needs, he still faces two major problems. First, how can he hope to compete with large companies for individuals with talent? After all, the salaries, security, fringe benefits, and retirement programs offered by the giants are hard to beat. Second, how can he make the people he wants aware of the fact that he has a job ready for them? It costs a lot in dollars and time to advertise a job opening.

Every small business has problems similar to those faced by Paul. You must determine the kinds of people you need; how to find qualified job applicants; how to attract them to work for your company; and, once you have a list of applicants for a particular job, how to pick the best one. Implied is still another problem: how to keep good employees once they are hired. This is important since every time someone quits, you will have to start the time-consuming and expensive process of hiring over again.

This chapter will help you to begin to solve these problems by analyzing the kinds of people you need, the mechanics of finding job applicants, and strategies for telling which job applicant is best for a job opening. Chapters 15 and 16 will continue the discussion by focusing on techniques for paying and keeping your employees.

If you own a business, you have probably had to deal with the problems we have identified in this chapter. Even if you are the only one in your business now, you may have to deal with these problems in the future if it becomes profitable for you to have employees. Hiring, therefore, is an important issue.

How can you diagnose whether or not you are hiring the right people? You must begin by analyzing how you hire people now (or would hire them if you do not now have employees). The best way to do this is to analyze your last hiring. Why did you hire someone? Exactly what is that individual doing

PROBLEM IDENTIFICATION

DIAGNOSIS

for you? How will he or she contribute to your firm's profitability? How did you pick the person you hired from all the applicants for the job? Could you have gotten someone better? How did you make the community aware that there was a job opening? Exhibit 14.1 lists several questions to help you with your self-diagnosis. A scoring guide follows.

Many small business owner/managers would score poorly on the hiring questions in Exhibit 14.1. If your score is low, it may indicate that there is a wide gap between your dream for a profitable company and what you are doing to make your dream a reality.

It should be noted that you may not be safe even if you have a high score. A wrong answer to any high point question may still be costing you a lot of money.

Exhibit 14.1   Do You Hire the Right People?

Instructions: Answer (Y) or No (N) to the following questions about the last person you hired:

About the Job:

Y__N__ **1.** Do you know how much this job is worth, i.e., how much the company stands to profit when it is done well?

Y__N__ **2.** Can you list the most important things that must be done well to do the job right? (Hint: Few jobs have more than five critical job behaviors. These behaviors relate to key job functions or activities.)

Y__N__ **3.** Can you list the special qualifications required to fill this job, such as experience, education, special skills, and physical requirements?

Y__N__ **4.** Do you have a written description of the job that includes the objective of the job, the work to be performed, the responsibilities involved, the skills needed, the working conditions, and the job's relationship to other jobs?

About the Selection Process:

Y__N__ **5.** Did you have the applicant fill out an application blank?

Y__N__ **6.** Did you have the applicant give references for you to check?

Y__N__ **7.** Did you require the applicant to take a physical exam that tested capabilities relevant to doing the job well, such as vision, movement, strength, stamina, and hearing?

Y__N__ **8.** Did you give the applicant any other tests?

Y__N__ **9.** If you did give other tests (Question 8), did these tests require the applicant to try out, i.e., to demonstrate key skills required for the job?

Y__N__ **10.** Did you interview the applicant for the job using a list of questions you had prepared in advance?

Y__N__ **11.** Do you have written recruiting and hiring policies?

Y__N__ **12.** Did you seek applicants for the job from five or more sources (e.g., ads, school placement offices, sign in window, etc.)?

About the Person You Hired:

Y__N__ **13.** Did you pick the person because he or she was willing to work for what you could afford to pay?

Y__N__ **14.** Did you pick the person because you figured he or she would be loyal and stay with the company for a long time?

Y__N__ **15.** Did you pick someone you will have to train?

Y__N__ **16.** If your answer to Question 15 was yes, do you have a formal on-the-job training program for this job?

Y__N__ **17.** Did you pick someone because he or she was truly needed and could produce the results desired, even though you may have had to pay more?

Y__N__ **18.** Did you orient the person hired to the job? Was the employee given a written description of the job requirements, work rules, and company benefits, introduced to new employees, shown the company layout and facilities, and shown how to do his or her job?

Y__N__ **19.** Do you expect your new employee to carry the ball right away and do the job well without asking you (or his or her supervisor) a lot of questions?

Y__N__ **20.** Did you oversell the job a bit to try to attract some good talent that may not have joined your company if you had been completely honest?

Scoring Guide

Instructions: Give yourself the points indicated below for each yes or no answer. A positive number adds to your score. A negative number subtracts from it.

Special Note: The points you can earn on each question reflect the relative importance to your business of the practice described in that question. Five-point issues are very important and should receive special attention.

Question	Yes	No
1	+ 5	− 5
2	+ 5	− 5
3	+ 5	− 5
4	+ 3	− 3
5	+ 2	− 2
6	+ 3	− 3
7	+ 2	− 2
8	+ 2	− 2
9	+ 4	− 4
10	+ 4	− 4
11	+ 3	− 3
12	+ 3	− 3
13	− 5	+ 5
14	− 3	+ 3
15	− 3	+ 3
16	+ 5	− 5
17	+ 5	− 5
18	+ 4	− 4
19	− 5	+ 5
20	− 4	+ 4

A perfect score is + 75.

A score of + 20 or above means you are on the right track since you understand most of the major concepts.

A score between − 20 and + 20 indicates you need several adjustments in your approach to hiring.

A score below − 20 indicates you have to rethink completely the way you hire.

In this section, we will explore why each of the twenty questions in Exhibit 14.1 is important to you. The five-point questions indicate what we think are the central principles of effective hiring, no matter what the size of your business. The hiring principles covered by the lower-point questions may be relatively unimportant when your business is very small but become increasingly important as you increase your number of employees.

Defining Company Goals and the Value of a Job

To hire effectively, you must begin by defining what you want each position to contribute to company goals and objectives. A yes answer to Question 1 means you have given a lot of thought to where your company is going and can define the return you expect from your investment in this employee. This return is worth more to you the sooner you get it, which explains our bias toward hiring experienced people that fit your business plan and paying them well. However, it is important to keep potential longterm uses for employees in mind. As Theodore Cohn and Roy Lindberg point out:

> A small business manager about to sign a ten-year lease understands the need to plan his space requirements. Similarly, buying machinery often entails long-term capital commitments and thus raises the question of long-term use and payback. But space and machinery are useless without the right people at the right time. The job of people planning requires not only a guess as to how many people will be needed and with what skills, but an even wilder guess as to the development of the individuals now on board.
>
> A tough-minded evaluation of the potential of present and projected management and supervisory people is one of the best ways of insuring survival in the small business.[2]

Distinctive Competencies Define the Kind of People You Need

Specifically, a yes answer to Question 1 means you have done a careful analysis of your company's distinctive competencies and the best markets for your products or services, as discussed in Chapter 10 (See Exhibit 10.2). This analysis is intimately tied to the people you have and the people you need. Your business goals and objectives help you to spell out job requirements. They enable you to recognize the kind of help you need. It is easy to see how. Asking questions aimed at identifying, protecting, and capitalizing on the company's competitive edge focuses your attention on setting the company apart. It makes you think about what specific performances are needed to serve existing customers in special ways or to attract customers with greater ease, at lower cost, and/or with greater profit than competitors.[3]

Listing the Most Important Job Goals

This company analysis can lead to straightforward, concrete answers to the second question in Exhibit 14.1 (i.e., listing the most important things that must be done to do the job right). For example, in one recent study, the owner of a small neighborhood grocery store boiled the jobs of his two clerks down to three observable goals, none of which was being reached consistently:

> (1) At least one of the workers should be in the store, i.e., within three feet of a display shelf, a meat or produce counter, or the meat refrigerator, whenever the store was open for business. (2) Whenever a customer was in the store, he/she should be assisted. That is, one of the workers should approach within three feet and, with a smile, ask the customer, 'May I help you?' When any customer requests assistance (e.g., weighing produce, asking for items), the assistance should begin within five seconds of the request. Anytime a worker is assisting a customer, he should acknowledge another customer's request by saying, 'I will be with you in a moment,' and within five seconds after finishing with one customer proceed to assist the next customer. (3) The merchandise display shelves, the produce counter, and the package meat counter should be filled to at least 50 percent of their capacity (assuming that sufficient quantities are available) at all times that the store is open for business.[4]

The owner discussed these goals with his employees and agreed to give them time off with pay when they consistently reached these goals during a pay period. Consistent attainment of the three goals by the two clerks meant, of course, that customers were being approached and served immediately, shelves and counters were rarely empty, and at least one worker was in the store except for those times both were needed in the storeroom to receive merchandise. Customers noticed and appreciated the resulting improvement in service, which contributed significantly to the competitive edge of the little store.

Specifying Qualifications

Once you have answered Questions 1 and 2 in Exhibit 14.1, Question 3 (listing special qualifications) becomes a relatively simple, though still critical, matter. Consider the clerks from the above example. With the store owner's three goals, it is possible to be very specific and realistic about the kind of person needed for these positions. For example, extensive experience and education are not necessary, but physical agility, clear speech, and the ability to read numbers and enter them correctly probably are. A basically grouchy or sullen attitude would be totally unacceptable. Some of these qualities are objective and can be tested by a written test or a brief trial simulating the key elements of the job. Others, such as attitude, are more subjective. In either case, you need to be realistic in your requirements to insure that your human resource investment is made wisely. Your physical agility requirement, for example, should not be set too low or too high. Standards set too high screen out applicants who could do the job well. Standards set too low defeat the job goals of the employer.

Writing Job Descriptions

Correct hiring is tied closely to adequate knowledge of the job to be filled. As Question 4 in Exhibit 14.1 implies, you should be able to describe the job in writing. Writing down job descriptions helps you double-check each job to make sure it fits your company plan. An honestly written job description is also useful for the prospective employee since it lets the applicant know what he or she is in for. Many unqualified people will withdraw their applications when they read an accurate job description. This saves everyone's time. Finally, job descriptions are a useful record of your expectations. They can be used as a basis for employee evaluation. Exhibit 14.2 presents two sample job descriptions from a recent *Small Business Reporter*.[5]

Can you write a job description for each job in your company? A good job description describes the objectives of the job, the work to be performed, the responsibilities involved, the skills needed, the working conditions, and the job's relationship to other jobs.[6]

Collecting Information About Job Applicants

Questions 5 through 10 in Exhibit 14.1 emphasize that correct hiring is also tied closely to adequate knowledge about the people available. In this regard, it is particularly important to collect as much relevant information about the applicants as possible, given your time and budget limitations. There are four sources of information about a job candidate: the applicant, the applicant's personal references, the applicant's previous employers (or schools), and the applicant's products (examples of his or her previous work). Typically, this information is collected by having the applicant fill out an application blank, checking out references, giving tests, and interviewing the applicant. You can save a great deal of time and money if you remember two basic principles when collecting this information:

1. Collect only information you really need. This means information directly related to the applicant's ability to accomplish present and future job goals. If the information cannot identify those individuals with the greatest probability of success, why collect it? Collection of unnecessary information not only wastes your time and money but also is illegal in some cases![7]

Exhibit 14.2   Sample Job Descriptions
(All requirements listed should be job related)

Receptionist-Typist

Duties—Greets and directs visitors; answers phone on call director; takes messages; sets up appointments; does light typing from written copy; picks up, opens, stamps and distributes mail and does assorted duties as asked.

Responsible to—Office manager.

Requirements—Applicants should: have a high school diploma and/or some business training; be able to type 65 w.p.m.; and be able to learn use of office machines. One year's previous working experience is desired.

Personal—Should be personable since the job requires public contact. Needs initiative to assume more responsibility as business grows; should be willing to take bookkeeping training.

Retail Salesclerk

Duties—Greets and waits on customers; discusses merchandise; rings sales; makes change; writes up charge slips; wraps for shipping and bags items; keeps shelves stocked; directs deliveries; follows procedures on opening and closing store when manager is away.

Responsible to—Store manager.

Requirements—Applicants must: be good at arithmetic; have previous sales experience; be available to work nights and weekends; be able to learn use of cash register and other store procedures as taught; often be bondable; be willing to join union within 30 days.

Personal—Must have an easy manner with people, like retailing, and be able to withstand long hours on the sales floor.

---

2. Assume stability of traits. To paraphrase two old sayings, a leopard will not change its spots, and a dog will not learn new tricks. Hire the person who can do the job now. It is often faster, cheaper, and safer to pay a little more for someone who already has the expertise the job demands than to experiment with training someone cheap who does not. An "old dog" that knows the tricks you need is worth a lot more than a litter of trainees.

Overview of Specific Hiring Strategies

Do you now understand why Questions 13 through 20 from Exhibit 14.1 are scored as they are? A small businessperson hiring cheap help is like a mechanic buying cheap tools. You get what you pay for; so it is best to pay enough to get what you need.

There is no need to hire people for life. People should be hired because they can produce the results you need and want. A topnotch employee who stays with you only a year or two is still effective and can be worth far more than a so-so applicant who stays with you a long time. In one recent case, a young entrepreneur hired a 72-year-old head chef for his restaurant. The chef only stayed for two years before retiring; but in the meantime, he put the restaurant on the map. He used his fifty years of experience to create culinary delights for the menu, keep food costs down, and select and train staff. He even used his industry contacts to help the owner to select his own replacement!

Our general advice is to hire experience; but if you have jobs planned that will grow with the company, it can pay to hire trainees and develop their skills as you need them. If you do this, you must make sure you follow through with your training plans to make sure your employees have a fighting chance to grow with their jobs. The object is not to subject employees to trial by fire, but rather to develop effective employees efficiently. A trial-by-fire approach hurts employee morale, leads to high turnover, and defeats your company goals. We will explore the relationship of training to morale in Chapter 16. For now, remember that even experienced self-starters need direction. There are no white knights in the small business world who can come into your company and solve all your problems on their own. In order to do their best for you, topnotch people need your help. They need to know the goals you want them to achieve. Make sure someone is available to answer their questions and keep them going in the right direction. Getting the most out of your employees is hard work—but very profitable work.[8]

Question 20 in Exhibit 14.1 refers to a mistake made all too often by the small business owner. Concerned that a top job applicant might turn down a job offer if the truth were known about the job, the small business owner stretches the truth a bit. Such overselling is almost invariably a costly mistake. Top applicants will soon learn the truth and are likely to resign quickly if you cannot deliver what you have promised. Although common sense indicates that this would be the case, overselling is often tried, possibly because owners see only the disadvantages their small businesses have relative to large companies when trying to recruit top applicants. Actually, the small business owner has several recruiting advantages that can be very attractive to top applicants. Capitalizing on these advantages allow the small businessperson to create jobs of real interest without stretching the truth.

As we noted above, many small business owner managers would score quite low on the hiring quesions in Exhibit 14.1. A good summary of why is given by Kenneth Rindt:

> Employers often have not defined the specific goals or objectives they have for the business; consequently, they have difficulty seeing the job requirements and kinds of people needed to accomplish these goals.
>
> Owner-managers sometimes do not recognize good help when it is referred to them for employment. Without special knowledge or skill in

personnel or human resource management, they may not see an employee's potential for further development and success. Too often they fire unsatisfactory performers, assuming they have been poor [selections]..., when the real difficulty is inadequate development of their potential through training.[9]

To summarize our discussion of hiring to this point, if you want to hire effectively, you must have sound answers to each of the three questions given at the beginning of this chapter: What kinds of people do you need? How do you find job applicants? How do you tell which applicant is best for the job?

As we have explained, a good part of the answers to the first and third questions lies in clear definition of your company's goals and the translation of these goals into a list of critical jobs and critical job behaviors that need to be done right to accomplish your goals. If you concentrate on doing those things that are essential to reaching your goals extremely well, you will keep your payroll lean; and you will thus be able to afford to hire qualified people. Further, clear definition of critical job behaviors provides you with a shopping list of job qualifications that you can focus on when you select employees. Even though some of your qualifications may be subjective, if they are critical to the job, they are an invaluable guide for your hiring decisions.

Even the second question is affected by how you define your goals and jobs. This is because your list of critical job qualifications will normally suggest where you should look for the job applicants you want.

After your company's goals and jobs are clearly defined, you are well armed to begin an employee search. We will now comment on several specific topics that will help you to recruit and select the people you need.

Recruiting Advantages of Small Businesses

It is a widely held misconception that small firms are at a disadvantage when competing with large firms for qualified job applicants. Actually, the reverse is true in most cases, especially when you are seeking people with high potential value to your company. According to Kamal Said and Keith Hughey, this misconception has prevented most small firms from developing a recruitment position competitive with that of the larger corporation. They argue that there are two factors or aspects of this misconception:

> (1) an external factor: the generally unfounded notion that the small firm is not able to offer as much security, prestige, and renumeration as the larger corporation; and (2) an internal factor: the small businessperson's belief that his or her firm is incapable of recruiting and retaining a stable work force because of its disadvantageous competitive position in the labor market.[10]

It is important for you to understand what the small business's potential recruiting advantages are and to make sure your job applicants are aware of the advantages of working for your company. These advantages do not exist automatically. They should not be promised unless you plan to work hard to make them a reality within your company. Exhibit 14.3 presents a list of ten advantages your small business can offer to key job applicants.

If you can create the advantages listed in Exhibit 14.3 for your company, many top job applicants will be yours for the asking. Even if you cannot afford to provide the higher starting salaries and fringe benefits larger companies offer, you can promise rapid organizational and economic advancement to those that prove themselves. You can offer a faster track to success, thereby attracting people with high potential who do not want to wait years for their competence to be recognized by a large company.

Exhibit 14.3   Ten Advantages of Working for a Small Firm[11]

1. **Richer Personal Relationships.** The employees of small companies are often neighbors. They share in recreational activities and are more likely to interact socially with members of top management. Everyone knows and is known by the top management team. Complaints and grievances can be solved at once rather than being referred to a committee. Small companies are more informal and more fun.

2. **Accelerated Experience.** Employees are more likely to be able to try different jobs since employers are more likely to pay close attention to their talents and desires. Since the company is small, the scope of each job assignment is naturally broader and more varied, using more of the employee's valued skills. In a small company, employees can quickly learn where their company is going and why.

3. **Involvement.** Top management can quickly learn about each employee's special skills. In the small company, employees are more likely to be asked for input on critical decisions early in their careers. Employees can expect to make meaningful decisions sooner.

4. **Faster Recognition and Reward for Good Work.** Owners of small firms can readily observe, compliment, and reward exceptional employee achievements. Feedback on performance is faster and more accurately reflects the true value of the employee's contribution. Rewards can be custom tailored to the employee's desires.

5. **Visibility.** Employees cannot become lost. They will not be overlooked and will not remain nameless. They will be able to show what they can do to top management.

6. **Quicker Assumption of Meaningful Responsibility and Authority.** Professional contribution and competence are highly valued in the small company, and the competent employee will be quickly rewarded with assignment of major responsibilities along with the authority necessary to get the job done. This leads to:

7. **Rapid Advancement.** The competent employee can look forward to a shorter path to the top of the company. There are fewer people to compete with for the top spot, and the odds in favor of becoming the chief executive are better.

8. **Roots.** Smaller firms tend to serve more concentrated geographic areas. This benefits employees who want to work in the area where they live. It means less travel, fewer moves, and more time at home with the family for the rising executive.

9. **Job Security.** Job security is surprisingly good for key employees in successful small companies. Such companies are less likely than large companies to overstaff in good times and therefore less likely to lay off in bad times.

10. **The Ownership Edge.** Employees in a small company often have the chance to become owners or at least to share significantly in the profits they produce for the company.

Where to Look for Employees

Once you have clearly defined the job and the qualifications required for the job, you are ready to search for the right employee to fill the position. Before you do, however, take another close look at the job and the qualifications. Do you need the job done year round? Does the job require high skill but few hours per week? Can employees you have now do the job well? Can a machine do the job? Can a more efficient paperwork system eliminate the need for the job?

You have several options besides hiring a new full-time employee. Remember the objective is to do those things essential to reaching your goals extremely well and to keep your payroll lean at the same time. What are your options? The following are some suggestions:

1. **Use Free Services**. A surprising number of free services are available to you from your suppliers, your banker, and your trade association in return for your patronage. Even your customers might be convinced to handle certain services it is more costly for you to provide.

2. **Reevaluate Work Loads**. Sometimes reorganizing the critical tasks that you need accomplished can eliminate the need for expensive new help. Are your key employees wasting a good portion of their time doing routine tasks? If a new secretary relieved them of this routine work, could they handle the critical tasks you had in mind? Can an inexpensive machine do the routine tasks, freeing staff time for critical tasks? Can your paperwork procedures be streamlined to free staff hours?

3. **Use Contract Services**. If you need a specific job done well but do not need a full-time expert on your staff, contract services make sense. Examples range from answering services to advertising agencies. Contract services provide you with expert help on a fee basis when you need it without the complications involved in hiring employees. Accountants, attorneys, consultants, and computerized accounting services fall into this category. You can often create your own pool of expert consultants

that you can call on when you need them. Key executives in large local firms, retired executives, trade association executives, and university professors often have the skills you need and are more than willing to serve as consultants. Appendix A to this chapter explains how to select consultants and how to make sure they perform well.

4. **Promote From Within**. One of your present employees with proven initiative may be capable of handling the job you have in mind. The job vacated may be easier to fill.

5. **Pay Overtime**. If there are temporary peaks in workload due to holiday seasons or contract due dates, paying overtime to present employees who wish to earn extra money may be cheaper than recruiting and training new help.

6. **Hire Part-Time Employees**. Two part-time employees can often meet your objectives better than a single full-time employee. If, for example, fast service is your goal during peak periods, seasonal employees are often available during peak seasons for many years, thus reducing training costs. Experts may be available part-time for a moonlight position. Highly qualified retirees may consider part-time, but not full-time, work.

There are several plans to look for new employees. Exhibit 14.4 is a list of traditional sources prepared by the Bank of America.[12] You should also explore several sources beyond the traditional ones. Sources we recommend in addition to those listed in Exhibit 14.4 include:

1. **Your Employees**. Post the job descriptions for the jobs you want to fill. Interested employees might apply, as noted above, or employees may refer a qualified friend to you. You might consider offering financial incentives for referrals that work out.

2. **Your Former Employees**. Keep in touch with qualified former employees. Keep track of their growth in your industry. Let them know about job openings that match their skills.

3. **Qualified Applicants You Once Turned Down**. Keep a record of people you were unable to hire in the past but were interested in at the time. Recontact them if they seem qualified for the job you are trying to fill now.

4. **Associations and Other Trade Sources**. Your industry and/or professional associations may provide job referral services. Association newsletters and trade journals often feature classified sections in which you can advertise job openings. Such ads are sure to be read by exactly the kind of people you need.

As you can see, the list of places to look for qualified employees is long. Careful analysis of the jobs you want to fill should suggest which of these sources will be practical for you. Once you know the kinds of people you need, go out and recruit. Limiting employee applications to people who happen to stop in and ask for a job is false economy.

Exhibit 14.4   Sources for Locating Employees

Source and Cost	Characteristics
Classified ads in the "help wanted" section of metropolitan newspapers, community shoppers, and trade publications are well read by job seekers. Costs vary with readership, number of times ad is run, complexity of copy and artwork.	Employer can choose to have applicants reply by telephone or write to a box number; the latter method allows for confidential replies and application screening before scheduled interviews. Trade publications are especially advantageous in reaching a specific industry audience.
Private employment agencies match job seekers and employers and may specialize in clerical, manual, executive, or other job classifications. A fee of 5% to 15% of the first year's salary may be paid by either the applicant or employer.	Many agencies prescreen applicants, ideally weeding out unsuitable candidates. The employer pays a fee only if the agency's applicant is hired or pays a temporary or reduced fee if the employee fails to stay a guaranteed length of time.
Temporary agencies recruit, test, and hire people in a number of job categories and place them with employers for limited periods of time. The employer pays a fee based on the number of hours worked. Rates vary depending on job classification.	Employer can obtain qualified people on short notice for emergency projects, seasonal relief. Hourly rates are more expensive than straight hire, although administrative costs are eliminated and the employer does not have to add another person to the payroll.
State employment agencies are under federal auspices with 2,000 offices throughout the U.S. Costs are paid by taxes on payrolls, and services are free to both employers and employees.	A nationwide network of offices enables wide recruitment. In some areas, computer job banks match jobs with applicants. Service may be somewhat less personal than with a small private agency.
Unions may have an excellent referral system, especially in metropolitan areas and in certain job categories. Referral services are free.	Referrals are usually experienced and have union approval, although some unions require that referrals be accepted sight unseen.
Schools—trade, professional, vocational, local high schools, and colleges—may have placement counselors or maintain job bulletin boards. Referral services are free.	While students may be inexperienced, they are often available part-time, on holidays, and for emergencies and are not looking for long-term employment or benefit programs.
Community organizations, both private and public, are set up to improve local community conditions and often have job-training programs. Referral services are free.	Applicants may lack previous experience and require special attention. Grants for training are sometimes available from the Department of Labor.

Job Application Forms

Each person you consider for a job should complete a job application. This application provides you with relevant personal data, work experience, job skill information, and references in a standard format that facilitates comparison of applicants. For those you hire, the application form becomes a convenient inventory of the applicant's entry level skills. Although you may not use all the applicant's skills initially, you may need more of them in the future. As noted above, even if you do not hire a qualified applicant now, you may want to consider the applicant when jobs open in the future. Application forms, properly indexed by job skill, can give you names to consider for new job openings.

For ideas for designing your application forms, we suggest you study those used by the larger firms in your industry. They are likely to be up to date in terms of including only nondiscriminatory questions. They also have been proven by experience, at least in regard to the collection of essential biographical data. You will want to custom design the questions you ask about experience and skills. We suggest you hire someone experienced in personnel to spend an hour or two reviewing your application before it is printed. (Perhaps the personnel director for a large local company would be willing to act as your consultant in this regard.)

Tests

Two types of test are of value to the small company: physical examinations and performance tests. Physical examinations are particularly important where the job requires above-average physical qualities, such as vision or stamina, or where the health and safety of the public or coworkers could be affected. Performance tests are sometimes useful for technical jobs or for jobs requiring special skills. The closer such tests simulate the actual employment situation, the better. Indeed, a tryout prior to actual employment is often a practical testing scheme.

Interviews

The main purpose of a job interview is to evaluate how well the applicant matches the set of qualifications you have established for the job. Your goal should be to discover job-related facts about the applicant that verify or expand the information in the application form. Another important purpose of a job interview is to give the applicant the facts about the job. Compensation, job duties, job potential, and company goals should be discussed frankly.

Generally, you will do a better interviewing job if you keep two guidelines in mind:

1. Prepare a list of questions you believe will draw out responses that will reveal how the applicant fits critical job qualifications. Use this standard list for all interviews. The applicant may volunteer the answers to some questions during the course of the interview. Others may have to be asked to get answers. Either way, make sure you get a complete set of answers from each applicant. A standard list of questions will give you a basis of comparison among applicants and improve your choice.

2. The more people that interview the applicant, the better. Interviews by more than one person tend to reveal more facts about the applicant and permit crosschecking of individual evaluations of the applicant's qualifications.

In addition to our two general guidelines, Forrest H. Frantz recommends five useful guidelines for interviews:[13]

1. Be natural and make the applicant feel at ease. Hold the interview privately and without interruptions.

2. Encourage the applicant to tell you about his (or her) previous work experience and training. Be prepared to lead him with questions but make the questions sufficiently *indirect* to encourage him to talk freely. Avoid direct questions that turn the interview into a question-and-answer period. For example, *say*, "You've been working for Ferguson Tool Company for three years, and you've had considerable previous experience. I'd like to know more about you and your working experience." *Don't ask*, "What was your first responsibility at Ferguson?" The approach to encouraging the interviewee to talk freely is called *nondirective* interviewing. (*Directive* interviewing, on the other hand, employs direct questions and encourages specific answers, thus tending to confine the conversation boundaries.)

   Once the nondirective interview is launched, you can keep the applicant talking with comments such as "I agree," "That's great," "Certainly," and "You finished that job in three hours?" Restatement of the interviewee's conversation in question form, as well as your verbal and nonverbal responses, tend to keep him talking.

   Your big job is to listen, and to listen well. It's preferable *not* to make notes in the applicant's presence because this tends to make some interviewees uneasy. Make notes after the interview out of the applicant's sight and place them in the applicant's file. This will help you to recall the individual and the interview when you prepare to make your final selection or wish to take any other action in the matter. This information will also be useful if the applicant is not selected for the job at hand but is to be considered for a future opening.

3. Have copies of the job description and specification available to show and to discuss with the applicant. Be sure that he understands what's expected and that he knows enough about your company and you to reach an intelligent decision if a job is offered.

4. If the talk turns to pay or incentives, let the person know the specific pay if it's nailed down. If otherwise—for example, if pay is to be

based on the applicant's experience, present salary, and so forth—say so and indicate that any offer, if made, will specify the pay.

5. Keep the objectives of the interview in mind. They are to determine the applicant's experience, ability, integrity, attitudes, fit to the job, and fit to your organization. You may have additional objectives. Again, employ nondirective techniques in exploring these areas.

Reference Checking

Employers, big and small, routinely ask applicants for previous employment records and references. Surprisingly, few small employers check such references thoroughly. Obviously, it is impractical to check the references on every application form, but it is important to check them for applicants who appear promising after initial testing and interviewing. Never take an application at its face value.

Generally speaking, work references are more useful than personal references. Former employers tend to be more objective than an applicant's friends. Information provided verbally by those listed as references also tends to be more candid. A personal visit to a former employer will produce more information than a telephone call.

All references should be taken with a grain of salt. On the one hand, irrelevant personality clashes with your applicant may lead a former employer to give a bad reference. On the other hand, former employers may be hesitant to mention your applicant's weaknesses if they feel it will prevent him or her from getting a job. Cohn and Lindberg suggest several questions you can ask to get useful answers: "If this employee hadn't left, would you have retained him or her? Why? How far would this employee have gone in your company in three years? What are the best things he or she did for you? On a scale of ten, how would you rate the employee's job performance? How could it have been improved?"[14]

CASE SOLUTION

Paragon Injection Molders, Inc.

Paul Green attacked his hiring problem on two fronts. First, he hired an inexperienced man named John who walked in one day asking for a job. Paul liked John and decided to train him to be his lead machine operator even though John had little mechanical knowledge. Second, he contracted with two independent manufacturers' representatives to sell his product. Each represented several different manufacturers and sold on a straight commission basis. One represented companies that made metal castings and did not have any previous injection molding experience. Paul knew very little about the second representative beyond the fact that he was interested in representing Paul's company.

Paul ran into several problems as a result of his hiring practices. An analysis of the way he spent his time revealed that 30 percent was used training John. Paul spent an additional 30 percent of his time doing most of the quality control work, which John could have done if he had been a more experienced operator. When Paul was questioned about John, he indicated John was a bargain since he worked for $4.50 an hour, when an experienced operator would have cost $8.50 per hour. Simple mathematics reveals the fallacy in Paul's logic. Since Paul worked fifty hours per week, thirty hours of his time could have been saved if he had hired an experienced operator who needed little training to maintain and operate the machinery and to carry out quality control activities. The extra cost of the experienced operator would have been $3.50 per hour, or $140.00 for a 40-hour workweek. This amounted to about $4.67 for each hour used of Paul's time that was sorely needed elsewhere to bolster the company's selling effort.

Although the use of manufacturers' representatives is an effective way for a company like Paul's to sell its products, the manufacturers' representatives Paul settled on had little specific knowledge about his product and had too many other clients. They simply did not have time to sell his products adequately. Further, the representatives had been given large sales territories that encompassed virtually all of Paul's potential customers. This prevented Paul from making sales without involving the representatives. One representative produced no orders and was dropped. The other produced a singificant number of orders, but his sales volume was far below the company's breakeven point.

Lack of careful hiring procedures had cost Paul dearly by strangling his direct sales to potential customers. Had Paul clearly established his goals for both his manufacturing operations and his sales operations, he could have avoided the above problems. Such an analysis would have led to clear job descriptions for himself and his employees and representatives and would have most likely led to a listing of critical qualifications for his machine operator and his sales representatives that would have helped him avoid the hiring mistakes he made. Armed with these qualifications, Paul could have recruited in the industry to get topnotch people instead of settling for three people who happened to show an interest in his company. He could have employed systematic selection procedures to insure that the people he selected were indeed well qualified. Once he had made his hiring decision, his list of critical job behaviors could have been used as a yardstick to measure performance and insure that his goals were met by his new employees.

Effective hiring practices would have made an enormous difference for Paul Green and Paragon Injection Molders, Inc. Instead of having financial problems, Paul and his company would most likely have made an excellent profit.

CHAPTER SUMMARY

If you want to hire effectively, you must have good answers to each of the three questions given at the beginning of this chapter: What kinds of people do you need? How do you find job applicants? How do you tell which applicant is the best for the job?

A good part of the answers to the first and third questions lies in clear definition of your company's goals and the translation of these company goals into a list of critical jobs and critical behaviors that need to be done right to accomplish your company goals. Focusing on critical jobs will keep your payroll lean. You will thus be able to afford to hire qualified people. Also, clear definition of critical job behaviors provides you with a shopping list of job qualifications that you can focus on when you select employees.

The second question is also affected by clear definition of your goals and jobs. This is because your list of critical job qualifications will normally suggest where you should look for the job applicants you want.

After your company's goals and jobs are clearly defined, you are well armed to begin an employee search. This chapter discusses several specific topics related to this search. Ten recruiting advantages enjoyed by small businesses are listed. Ideas concerning where to look for employees are reviewed. The chapter concludes with a discussion of the three major ways to collect data about the qualifications of job applicants: job application forms, tests, and interviews.

DISCUSSION QUESTIONS

1. **Short Case: Nichelson's Shoes I**

    Michael Manin has built up Nichelson's Shoes from a single old storefront to three good-sized, mall stores since he bought the original store from Fred Nichelson four years ago. Nichelson's Shoes had always had a good reputation in the community for quality goods and service. Michael has kept this reputation alive and has added to it. His problem is that he has not been able to find what he terms "decent managers" for any of his stores. He is managing all three stores himself, making do by giving certain, routine management responsibilities to sales people in each store. He is really in a bind because the shortest driving distance between the three stores is forty miles. It seems he is constantly on the road. Still, he cannot seem to hire the kind of manager he wants. The people he hires seem unwilling to do things his way, or they quit after a few months. So far, he has tried out ten managers, none of whom has worked out.

    a. Based on what you have read in this chapter, why do you think Michael is having this problem?

    b. Devise a systematic, step-by-step scheme for finding Michael the store managers he needs.

2. As noted in this chapter, sometimes the best solution to what appears to be a hiring problem does not turn out to be a new full-time employee. What other choices might be possible for the following jobs?

    a. Maintenance Man—Property Management Company.

    b. Accounting Clerk—Construction Firm.

    c. Market Research Specialist—Fire Engine Repair Company.

3. What are the five most critical job behaviors for the following two jobs?
   a. Waitress—Exclusive Restaurant.
   b. Salesperson—Computer Store.
4. Based on your answer to Question 3, write a job description for each job.
5. Assume you are about to open an auto parts store. Based on what you know about your own skill and background, write a job description for the one key employee you can afford to hire.

REFERENCES

Bruckman, John C. and Iman, Steve. "Consulting with Small Business: A Process Model." *Journal of Small Business Management* 18, 2 (April, 1980): 41–47.

Cingolani, Melodie. "Personnel Guidelines." *Small Business Reporter* 14, 2 (1978).

Cohn, Theodore, and Lindberg, Roy. *Compensating Key Executives in the Smaller Company*. New York: AMACOM, 1974.

Cohn, Theodore, and Lindberg, Roy. *Survival and Growth: Management Strategies for the Small Firm.* New York: AMACOM, 1974.

Frantz, Forrest H. *Successful Small Business Management.* Englewood Cliffs, NJ: Prentice-Hall, Inc., 1978.

Steinhoff, Dan. *Small Business Management Fundamentals,* 2nd ed. New York: McGraw-Hill Book Co., 1978.

FOOTNOTES

1. This case was prepared by one of the authors based upon a Small Business Institute counseling report completed under his supervision. In order to maintain client confidentiality, the facts given here are somewhat different from the original case.

2. Theodore Cohn and Roy Lindberg, *Survival and Growth: Management Strategies for the Small Firm* (New York: AMACOM, a division of American Management Associations, 1974), p. 136.

3. Theodore Cohn and Roy Lindberg elaborate on this point in their book, *Compensating Key Executives in the Smaller Company* (New York: AMACOM, 1974). They also point out that analyzing your business plan lays the groundwork for designing compensation plans that focus workers' efforts on what needs to be done in order to make the company succeed.

4. Jui Komaki; William H. Waddell; and M. George Pearce, "The Applied Behavior Analysis Approach and Individual Employees: Improving Performance in Two Small Businesses," *Organizational Behavior and Human Performance* 19 (1977): 339.

5. Melodie Cingolani, "Personnel Guidelines," *Small Business Reporter* 15: 3, © 1978, 1981. Reprinted with permission from Bank of America, NT & SA.

6. Dan Steinhoff, *Small Business Management Fundamentals,* 2nd ed. (New York: McGraw-Hill Book Company, 1978), p. 253.

7. Equal Employment Opportunity (EEO)legislation, for example, affects all means of choosing among job applicants. It is unlawful for employers to fail or refuse to hire any individual because of such individual's race, color, religion, sex, national origin, age, or handicap unless it can be demonstrated that such characteristics fairly screen out those individuals with the greatest probability of job failure. Jack English dis-

cusses the best approach to meeting EEO requirements when recruiting and selecting employees in "How to Pick the Best People Under EEO," *S.A.M. Advanced Management Journal* 44, no. 3 (Summer 1979): 23–30. Jerome Siegel presents a very detailed discussion in *Personnel Testing Under EEO: An AMA Research Study* (New York: AMACOM, 1980).

8. Cohn and Lindberg, *Survival and Growth*, p. 153, note that, "In the enthusiasm of hiring specialists, small business managers are often guilty of the white-knight delusion: Get the new man on board fast, and don't bother with job details; just turn him loose, and he will solve all our problems. Instead, the new employee should be told the tasks he is to perform, the results expected, the standards for measuring performance, the order of priorities, the review and communication procedures, the person he reports to, the employees who report to him, and the kinds of money and personnel decisions he can make without approval."

9. Kenneth E. Rindt, "Small Firm Personnel Problems and Management Assistance," *Journal of Small Business Management* 13, no. 3 (July 1975): 15. This article reports on research conducted concerning the use of employment agencies by small businesses.

10. Kamal E. Said and J. Keith Hughey, "Managerial Problems of the Small Firm," *Journal of Small Business Management* 15, no. 1 (January 1977): 38.

11. This list was compiled from a variety of sources but owes much to four sources in particular: Said and Hughey, "Managerial Problems of the Small Firm," p. 38; George W. Rimler and Neil J. Humphreys, "The 'New Employee' and the Small Firm: Some Insights to Modern Personnel Management," *Journal of Small Business Management* 14, no. 3 (July 1976): 25–27; Cohn and Lindberg, *Survival and Growth*, pp. 129–130; and Steinhoff, *Small Business Management Fundamentals*, pp. 250–251.

12. Cingolani, "Personnel Guidelines", p. 3.

13. Forrest H. Frantz, *Successful Small Business Management* (Englewood Cliffs, N.J.: Prentice-Hall, Inc. 1978), p. 366. Reprinted by permission of the publisher.

14. Cohn and Lindberg, *Survival and Growth*, p. 133.

Appendix A

CONSULTANTS: HOW TO SELECT THEM AND MAKE SURE THEY PERFORM WELL

If you need a specific job done well but do not need a full-time expert on your staff, it often pays to hire a consultant to do the job for you. Consultants can provide the services you need on a fee basis, without all the complications involved in hiring employees. Consultants are not, however, white knights who can come into your company and solve all your problems for you. You need to know which problems consultants can help with, how to find consultants with expertise to solve these problems, and how to monitor the consultants' activities to make sure you get your money's worth. The purpose of this appendix is to answer these three questions.

What Kinds of Problems Can Consultants Help You With?

The reason for using consultants is to obtain expertise you do not have within your own organization. It is commonly recognized that successful small business owner/managers make frequent use of outside help from financial, legal, and accounting specialists; less successful firms use such outside help only occasionally, when immediate pressures, such as tax deadlines, require it.[1] Kenneth E. Rindt adds personnel experts to the list of needed specialists. He argues that the typical business owner/manager has limited knowledge in the area of personnel and needs ongoing outside advice on hiring and training activities.[2]

Other consultants suggest that they are useful in less technical areas, such as sales, operations, productivity, and financial control—the dynamics of running your company. Thomas Faulhaber, for example, argues: "I don't know more about your business than you do, but I do know management. Also, I'm not so close to your operations that I know the business too well. I am in a position to see the forest as well as the trees. The right consultant brings certain ways of looking at things, analyzing problems, finding solutions that many small companies don't have."[3]

What kinds of problems are consultants particularly good at solving? John C. Shaw suggests consultants should be used for (1) gauging the feasibility of a new idea, (2) confronting a problem that may require a redirection of corporate strategy, such as a significant loss of market share, and (3) solving a specific problem or filling a special technical need on a limited basis.[4] If a problem you face is one you do not have time to solve on your own, if you feel solving the problem requires specialized knowledge or experience you don't have, if you feel the problem could benefit from an independent and objective outside point of view, and/or if you feel the problem lends itself to a methodical scientific approach to solution, then you should consider using a consultant.

There are two things to remember. First, if you have a problem you have not been able to solve, you may not really understand the true nature of the problem. It may be different from what you think. Consultants are useful for helping you define what the problem really is. Second, it can be profitable to have your operations checked periodically by an outsider even if you think things are running smoothly. An independent view may reveal hidden pitfalls or opportunites that currently exist or are just now coming over the planning horizon.

How Do You Find Consultants With the Expertise to Solve Your Problems?

Not all management consultants are professionals. There are several thousand consultants or consulting firms in the United States. Some are incompetent. Some are excellent. How do you tell the difference? The answer is to take the same precautions you would if you were hiring a management employee. Perhaps the best starting point when looking for a consultant is to seek referrals from business associates or other professionals you trust, such as your banker, your accountant, or your industry association representative. If good referrals are not available, you can try your local university or contact two consultants' associations that restrict their membership and accredit their members:

> The Association of Management Consultants
> 500 N. Michigan
> Chicago, Illinois 60611
> (312) 661-1700
> (Membership is composed of small consulting firms.)

> The Institute of Management Consultants
> 19 W. 44th Street
> New York, New York 10036
> (212) 921-2885
> (Member is made up of individual consultants.)

Once you line up a prospective consultant, there are four rules you must follow to evaluate him or her. The first is to ask for recommendations from satisfied clients. Check with these clients to determine the quality of the consultant's work. Ask them whether or not the consultant completes projects on time, what the consultant's strengths and weaknesses are, what the consultant's style (approach to people) is, and whether or not the consultant has been or would be awarded repeat business. The second rule is to evaluate expertise. Is the consultant recognized as an expert in your problem area? What experience does the consultant have with your industry and with your type of problem? The third rule is to watch out for consultants who promise results before having had a chance to study your business carefully. The fourth, and final, rule is to pick a consultant you feel comfortable with. You will have to be able to work well with the consultant, or nothing will get done.

Once you think you have found the consultant you want, we suggest you try him or her out on a small part of the project before making a full commitment. Observe how much of your time the consultant takes and how he or she works with your people. See if the consultant identifies practical ways for you to implement suggested solutions. Don't be hesitant to question the consultant closely if you think his or her proposals do not make good business sense.

How Do You Get Your Money's Worth from a Consultant?

There are six steps to getting the most out of a consultant. The first is to define the task. The scope of the work cannot be defined exactly at the outset, but you can write an informal contract describing what is expected of the consultant and what the consultant expects of you. The more complex the project, the more formal this contract should be in regard to necessary meetings, nature of the work, timetables, and fees. Generally, the consultant should be able to give at an early date a reasonably accurate projection of the cost and time required for the following phases of the project: defining your problems, planning necessary research, collecting data, analyzing data, developing and evaluating alternative responses to the problem, preparing a plan for solution, and implementing the plan.[5] It is a good idea to have the consultant update the cost and time projections at the end of each phase. This permits you to weigh the cost of further work against the potential benefit to you at each step. If the project will take considerable time, you should require progress reports and revised time and cost estimates at least every two months.[6]

The second step for getting the most out of a consultant is to disclose fully to him or her all relevant company information. This includes your candid assessment of the financial, physical, and human resources of the firm. If you are concerned about secrecy, we recommend that rather than keeping some information from the consultant, you use a secrecy agreement to hold the consultant accountable if the secret is made public. The consultant must have full information to diagnose your problem accurately and solve it effectively.

Step three is to make it clear to the consultant that you want a frank, unbiased assessment of your situation. This is the reason you are spending money on a consultant. You are not hiring the consultant to agree with you on everything.

The fourth step is to insist that all solutions suggested by the consultant include practical, concrete steps for implementation. Make sure you understand clearly how you can use these steps to reach the solution. Make it clear you do not consider the consultant's job to be over until he or she has helped implement the solutions in a practical manner.

Step five is never to accept the consultant's solution at face value. Question it. Make sure it will work for your company with a reasonable expenditure of money, time, and effort. If the plan seems too costly or requires the use of resources you don't have; make the consultant specify why the plan is worth it and where you can find the resources you need.

The last step is to act. Once the consultant has developed a solution you have confidence in, commit yourself to it and do what is necessary to make it work. Remember the consultant's recommendations are worthless unless you follow them.

APPENDIX FOOTNOTES

1. Kenneth E. Rindt, "Small Firm Personnel Problems and Management Assistance," p. 13.

2. *Ibid.*, p. 15

3. Paul W. Kellam, editor, "A Small Company President Talks Back to Consultants," *Inc.* 2, no. 5 (May 1980): 84.

4. John C. Shaw, "Hiring Consultants: Common Sense for Clients," *Boardroom Reports* 9, no. 6 (March 24, 1980): 6. Mr. Shaw heads the New York office of Touche Ross and Co.

5. These steps or phrases of a typical consulting project were suggested by John C. Bruckman and Steve Iman, "Consulting with Small Business: A Process Model," *Journal of Small Business Management* 18, no. 2 (April 1980): 41–47. This article is an excellent discussion of what to expect from a professional consultant and gives useful insights on how to organize yourself to get the most from the consulting project.

6. Shaw, "Hiring Consultants," p. 6.

Pay | 15

☐ **What should you pay your employees?**

☐ **What fringe benefits should you offer?**

☐ **What incentive programs can make your employees more productive?**

CASE
PROBLEM

*Interiors,
Inc.*[1]

Interiors, Inc. was founded by Mr. and Mrs. Stein. The company operates a retail store that sells a full line of home-decorating products, including drapes, floor coverings, paint, wallpaper, and accessories. The company also provides advice on interior design. Its target market is upper middle class do-it-yourselfers. To date, the store has been very successful. It appears that this is due to a variety of factors, including friendly, well-trained employees who notice when customers need help; a wide selection of samples to choose from; and a neat, well-decorated store.

Encouraged by the success of their store, Mr. and Mrs. Stein recently decided to begin a franchise operation. The Steins reasoned that franchising would permit them to expand on their success rapidly with a minimum capital outlay. Their objective is to help others to succeed in their industry in return for a small percentage of the profits.

The decision to franchise raised several questions about pay. How much should the franchises pay their sales people? Should sales people be paid commissions? What benefits should they be offered? How should store managers be compensated? Should bonus plans or profit sharing be recommended? Also, the franchises will require a central administrative staff, including field representatives to advise franchises. How should these representatives be compensated?

PROBLEM
IDENTIFICATION

The pay problem faced by the Steins is somewhat more complicated than it might first appear. Several factors must be considered when deciding on compensation for employees. For example, what the employee is worth, what you can afford to pay, and what your competitors pay are three important factors. Even more basic are the level and kind of compensation you will need to offer to attract and keep good employees. You must consider both the impact of pay on employee motivation and the investment aspects of pay.

How much you pay and how you pay your employees have a strong impact on their motivation. If we review the marketing strategy of Interiors,

Inc., we can see how the choice of compensation could affect employee motivation and consequently the company's profitability. Consider, for example, the idea of paying salespersons commissions. On the one hand, commissions might motivate the salespersons to provide prompt attention to customers and to try to sell more of those items that earn the most commission. On the other hand, commissions may discourage patient assistance to difficult customers, who do not look like good candidates for an immediate sale but who, in the long run, might buy more. Since personalized service is a major competitive edge for Interiors, Inc., any compensation plan used must encourage the sales people to provide personalized service.

Another aspect of the company's marketing strategy is to have knowledgeable sales people wait on customers. It takes time and effort for salespersons to acquire the knowledge they need. Does the compensation system give them an incentive to learn what they need to know quickly and well? Is compensation adequate to prevent the loss of experienced employees to the competition?

A third aspect of the Steins' marketing strategy is to keep the store neat and orderly, the theory being that a well-organized store appears more professional, is more inviting to browsers, and helps customers find what they want more easily. The sales people need to pick the store up constantly to maintain its neat appearance. As we saw in the last chapter, compensation can affect even routine matters, such as keeping the store neat. In the research study we discussed in that chapter, two clerks at a small grocery store received time off with pay for consistent attainment of three goals, two of which involved customer service and one of which was keeping shelves stocked with merchandise.

As noted in chapter 14, hiring a new employee is a human resource investment. Because hiring is an investment, many of the same rules that apply to purchasing a new machine also apply to hiring a new employee. Cost must be weighed against worth. Worth is defined in terms of the value of the job to be done. The value of the job depends on its contribution to your company's competitive edge—to your company's bottom line.

The comparison of a new employee with a machine is useful only to a certain point. Unlike machines, people have aspirations. They have a complex set of needs. Their needs vary in intensity, and they vary over time. Pay is an investment for you, but it is a means to satisfy needs for your employees. The return on your investment depends on human emotion.

DIAGNOSIS

Diagnosis of the effectiveness of your pay system actually begins with Questions 1 through 4 in Exhibit 14.1. If you have carefully analyzed the jobs in your company and prepared written job descriptions, you should now be able to answer yes to these questions. Yes answers give you a solid foundation for an effective pay system. Can you honestly answer yes to all four? If so, you are prepared to make sound human resource investments, once you adjust for the unique needs of each person you hire. If not, your profits and the morale of your employees may well be in jeopardy. If you do not know how much something is worth, you may pay too much or offer too little and miss a golden opportunity. If you do not know what an employee is worth, you can easily be unfair. You may pay too much, which is unfair to other employees, or too little, which is unfair to a good employee. How can you reward employees for good work if you do not define what constitutes a job well done?

There are several other factors that determine the effectiveness of your pay system. They relate to the employee's *perception* of the need fulfilling potential of the pay you offer. Your answers to the following ten questions will help you diagnose how effectively your pay system deals with these factors. Write down your answer to each before reading further.

1. How would you determine the pay for two employees working at similar jobs?

2. Can you list the key employees in your company who would be very hard to replace?

3. In percentage terms, how much more do your key employees make than your average or marginal employees doing the same work?

4. Do you know if your key employees are satisfied with—
   a. their pay relative to what others make (Question 3)?
   b. their pay relative to what they think they are worth to the firm?
   c. their fringe benefits?
   d. their chance to make more money?

5. When is the last time you checked around to see what workers like yours are paid by other companies in your industry?

6. What is your method for figuring out who should be given a raise or bonus?

7. Do you offer some or all of your employees extra pay for extra output? If so, describe how the extra pay is calculated, who gets it, why they get it, and when they get it.

8. Do you give across-the-board pay increases? Why or why not?

9. Are owners or owners' family members on the payroll of your company? If so, describe how you calculate salaries for these people.

10. Is your company unionized? How do unions affect the way you pay your employees?

Now that you have written down your answers to the above ten questions, it is time to compare your pay practices with those recommended by experts in motivation and compensation. The "Understanding" section summarizes what the experts think. How do your pay practices measure up?

How much you pay your employees and how you pay them have a major impact on your company's profitability. There is no doubt that the level and kind of compensation you offer influence employee productivity and your ability to hire and keep good people. As we will see in chapter 16, your ability to attract and keep productive help depends on many factors in addition to how much and how you pay. Still, in our society, pay is probably the single most powerful tool you have at your disposal for getting others to do what you want them to do.[2]

What Pay Is

In order to understand what will make your pay system effective, you must first understand what pay is.[3] Pay is money—money you give directly to employees and money you spend on their behalf to purchase fringe benefits, such as health insurance. When you offer to pay someone to work for you, you are offering to exchange money for his or her time and talents. Your offer and the employee's acceptance creates a contract. Written or unwritten, this contract governs the working relationship. To be sure, your offer of employment probably includes other inducements besides money, such as good working conditions, fair supervision, a chance to develop skills, appreciation of good work, rapid advancement, and status; but the money you offer initially, the amount and nature of bonuses and raises you give, and the timing of these bonuses and raises have a strong impact on the success of the contract. The pay the employee receives from you is a concrete, unequivocal statement of how much you value the employee's work. Verbal praise for an exceptional job is certainly important, but a bonus in the pay envelope to reinforce what you say will do a lot to insure that the employee does an exceptional job in the next pay period.

Pay also expresses how much you value an employee's work relative to others. Questions of fairness and equity become involved not only because of the economic value of the dollars involved but also because of the importance the employee places on your valuation of him or her relative to other employees. How much extra is the employee getting, for example, for exceptional productivity relative to a marginal performer? If the answer is peanuts, the employee may well say, "Why bother to work hard? The boss doesn't care. Otherwise I would be paid well for the extra value I contribute. The whole thing is unfair."

Keep the above observations about the nature of pay in mind as we review the characteristics of an effective pay system. They dictate what will work and what will not.

The Characteristics of an Effective Pay System

The characteristics of an effective pay system are fairly well agreed upon. William J. Kearney echoes the beliefs of many motivation experts when he summarizes four conditions that must be met if pay or any other motivator, such as praise or recognition, is to encourage workers to perform at high levels. These four conditions are described below:[4]

1. The employee must believe that his or her additional effort will improve performance. Obstacles to a clear relationship between effort and performance, such as vague work objectives, hazy job definitions, inadequate tools, and inadequate training, must be eliminated.

2. The employee must perceive that better performance will be noticed.

3. The employee must see that better performance leads immediately to rewards that he or she wants and values and perceives as equitable, given the effort required to achieve the improvement in performance and what others are paid for a similar level of performance. The employee must see good performance as the most attractive of all possible behaviors.

4. The rewards the employee receives for achieving results must not come at an unacceptable cost in terms of the employee's other goals. Positive consequences from good performance must exceed negative consequences. Generous overtime pay and productivity bonuses, for example, lose their value as fatigue increases and health deteriorates from overwork.

In short, to influence performance significantly, you must use rewards that are contingent upon performance. Pay is a major reward, and your company should pay for performance.[5] This is so obvious that it is almost a truism. However, as we shall see, it is a prescription that is very difficult to follow in the real world of small business.

Obstacles to Paying for Performance

Why is it difficult to pay for performance? There are several obstacles in your way. You must overcome them before you can build an effective pay system. These obstacles and ways of overcoming them are discussed below.

Money.   You need topflight people to make your company's sales and profits grow rapidly, but you will not have the money to pay them well until they do a lot of hard work to make your company successful. You need cash to grow, but you also need good people. Will they accept a pile of IOUs in return for outstanding performance?

A two-step strategy can be used to overcome this obstacle.[6] First, you must identify the two or three key jobs needed to make your company grow. These jobs must be occupied by people who have the drive, the knowledge, and the vision to identify profit opportunities and capture them for your company. These people are a lot like you in that they see your company's potential and will work hard to reach it. They will not be easily replaced.

The second step of the strategy is to offer your key people substantial incentive pay. There are a couple of ways to do this. One relatively formal approach is to offer your key people relatively low salaries but agree to pay them a substantial share of your pretax profits after an agreed amount of money is set aside to meet company needs. This arrangement costs nothing if the key employees turn out to be average performers; and since there are only a few of these key employees, it costs little relative to your profits if they make you very successful. Another, more informal, way to give incentive pay is to use bonuses.[7] Again, the relatively low (but not too low) salaries are guaranteed, and periodic bonuses are paid for outstanding performance. No performance, no bonus. If you use the more informal approach, be sure employees understand what they have to do to earn a bonus of a given size.

What about employees who are less committed to your company goals and easier to replace than key employees? Fair salaries are important, and bonuses may help. Generally, though, such employees will pay more attention to their base salary, and the promise of a significant bonus will do less good. This is partly because their commitment to the organization is not as strong as that of key personnel. It is primarily because they do not have as much influence over the destiny of the company as your few key people. They do not create the company's growth. The limit on their potential contribution to profits is reached relatively soon, no matter how big the bonus or how hard they work to try to earn it. Bonuses to these employees should be paid for competency and efficiency and should be in line with the extra value for you of a good worker relative to a marginal worker in a given job. Again, continued bonuses should be contingent on continued high competency and efficiency.

Measuring Performance. For rewards to be fair and motivating, they must be tied to key results accomplished by the employee. Defining key results and measuring their accomplishment is hard work. Behavioral requirements of the work must be spelled out, with job performance goals stated in measurable terms, such as number of parts to be produced, quality standards to be satisfied, or deadlines to be met. Decisions have to be made about when to measure performance and someone has to take the time to measure performance accurately. Differentiation is necessary between good performers and outstanding performers so that rewards can be meted out fairly.

You should already have a good portion of this obstacle overcome based on the discussion in chapter 14. If you have analyzed the job carefully before hiring, you will not have a great deal of difficulty identifying performance measures. More is required, however, since you must also devise means to measure accomplishment of results accurately.

Competition. In order to attract and keep the help you need, your pay must be competitive with pay rates prevailing in your area. As noted above, people may accept less than the average pay for their skills if the prospects are good for bonuses, but you still have to be in the ballpark with your pay scale. You know, or should know, what an employee is worth to you. You also need to know what he or she is worth to other companies.

Can you afford to pay competitive wages? If not, something is wrong. Either your chosen business does not have sufficient profit potential given your investment, or you are hiring more people or more highly skilled people than are really required to get the job done.

One last point about meeting the competition needs to be added. If you decide to adjust your employees' wages upward to make them competitive, make it clear to employees that you are doing so to be fair, not to reward merit. Pay for exceptional performance should be kept separate from across-the-board pay increases.

Family Employees. Your pay system includes you and family members who work for you. Often small business owners have the illusion that what they pay themselves and family members is none of other employees' business. Actually, what you pay and how you pay family members has a tremendous influence on other key employees. Pay to family members working for the company should match their ability to accomplish key results. Pay them what they are worth. Don't pad the payroll with highly paid, but relatively incompetent, family members, particularly if a bigger payroll reduces the profits on which bonuses are calculated for top nonfamily employees.

Unions. Many union contracts do not provide for merit increases. They set a single rate structure for similar jobs or a narrow range of rates. Such a wage structure is designed to protect all union members. However, it leaves little room for you to reward top performers with significant amounts of extra money. Even if you are a nonunion company, union contracts with other firms in your industry can affect you since the other firms compete with you for employees. Bonus plans may help you if you are nonunion. If you are unionized, there may be no easy way around this obstacle to an effective pay system.

Inflation. As the cost of living increases, employees find their buying power eroded. They demand cost-of-living adjustments (COLAs) to their wages. Two observations can be made about this obstacle. First, it may be possible for you to pass on the increased salary costs created by a COLA by increasing your prices. Second, COLAs should be kept separate from merit pay. COLAs should be clearly identified as such and should be implemented and communicated to employees at a different time from merit increases.

The Hidden Paycheck. Large companies typically do a much better job than small businesses of informing their employees about the paycheck hidden in fringe benefits. Although more that 35 percent of a small company's payroll dollar will probably go for fringe benefits, few do more than tack memos about benefits on a bulletin board or give brochures to employees.[8]

Fringe benefits include medical and dental insurance, life insurance, additional accidental death and dismemberment insurance, long-term disability, social security, workmen's compensation, unemployment insurance, pension plans, and items such as paid vacations. Employees tend to take such benefits for granted unless they are reminded about them. Also, employees are usually ignorant of the true value of benefits unless they are explained carefully.[9] One way to bring home the value of fringe benefits dramatically is to note that the company adds fringe benefits to the employee's salary, whereas, if the employee were working for himself, the cost of these benefits would be subtracted from earnings. For example, assume the employee earns $15,000 and fringe benefits have a total value of $5,000 . Total effective compensation is $20,000. If the employee worked for himself, earned $15,000, and purchased the same benefits out of his own pocket, he would have a net spendable income of $10,000.[10]

Remember the *potential* for high earnings, through incentive pay, merit, and bonuses is a significant fringe benefit, particularly when competing companies do not offer the opportunity to earn such bonuses. Such incentive plans, like other fringe benefits, must be explained carefully to insure that employees understand them.

Practical Dos and Don'ts for Designing an Effective Pay System

At this point, you should understand the four conditions that must be met if pay is to motivate workers to perform at high levels. You should also understand the obstacles that will stand in your way when you attempt to pay for performance and what you can do to overcome these obstacles. To be effective, a pay system must satisfy the four conditions and overcome the obstacles.

How do you design an effective pay system for your company? How do you decide how much and how to pay? The above discussion of motivational conditions and practical obstacles can be translated into a list of dos and don'ts for developing the best answers to these questions for your company:

1. Do perform a careful analysis of what makes your company special, and do translate your competitive edge into specific jobs that must be done. (See chapters 10 and 14 on how to do this.)
2. Do define the key results each job must deliver and how each job must interact with each other job to make delivery of key results possible.

3. Don't define more than three to five key results for each job.

4. Don't hold the employees accountable for key results beyond their control. Make sure you give employees what is needed to get the job done.

5. Do establish means to measure each employee's progress toward key results.

6. Don't rely solely on quantitative measures, or hard numbers, to indicate progress toward key results, even if they are easier to compile. Qualitative results, such as friendly service and cooperation, are also important.

7. Do measure progress as well as end results so that you can take corrective action if progress is not in the right direction.

8. Do pay competitive wages by matching the wages paid for similar jobs by your competitors, but make sure across-the-board pay adjustments to meet the competition or to adjust for inflation are kept separate from rewards for high productivity.

9. Don't pay someone more than he or she is worth to your company.

10. Don't pay someone less than he or she is worth.

11. Do design your reward system to pay employees extremely well for accomplishing key results that are extremely profitable to you.

12. Do give rewards promptly and specify what key results you are rewarding.

13. Do try to give rewards that meet the personal needs of the employee, especially if the individual is one of your key people.

14. Don't offer rewards to one employee without considering the impact of the proposed rewards on other employees. It is important for employees to view the reward structure as fair and equitable.

15. Do discuss your pay plan with your employees:
    a. Explain what you have in mind concerning key results.
    b. Explain why the key results are important to you.
    c. Explain how the employee's progress toward key results will be measured.
    d. Explain what rewards the employee will receive for obtaining key results.
    e. Explain all rewards to be given, including fringe benefits.
    f. Explain why the rewards an employee will receive are the same, more, or less than what other employees will receive.
    g. Have the employee restate his or her understanding of your pay plan.
    h. Listen to the employee's reaction to your plan.
    i. Revise your pay plan to incorporate good ideas your employees bring up (which they nearly always do if you give them a chance).

16. Do be willing to amend your pay plan as you learn more about the jobs being done, what your key employees want, and what your competitors pay employees similar to yours.

The Steins had not really given much thought to pay issues prior to putting together their franchising package. In fact, a review of their franchising materials and interviews with their employees revealed several discrepancies needing correction.

First, although the Steins had compiled an operations manual for franchises and a training manual for their employees, no explicit job descriptions had been developed, and key results for each job had not been specified. Second, the employees had been loyal to the company, partly because of the possibility for advancement as the company grew and partly because of some rather vague bonus promises made by the Steins. However, interviews revealed that although the employees liked the work, they felt their pay and fringe benefits were lower than what they desired and what they deserved. Low pay, lack of a medical insurance plan, and too little vacation time were cited as issues. Third, it was determined that there had been no attempt to tie compensation to achievement of results. Fourth, employees reported that they had not been approached concerning what kinds of benefits they wanted: increased wages, an insurance plan, vacation pay, or a combination of all three. Fifth, even though one of the employees was in line to be promoted to a field management position, it had not been clearly specified how many stores would be serviced by the field representative, what the key job results were, or how compensation would be determined. Sixth and last, it was observed that the Steins were taking substantial draws from the company's earnings each month. These draws had the double impact of reducing working capital and weakening the company's financial ratios.

The six discrepancies listed above violate several of the sixteen dos and don'ts outlined earlier. Specifically, it is clear that dos and don'ts 1, 2, 8, 10, 11, 12, 13, and 15 are being violated. One also suspects that numbers 3, 4, 5, 6, 7, and 14 are not being handled as well as they could be; 3, 4, 5, 6, and 7 are probably being handled adequately, however, since employees appear to like their work.

What should be done? It is clear that the Steins must begin with a careful job analysis that specifies the key results they desire to maintain their competitive edge. Value has to be attached to these key results and pay levels set that both meet the competition and provide the employees with incentives to get results. The Steins may get away with paying less for a while; but if rewards are delayed too long, the employees will lose faith.

Once the Steins outline their pay plan, they should discuss it with their present employees and listen to their reaction. They should explore carefully what kind of compensation is of particular interest to their employees and tailor their compensation program accordingly. Dos 15 and 16 will be helpful here.

CASE
SOLUTION

*Interiors,
Inc.*

Unless the Steins take corrective action to improve their pay plan, their franchises may not prove nearly as successful as they hope. Their present pay plan (or lack thereof) may be working after a fashion for their own store. It does not, however, provide much guidance to franchise owners who are new to the business and unfamiliar with the key results each employee must accomplish.

CHAPTER
SUMMARY

This chapter deals with pay issues. Pay is money—money you give directly to employees and money you spend on their behalf to purchase fringe benefits such as health insurance. Pay is probably the single most powerful tool you have at your disposal for getting others to do what you want them do do. Basic pay considerations include what the employee is worth, what you can afford to pay, and what competitors pay. Perhaps the most basic pay consideration, however, is what level and kind of compensation will allow you to attract and keep good employees.

It is argued in this chapter that pay is both a motivator and an investment in your company's future. How you pay and how much you pay are both important. The "Diagnosis" section of this chapter helps you analyze the effectiveness of your pay system. The "Understanding" section explains what pay really is and points out the characteristics of an effective pay system. It also describes seven obstacles to designing an effective pay system and provides a list of sixteen dos and don'ts to help you to design an effective pay system.

DISCUSSION
QUESTIONS

1. **Short Case: Nichelson's Shoes II**
   Question 1 at the end of chapter 14 presented information about Michael Manin's problems in hiring shoe store managers.
   a. Based on what you have read in this chapter about pay, what type of compensation package do you think Michael should offer to prospective new managers?
   b. Can you think of a way that Michael could minimize his investment in each new manager until he or she proves capable of performing the job?
2. What would an effective pay system be for the following workers at a secretarial service with ten employees? (Assume you own the business.)
   a. Secretary receptionist (your spouse).
   b. Secretary who knows how to operate all the computerized word-processing and mailing equipment.
   c. Yourself as the business owner.
3. Assume you are about ready to open a small manufacturing company. How would you go about finding out what your competitors pay their employees?

4. One of the dos listed at the end of this chapter states, "Do design your reward system to pay employees extremely well for accomplishing key results that are extremely profitable to you." Does this really make sense, or is it probable that employees would settle for their normal paychecks or small bonuses, thereby leaving more profits for you?

5. Explain in your own words why each item listed under number 15 in the list of dos and don'ts is necessary.

REFERENCES

Belcher, D. W. and Atchison, T. J., "Compensation for Work." *Handbook of Work Organization and Society.* Edited by Robert T. Dubin. Chicago: Rand McNally College Publishing Co., 1975: 567–611.

Cohn Theodore, and Lindberg, Roy A., *Compensating Key Executives in the Smaller Company.* New York: AMACOM, 1979.

Fein, Michael. "Wage Incentive Plans." *Industrial Engineering Handbook*, 3rd ed. Edited by H. B. Maynard. New York: McGraw-Hill Book Co., 1971: 6-15–6-50.

Gellerman, Saul W. *Managers and Subordinates.* Hinsdale, IL: The Dryden Press, 1976.

Hill, Frederick S. "The Pay for Performance Dilemma." *Personnel* (September-October, 1979): 23–31.

Kearney, William J. "Pay for Performance? Not Always." *MSU Business Topics* 27, 2 (Spring, 1979): 5–16.

FOOTNOTES

1. This case was prepared by one of the authors based upon a Small Business Institute counseling report completed under his supervision. In order to maintain client confidentiality, the facts given here differ somewhat from the original case.

2. Our position concerning the importance of pay is controversial. Some well-known psychologists, such as Harold J. Leavitt and Victor R. Vroom, have agreed with us, arguing that money occupies a central place as an incentive. Perhaps this is because money is a common currency that can be used to satisfy a complex array of needs, ranging from hunger to status and recognition. See Harold J. Leavitt, *Managerial Psychology* (Chicago: University of Chicago Press, 1964) and Victor H. Vroom, *Motivation in Management* (New York: American Foundation for Management Research, 1965). Other equally well-known psychologists have been more skeptical about the importance of pay. William F. Whyte argues, for example, that economic incentives tap only a small portion of the reservoir of productivity contained in the industrial worker. Saul W. Gellerman argues that pay has little or no motivational impact unless it is perceived as unfair, which has an unfavorable impact. See William F. Whyte, "Economic Incentives in Human Relations," *Harvard Business Review* (March-April, 1952) and Saul W. Gellerman *Managers and Subordinates* (Hinsdale, Ill.: The Dryden Press, 1976), pp. 17–22. Mitchell Fein sums up the controversy, "Managers looking for clear recommendations from psychologists will be disappointed; support can be found for and against (financial) incentives in their writings." He also points out that, "it is generally believed by managers that money is the prime rea-

son that people work and that people in general endeavor to maximize their earnings." Mitchell Fein, "Wage and Incentive Plans," in *Industrial Engineering Handbook*, 3rd ed., ed. H. B. Maynard (New York: McGraw-Hill Book Co., 1971) pp. 6–21. We contend that these two beliefs are facts.

3. This section owes much to an excellent discussion of pay found in Theodore Cohn and Roy A. Lindberg, *Compensating Key Executives in the Smaller Company* (New York: AMACOM, a division of American Management Associations, 1979). You will find, as we did, chapters 1, 2, and 6 of their book particularly useful.

4. William J. Kearney, "Pay for Performance? Not Always," *MSU Business Topics* 27, no. 2 (Spring 1979): 5–16. Reprinted by permission of the publisher, Division of Research, Graduate School of Business Administration, Michigan State University. These four principles make up an "expectancy theory" of motivation. For a detailed discussion of the development of this theory see D. W. Belcher, and T. J. Atchison, "Compensation for Work," in *Handbook of Work Organization and Society*, ed. Robert Dubin (Chicago: Rand McNally College Publishing Co. 1975), pp. 589–595.

5. Several empirical studies support this view. For example: David J. Cherrington, H. Joseph Reitz, and William E. Scott, Jr., "Effects of Contingent and Noncontingent Reward on the Relationship between Satisfaction and Task Performance," *Journal of Applied Psychology* 55, no. 6 (1971): 531–536; Judi Komaki, William M. Waddell, and M. George Pearce, "The Applied Behavior Analysis Approach and Individual Employees: Improving Performance in Two Small Businesses," *Organizational Behavior and Human Performance* 19 (1977): 337–352; Philip L. Cooley, "Managerial Pay and Financial Performance of Small Business," *Journal of Business Research* 7, no. 3 (1979): 267–276; David J. Cherrington, "The Effects of a Central Incentive-Motivational State on Measures of Job Satisfaction," *Organizational Behavior and Human Performance* 10 (1973): 271–289; and Fred Luthans and Jason Schweizer, "O.B. Mod in a Small Factory: How Behavior Modification Techniques Can Improve Total Organizational Performance," *Management Review* 68, no. 9 (September 1979): 43–50.

6. This strategy was suggested by Cohn and Lindberg, *Compensating Key Executives in the Smaller Company*, p. 118.

7. This strategy was suggested by Frederick S. Hills, "The Pay for Performance Dilemma," *Personnel* (September-October 1979): 30.

8. Ernest H. Schnell, "Take the Wraps Off Your Employee Benefits Package," *Inc.*, 2, no. 8 (August 1980): 72.

9. Vance Jacobson, cited by Thomas N. Richman, "Show Employees What They Earn," *Inc.*, 2, no. 8 (August 1980): 55.

10. Schnell, "Take the Wraps Off," p. 72.

Keeping Good Employees

16

☐ **Can you afford to give your employees what they want?**

☐ **What else do your employees want besides money?**

☐ **What can you do to reduce employee turnover?**

CASE
PROBLEM

*A Swensen's
Ice Cream
Franchise*[1]

PROBLEM
IDENTIFICATION

The Nelson family purchased their Swensen's Ice Cream franchise in 1978. Swensen's stores sell high-quality ice cream, ice cream fountain items, ice cream specialty items, beverages, and sandwiches. Each franchise is independently owned and operated. The Nelsons' store was located in a new neighborhood in southern California. Tracts of attractive, middle-class homes were being constructed in the area, making the location very desirable.

In the fall of 1979, the Nelson family faced a difficult problem. Several of their employees had recently quit. As a matter of fact, 34 percent of their employees had turned over (quit and had to be replaced) since September. The Nelsons were concerned by this high labor turnover. They wondered how they could keep more of the employees they had taken so much time to train.

Since September is the beginning of the school year and most of the Nelsons' employees were students, they speculated that many had quit to spend more time on school. They also guessed that other companies could afford to pay better wages and thus were attracting some of their more ambitious employees. However, the Nelsons were not sure these were the real reasons for their high turnover. Also, they were not sure what they could do about the high turnover even if they knew exactly what was causing it.

The Nelsons' high turnover is a good example of the difficulties a small business can have in keeping good people. Both high turnover and absenteeism are usually symptoms of more basic problems. The causes of high turnover and/or absenteeism are numerous. Some are unavoidable, such as a change in residence. Many cases, however, relate to motivation: the employee does not like the work, does not like the boss, or does not really know what he or she does like but is pretty sure it is not this job. These causes can be controlled by managing motivation.

Certainly the fact that the Nelsons were hiring young, unproven employees for the minimum wage contributed to the turnover rate, as can be inferred from our discussion in chapters 14 and 15. Still, many restaurant operations draw on this inexperienced pool of relatively cheap labor, and some are able to avoid high turnover rates. How do they do it? The answer lies in how they manage motivation. Managing motivation involves understanding what employees want and entering into an agreement with them to satisfy *their* wants in return for their work. As we noted in chapter 15, this employment contract is formed by your offer and the employee's acceptance. What you offer and how you offer it is the key to managing motivation.

The three questions that opened this chapter all relate to the management of motivation. You need to know what your employees want and how you can give it to them in a manner that will allow you to develop a stable, hard-working labor force. This chapter will use the concepts introduced in chapters 14 and 15 to develop ten guidelines to help you to manage motivation.

DIAGNOSIS

How well do you manage the motivation of your employees? This question is very difficult to answer by yourself since it requires a subjective self-analysis of how you are doing in regard to a vague, elusive concept. You can, however, do several things to diagnose how well you are doing.

First, if you did not do well on the questions in Exhibit 14.1 and on the ten questions in the "Diagnosis" section in chapter 15, you probably are not managing motivation well. Your approach is flawed; and if it has not caused you significant problems already, it will cause problems for you soon. This is true even if you feel you have gone out of your way to be courteous and friendly to your employees.

A second way to get an idea of how well you are managing the motivation of your employees is to look at employee turnover and absenteeism. Are these figures high? Are employees quitting or staying home more than you would like?

A third, and perhaps the best, way to find out how well you are managing motivation is to conduct an attitude survey. Instead of asking yourself if you are doing a good job managing motivation, ask your employees. The answers you get, in combination with the ten guidelines discussed later in this chapter, can give you some excellent insights into improving your management techniques.

What questions should an attitude survey include? The questions used to interview employees at the Nelson family's ice cream parlour are listed below:

1. Age?
2. How long employed?
3. What were your reasons for obtaining this job?
4. Do you think you had proper training? If no, why?
5. Do you think the workload is heavy? If yes, why?

6. Do you feel the pay is adequate? If no, why?

7. Are you happy with the scheduling?

8. Do you think the management is efficient? Why?

9. What areas do you think need improvement?

10. Do you have any interest in advancement? Why?

11. What are your personal feelings about Mr. and Mrs. Nelson?

12. Do you think your job is boring? If yes, why?

13. How are you rewarded for doing good work?

14. How are you reprimanded for poor work?

15. Is there an open line of communication between management and employees?

16. Do you think there is favoritism toward certain employees?

Since it was felt that employees would be hesitant to give frank answers to the above questions if they were asked by the Nelsons, an outside consultant conducted the employee interviews. The consultant promised all employees that their answers would remain confidential. The consultant compiled the responses in summary form for review by the Nelsons. When the number of emloyees permits (i.e., when more than one is interviewed), confidentiality is a good idea.

The above sixteen-question attitude survey used open-end questions to solicit written or oral responses. Closed-end questions, which require the employee to select from three to five possible responses, can also be used. Cohn and Lindberg have developed an excellent attitude survey using closed-end questions.[2] Three sample questions from their survey are:

Do you think the firm offers you the chance to have the kind of job you will want five years from now? (1) Yes _____ (2) No _____ (3) Not Sure _____

When you want information or help on a difficult problem, how likely are you to get the help you need? I get (1) Very little help _____ (2) Fairly good help _____ (3) All the help I need _____

Are you encouraged to offer ideas and suggestions for new or better ways of doing things? (1) All the time _____ (2) Often _____ (3) Sometimes _____ (4) Rarely _____ (5) Not at all _____[3]

UNDER-STANDING

What Is Motivation?

Since this chapter defines the problem of keeping good employees as one of managing motivation, it is important to understand what motivation is. "Motivation" is a vague term that refers to whatever it is that influences the direction and strength of human behavior.

Three Theories of Motivation.   There are three theories that can be used to explain employee motivation. Some people feel that it is management's job to motivate employees.[4] This is the pin-in-the-frog theory. The basic model for it is a stimulus followed by a response. You stick the pin in the frog and it jumps. According to this theory, a lifeless lump reports to work on Monday morning and says to you, "Here I am, boss. It's 8:00 A.M. Motivate me!" What you need is a good supply of pins, or better yet, knitting needles.

Other people feel that motivation comes only from within. This is the noble frog theory. The noble frog is somewhat like the noble savage. What makes a good jumper is the inner fire to achieve. The frog that wants to jump will overcome every obstacle to do so. The frog that doesn't want to jump won't. According to this theory, what you must do is hire self-starters.

We believe the truth about motivation lies somewhere between these two theories. You could call it the jumping frog theory. This theory assumes that most frogs like to jump. If yours is not jumping, it may be that it is unsure about the best direction to jump; or, even worse, it may be that you or your company has inadvertently filled the frog's belly with buckshot, and it can't move. In either case, there is a lot you can do to get your frog jumping.

The Practical Meaning of Motivation.   What the jumping frog theory really says is that most people want to look back at their work life when they retire and be able to say to themselves, "What I did counted for something. I made a difference. I was worth what they paid me." They want to be able to do what they consider a job worth doing or a job well done.[5]

As a supervisor, your job is to help your employees to translate this basic desire into effective action. Often their desire is ill defined or has been weakened by bad job experiences. Changes cannot be accomplished overnight. It takes patience and persistence on your part to get the most out of your employees.

In chapter 15 we introduced four conditions that must be met if pay or anything else is to motivate workers to perform at high levels:

1. The employee must believe that his or her additional effort will improve performance.

2. The employee must perceive that better performance will be noticed.

3. The employee must see that better performance leads immediately to equitable rewards that the employee wants and values.

4. The rewards the employee does receive for achieving results must not come at an unacceptable cost in terms of the employee's other goals.[6]

These four conditions, combined with the jumping frog theory, are the cornerstones of the ten guidelines for managing motivation given in this chapter.

As you read the ten guidelines for managing motivation, keep in mind that small business owners have the opportunity to manage motivation more effectively than large business managers. The same personal touch used to develop loyal customers can be used to keep good employees. In Exhibit 14.4 we listed ten advantages of working for a small firm. Many of these advantages must be consciously created by the small business owner. If you follow our ten guidelines for managing motivation, you will create most of these advantages for your company and thus insure that your employees will work as hard as possible for your company. There is no easy and fail-safe way to get your employees to achieve and maintain high productivity, but our guidelines will provide you with a sound approach to the problem of keeping good employees.

Ten Guidelines for Managing Motivation

Let's go over the ten guidelines:[7]

Guideline 1. Establish an organizational climate that fosters positive work values and a commitment to excellence. This sounds technical, but by concentrating on the following factors, you should be able to achieve the recommended climate:

Your Example: What you do is more important than what you say. You are a model for your employees. If you display excellence in your work, you will encourage your employees to pursue excellence. Your concern about quality craftsmanship and your sense of urgency about accomplishing important goals is infectious. Be urgent and concerned.

A Worthy Organizational Mission: Your organization's mission statement should explain how the organization serves society. This shows your employees that their efforts go for a worthy purpose. Their efforts contribute to the good of society in addition to putting money into the pockets of the company owners. A worthy organizational mission allows employees to feel good about their work for your company.

Organizational Efficiency: You should strive to maximize the productive social benefits derived from the efforts of the workforce. Plans should be well laid out, and priorities should be clear. A major aspect of achieving efficiency is listening to, being interested in, and following through on employee suggestions. It is particularly important to check out complaints about procedural inefficiency or managerial sins of commission or omission. Check out suggestions and complaints carefully and report back to employees about what, if anything, you plan to do and why. Give quick recognition and rewards for good comments, explaining specifically how these comments assisted in the improvement of organizational efficiency.

Supportive Group Norms: Work groups tend to establish standards or norms for their members. Individual employees tend to conform to the work group's expectations. Your task is to foster group norms that encourage and support excellence. Recognition and rewards should be provided for outstanding group performance. Cooperative efforts or teamwork should be encouraged. When employees cooperate or form teams on their own to do work better, recognize this as a positive behavior and be quick to reward it.

Guideline 2. Make sure each employee fully understands his or her job.[8]
This involves (1) carefully defining what you think the employee's job should
be in terms of key results expected for a given period of time, (2) discussing
these expectations with the employee and modifying the list of key results expected based on the employee's suggestions and comments, (3) Once an
agreement on what will constitute adequate performance is reached, establishing with the employee how you both will recognize this performance, or,
in other words, spelling out the yardsticks you both will use to measure accomplishment of key results.

If you think you have already done a good job of following this guideline, there is a simple test. Ask a few employees the following question:
"What do you think is expected of you in this job?" Are the responses you get
a list of duties and responsibilities or a list of key results expected for a given
period? If key results are given, are they the same ones you had in mind? Remember that the employee who answers differently from what you expect is
not wrong and should not be put down. Unexpected answers give you the
opportunity to begin a discussion that can clarify the employee's job for both
you and the employee. Clarification of what is expected in terms of key results boosts employee morale and makes your job of evaluating employee
performance easier. Clarification begins with the employee's restatement of
what is expected to result from the work being done. Listen carefully.

The objective of Guideline 2 is to establish individual accountability for
key job results. The focus on results rather than activities allows the individual to adapt to the unexpected. Accountability is established by the agreement between you and the employee on the results to be accomplished. Accountability is maintained by your periodic review to evaluate progress and
your approachability to provide guidance and support as needed. Remember
that time spent discussing the difficulties the employee encounters on the job
is almost never time wasted. You don't have to worry about the subordinate
asking questions to avoid responsibility if you make it clear that the assumption is that the employee is responsible for the final outcome. The employee's
personal commitment and involvement are developed by providing opportunities for individual choice and participation—by asking, rather than telling, the employee to perform his or her tasks and by encouraging individual
participation in redesigning jobs and setting goals.

Two key observations are in order about techniques for implementing
Guideline 2. First, you may have to ask employees for their views several
times before they will begin to open up. You often have to earn the right to
good responses by consistently asking for input and following through on
what input you do get. You have to prove that you are sincere and that you
really want employees to make candid remarks.

A second observation is that performance expectations tend to be self-
fulfilling. If you assume someone will perform at a high level, you tend to
work harder to provide the instruction and support necessary to get the individual to attain that level of performance. If you assume performance will be
marginal, you tend to skimp on the time and resources you devote to helping

the individual try to perform above the acceptable minimum. Similarly, employees tend to respond to expectations. Your expectations affect the worker's on-the-job performance goals, the worker's self-concept, and even the worker's personal aspirations and goals. Performance expectations can be effectively communicated; this is best done when the job is assigned during the new employee orientation.

Guideline 3. Recognize and comment on good work. This involves monitoring employee performance, recognizing when an employee's actions are contributing to the results desired, and telling the employee so. Verbal acknowledgement of good work costs next to nothing; yet it accomplishes many useful things:

> It lets the employee know you know how he or she is performing.
>
> It lets the employee know he or she is performing well. It reassures. It indicates progress is being made in the right direction.
>
> It tells the employee that you value his or her contribution enough to take the time to comment on it.
>
> It builds the employee's perception of you as a fair and equitable boss.

It is helpful to keep four things in mind when recognizing and commenting on good work. First, particularly for inexperienced or marginal workers, reinforce any improvement in behavior. Waiting for momentous improvements may frustrate both you and the employee. Second, frequent day-to-day feedback should be given to the employee on three aspects of performance: job-relevant personnel data such as attendance and punctuality, production data concerning the quantity and quality of work, and judgments of others regarding spontaneous and innovative behaviors beyond the normal job requirements. The third thing to keep in mind when recognizing and commenting on good work is that formal feedback to employees on their performance should be divided into two separate appraisal sessions. Both are needed, but they should not be done at the same time. The two types of appraisal review are a contributions appraisal and a personal development appraisal. The contributions appraisal should evaluate and reward past performance. The personal development appraisal should evaluate strengths and weaknesses and encourage growth and learning. Fourth and finally, when recognizing good work, remember that day-to-day feedback on contributions and patient day-to-day coaching on possibilities for improvement are far more effective than biannual or quarterly formal review interviews.

Guideline 4. Reward effective performance. Pay and other social reinforcers should be used to reward good performance. People do what they are reinforced for doing.

Pay should be based on the concept of appropriate reinforcement for accomplishment of key job results. High performers should be paid significantly more than lower performers based on the extra value contributed by the high performers. Pay gives a clear message to the employee about what you think of his or her work. Pay should be used to reinforce the significance and social usefulness of the job and should be clearly linked to the accomplishment of the key results you desire.

Effective performance should also be highly rewarded with praise and recognition. The employee needs to know others recognize and appreciate the quality of work he or she is doing. The best source of such recognition is the people the employee works closely with on a day-to-day basis, such as immediate supervisors or peers in the department. A recognition program that gives awards, such as jewelry with the company logo on it, for outstanding individual performance may seem corny, but it works.

Guideline 5. Highlight personal impact. Show employees how their personal efforts affect performance of the company. Explain to them what specific actions they can take to make meaningful contributions to the company. Employees need to know why their jobs are important and why their actions make a difference to the company. The desire to perform well can be dampened quickly if employees do not see the linkage between personal effort and performance. If the linkage is not clear, employees tend to assume that there isn't one. Instead, they think of the organization as a political arena or bureaucratic maze where appearance is more important than performance and inefficiency is rampant, and they see little opportunity for an individual worker to change the situation.

Guideline 6. Dangle the carrot. Make sure the employee understands exactly what he or she stands to gain in return for doing a good job. For a reward like a pay raise, a bonus, a choice of job assignments, a promotion, or a special privilege to be an effective inducement to improved performance, four conditions must be met. First, the employee must know in advance that the reward is available. Second, the employee must want the reward. Third, the employee must know what must be done to get the reward; and fourth, the employee must perceive that the reward is obtainable with reasonable effort.

In regard to the second condition, employees must consider a reward meaningful before they will work for it. Each employee is an individual with unique preferences. What one employee enjoys doing, another may despise. The trick is to know each employee well enough to understand his or her likes and dislikes. Listen to what employees talk about; observe what they enjoy doing. Custom tailor the rewards you offer accordingly. Remember, however, that other employees must perceive the rewards you offer as fair and equitable, given the performance involved in earning them.

Concerning the fourth condition, keep in mind that many of the rewards you offer are not immediate. They require a long period of high performance before they are earned. This means that you must periodically assess the progress a worker is making toward the reward: for example, "You are performing at level X because of your specific job behaviors A, B, C. If you continue to perform at this level until time Y, here is what you stand to gain." Periodic assessments can often be accomplished by charting key job behaviors and pinning them up on the wall.

Guideline 7. Give employees the sweet taste of success. This guideline refers to creating pride in accomplishment. Even if you have followed Guidelines 1 through 6 carefully, many employees still will not make the linkage between a good personal performance and a feeling of success or pride without some help from you. This is because they do not feel responsible for the outcomes of their work. They feel that successes or failures on the job are most often due to the good work or incompetence of other employees or supervisors. You want to make sure that when your employees do a good job, they equate their feelings about the work done with a sense of personal pride and accomplishment. Employees need to know that they did make a difference or that they did do a good job, or that they did a better job this time.

Achieving this guideline involves teaching and explaining the value of work, the dignity of labor, and the job of service. Setting a good example is an important aspect of this teaching process. You need to act as a model for your employees. You need to make it clear that you have high standards for your work and that you get a sense of personal pride or accomplishment from meeting these standards. Beyond being a good model, you must seek opportunities to make enlightening comments at times when employees appear receptive. Such comments tend to be better teaching tools than detailed discourses on the puritan ethic. The key is to comment consistently and patiently on the personal satisfaction employees should be deriving from their accomplishments.

Guideline 8. Crystalize your employees' personal goals. Many of your employees are unclear about how working for you can contribute to their personal growth and development. They are ships without rudders. They have no personal career goals and, as a result, see little in their jobs that is suited to their talents, skills, abilities, or interests. Their lack of direction and purpose carries over to their work and causes them to seek the path of least resistance to the income and job security your company offers. Certainly many lower level jobs in your company do not offer much of a future. In and of themselves, they are dead-end jobs. They are a lot like jobs your employee could get almost anywhere in town. Even the pay is about the same as elsewhere.

What can you do to help your employees grow and develop? Obviously, you need to work with individual employees to help them define personal goals that line up with your organization's goals. There are three steps involved in doing this:

1. Helping the individual identify what he or she wants from work now and in the future.

2. Pointing out to the individual what he or she is currently getting from the organization that satisfies his or her goals.

3. Helping the individual design a career strategy to achieve further goals through working for your company.

There is more to crystalizing your employees' personal goals than these three steps, however. Workers should also be encouraged to develop and follow their own self-improvement plan. Continually encouraging your employees in their personal growth and skill development is a positive demonstration of your concern for each employee as an individual. Although it may be difficult to demonstrate statistically a direct linkage between your continual encouragement of the employee's personal development and improvement in the employee's on-the-job performance, there is some evidence that such a linkage exists. What can be covered by a self-improvement plan? David Cherrington suggests the following:[9]

Physical exercise to improve the condition of the employee's health.

Social development to increase the employee's interpersonal skills.

Emotional maturity to develop a greater sense of self-awareness and emotional stability.

Intellectual development to further the employee's knowledge, wisdom, and practical skills.

Character development to further his or her ethical and moral behavior.

Spiritual development for a greater awareness of the meaning of life and the purpose of existence.

Guideline 9. Try to match job requirements with employee motives. This guideline does not require you to install a couch in your office and become an amateur psychiatrist. It does, however, require you to get to know your employees well enough to understand their behavior and use it to your advantage. David McClelland has suggested, for example, that some people have strongly held motives that you can capitalize on.[10] Three specific motives that McClelland has identified are the need to achieve, the need for power, and the need for affiliation. The achiever is turned on by challenge and derives considerable satisfaction from success. The power seeker obtains satisfaction (not necessarily malicious) through influencing or controlling others. The affiliation seeker finds satisfaction in being accepted and respected and in interacting on a personal basis with others.

To the extent that you have a variety of jobs to be done under your supervision, you can make work assignments based on the differing motives of your employees. To the extent that you can match motives and jobs, you can make each employee more interested in his or her work and more of a self-starter. For example, the clerk with a strong need for achievement might be given special projects or assignments as a trouble-shooter. If someone on your office staff has a strong need for affiliation, he or she may be given major responsibilities for public contact at the front desk. A power seeker enjoys negotiating and therefore might serve you well as a collector of accounts receivable.

Guideline 10. Remove roadblocks. Roadblocks are significant and persistent obstacles that prevent employees from attaining a sense of a job well done. Your job is to tear down as many of these roadblocks as you can and to avoid erecting any unnecessary roadblocks.

Frank Hoffman has suggested that there are two major types of roadblocks that a company or a supervisor can create for employees.[11] The first kind is a roadblock to performance. This is a condition which affects actually doing the work that keeps the employee from performing at a high level of excellence over an extended period of time. Examples of this kind of roadblock include: inadequate tools, poor training, constant interruptions, distracting shop conditions, delays in getting necessary data from other departments, unrealistic deadlines, unclear or nonexistent standard operating procedures, and understaffed operations.

The second kind of roadblock suggested by Hoffman is a roadblock to work gratification. This kind of roadblock does not prevent employees from performing, but it makes them ask themselves, "Why bother?" Examples of this kind of roadblock are:

Lack of recognition for accomplishment of the things that matter in job performance.

Inconsistent or inequitable rewards, such as flat rate pay for a job classification that does not tie rewards to important aspects of job performance in an honest and genuine way.

Lack of backing from the boss for actions involving a reasonable exercise of judgment (even if rules are violated or mistakes made). If you expect loyalty from your employees, you have to be loyal to them.

Organizational policies and administrative procedures that divert excessive energy from productive ends for the sake of uniformity or conformity.

The above ten guidelines embody our jumping frog theory of motivation. They do not offer quick-fix solutions to high turnover and low productivity. Changes in employee work values, in particular, take an extended period of time. You simply cannot change an employee's view of what is important and why it is important overnight. The key to the successful use of the ten guidelines is patient and persistent supervision.

CASE
SOLUTION

A Swensen's Ice Cream Franchise

As noted in the case problem, an outside consultant was brought in to interview employees at the Nelsons' business. The consultant recorded the employees' confidential responses to the sixteen questions in the attitude survey. These responses gave the consultant several clues concerning which of the above motivational guidelines were being violated.

The responses to the attitude survey can be summarized as follows:

The majority of employees obtained their jobs because they wanted work experience and money for school.

Most employees felt that their training was good but could be much better if defined in written form.

Many employees did not know where needed supplies were stored, which proved frustrating from time to time.

The employees unanimously agreed that the workload was light and that they actually had nothing to do when business was slow.

Most employees thought the pay was fair except during the training period.

Several employees considered the three-month duty schedule too inflexible, as trading of hours and days among employees was causing confusion and errors.

The majority of employees considered Mr. and Mrs. Nelson informative and helpful but complained that the salaried managers, and in particular one manager, were unorganized and had let the power of being managers go to their heads, turning into authoritarian dictators in the absence of the owners.

The employees felt that they did not know what was expected of them in certain instances.

They felt uninformed concerning the reasons for certain policies and rules.

It was also noted that the Nelsons and their salaried managers often gave contradictory orders.

Several of the employees complained that the cleanliness of the kitchen and the eating areas was not as good as it should be.

Many employees expressed interest in possible advancement to a managerial position.

All employees liked the family type atmosphere, but some felt that the atmosphere was too loose and that things got out of control at times.

Most employees were not bored unless business was slow.

A significant number of employees stated they were never rewarded for good work.

Most employees found reprimands to be congenial and constructive in nature, but a significant minority reported receiving only disgusted looks without any verbal communication.

Favoritism was not seen as a problem.

Finally, several employees did not want to work weekend nights.

Before reading further, take a moment to compare the survey results with the ten guidelines for managing motivation. Can you describe what was going wrong in terms of the ten guidelines? Can you guess what the consultant recommended to the Nelsons?

Beginning with Guideline 1, several mistakes were made: managers were unorganized; contradictory orders were given; cleanliness was not emphasized enough; the workload was light; and the family type atmosphere was too loose. The sum of these observations implied a climate that did not foster positive work values and a commitment to excellence. Bad examples were set. The worthy organizational mission was counteracted by the perceived lack of cleanliness, and the organization appeared inefficient. It is not hard to imagine how the managers reacted to employee suggestions in the absence of the owners.

Guideline 2 was also violated. Although the Nelsons had defined key results for each job, this information was not reaching the employees in a way that made them feel they fully understood their jobs. The employees felt certain policies and procedures should be written down so that they could study them. They wanted to know where supplies were kept. They felt the managers were not approachable for help and were telling employees what to do rather than asking them to do it. They did not always know what was expected of them. Even reprimands were unclear in certain cases. Because of these problems, individual accountability was not being established.

Guideline 3 was violated for a significant number of employees, who felt they were not rewarded for good work. On the other hand, some employees viewed controls as too loose, which implies that they felt some employees were not doing their job and were getting away with substandard performance.

Similarly, Guideline 4 was violated since the family type atmosphere created by Mr. and Mrs. Nelson included everyone. No distinctions were perceived between top performers and marginal performers by many employees. No recognition program was in force. Since the linkage between personal effort and performance results was blurred by violations of Guidelines 1 through 4, Guideline 5 was not being followed either.

Guideline 6 was also violated. Employees viewed the lower wages they received during training as unfair since they stayed at the same low level during the whole two-month training period regardless of performance. Even after the training period was over, carrot dangling was not done effectively due to the lack of control and recognition.

Guideline 7 was violated due to the lack of perceived ownership by the employees of the outcomes of their work. Operating the store is, of course, a team effort. When good employees perceive their managers as unorganized and arbitrary and feel that certain of their fellow workers are getting away with murder, they lose a sense of personal pride in a job well done. Instead, they rationalize that at least they are not responsible for the way things are being messed up.

Guideline 8 can be a very powerful tool for motivating young people; yet it does not appear that the Nelsons attempted to crystalize their employees' personal goals. In particular, although many employees were interested in the manager's job, they were not sure how to groom themselves to compete for it. The inflexible three-month schedule also suggests that employee educational goals were not being accommodated. Similarly, the matching of job requirements with employee motives suggested by Guideline 9 was not attempted.

Finally, there were several roadblocks that should have been torn down, according to Guideline 10. These included lack of a written training manual; employees' lack of knowledge about the location of needed supplies; lack of clear job assignments, especially for slow periods; an inflexible three-month duty schedule; lack of recognition; and lack of consistent rewards, particularly during the training period.

What did the consultant recommend? The following recommendations were made to help the Nelsons follow the ten guidelines for managing motivation more closely:

1. It was suggested that a written training manual be put together to aid in the overall training process and to serve as a reference when doubts about policy and procedure arose. It was felt that compilation of the manual would also help clarify for the Nelsons what constituted an equitable workload for each job.

2. It was recommended that lists of tasks to be accomplished during slow periods be compiled, emphasizing the key result of cleanliness.

3. It was recommended that wages during training be gradually increased as the trainee demonstrated increased competency. It was also recommended that the length of the training period be made flexible, depending on the learning speed of the trainee. This meant that instead of all trainees receiving the same low trainee's wage for the entire two-month training period, exceptional trainees could advance quickly to full pay status as they learned all facets of the job. Frequent reviews of trainees' work were suggested to implement this procedure.

4. It was suggested that three-month work schedules were too inflexible, given the employees' needs. More frequent schedule adjustments were recommended, based on input from employees, particularly around the beginning of the school year.

5. Related to scheduling was the reluctance of employees to work weekend nights. The consultant noticed that tips were pooled and split among employees on a weekly basis. Therefore, even though weekend

nights were busier (and generated more tips), an employee received his or her share based on hours worked, not nights worked. The recommendation was to pool tips on a daily basis so that people who did work the busy nights would get paid a little more. As a result, employees no longer mind working on the weekends.

6. It was recommended that more frequent informal meetings be held between the Nelsons and their managers to clarify policy and to discuss how to handle problems brought up by the managers or observed by the Nelsons. Emphasis should be on coordinating views and deciding how to communicate agreed solutions to employees.

7. It was suggested that the Nelsons meet with employees at least monthly to determine it they need information or have suggestions. Naturally, day-to-day contacts are also important. The objective is not to undermine the managers but to see if issues arise that the manager can resolve after a private discussion with the owner. These frequent meetings are a form of control, in that they make the owner aware of what is actually happening in the store. Based on this knowledge, schemes for corrective action can be devised. Special attention was given to the fact that most of the employees were young and therefore hesitant and unsure of themselves when talking with older, more knowledgeable bosses. This meant that it would take a special effort to get the employees to air their views.

8. It was also suggested that oral employee evaluations be carried out frequently on a one-to-one basis by the managers, with an emphasis on verbal praise for work well done and coaching in areas that needed to be improved. The managers should be impressed with the need to use a positive approach and to listen to the employees. It was emphasized that, as much as possible, daily feedback and recognition should be implemented. Where reprimands were required, it was recommended that they be carried out quickly and impartially, carefully spelling out what the infraction had been and how to avoid future infractions.

To be sure, the consultant's recommendations were just a beginning. However, they paved the way for a dramatic reduction in turnover. Should the Nelsons be content with the average labor turnover rate for Swensen's franchises or other local restaurants that rely on young, inexperienced students to fill most positions? We think not. The survey of the Nelsons' employees indicated they wanted work experience and expected to do more than they were required to do. They had work values. These employees could be led well by a manager/owner who took a personal interest in their work and in their future within the framework of the ten guidelines for managing motivation.

This chapter defines and deals with a vague, intangible concept—motivation. Motivation refers to whatever it is that influences the direction and strength of human behavior. This concept has a lot to do with how hard your employees will work for you. It also affects how long they will stay with your company and how often they will show up on time for work. There is quite a bit of debate about what motivates people. This chapter presents three theories: the pin-in-the-frog theory, the noble frog theory, and the jumping frog theory. In this chapter we give our views about what people really want and present ten guidelines for managing the motivation of employees. These guidelines can work especially well for a smaller company. They are:

CHAPTER SUMMARY

1. Establish an organizational climate that fosters positive work values and a commitment to excellence.
2. Make sure each employee fully understands his or her job.
3. Recognize and comment on good work.
4. Reward effective performance.
5. Highlight personal impact.
6. Dangle the carrot.
7. Give employees the sweet taste of success.
8. Crystalize your employees' personal goals.
9. Try to match job requirements with employee motives.
10. Remove roadblocks.

As we note in this chapter, there is no easy and fail-safe way to get your employees to achieve and maintain high productivity, but our guidelines will provide you with a sound approach to the problem of keeping good employees.

1. **Short Case: Nichelson's Shoes III**
   Question 1 at the end of chapter 14 introduced Michael Manin's three-store company to you as a hiring problem. Question 1 at the end of chapter 15, had you consider how Manin should compensate his managers. Based on the ten guidelines presented in this chapter.
   a. What can Manin do to keep good managers?
   b. What can Manin do to keep good salesclerks?
   In answering these two questions, remember that money is only one aspect of the motivation problem.

2. One of the most controversial of the ten guidelines presented in this chapter is to crystalize your employees' personal goals. How workable do you think this guideline is? Why?

DISCUSSION QUESTIONS

3. Select a job that you are familiar with in a small company (yours or a friend's). What roadblocks are present in this job? What could be done at little or no cost to remove these roadblocks?

4. Select an employee of a small company who is excited about his or her work and the company. Evaluate how effectively the ten guidelines discussed in this chapter are being applied to this individual.

5. Select an employee of a small company who hates his or her job and is looking for another job. Evaluate how effectively the ten guidelines discussed in this chapter are being applied to this individual.

REFERENCES

Cherrington, David J. "Teach the Work Ethic at Work," *The Personnel Administrator* 21, 7 (October, 1976): 24–28.

Cohn, Theodore and Lindberg, Roy A., *Survival and Growth: Management Strategies for the Small Firm*. New York: AMACOM, 1974.

Cook, Curtis W. "Guidelines for Managing Motivation." *Business Horizons* 23, 2 (April, 1980): 61–69.

Fein, Michael. "Motivation for Work." *Handbook of Work, Organization and Society*. Edited by Robert Dubin. Chicago: Rand McNally College Publishing Co., 1976: 465–530.

House, Robert J. and Mitchell, Terence R., "Path-Goal Theory of Leadership." *Journal of Contemporary Business* (Autumn, 1974): 81–97.

Mayer, Robert F. and Pipe, Peter, *Analyzing Performance Problems or 'You Really Oughta Wanna'*. Belmont, Calif.: Fearon Publishers/Lear Siegler Inc., Education Division, 1970.

FOOTNOTES

1. This case was prepared by one of the authors based upon a Small Business Institute counseling report completed under his supervision. In order to maintain client confidentiality, the facts given here differ somewhat from the original case.

2. Theodore Cohn, and Roy A. Lindberg, *Survival and Growth: Management Strategies for the Small Firm* (New York: AMACOM, a division of American Management Associations, 1974) pp. 211–214. This thirty-five question survey is highly recommended as a guide to the preparation of your survey.

3. *Ibid.*, pp. 211–212.

4. Michael Fein, "Motivation for Work," in *Handbook of Work, Organization and Society*, ed. by Robert Dubin (Chicago: Rand McNally College Publishing Co., 1976), pp. 465–530. On pp. 465–66 of this article Fein discusses the popular behavioral motivation concepts summarized here by our three frog theories.

5. This description of what most people want was first described to us in this manner by Frank Hoffman in a speech given at the Western Regional Meeting of the American Society for Personnel Administration in San Francisco on December 1, 1977.

6. William J. Kearney, "Pay for Performance? Not Always," *MSU Business Topics* 27, no. 2 (Spring 1979): 5–6.

7. These ten guidelines have been compiled from a variety of sources. Two that contributed a great deal to the outline of our discussion were: Curtis W. Cook "Guidelines for Managing Motivation," *Business Horizons* 23, no. 2 (April 1980): 61–69 (Guidelines 2, 3, 5, 6, 7, 8, 9, 10) and a seminar presentation entitled "Motivation" given by David J. Cherrington to the National Meeting of the American Society for Personnel Administration in Salt Lake City, Utah on June 17, 1980 (Guidelines 1, 2, 3, 4, 7, 8). Cherrington's viewpoints are available to you in written form in his article, "Teach the Work Ethic at Work," *The Personnel Administrator* 21, no. 7 (October 1976): 24–28. A third work that influenced our motivational guidelines and is well worth reading is Robert J. House and Terence R. Mitchell, "Path-Goal Theory of Leadership," *Journal of Contemporary Business* (Autumn 1974): 81–97.

8. Robert F. Mayer and Peter Pipe present an interesting discussion of how this guideline applies to new employees in their book, *Analyzing Performance Problems or 'You Really Oughta Wanna'* (Belmont, Calif.: Fearon Publishers/Lear Siegler Inc. Education Divison, 1970). As they say, "If you want someone to perform in a particular way, let him in on the secret." (p. 85).

9. Cherrington, "Motivation" seminar.

10. David C. McClelland, *The Achieving Society* (New York: Van Nostrand, 1971), as referenced in Cook, "Guidelines for Managing Motivation," p. 64.

11. Hoffman, speech at ASPA meeting.

Opportunities and Pitfalls

PART V

Taxes and Insurance

17

□ **Taxes are inevitable, but which ones apply to you?**

□ **What kinds of insurance do you need, and how much?**

□ **What is an effective risk management plan?**

CASE
PROBLEM

*Barbara's
Swimming
Schools[1]*

Barbara Johnson has been a swimming instructor for fifteen years. During this time she has developed a successful method for teaching people how to swim. She uses a flotation belt to overcome their basic fear of sinking. This belt, combined with her instruction, makes her students more willing to get into the water and more enthusiastic about learning their basic swimming strokes. Although Barbara's method of instruction does not follow Red Cross methods, her rate of success and the increased enrollments in her school have led her to consider expanding her business. Since she is located in southern Florida, where swimming is a year-round activity, she thinks she can be successful.

Barbara has already taken some steps to check into the possibility of expansion. Her first step was to try to acquire additional flotation belts. She found that they were not available any longer. The manufacturer had phased them out of production because they no longer met Coast Guard standards, and he was unwilling to make the additional investment required to redesign and update the belts and manufacturing equipment. However, he was willing to sell the license and equipment to Barbara.

When she found that the equipment was available, she wanted to know whether she could manufacture and market the belts herself. Her study indicated that the cost of raw materials and overhead costs made this infeasible. However, she did find a job shop that would manufacture the belts in limited quantities for a reasonable cost.

She also found that the retail market for her product is very limited. Although there is a market for swim aids, it is already dominated by large manufacturers with less expensive products. However, it does appear feasible for her to develop a franchise of swimming schools that would use the swim aid as part of a package.

Barbara likes the idea of a swimming school franchise. It would enable her to start a successful business and to spread her instructional method. However, there are a number of issues that she needs to address before she opens her franchise:

1. How can she protect herself from liability actions that might arise as a result of using her swim aid or instruction method?

2. Does she need an endorsement for her method and equipment from a recognized agency, and how can she get it?

3. Does she need to incorporate in order to protect herself from personal liability? What would be the impact on her income taxes if she were to incorporate? Does she have any options that would protect her from personal liability without placing a corporate tax rate on her business?

4. Are there any unique tax problems that could arise because of her franchise or sales of her product?

Barbara's questions relate to taxes and insurance. These two issues probably do not rank very high on the list of issues that need to be taken care of when going into business; but if Barbara were to ignore them, she would soon run into trouble. Proper analysis of your taxes and insurance is like preventive maintenance on your car. If you see that it gets done, you won't have any trouble; but if you ignore it, you will run into problems. Barbara has already asked some pertinent questions about insurance. She has also recognized that corporate taxes could cost her more. Among the unique tax problems she may encounter will be employment and sales taxes.

PROBLEM IDENTIFICATION

The specific tax issues that affect you depend on your type of business, its legal form of organization, and whether or not you have any employees. Basically, business taxes include income taxes, employment taxes, and sales and excise taxes. Some of these taxes need to be paid out of the business. Other taxes, such as sales taxes and employee withholding, are collected and passed on to the tax collector.

Insurance is part of the broader issue of risk management. Risk management includes preventing or limiting your risks and protecting yourself from the damages resulting from risk. One way of protecting yourself from damages and losses is by insuring yourself.

Barbara Johnson's primary risk management problem is to protect herself from personal liability for damages resulting from the use of her flotation device. She might also wish to consider other forms of insurance, such as health or life insurance or a retirement plan. If she actually opens her business, she will want to consider property insurance to protect her business's assets.

There are several steps you need to take to address the issues of taxes and risk management. First, identify the taxes that you are subject to and the risks that you may encounter. Then, evaluate the various ways of handling these taxes and risks and select the best way in each case. Finally, take the actions necessary to pay your taxes and control your risks.

Taxes are inevitable. The main question that you need to ask yourself is what kinds of taxes are you responsible for. The answer is extremely important. Failure to pay your taxes or late payment of taxes can have much more serious consequences for a business than for an individual.

DIAGNOSIS

Taxes can be classified into three major catagories: employment taxes, income taxes, and other taxes, such as sales taxes and excise taxes. The following questions should help you determine which taxes apply to you:

1. *Do you have any employees?* If you have any employees, you are subject to employment taxes. In addition to other taxes that you need to pay, such as social security and unemployment taxes, you also need to deduct an amount from your employees pay checks for their taxes. Generally, these deductions are for the employees' share of social security and income tax withholding.

2. *Does your business have to pay income taxes?* The answer to this question depends on the type of business organization that you have chosen. If your business is a corporation, then it will have to pay taxes. Additionally, you will have to pay personal income taxes on your income from the corporation. If your business is a sole proprietorship or a partnership, then the business itself does not pay income taxes. However, your share of all of the business's profits is reportable as personal income for yourself. You need to declare this income on your annual tax return. Additionally, partnerships need to file an information return, although taxes are not paid by the partnership. There is a special type of corporation called an S Corporation. This allows you to have the legal safeguards of a corporation, but taxes are levied as for a partnership. There are very specific rules that govern a corporation's eligibility for Subchapter S status.

3. *Are there any other kinds of taxes that you must pay?* The other kinds of taxes that your business may be subject to depend on the kind of business that you are in and where you are located. The most common types of other taxes include sales taxes, excise taxes, and property taxes. Many of these taxes are levied at the local level.

4. *When do you need to pay your income taxes?* Generally, income taxes are due on the fifteenth day of the fourth month after the end of the tax year. For most of us, that is the infamous April 15. A tax year is twelve months long. However, it need not be a calendar year. Many businesses report their taxes on a fiscal year basis. A fiscal year is any twelve consecutive months ending on the last day of any month except December. Your tax year is generally determined when you file your first tax return. To change a tax year, you need to get the permission of the Commissioner of Internal Revenue.

5. *When do you need to pay your employment taxes?* Payroll taxes need to be paid on at least a quarterly basis. That is when you need to file your quarterly tax return (federal IRS Form 941). If you have withheld more than a certain amount from your employees in any given quarter, you are required to make timely deposits of these funds. These deposits are made to an authorized financial institution or a Federal Reserve Bank (federal Form 501). Unemployment taxes are paid on a quarterly basis (federal

Form 508) and reported annually on the annual unemployment tax return (federal Form 940.) Unemployment taxes are reported on a calendar year basis, regardless of your fiscal year.

Your business is going to encounter a wide variety of risks and hazards, including fire, theft, burglary, robbery, accidents, injuries, and illnesses. Because all of these hazards can be costly to your business, it is important that you manage these risks. Risk management is the identification and control of the hazards of your business. How do you go about developing an effective risk management program?

1. Make a list of all of the hazards that face your business.

2. Examine each hazard that you have identified. This examination should evaluate the chance of each hazard occurring and estimate the cost of such an occurrence.

3. Select the best way to handle each hazard and develop a plan to control your risks. The various ways to handle a risk include:
   Avoiding the risk
   Spreading the risk
   Preventing the risk
   Transferring the risk to someone else (through insurance).

Taxes

UNDER-STANDING

Required Records.   A business needs to keep accurate records of all of its transactions. It is good business sense to keep good records. They not only provide support for your tax return but also tell you what is happening to your business. It is important that your records provide an accurate, complete, and permanent record of your business. They are used to support your claims for income, deductions, credits, and employee information.

One of the easiest ways to keep records is with a checkbook. If each of your businesses has a separate checkbook and all of your business expenses are paid through these accounts, you will have readily accessible documentation for all of your transactions.

To be effective, your record-keeping system should do the following:

Identify the sources of your income

Identify, document, and substantiate deductions

Provide the information needed to use special tax advantages, such as capital gains and investment tax credits

Determine your self-employment earnings if applicable

Support the information reported on your tax return

If you are an employer, you have additional documentation and reporting requirements. You will need to keep an account of your employees' withholding and social security information. Your employee record-keeping system should provide the following minimum information:

Income Tax Withholding. Employee identification information, including social security number, amount and date of each wage payment, amount of each payment subject to withholding, and amount of withholding tax collected

Social Security Taxes. Amount of wage payments subject to withholding and amount collected for social security. Good information is needed because you, as an employer, need to match all of your employees' contributions.

Federal Unemployment Taxes. In addition to the above information, you need to report the total amount paid to employees during the year, the amount subject to unemployment tax, the amount paid into a state unemployment fund, and any employee deductions made for these payments.

Business Income Taxes.   In order to be a business for tax purposes, you must conduct regular economic activities that have a profit motive. Your business can take any of several forms, the most common being a sole proprietorship, a partnership, or a corporation. Regardless of your form of organization, taxes need to be paid on your profits. However, the way in which these taxes are assessed varies, depending on your form of organization.

Sole Proprietorship.   A sole proprietorship is the simplest form of business organization. There is only one owner. Income for a sole proprietorship is reported as ordinary income on the owner's income tax return. Sole proprietors report business income on Schedule C of Form 1040. This schedule is attached to their regular income tax forms when the tax return is filed. If you own more than one business, you need to file a separate Schedule C for each business.

As a sole proprietor, you probably need to file two other tax forms: Form SE for self-employment taxes and Form 1040-ES for estimated taxes. Form SE is used to report social security taxes for self-employed persons. Because, as a sole owner of a business, you do not collect wages as an employee, you do not withhold any money for taxes from your withdrawals from the business. Therefore, it is necessary for you to estimate the income taxes that you owe and file an annual declaration of estimated taxes.

Partnership.   A partnership is like a sole proprietorship in that it does not pay taxes. The profits of the partnership are divided among the partners, and they declare them as income on their personal tax returns. The partnership calculates its income and reports it on an information return (Form 1065). This income is distributed to the individual partners in any way that they choose.

Each individual partner's share of the partnership income is reported on Schedule K-1 of the partnership return. Copy A is attached to the partnership return, and Copy B is attached to the individual partner's annual tax return. Since partners must pay taxes individually on their share of partnership income, they may be subject to self-employment taxes and estimated tax payments like sole proprietors.

Partnership profits are distributed as described in the partnership agreement. This agreement is used to document that a business partnership exists and to support the profit distributions that are made.

Corporation. A corporation is considered a legal entity. As such, it has the privilege of paying its own taxes. Therefore, corporate profits are taxed directly. Any profit distributions that are made to the business's stockholders (dividends) are considered personal income and are subject to additional taxation. Some corporations are entitled to claim what is called Subchapter S status. This permits stockholders to claim the business's income directly so that the corporation is not directly taxed.

A corporation must file its own tax return (Form 1120) and pay its own taxes unless it elects Subchapter S status. The income taxes paid on the profits of sole proprietorships and partnerships depend on the tax brackets of the individual owners. However, corporations have separate tax rates. The corporate tax rates for 1982 were as follows:

16% on the first $25,000

19% on the next $25,000

30% on the next $25,000

40% on the next $25,000

46% on any taxable income over $100,000

Corporations are also required to file their own estimated income tax returns.

Some corporations may elect not to be subject to the corporate income tax. These are known as S Corporations. If a corporation qualifies for this status, taxes on income are usually paid by the individual stockholders. The requirements for Subchapter S status are discussed in more detail in Chapter 3.

The effect of a Subchapter S election is that the corporation's profits are essentially taxed like those of a partnership. The advantage to the taxpayer lies in the legal advantages of corporate status that are gained without incurring the tax obligations of a corporation.

Taxpayer Identification Number. Businesses have taxpayer identification numbers, which serve the same function as social security numbers for individuals. These numbers must be shown on all business tax forms and all tax-related documents for both income taxes and employment taxes. They are available from the IRS.

Employment Taxes.   As the owner of a business, you may be subject to employment taxes. The principal employment taxes are the self-employment tax and taxes on employees, mainly social security and unemployment taxes.

Self-Employment Taxes.   The self-employment tax is the social security tax that is applied to those who work for themselves. The income limits for the self-employment tax are the same as for social security taxes on wages (up to $32,400 for 1982). If you are subject to social security taxes on earned wages, your self-employment tax obligation is reduced. Self-employment taxes are paid on the income of a trade or business. Schedule SE (Form 1040) is used to calculate the amount of your self-employment tax. The rate for the self-employment tax was 9.35 percent for 1982.

Social Security Taxes.   If you have one or more employees, you probably need to pay social security (FICA) taxes. Questions frequently arise as to whether or not a person working for you is an employee or not. When you control both the method and the results of a person's work and services, that person is an employee. If you have the right to discharge a person and supply tools and a place to work, then that person is probably an employee.

FICA taxes are levied on both the employee and the employer. The rate for both was 6.70 percent on the first $32,400 for 1982. You must withhold both social security and income taxes from your employees' paychecks. However, your share of the FICA tax is above and beyond this withholding deduction. You are also liable for the employees' withholding amounts, whether or not you collect them from your employees.

FICA Tax Rates for 1982–1990	
1982–84	6.70% on $32,400
1985	7.05%
1986–89	7.15%
1990	7.65%

If you are required to collect income taxes and social security taxes, you must file a quarterly tax return, Form 941. You must make deposits for these taxes on at least a monthly basis using Form 501 unless your total liability is less than $500. As soon as possible after December 31 of any calendar year and no later than January 31, you must provide each employee with Form W-2.

Federal Unemployment Taxes.   You are generally liable for federal unemployment taxes (FUTA) if you pay wages in excess of $1,500 in any calendar quarter or have one or more employees for some part of at least one day during twenty different calendar weeks. The rate for FUTA is 3.4 percent on the first $6,000 of wages per employee. However, you may receive a credit of up to 2.7 percent for state unemployment taxes that you pay. Form 940 is used to report unemployment taxes.

Information Sources.   One of the most comprehensive sources for business tax information is the IRS. Publication 334, Tax Guide for Small Business, is a complete and readable source of information on business taxes. It will also provide you with additional sources of information. Appendix B is a list of other documents available from the IRS that can give you specialized information on your tax questions. Publication 15, the *Employers Tax Guide* (Circular E), will be especially helpful if you have any employees.

If you would like further information or if you do not trust IRS publications, you might want to check commercial sources. Both Commerce Clearing House and Prentice-Hall publish extensive tax information. Generally, you can find this information at your public library. West Publishing also publishes annual editions of *West's Federal Taxation*. These volumes are available for either individual income taxes or corporations, partnerships, estates, and trusts.

Insurance

As was mentioned earlier, insurance is a system of protection against the losses that your business may suffer. There are a number of different kinds of insurance protection that you may be able to buy. To understand the different types of insurance, you must first understand some of the commonly used insurance terms.

Definition of Insurance Terms.   You will probably come across some or all of these terms when you buy an insurance policy. You will be a better buyer if you understand them.

Coverage.   The coverage of your insurance policy is the type(s) of loss for which the policy will pay. Generally, a policy will cover the amount, with limitations, of your loss or liability. Policies may also cover the expenses of settling any suits that may arise in conjunction with your loss.

Exclusions.   Exclusions are the kinds of loss that your policy will not pay for.

Limitations.   Limitations are the maximum amounts of coverage provided by a policy. For instance, a $25,000 life insurance policy is limited to paying $25,000. Other limitations may apply to the number of instances covered, the amount of coverge per occurrence, or any other kind of limit that is agreed upon.

Deductibles.   Deductibles are used to reduce the cost of your insurance. If you accept a deductible, you are assuming some of the risk of loss. A deductible is a specific amount or percentage of loss. The insurance coverage will cover only losses above this deductible amount.

Indemnity.   Indemnity is an insurance principle. It limits your coverage to the actual amount of your loss, regardless of the amount stated in the coverage. Therefore, if you insure a truck worth $2,500 for $8,500, you can collect only for the actual amount of the loss (maximum $2,500). Indemnity prevents excess insurance coverage for profit. Actual losses are generally determined by insurance adjusters.

Types of Insurance.   There are three general types of insurance coverage available to business: liability, life and health, and property insurance. It is also possible to purchase supplemental and special purpose insurance for other kinds of hazards.

Liability Insurance.   Liability insurance protects your business against injuries or other kinds of damage for which your business may be legally responsible. As a business owner, you are subject to the laws regarding negligence. The laws apply to customers, employees, and anyone else who may do business with you. Negligence is the failure to exercise adequate care to protect these persons. There are two general types of liability insurance—one to cover members of your firm and the other to cover nonmembers.

Nonmember liability coverage is designed to protect you from losses involving nonemployees. These losses include injuries to others while they are on your property and injuries that you may make to others' property. Some liability coverage is also available for damages that occur as a result of the use of your business's product or service. Much of this coverage can be obtained through a multirisk, or comprehensive, liability insurance policy. However, even a comprehensive policy may not protect you from all of the liability risks you may be subject to. Therefore, it is often necessary to obtain additional coverage to protect your business from automobile and product liabilities.

Automobile liability insurance for a business is similar to that which you have on your personal car. However, it may provide additional coverage in that it covers your liability for accidents that occur when the vehicles of your employees, customers, or sub-contractors are being used on behalf of your firm. Such accidents could occur if you were renting vehicles or if your employees were driving customers' vehicles for some reason.

Product liability insurance protects you against damages arising from the use of your product or service. As consumer protection laws have become more stringent, this type of coverage has been increasingly important. It can cover losses if your product causes injury or damage to a user. For instance, if you run an auto repair shop and a brake cylinder fails on a customer's car, the problem could have been in either the manufacturing or the installation. Therefore, both the manufacturer and the installer would need product liability coverage.

Member liability coverage applies to your employees. The most common type of this coverage is workmen's compensation. However, there is a growing trend to provide disability, health, and other types of insurance also.

Workmen's compensation insurance protects employers against liabilities from accidents that happen to their employees. The laws that require workmen's compensation insurance insure that employees will have a safe place to work, have safe tools, and be forewarned of dangers on the job. The insurance provides for payment of doctor, hospital, and medication bills and income payments for time lost from work beyond some minimum period. The laws governing workmen's compensation vary from state to state in regard to the amount of coverage required and the method of determining the amount of liability.

Life and Health Insurance.   Many businesses carry group life and health insurance coverage on their employees. Although it is not often required by law, this coverage is increasingly being provided to employees as an employment benefit. The choice of whether or not you provide this coverage is up to you as a business owner. However, if your competitors offer it to their employees, you may need to offer it also to remain competitive. Group policies are generally less expensive than individual policies. The cost of the policies may or may not be shared by the employer and the employees.

Life insurance provides for the financial protection of an employee's family in the case of the employee's death. Usually this protection is coupled with a health insurance plan. This type of group insurance is usually available for even a small number of employees.

Health insurance plans come in three types: basic hospitalization and medical insurance, major medical insurance, and disability insurance. *Basic hospitalization* insurance covers the cost of hospitalization, medical care, and medicine while an employee is in the hospital. It may also pay for some outpatient services and diagnostic services, such as x-rays. *Major medical* plans cover employees for medical costs over the basic medical and hospitalization plan coverage. They are designed to cover the costs of catastrophic illness. *Disability* insurance is used to pay an employee a portion of his or her salary if the employee is away from work because of an illness or injury that was not work related.

You should not forget yourself or your family when you are investigating life and health insurance. What would happen to your business if you or a critical employee died? To provide for such an event, there is a type of insurance called "key man" insurance. This insurance is owned by and payable to your company in the event of the loss of you or another insured key employee. The advantage of this type of insurance is that it gives your business an additional financial resource to fall back on until you can replace your key employee or until your family can arrange for the continuation of the business after your death.

Pension and retirement insurance provides for income to employees after they retire. These plans can be very complex and expensive and should be investigated carefully. Because a pension plan may involve federal laws and tax regulations, you should obtain competent advice before you adopt one. In recent years, the tax laws have provided for Individual Retirement Accounts (IRAs) for employees and Keogh plans for self-employed individuals. These plans allow you to shelter some of your income until after you retire. They can be easy to use and are less expensive than a pension plan.

Property Insurance.   Property, or casualty, insurance protects you from losses arising from the destruction of property. Casualty insurance includes the following types of coverage:

Fire insurance

Comprehensive property insurance

Crime insurance (theft, burglary, or robbery)

Vandalism

Hail, wind, and flood insurance

Vehicle insurance (collision)

Fire insurance covers your business against losses from fire, lightning, or the removal of goods from your property because of fire (looting). Often you can extend your fire insurance policy to include coverage for related losses, such as damage from explosions, riots, or smoke.

Comprehensive insurance is used to cover gaps that may occur in specific types of casualty insurance. It generally covers all losses except those specifically exempted. Comprehensive policies reduce the possibility of duplicated coverage from several types of policies and can make collecting on a loss easier than if several different types of coverage had been purchased.

Some coverage for crimes may be provided by a comprehensive insurance policy. However, additional coverage may be needed to cover off-premises robberies, employee theft, or embezzlement. Since employee theft is one of the most rapidly increasing crime areas, it is a good idea to carry this kind of coverage. If your business needs to handle large amounts of cash, you may also want to get a fidelity bond. This is a specific insurance to cover employee theft and embezzlement.

Vehicle insurance covers your losses associated with vehicle damages over and above liability losses.

In addition to the types of insurance mentioned above, it is also possible to obtain named-peril coverage. This insurance is used to provide protection for a specific type of property or occurrence. An example of a named-peril policy would be the one on Betty Grable's legs.

Supplemental and Special Purpose Insurance.   Supplemental insurance coverage is used to provide protection over and above that provided by liability and casualty insurance for potential large losses. Examples of supplemental insurance are transportation, business interruption, and credit insurance.

Transportation insurance is used to cover losses that are not the liability of a common carrier. Common carriers include trucking firms, railroads, and air freight companies. These include collision, derailment, and "acts of God."

Business interruption insurance protects you if your business is shut down because of a disaster. It allows you to continue to pay your operating expenses, even though there is little or no income. It can also provide for payment of part of your profits and fixed expenses. This kind of insurance has a high coinsurance requirement and will not cover the full amount of your loss.

Coinsurance requires that you carry a specified proportion of the value of the property in insurance or bear part of the loss. This requirement may be 80 percent or 90 percent of the cash value of the property.

There are three types of credit insurance available: credit life insurance, commercial credit insurance, and installment sales floaters. *Credit life insurance* is used to insure that outstanding debt will be paid in the event of the death of a customer. *Installment sales floaters* protect you against losses when a purchaser does not insure goods purchased on credit. The floater insures that you will be able to collect payment for those goods. *Commercial credit* insurance protects you if you sell to only a few commercial customers and carry a large amount of these sales in credit. This insurance provides payment if one of your customers is unable to pay a bill, causing severe financial strain for you.

There are also other forms of insurance available. They include rent insurance (if a tenant fails to pay), profit and commission insurance (if property is destroyed), sprinkler leakage insurance, glass insurance, fidelity bonds, and key employee insurance. An insurance agent can advise you of the types and costs of the available insurance coverages.

How To Buy Insurance.   The purpose of insurance is to protect you from losses. However, if you attempt to cover yourself from every type of hazard possible, you may find yourself insurance poor or insurance broke. You need to take some precautions to insure yourself against some of the hazards and risks faced by your business, but you also need to be careful when you purchase insurance coverage. You should use the following techniques:

1. *Determine the type and amount of coverage necessary.* The checklist in Appendix C might help you to determine the type of coverage needed. When determining the amount of coverage, you should consider the amount of insurance, the coinsurance required, the level of deductibles available, and the cost of the premiums for the coverage available.

2. *Select an insurance agent.* Insurance agents can advise you on the type and amount of insurance needed and can help you with the details of a policy. They can also provide assistance in reducing premium costs, getting the best protection, and helping you to settle claims. Because agents work on a commission basis, you need to select an agent who has a considerable amount of personal integrity and in whom you have confidence. Some agents are independent and may be able to provide coverage from several different companies. Other agents work directly for an insurance company

and are employees of it. Independent agents may have a higher desire to obtain and retain clients because they are dependent on commissions. Direct writer agents may have a more in-depth knowledge of the full details of a particular company's coverage. Each type of agent has its own advantages.

When selecting or reviewing an agent, you can use the following guidelines for your evaluation:

Use a competitive bid to select the lowest-cost coverage that provides the given level of protection you need. In a competitive bid, you give several agents an opportunity to "bid" on the cost of providing you with insurance. This will provide you with information on the range of coverage offered and its cost.

Review the specific types of insurance provided to see if any areas have been overlooked by one agent or the other.

Evaluate the effectiveness of the agent in getting claims settled quickly and fully.

Evaluate the supportive services and advice provided by the various agents.

Review your insurance program and your agent on a regular basis.

3. *Make sure your coverage is appropriate.* An important part of proper insurance coverage is taking the steps necessary to protect yourself. The following steps can simplify your insurance program:

Notify your insurer promptly of any losses.

Keep a good set of records to document any losses.

Avoid insuring a property or occurrence more than once (overlapping coverage).

Avoid noncurrence (covering the same property with nonidentical coverage). All risks should be covered with one policy, or coverage should be identical.

Avoid spreading coverage over several agents. (Deal with one agent.)

Do not insure your property for too much or too little. Overinsurance will increase your costs without increasing your protection. Underinsurance will not adequately cover your losses.

Risk Management.   Up to this point, we have focused on the different types of insurance available to you. However, insurance is only one dimension of an effective risk management system. Insurance manages risks by transferring them to someone else. A comprehensive risk management system also handles risks by avoiding them, spreading them, and preventing them. If you use such a system in your business, you will reduce your need for insurance or at least the cost of the insurance that you do need.

There are three steps to developing a comprehensive risk management system: 1. identifying your risks; 2. evaluating the probability and cost of their occurring; and 3. controlling each risk by selecting the best way to handle it (avoid, spread, prevent or transfer).

Risk Identification.   Risk identification is the process of examining your business to determine the potential threats of loss, damage, and expense to it. This identification process should start with your financial statements and organizational papers. You need to examine the following:

    Balance sheet

    Income statement

    List of employees, their hours, tasks performed, and rates of pay

    List of equipment, buildings, and materials

From this information, you should begin to prepare a schedule of possible risks. For instance, you could use the following format to help you to identify the risks associated with each item you have examined.

Item (from the balance sheet)	Risks	Cost Probability
CASH	Pilferage Robbery Fire/flood loss	
ACCOUNTS RECEIVABLE	Death of customers Nonpayment	
INVENTORY	Employee theft Burglary/robbery Fire/flood loss	

You should be able to expand this list and add to the different types of risk you could expect in your business. The important thing for you to do is to let your imagination roam and put down every kind of possible risk that you can come up with. All that you are trying to do at this point is to identify all of your potential risks.

Risk Evaluation.   The second step in risk management is to evaluate the risks you have identified. You will notice that the risk identification form above has a column for probability and cost. This is your evaluation step. After you have identified each of the risks that your business could face, you need to determine what the chances are that this event will occur. Although this is subjective, it will help you to develop your risk management plan. The evaluation also needs to look at the cost of each risk. For instance, a particular risk might have an 80 percent probability of occurring. However, if the cost of that occurrence is five dollars, then you probably will not want to look at insurance as the way to manage that risk. In your evaluation, you should also examine the potential for several risks occurring at the same time. For instance, a burglar might start a fire to cover the crime.

Risk Control.   Control of risks involves the four methods of handling risks mentioned earlier: avoiding, spreading, preventing, and transferring risks. You control your risks by trying to make certain that they do not occur. At the same time, you make certain that you have selected some method to handle them if they do occur.

Risk transfer has been dealt with under insurance. Risk avoidance is avoiding situations where the risk could occur. For many risks, this may not be possible.

Spreading risk generally involves having duplicates or back-up systems. For instance, you might want to have photocopies of your deeds, partnership agreements, and tax records in a safe deposit box. Then, if the original record is destroyed, you will have back-up material. Back-up systems can also be used to reduce potential loss. For instance, a grocery store might have an auxiliary generator to provide electricity to its cold storage facilities in the event of a power failure.

Risk prevention methods can reduce both the chances of loss and the cost of some kinds of insurance that may also be a part of your risk management plan. The following are examples of preventive activities that you might use to control risk:

Sprinkler systems for fire suppression

Burglar alarms

Safety devices for machinery

Quality control procedures to test products

Store security to prevent shoplifting

Closed circuit TV to prevent shoplifting and employee pilferage

Frequent inventory checks on high-value merchandise

Identification procedures for accepting checks and a charge for returned checks

After you have identified the types of risk you expect to encounter in your business, you may come up with your own list of preventive measures. Insurance companies also have loss and safety consultants who can give you additional guidance on both prevention and avoidance methods.

CASE
SOLUTION

Barbara's Swimming School

Barbara's most effective course of action is to set up a model swimming school that she can then franchise out. Since she can sell her swim aids as a part of the franchise package, she will be able to generate a profit on the investment that she has already made. However, there are several important steps that need to be taken before she attempts to set up a franchise.

1. She needs to protect herself from personal liability for any injuries or deaths connected with the use of the swim aid. Setting her business up as a corporation would provide some of this protection.

2. She should secure product liability insurance for the swim aid. This task will be easier if she can get certification for the aid from the Coast Guard.

3. She needs to acquire the services of an attorney familiar with setting up franchises. She should also get the services of a patent law office to protect the product design.

4. She should look into the tax advantages, if any, afforded by Subchapter S election. This would enable her to get the protection of a corporate legal form without the tax obligations associated with a corporation.

CHAPTER SUMMARY

Although taxes are inevitable, you need to determine which taxes your business is subject to. Because failure to pay your taxes can result in the loss of your business, you should be fully aware of your tax obligations. The major kinds of taxes that you could be subject to are employment taxes, and income taxes.

Business income taxes are assessed according to the organizational form of your business. The profits of sole proprietorships and partnerships are taxed as income on the owners' individual tax returns. Corporations are taxed as separate entities. All businesses need to keep accurate records that tell how they are doing and support the data on their tax returns.

Employment taxes are assessed to businesses with employees. The principal employment taxes are social security and unemployment. Employers are also required to withhold their employees' social security and income tax payments.

Risk is part of business. An effective risk management program does three things. It identifies the risks. It evaluates the chance and cost of the hazards. It controls the risks by selecting the best way to handle each one. Risks can be handled in four ways: avoiding them, spreading them, preventing them, or transferring them through some type of insurance program.

There are three major types of insurance coverage available to business: liability insurance, life and health insurance, and property, or casualty, insurance. Many companies also provide special and supplemental insurance coverages.

DISCUSSION QUESTIONS

1. What federal tax forms are used to report business income for:
   a. sole proprietorships
   b. partnerships
   c. corporations

2. What kind of information or records should you keep for your business to help you prepare your tax return?

3. What federal taxes are you required to pay if you have employees? What federal forms are required to be filed when you pay these taxes?

4. Define the following terms:
   a. indemnity
   b. exclusion
   c. deductibles
   d. coinsurance

5. What are the three steps in designing a risk management program?

6. Theft is a common risk encountered by business. List several different ways of managing this risk.

7. List four types of liability that a business needs to protect itself against.

8. What types of coverage can be provided by a typical property insurance plan?

9. What options are available to protect against business risk other than commercial insurance?

REFERENCES   Commerce Clearing House. *U.S. Master Tax Guide: 1982 Edition.* Chicago, 1981.

Federal Tax Course. Englewood Cliffs, N.J.: Prentice-Hall, 1979.

Federal Tax Guide, 1982. Englewood Cliffs, N.J.: Prentice-Hall, 1981.

Greene, M. A. *Insurance Checklist for Small Business.* Small Marketers Aid No. 148. Washington, D.C.: Small Business Administration, 1976.

Hoffman, W. H., and Phillips, L. C. *West's Federal Taxation.* St. Paul: West Publishing Co., 1982.

Internal Revenue Service. *Tax Guide for small Business.* Publication 334 (Annual Revision). Washington, D.C.

Research Institute of America. *Federal Income Tax Guide, 1982.* New York: Ace Books, 1981.

Small Business Administration. *Risk Management and Insurance.* Business Basics Series No. 1018. Washington, D.C., 1980.

FOOTNOTES   1. This case was prepared by one of the authors based on consulting work done for one of his clients. In order to maintain client confidentiality, the facts given in this case differ somewhat from the actual case.

Appendix A

CHECKLIST FOR
TAXES

Some of the federal taxes for which a sole proprietor, a corporation, or a partnership may be liable are listed below. If due dates fall on a Saturday, Sunday, or legal holiday, they are postponed until the next day that is not a Saturday, Sunday, or legal holiday. For more information see Publication 509, Tax Calendar for 1982.

You may be liable for	If you are:	Use Form	Due on or before
Income Tax	Sole proprietor	Schedule C (Form 1040)	Same day as Form 1040
	Individual who is a partner or Subchapter S corporation shareholder	1040	15th day of 4th month after end of tax year
	Corporation	1120	15th day of 3rd month after end of tax year
	Subchapter S corporation	1120S	15th day of 3rd month after end of tax year
Self-employment tax	Sole proprietor, or individual who is a partner	Schedule SE (Form 1040)	Same day as Form 1040
Estimated tax	Sole proprietor, or individual who is a partner or Subchapter S corporation shareholder	1040ES	15th day of 4th, 6th, and 9th month of tax year, and 15th day of 1st month after the end of tax year
	Corporation	1120W	15th day of 4th, 6th, 9th and 12th month of tax year
Annual return of income	Partnership	1065	15th day of 4th month after end of tax year
FICA tax and the withholding of income tax	Sole proprietor, corporation, Subchapter S corporation, or partnership	941	4–30, 7–31, 10–31 and 1–31
		501 (to make deposits)	
Providing information on FICA tax and the withholding of income tax	Sole proprietor, corporation, Subchapter S corporation, or partnership	W-2 (to employee) W-3 (to the Social Security Administration)	1–31 Last day of February

You may be liable for	If you are:	Use Form	Due on or before
FUTA tax	Sole proprietor, corporation, Subchapter S corporation, or partnership	940 508 (to make deposits)	1–31 4–30, 7–31, 10-31 and 1–31, but only if the liability for unpaid tax is more than $100
Annual information returns	Sole proprietor, corporation, Subchapter S corporation, or partnership	See Publication 15	
Excise taxes	Sole proprietor, corporation, Subchapter S corporation, or partnership		

Source: IRS Publication 334, revised 1982

Appendix B

TAX PUBLICATIONS

The discussions in this book generally will answer your questions about the federal tax laws that apply to business. However, sometimes other IRS publications on individual topics are suggested for more information. You will find the titles and numbers of these publications listed below. You can order these free publications, and any forms you need, from the IRS Forms Distribution Center for your state. The address is in the instructions to your tax return. Or you can call the Tax Information number listed in your phone book under *United States Government, Internal Revenue Service.*

General Guides:

Your Federal Income Tax (an income tax guide for individuals) 17
Agricultural Employer's Tax Guide (Circular A) . . . 51
Employer's Tax Guide (Circular E) 15
Farmer's Tax Guide . . . 225
Tax Guide for Commercial Fishermen 595

Specialized Publications:

Accounting Periods and Methods 538
Administrators, Survivors, and Executors, Tax Information for 559
Aliens, U.S. Tax Guide for 519
Annuity Income, Pension and. 575
Annuity Programs, Tax-Sheltered, for Employees of Public Schools and Certain Tax-Exempt Organizations 571
Appeal Rights, Examination of Returns, and Claims for Refund 556
Assets, Sales and Other Dispositions of 544
Bad Debts, Deduction for 548
Basis of Assets 551
Business Expenses and Operating Losses 535
Business Use of Your Home 587
Casualties, Disasters, and Thefts, Tax Information on 547
Casualty Loss Workbook, Disaster and 584
Child and Disabled Dependent Care 503
Claims for Refund, Examination of Returns, and Appeal Rights 556

Clergy and Religious Workers, Social Security for Members of the 517
Collection Process, The. 586A
Community Property and the Federal Income Tax. 555
Condemnations of Private Property for Public Use. 549
Condominiums, Cooperative Apartments, and Homeowners Associations 588
Contests and Sporting Events, Tax Information for Sponsors of 558
Contributions, Charitable 526
Cooperative Apartments, Condominiums, and Homeowners Associations 588

Other Helpful Publications:
The Small Business Administration has a number of informative publications. SBA 115A contains a list of free publications, and SBA 115B provides a list of the ones for sale. Both are available through SBA's Washington and field offices. Or wrtie to the Small Business Administration, Washington, DC 20416.

Source: IRS Publication 334, revised 1982.

Appendix C

CHECKLIST FOR INSURANCE

Which of the following hazards do you have and need coverage for?

PROPERTY INSURANCE

Aircraft damage ———

Boiler and machinery ———

Civil commotion ———

Commercial property ———

Explosion ———

Fire ———

Flood ———

Hail ———

Lightning ———

Riot ———

Strike ———

Smoke damage ———

Theft   _____
Vandalism   _____
Vehicle damage   _____
Water damage   _____
Wind   _____

Floaters
Business interruption   _____
Credit   _____
Glass   _____
Installment sales   _____
Signs   _____
Rent   _____
Sprinkler leak   _____
Transportation   _____

LIABILITY
Automobile   _____
General liability   _____
Product   _____
Comprehensive (Umbrella)   _____

LIFE AND HEALTH INSURANCE
Basic health   _____
Disability   _____
Group life   _____
Key employee   _____
Major medical   _____
Workmen's compensation   _____

Computers 18

□ **What can a computer do that can't be done by hand?**

□ **How can you get the advantages of a computer—do you need to buy one, or are there other options?**

□ **How do you go about buying a computer?**

Joselyn's Designs was started by Joseph and Lyn Fredrickson in 1973. They design and manufacture needlepoint and crewel kits for craft work. At the present time, they distribute 450 different kits through approximately five hundred craft stores in the Southeast. They also have a rapidly growing mail-order business, all of which is developed through ads in general circulation magazines, such as *Family Circle* and *Good Housekeeping.*

After seeing advertisements for different kinds of computers, the Fredricksons began to wonder whether or not one would be useful in their business. They thought there were several areas in the business that could effectively use a computer. These included accounts receivable and payable, inventory information and control, kit making, and sales analysis. They developed the following plan for how they could use a computer:

Accounts Receivable: All sales to the five hundred craft stores were being handled as credit sales. Since several of their customers had begun paying on a much slower schedule, the Fredricksons felt a computer would be helpful in keeping a better watch on their accounts receivable. They also wanted to use it to help to manage their accounts payable so that they would be able to take advantage of all discounts they were eligible for.

Inventory Information and Control: Their product line required an inventory of approximately two thousand different items. They needed information on the current level of inventory for each item, the amount of material that had to be reordered for each inventory item, and the value of the inventory and each item in it. Because the demand for each inventory item was different, the system was very difficult to manage. The business had a policy of filling orders within one day, and it was very important that all items for a particular kit be readily available.

Kit Making: Each kit required a unique combination of materials. Besides the design itself, each kit included the appropriate amounts and colors of yarn to complete the project. The Fredricksons felt that if they could call up the composition of a kit on the computer, they would be able to speed up kit assembly. They had been making up each kit as the order came in. This policy kept the finished goods inventory very low.

Sales Analysis: The Fredricksons did not have a solid grasp on their sales composition. Although they could readily identify their top fifty designs, they were unable to get quick information on the remainder of their inventory. They had recently dropped two hundred designs from their product line because they felt these designs were unproductive. The Fredricksons felt they needed accurate and timely information on what items were selling, what quantities they were being sold in, and where they were being sold. With this information, they felt they would be able to forecast sales trends, estimate production and purchasing requirements, and minimize their inventory investment.

The temptation to buy a computer is an easy one to give in to today. Just a few years ago, it could have cost thousands or even millions of dollars to buy one. Now you can go down to the corner and buy one for a few hundred dollars. Even a fairly sophisticated business system can be purchased for a few thousand dollars. What was once a luxury for big businesses is now an affordable tool for many small firms. However, even though it may be within your reach, you may not be able to use a computer efficiently in your business. Would you spend $4,000 on the latest piece of equipment for your business if you were not going to use it? Probably not. You should examine the use of computers in your business in the same way. You should determine whether you need to use a computer and whether it can be a productive and profitable tool for you. The Fredrickson's were attracted to computerization of their business because computers have the kinds of abilities that they needed. Businesses are attracted to computers because of the following factors:

They have a high volume of straightforward and repetitive transactions; many of these transactions are additions or subtractions.

They employ many people in general processing activities, such as payroll and accounts receivable.

They serve a large number of active customer accounts, or have a large number of creditors and vendors.

They maintain an extensive inventory, especially one with many low-cost items.

They operate in more than two or three locations.

They spend more than five hundred dollars on outside computer services or services that use computers (such as a payroll system).

They have to cope with unique problems, such as lengthy mailing lists, complicated lead and delivery times, or complicated transactions such as bidding.

As you do your analysis of computers, you need to keep in mind that the computer is only a tool. Just because you have a computer, you are not going to become more efficient or more profitable. You need to buy the right computer for your business, and then you need to use it in the right way. If you buy a system that is too small, it will not do what you want it to do. If you buy more than you need, you will have excess funds tied up unprofitably. Having a computer and not using it is like buying a car and not driving it: it may be pretty, but it isn't doing you much good.

DIAGNOSIS
A commonly mentioned reason for buying a computer is to improve business. Although a computer can improve your business, it can also be a drag on your business if you don't use it the right way. Like any tool, a computer does some things very well. However, it does not do everything, and it does not think for itself. Before you jump into the computer marketplace, there are a number of questions you need to answer.

1. What is a computer? What can it do? What are the different parts of a computer, and what do they do?
2. Do you have any options other than buying a computer?
3. What questions should you ask yourself about computers and how they fit into your business?
4. How do you select the best computer for you and your business?

The reason for using a computer is to improve your ability to meet the needs of your business. A computer should help you do a better job of managing your business. If you are getting a computer to improve your business but are not sure exactly how it can help, then you could be making a mistake. You need to be able to answer the following questions before getting a computer:

1. *Can you quantify the major operations of your business?* An earlier chapter identified the record-keeping requirements of a business. If you do not have those systems in place, you are not ready for a computer. The computer will not keep the records that you refuse to keep for yourself. Do you know how much your sales are? How many of your customers are overdue in paying their bills? How many parts do you have in your inventory? If you do not have a set of systems already in operation to answer these questions, then the computer is not going to do much good for you. The computer can speed up your paper flow and fill your data needs more quickly, but it cannot give you information it does not have.

2. *Are your business procedures standard and orderly?* A computer does what it is told to do—quickly and consistently. Your business procedures must be consistent and standard to take advantage of these qualities. The computer requires that information be fed into it in a certain way. If your business is not set up to handle operations in a standard, fixed manner, then it may not be able to use a computer.

3. *Do you know what the capabilities of a computer are?* Do you know what a computer can and cannot do? If you want to run down to the corner computer store and buy a pocket-sized computer to handle your accounts receivable, you are making a big mistake. You need to know your requirements and what a computer needs to meet those requirements. You should visit other small companies that have installed small computers. You should also get demonstrations of the equipment that you are considering. Many computer suppliers and stores will give you a hands-on demonstration so that you can experiment.

4. *Could you manage your operation better with more accurate and timely information?* One of the biggest advantages of a computer is that it can process and return information to you much more quickly than manual methods. Do you need this kind of speed? A computer can also give you access to more and better information than you may have had before. Many managers make decisions based on intuition and sketchy information. If you can reduce your reliance on intuition and increase the data available to you, you may be able to make better decisions. A computer can help you to do comparisons of sales by area, by product, and by customer; and it can do this quickly and accurately. You can get a comparative report in minutes rather than days. It can also help you to keep track of your inventory levels, customer delivery times, and myriad other statistics that can help you to spot potential weaknesses and strengths in your business.

5. *Could you get more productive work out of your employees?* A computer will probably not decrease your workforce. In fact, it may increase it. However, the computer can make your staff more productive. It can eliminate much of the repetitive and routine work they do so that they have more time for more analytical work. Your bookkeeper might be able to spend more time analyzing your financial statements to find potential problems rather than spending hours posting journal entries to a ledger, for example. Although you may not get more work out of your employees, you might be able to get better work out of them.

6. *Do you expect to grow?* If you expect your business to grow, you may need a computer in a few years, even if you do not need one now. However, it takes time to install and integrate a computer into your normal business operations. You might find spending time to integrate a computer now worthwhile. It could save time later, when it might be more critical to have a computer.

7. *Will you be able to get a good return on a computer investment?* This is the bottom line and probably the most critical question. It might be nice to have a computer. It could impress your customers and even your creditors. But will it do the job that it should? You should think about the computer in the same way that you think about a new employee. It should help you to cut costs or to increase your sales or both. Before you hire a new employee, you develop some expectations of what that employee will do for you. You should also develop a set of expectations for your computer.

UNDER-STANDING

The Parts of a Computer

A computer system consists of equipment that performs the following four functions:

1. Input   3. Storage
2. Processing   4. Output

Information is fed into a computer by means of various input devices. The computer then processes the information in its central processing unit (CPU). After the processing is completed, the information either is stored in some kind of storage device or becomes output through some type of output device. The output device is sometimes the same one used for input. Figure 18.1 shows how the parts of a computer are related to one another.

Input. There are two major ways of feeding information into a computer: batch processing and real-time processing.

In a *batch-processing system*, information is first put onto a medium that is not connected to the computer. The most widely known batch medium is the computer punch card. The punch card has a pattern of punched holes that is interpreted by the computer. Other batch media include magnetic tape and discs. After the information has been put onto the medium by the keyboard, the medium (card, tape, or disc) is put into a reader for input into the computer.

In *real-time systems*, input is fed directly into the computer. This allows you to communicate and interact directly with the computer. Real-time systems are becoming more and more popular. The most common type of real-time input device is a CRT (cathode ray tube). A CRT is like a typewriter keyboard with a TV screen attached. Other types of real-time input include the reservation systems used by airlines, cash registers that automatically update inventory records, wands used in retail stores to scan price tags, and magnetic ink readers used by banks to process checks.

Output. Output devices take information from a computer and give it to you in a form that you can understand. Some output can come back to you through the input device. For example, the seat availability listing at the air-

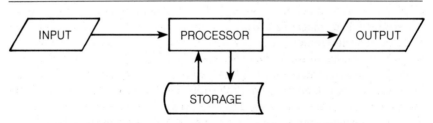

Figure 18.1 How the Parts of a Computer Relate

line counter works this way. The other kind of common output is the computer print-out that comes out of a printer. These printers can also be used to print checks, write letters, and perform most other kinds of tasks required to obtain output. Computer output can also be generated on punched cards and magnetic tape or discs for storage and retrieval later.

Storage.   Both computer input and output can be stored for later use. Storage can be either on-line or off-line. *Off-line* storage is storage that is not connected to the computer. The computer can only use it if it is connected or reentered through an input device. *On-line data storage* is always connected and the computer can get access to the data whenever it is needed or requested. On-line storage can be on magnetic tape, discs, or in the CPU itself. The stored information can be retrieved through either random access or sequential access. Random access provides instantaneous retrieval and requires some type of disc storage. Discs can be either hard discs or what are commonly called "floppy discs," or "diskettes." A floppy disc looks like a 45 r.p.m. record and is often used on small computer systems. Hard discs hold much more information and are generally used with larger systems. Magnetic tape storage gives you sequential access to data. This means that the data are stored at a particular location, and you need to run through the tape until you get to that storage space. Sequential access is like a tape player that you need to advance or rewind to find your favorite song. Random access, on the other hand, is like a record on which you just need to place the needle at the right spot. One way may be faster than the other, but both systems give you what you need.

Central Processor.   The central processing unit, or CPU, is the real computer. It is what does all of the work. The CPU has three major parts: the arithmetic unit, the control unit, and the memory. The arithmetic unit does the work of the computer—the actual calculations. The control unit coordinates and controls the activities of the computer operations. It takes information out of memory or from input, sends it to the arithmetic unit, puts data back into memory, or sends it to output. (It's really a fancy traffic cop.) The memory unit holds the information until it is needed by the arithmetic unit or the control unit. The memory unit can hold both the data being used or processed and the program being used.

A computer program is a set of instructions that tells the computer what to do. Without a program, a computer will just sit there. Computer programs are written in several languages. The computer itself understands only something called "machine language." Machine language is a set of positive and negative electronic impulses. Computer languages allow you to write a set of instructions in something that resembles English. The compiler then translates these instructions into machine language so that the computer can understand them. Common computer languages are: COBOL (one of the most common business languages in use), RPG (often used for statistical reports and business applications such as accounts receivable/payable), FOR-

TRAN (primarily used in scientific, engineering, and mathematical applications), BASIC (a simplified, easy-to-learn language, which is the most common system in small computers), and PASCAL (a newer language for scientific research and other advanced applications). There are also other languages in use today. However, those listed above are the most common ones.

What a Computer Does

A computer processes information, stores it, and gives it back to us when we need it. In essence, a computer does the jobs that you normally do in the everyday operation of your business. In order to understand more fully what a computer does, you need to look first at the steps required to process information and then at how the computer handles these steps.

Steps in Processing Information.   One of the main functions in a business is the processing of information. The computer is just one way in which this information can be processed. Originally, all information was processed manually. Later, machines such as typewriters and adding machines were developed to assist with the manual process. These machines were refined and developed until today we have electronic methods of processing information. Regardless of which method is used—and all are currently in use—the steps used to process data are the same.

1. *Origination*. Your data need to come from somewhere. They can be from a cash register, your personal observation, or any other source.
2. *Classification*. After the data have been originated, they are put into some system of classification. Financial information, for example, is put into a system of accounts.
3. *Sorting*. After the information is classified, it is sorted into a system that can be used for retrieval later. In accounting, this sorting process is the posting of information into a ledger. If you are doing a market study, you might sort a potential buyer into one of your target markets.
4. *Calculation*. If necessary, arithmetical operations may be performed to make the data more useful
5. *Summarization*. Summarization collects bits of information into useful clusters, such as the total sales for the day.
6. *Communication*. Communication conveys the data to someone who can use them.
   There are three additional steps in processing that are often used.
7. *Storage*. Storage is the retention of data for later use.
8. *Retrieval*. Retrieval is the process of taking data out of storage.
9. *Reproduction*. Reproduction is the duplication of data for several users.

Computer Processing of Data.   A computer follows the same steps given above. However, most of the functions are done electronically rather than manually. Figure 18.2 illustrates how a computer and a manual system perform the same processing functions.

Data-Processing Options

Your business will need to process information. You will need this information to keep your fingers on the pulse of your business. The information will also need to be available for other users, such as your banker. Essentially, you have three options available to you: a manual system, a service bureau, or an in-house computer.

Manual Systems.   Manual systems have been around since man started keeping records. Although most manual systems also use some type of machine assistance, most of the information is processed by people. For many businesses, manual systems are excellent. If your business does not have most of the characteristics mentioned in the problem identification, then you will probably find that a manual system will easily fill your information-processing needs.

   If you decide that a manual system is inadequate for your needs, you have several options open to you. We are making the assumption that mechanical aids, such as typewriters, copiers, calculators, and other related equipment, are part of a manual system and will not meet your needs. The next level of information processing is some type of electronic system. There are two ways to gain access to an electronic system—by using a service bureau or by leasing or purchasing your own computer.

Service Bureaus.   A service bureau is a business that uses its own computer to provide a variety of services to its customers. These services include accounts receivable, inventory management, payroll processing and record-

STEP	MANUAL	COMPUTER
Origination	Observation/writing	Input device (cards, tapes, discs, CRT)
Classification/Sorting	Hand posting	Computer program
Calculation/ Summarization	Brain/hand calculation	Computer (CPU)
Communication/ Reproduction	Written reports, etc.	Computer output (printouts, CRT displays, etc.)
Storing/Retrieval	Files, journals, ledgers	Tapes, discs, etc.

Figure 18.2 Processing Information

ing, and general ledger services, among others. The level of service available from these bureaus varies. Some offer comprehensive services that include all phases of the data-processing operation. Others offer only partial services.

Service bureaus may also offer the option of time-sharing. In a time-sharing operation, you share a computer with other users. You may use your own programs or share common programs with other users. Because the computer does its processing operation with incredible speed, a number of users might share the computer and never be aware of one another.

Generally, service bureaus will bill you for the services or time used. There may be a flat fee for the basic use of the service plus an additional charge based on actual use. When you evaluate a service bureau, you should consider several factors: cost, error correction, and turnaround time.

How much will it cost you to use the service bureau, and what will you get for your money? You should carefully investigate the full cost of several services and compare these costs and the actual services offered. You should also check with other users of the system to determine their costs and satisfaction with the service.

One of the major rules of computer use is GIGO (Garbage In, Garbage Out). If information is incorrectly entered, it will usually come out incorrect. As you investigate a service bureau, you need to ascertain the arrangements for detecting and correcting errors. The correction of errors needs to be done accurately and quickly.

Turnaround time is the time between the entering of data and the receipt of the information that you requested. For instance, if you process your employees' information on a Tuesday and receive their printed payroll checks and payroll information on a Wednesday, then you have a one-day turnaround time. Some data may not be needed immediately. Other information may be needed right away. You need a clear understanding of the time involved in turnaround. You must then decide whether that time is adequate for your needs. Generally, a time-sharing operation has a much faster turnaround time than a comprehensive service. Your own needs and the cost of the service will dictate an acceptable turnaround time for you.

In-House Computers.   An in-house computer is one that you have in your business and control and operate yourself. A typical small business computer consists of a CPU, disc file, a printer, and one or more entry devices, usually CRTs. Many small business computers are microcomputers, such as the Apple, Tandy's Radio Shack TRS-80, and the Commodore Pet. Other manufacturers are entering this market constantly. These systems provide the small business with the convenience and power of computers without the high cost usually associated with them. However, they do have their limits.

You can acquire an in-house computer either by leasing one or by purchasing one. You should not let the cost of the system dictate which type of computer you get. You should do a thorough investigation of your requirements and resources. Then, you should get the computer that meets your needs and is flexible enough to grow with your business. The decision to lease or buy should be a financial one rather than an economic one. A financial decision dictates how you will pay for it. The economic decision dictates how much you will pay.

One of the major considerations in getting a computer is support, both for the hardware (the computer itself) and the software (the programs that the computer uses to do its job). Hardware support means being able to get the equipment serviced by a qualified technician when necessary. If your printer goes on the blink during your monthly billing, you might be in real trouble if it takes three weeks to get it fixed. In the same way, if the program that does the billing is not doing what you need, you need someone who can get it going again. There is a wide variety of software available for the many microcomputers currently on the market. If you know nothing about how it was developed or how it works, you may find yourself with a computer system that does not do what you need done.

When you go out to get a computer system, you will find an incredible variety to choose from. There are a number of manufacturers available, and each one can offer you a variety of options for both your hardware and software needs. When you get ready to choose a system, you should have a method to help you make the best choice. The first thing you need to do is to determine whether you are ready for a computer. Then you need to make certain that you get the right computer.

Comparison of Computer Options.   As you consider whether you should computerize your business, you should carefully consider the advantages and benefits of each system in relation to its cost. The following financial considerations might help you in this analysis.

Leasing a computer gives you the benefit of totally deducting your lease costs as an expense. The lease may also cover maintenance and updating of your system, depending on the type of lease that you have. The right kind of lease can also make it easy for you to convert and upgrade your system.

A service bureau can give you the same financial benefit as a lease. In addition, you may be able to benefit directly from new software developments and additional hardware capacity as your service bureau upgrades its equipment and services.

Purchasing your computer has the obvious advantage of ownership. However, when you are comparing the cost of ownership with the cost of other options, you need to consider some of the hidden costs you may encounter if you own a computer. These costs include:

Maintenance

Parts

Software development, maintenance, and upgrading

Your hardware and software may become obsolete or inadequate for your needs. If so, you will find yourself facing the possibility of expensive conversion costs. Your old equipment may also be of minimum value, and you may lose your entire investment in software.

How to Select a Computer

If you have decided that a computer is a good investment for you, how should you go about getting one? There are several steps that should be followed in selecting a computer.

Establish objectives. Chapter 2 emphasized the need to set goals and objectives for your business. Goal setting is also important when you are considering a computer. You expect your computer to fit into the future of your company, but do you have any idea of what that future is? Will you be maintaining the status quo, will you be growing, or will you see a decreased level of activity? Will you be expanding your product lines, adding new employees, or spreading into new marketplaces? All of these goals affect whether or not you need a computer, what you will require from your system, and how you will use it.

Once you have determined your business's objectives, you should decide how your computer will fit into those objectives. Specifically, you should determine how your computer can help you to achieve those objectives. This will help you to plan the kind of computer you need and the capabilities you want it to have.

Determine Your Business's Capabilities to Install and Operate a Computer System. We have already indicated that your company needs to have orderly and systematic record-keeping procedures before a computer system is installed. If you have these procedures in place, you then need to look at your business's data records, organization, and personnel.

The data that your business collects need to be in a form that can be accepted by the computer. Generally, this means that you need to have numbering systems for the processes that you computerize. Therefore, your inventory items, accounts receivable records, and personnel records, among others, need to have appropriate numbers attached to them. Without these numbers, it will be difficult to process the information fed into the computer and retrieve it when you need it.

Data need to be collected systematically and consistently. Therefore, your business needs to have clearly defined roles and responsibilities for all of your employees. You will then be able to assign appropriate tasks to insure that useful and accurate data flow into your computer system. You will also be able to assign responsibility if there is a problem with the system.

Personnel problems can be your biggest stumbling block in putting a computer into operation. Many of your employees will be intimidated or frightened by the machine. You need to insure that your employees will accept and use the system that you install. You also need to insure that you have personnel who are able to operate the computer. This may mean that some of your employees will need to be trained in its use. You may also need to think about hiring a staff. You need to insure that you have people available who can operate the system and that the rest of your company will accept the system and cooperate in using it effectively.

Determine Your Requirements.   What information does your business need? You should decide this before you choose and install your system. By knowing your information requirements, you will be able to select the right amount of equipment with sufficient growth capabilities for the future. This will save you the time and expense involved in system conversions in the future. To determine your needs, you should answer these questions:

What kind of information do you need?

What form do you need it in?

Where does the information come from?

How much information do you need?

When do you need it?

Establish a Plan to Install and Operate the System.   The installation of a new computer system will, at a minimum, be extremely disruptive to your business. Therefore, the installation and integration of the computer into your normal operations need to be carefully planned. You should have some ideas as to when the computer will arrive and be installed. You need to insure that your facilities will be ready. If any physical modifications are necessary, you should plan to have them ready when the computer arrives. You may also need to schedule training for your personnel so that they will be able to operate the system. The most important part of the plan will be arranging to have the various subsystems put into the computer system. This may include some special programming.

Along with your plan, you should include a budget so that you will have an idea of the cost of implementing the system. This budget should include some funds for unforeseen problems. The computer system will certainly develop some type of hitch requiring special attention.

Evaluate and Select Your System.   You may not actually put your computer system out to bid. However, you should develop a set of specifications based on the requirements that you have established. You should then compare several manufacturers. Each should be able to provide you with a system to meet your requirements. You can then evaluate these proposals and select the most cost competitive of those that meet your needs. It is a serious mistake to talk to only one manufacturer.

After you have narrowed your search to a few potential vendors, you should carefully check out each possibility. You should not only talk to the supplier but also ask for a list of previous buyers. Then go to these buyers and ask them how satisfied they are with the system and the service they receive from the vendor. You would also be well advised to get all sales promises in writing. A careful examination of your purchase contract will tell you exactly what you are getting for your investment. If you are buying your system on the installment basis, you should carefully review your options and remedies if a third party carries the installment contract. Otherwise, you could find yourself paying for a system that does not deliver what you require.

Test Your System.   After your computer system has been selected and installed, it is necessary to test it. Your test should put the computer through the complete processing sequence needed to perform a particular job. The harder you can make the system work, the more comfortable you will feel when you accept the machine.

Use Your System.   You have done all of your testing. You have thoroughly considered all of the ramifications of your decision to acquire a computer. Now you have one. Go ahead and use it—and enjoy it.

CASE
SOLUTION

Joselyn's
Designs

The Fredricksons needed to answer two major questions before getting a computer. First, they needed to determine whether their operations were sufficiently systematic and orderly so that a computer could be effectively used in the business. Second, they needed to determine what kind of computer system was needed for the company.

Their inventory and sales data were already being managed in a thorough, although cumbersome, manual system. Each item of inventory was coded with a five-digit number. A daily tally sheet was used to keep track of the orders by kit number. This information was then transferred to index cards, which kept track of the monthly sales for each kit. Also, each item in the raw materials inventory was coded by number, and an index card was maintained on each item. Each bin was checked on a weekly basis, and the amount of material was entered onto the appropriate card.

Each kit was assembled from a materials list for that kit. Each set of kit instructions also had this materials list printed on it. When an order was received, the design and its accompanying set of instructions were pulled. Then, the rest of the kit was assembled based on the set of instructions.

The inventory and sales information systems of Joselyn's Designs were sufficiently well organized to be readily adaptable to some form of computer management. The next step was to determine the type of computerization that was available to the firm.

There were two major options open to the Fredricksons. The first option was to affiliate with a time-sharing system. The other option was to get an in-house computer.

There were two time-sharing options open to the company. The first used a set of canned programs that the company would be able to tap into. Although these programs were useful for accounts receivable and payable and for payroll, they did not meet the Fredricksons' inventory and sales information needs. The Fredricksons also found that if they used the second option, a flexible time-sharing system, they would have to pay the programming costs necessary to set up a system to meet their needs. Although the time-sharing system would not require a large initial capital outlay, the monthly service charge was five hundred dollars per month. The high monthly cost made this time-sharing option unattractive.

An in-house computer system, therefore, became the more attractive option. However, the Fredricksons were unsure of what was required. They needed to determine the cost of getting a system that would be adequate for their needs. They also needed to know about the kind and cost of software required to operate the system.

An investigation led them to a computer consultant, who was able to do two things for them. First, the consultant ascertained that the microcomputers generally available in the marketplace were adequate for their needs. It also appeared evident that microcomputer technology was growing quickly enough to keep up with their needs for the foreseeable future. Second, the consultant arranged for a programmer who would be able to set up a special system to manage their inventory and sales information requirements. The programmer was also able to modify some existing software to take care of their accounts receivable and payable needs.

The total cost of the new computer and the related software was $11,300. Because the Fredericksons chose a nationally known computer system, they were only a few miles from a service center that would be able to repair all of their hardware. The programmer was available as a consultant on a retainer basis to maintain the software systems of the computer.

The computer, which was once the luxury of big business, is now an affordable tool for many small businesses. However, before you buy one, there are a number of important questions that you need to ask yourself.

Before you jump into the computer market, you need to have some knowledge of what a computer is. You should know what the various parts of a computer are, what these parts do, and what kinds of work the computer is especially suited for.

CHAPTER SUMMARY

Computers process data quickly. They take the information that you may be processing by hand now and do the same tasks much more quickly. There are several ways in which you can get the services of a computer. The obvious way is to buy one. However, you might also be able to lease one. A computer service bureau is also an excellent way to get computer services without the problems of ownership.

Before you look for a computer or a service bureau, there are a number of things that you need to know about your business. Can you quantify the major operations of your business? Do you have standard and orderly business procedures? Do you know what a computer can and cannot do? Could you manage your business better with more accurate and timely information? Do you expect to grow, and can you get a good return on your investment?

When you select a computer, you should follow these steps:

1. Establish your objectives.
2. Determine your business's capabilities to install and operate a computer system.
3. Determine your requirements.
4. Establish a plan to install and operate the system.
5. Evaluate and select your system.
6. Test your system.
7. Use your system.

DISCUSSION QUESTIONS

1. What types of computer devices are used to perform the following functions?
   a. Input
   b. Output
   c. Processing
   d. Storage
2. How does a batch-processing system differ from a real-time system?
3. What is the difference between a random access storage system and a sequential system?
4. What are the three components of a computer's central processing unit? What is the function of each of these components?
5. What are the major factors that you should consider when investigating a computer service bureau?
6. What steps should you follow when selecting a computer?
7. Name three computer languages commonly used in business computer systems.

REFERENCES

Bulkeley, W. M. "In Buying that First Computer, Some Homework Can be Crucial." *Wall Street Journal*, 6 October 1980. p. 29.

_____. "Business Programs Can Be Used: For Most Buyers of Personal Computers, There's a Hard Time Finding Software." *Sacramento Bee* (New York Times News Service), 7 December 1980, p. F7.

Cohen, J. A., and McKinney, C. S. *How To Computerize Your Small Business*. Englewood Cliffs, N.J. Prentice-Hall, 1980.

Egan, M. J., and Fioravante, J. "First Time Buyers Urged: Get Advice, Study Needs." *MIS Week*, 26 November 1980, pp. 1 and 14.

Frederick, S. "Ready for your First Computer?" *Inc.*, April 1979, pp. 65–66.

Goldfinger, E. "A Manager's Guide of Computer Systems" (a three-part series). *Inc.* May 1980, pp. 101–109; June 1980, pp. 79–87; July 1980, pp. 71–76.

Hedberg, A. "Choosing the Best Computer for You—What to Buy." *Money,* November, 1982, pp. 101–115.

Jacobs, S. L. "Experts Say Computerization Raises Risk of Embezzlement." *Wall Street Journal*, 23 February 1981, p. 25.

Press, L. "Getting Started in Personal Computing." *Inc.*, Spring 1981, pp. 8–17.

Sippl, C. J., and Dahl, Fred. *Computer Power for the Small Business*. Englewood Cliffs, N.J.: Prentice-Hall, 1979.

FOOTNOTES

1. This case was prepared by one of the authors based on consulting work done for one of his clients. In order to maintain client confidentiality, the facts given in this case differ somewhat from the actual case.

Special Problems with Special Businesses

19

□ **Is your small business really several small businesses under one roof?**

□ **What are the major types of small businesses, and what are the special opportunities and pitfalls of each?**

□ **What special problems do you encounter if you try to operate more than one type of small business at once?**

CASE
PROBLEM

*Sunnymead
Supply
Company[1]*

Sunnymead Supply Company was founded in the early 1970s as a janitorial supply company by Jack Black. Jack had been an experienced field sales representative of a large wholesaler of janitorial supplies. Jack reasoned that with his contacts he could deal directly with the manufacturers of the supplies he sold and open his own warehouse and wholesaling operation to serve his community. In this way, he could provide quicker deliveries and better service. Because his warehouse was local, for example, many of his customers could drop by on their way to work and pick up needed supplies. Also, because he was covering a smaller territory, he had the time to provide advice on tough cleaning jobs, which he thought would win loyal customers. Although his prices were not always lower than those of his former employer, Jack did very well.

A few years later, another janitorial field sales representative, Bill Bush, bought into Jack's company. With two persons selling, Sunnymead was able to cover a larger territory. Jack and Bill also began bidding on janitorial supply contracts put out to bid by larger companies and government agencies. After losing a few large bids, they discovered that such organizations were more interested in price than in quality or service. They adjusted accordingly but still found their contracts with large organizations vulnerable to price competition from other suppliers.

In 1978 a third individual, Dave Harding, bought into the company. Dave's background was in packaging (cartons, staples, tapes, etc.). He had been a field sales representative in the area for a number of years. Dave liked Sunnymead Supply's approach of keeping local stocks of merchandise to insure prompt deliveries. Soon Sunnymead's warehouse, which had been more than big enough for the janitorial supplies, was filled to overflowing with cardboard cartons and tapes. Sunnymead then moved to larger, much more expensive quarters.

Dave was not the kind of fellow to let grass grow under his feet. He was always seeking new profit opportunities. Shortly after buying into

Sunnymead, he noticed that the manufacturer's markup on liquid detergents and cleaners used for the janitorial supply business was outrageous. He did some checking around and discovered that a company in Chicago sold both the equipment to make the liquid cleaners and the basic chemicals to do so. He urged Bill and Jack to buy the equipment and manufacture their own cleaners. The equipment was purchased soon after the company's move to its larger quarters.

Once into their new quarters, Dave noticed that some of the office space in the front of the building was not needed. He suggested that the company open a retail carpeting and drapery store in the excess space, using their industry contacts to get good prices and display samples. Since no inventory would be carried beyond the sample books, Dave reasoned this would be another good use of the company's wholesale buying power. Once again, Bill and Jack went along.

Recently, Dave noticed that it was hard to buy odd-width tapes locally. These widths are used for special packaging applications in a variety of industries. Local users of these specialized tapes were experiencing long delivery delays. Once again, Dave searched for a solution. He discovered sources of supply for the specialty tapes in rolls, or "logs," six feet in length. He then found a local company that had the equipment necessary to slice tape logs into the required sizes and began discussing a merger. If the merger were completed, Sunnymead would once again have to move to larger quarters to provide space for its diverse operations.

At this point, Bill and Jack were becoming a bit concerned. Their overhead seemed to have greatly increased since they moved to their present location. Their private label of soap was not selling very well despite their investment in chemicals, equipment, plastic bottles, and labels. The carpet and drapery business took much of their time but did not seem to be going anywhere. Further, their sales literature had so many different kinds of cleaning and packaging products listed that the customers seemed more confused than interested. Bill and Jack had to point out which part of the product list a customer should look at. Now Dave wanted to bring in a new partner, go into tape slicing, and move to larger quarters. This made Bill and Jack very nervous.

Sunnymead Supply Company has a problem that is surprisingly common among small businesses. In terms of the small business marketing disadvantages discussed in chapter 9, Sunnymead Supply has fallen into the trap of offering too much choice. By trying to handle all of the different markets it has entered, this company finds it difficult to satisfy fully the needs of the customers in any one market. It has become confused about whom it is really aiming to please. This has hurt its profitability.

**PROBLEM
IDENTIFICATION**

The implications for Sunnymead Supply of offering too much choice go beyond the marketing issue of offering too large an assortment and lacking a clear-cut mission, or market focus. Sunnymead Supply Company is actually a collection of several dramatically different kinds of businesses. Each offers its own special opportunities, and each has its own special problems. Sunnymead Supply was lured into each type of business by tempting opportunities. Unfortunately, the company soon found that it is extremely difficult to run so many businesses efficiently and profitably at once. The marketing of each type of business must be approached somewhat differently. Operating strategies that work cheaply and efficiently for one type can waste money and create cash flow problems for another type. The different types do not mix well. It takes considerable skill to make such a complex company recipe produce profitable results.

Have you fallen into the same trap that has snared Sunnymead Supply? Are you having a hard time running your company and losing profits because you are really several different and incompatible companies under one roof? If so, what can you do about it? If you have avoided this trap so far, what do you need to know to protect your company's profits from it in the future? The remainder of this chapter will help you to answer these questions.

DIAGNOSIS   Exhibit 19.1 presents a series of questions for you to answer. The numbered questions are designed to identify the type(s) of business you are in. The indented and lettered questions under each numbered question are designed to discover if you are experiencing the special problems of this type of business. If you answer no to a numbered question, you can skip the indented questions below it. If you answer yes, answer yes or no to each indented question. If you answer no to an indented question, we also recommend that you write down in your own words on a separate sheet of paper an example of the problem as it affects you. Please answer the questions in Exhibit 19.1 before reading further.

Exhibit 19.1   What Type of Business Are You In?
Are You Experiencing Its Special Problems?

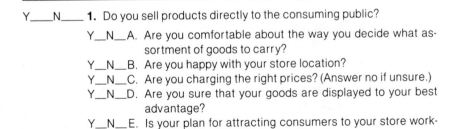

Y____N____ **1.** Do you sell products directly to the consuming public?

    Y__N__A. Are you comfortable about the way you decide what assortment of goods to carry?

    Y__N__B. Are you happy with your store location?

    Y__N__C. Are you charging the right prices? (Answer no if unsure.)

    Y__N__D. Are you sure that your goods are displayed to your best advantage?

    Y__N__E. Is your plan for attracting consumers to your store working as well as your would like?

Y__N__ F. Are you happy with the way your products are sold to customers once they enter your store?

Y____N____ **2.** Does your company convert raw materials and/or components into useful products?

Y__N__A. Is it easy for you to decide how to design your products and/or how to make them in the quantities needed?

Y__N__B. Do you find it easy to figure out what materials will be needed when?

Y__N__C. Is it easy for you to determine how labor and equipment can best be used to make your products?

Y__N__D. When you have a lot of orders, do you find it easy to figure out which product should be made first?

Y__N__E. Do you find it easy to assure that your products are made with acceptable quality built in?

Y__N__ F. Do you find it easy to determine what to charge for your product? (i.e., are you sure you are making a good profit on each order?)

Y____N____ **3.** Do you perform services for your customers on a fee or contract basis, as opposed to making a product?

Y__N__A. Is your method of getting to your customers and selling to them working out?

Y__N__B. Do you find it easy to schedule and control the provision of your services?

Y__N__C. Do you feel as though your reputation in the community matches your expertise?

Y____N____ **4.** Do you act as a middleman between business buyers and sellers of products? (i.e., do you deal with commercial and industrial firms rather than the general public?)

Y__N__A. Have you not been losing customers to price competition from larger firms? (i.e., are you not being undersold?)

Y____N____ **5.** Do you act as a middleman by contracting to provide specific materials, equipment, and labor to do a job for another party and then arranging for the materials, equipment, and labor to be supplied?

Y__N__A. Do you find it easy to coordinate all the jobs you are doing at once?

Y__N__B. Do you find it easy to keep track of progress on each job and the costs incurred on each job?

Y____N____ **6.** Do you export domestically produced goods or import foreign-made goods?

Y__N__A. Are you experiencing little or no delays in getting paid for orders?

Y__N__B. Are shipping expenses what you expected?

Y__N__C. Are the products you handle selling as expected?

The numbered questions in Exhibit 19.1 are keyed to the classification of business types given in Exhibit 19.2 and discussed below. The indented and lettered questions correspond to the special problems of each business type discussed below. These cross-references will permit you to skip sections of this chapter that do not apply to your type of business. However, if you expand your business in the future, we recommend that you come back and take another look at Exhibit 19.1. If the questions indicate that your expansion is really entry into a new type of business, we suggest you read the relevant sections of this chapter that point out the special problems and special solutions relating to your new venture.

Exhibit 19.2   Classification and Definition of Major Types of Small Businesses

TYPE	DEFINITION
1.0 *Retail*	Sells products directly to the consuming public, usually from a fixed store location. Basic retailing, or merchandising, strategy involves selecting an assortment of goods designed to meet the needs of a target market of consumers, making these goods available at attractive prices, and convincing the target consumers that the goods will meet their needs. Examples: children's wear shop, furniture store, drugstore, toy store, stationery store.
2.0 *Manufacturing*	Sets up and operates manufacturing processes to convert raw materials into useful products. May invent and manufacture its own product or build products to customer specifications. Some sell directly to the general public, but most employ middlemen to distribute their products. Manufacturing tends to take place at a fixed plant location. Basic strategy is to efficiently produce products with a good balance of the attributes, quality, price, and delivery dates desired by the customer. Examples: garment manufacturer, leather chair manufacturing company, injection molder who produces vinyl heads for toy dolls, printer who makes stationery.
3.0 *Service*	Performs activities for customers or clients on a fee or contract basis. Distinguished from manufacturing by the fact that there is no end product. Rather, something is repaired or cleaned, advice is given, or a concept is created. Raw materials used to provide the service can be minimal. Service companies tend to go to their customers to provide services rather than requiring their customers to come to a fixed store location. Basic strategy is to convince customers that the service will be performed quickly and efficiently and that, once completed, it will meet the customers' needs at a reasonable price.
3.1 *Wholesaling*	Acts as a middleman between buyers and sellers in a product distribution channel. Distinguished from a retailer by the fact that sales are made to merchants and industrial or commercial users rather than to the general

TYPE	DEFINITION
	public. Also, unlike retailers, a wholesaler may not actually stock merchandise. Rather, the seller gives title to the products directly to the buyer, and the wholesaler receives a fee for bringing buyer and seller together. Examples: merchant wholesalers, distributors, brokers, merchandise agents, and manufacturers' representatives.
3.2 *Contracting*	Acts as a middleman by contracting to provide specific materials, equipment, and labor to do a job for another party and then arranging for the materials, equipment, and labor to be supplied. The contractor may be skilled enough to provide the required labor or may subcontract the work by hiring people or companies with the skills necessary to do certain aspects of the job. Examples: building contractors, pool contractors, labor contractors for the garment industry, and landscape maintenance contractors.
3.3 *Export-Import*	Acts as a middleman to export domestically produced goods to foreign markets or to import foreign-made products for domestic distribution. Generally speaking, the exporter-importer is simply a wholesaler specializing in making markets by bringing commercial/industrial buyers and sellers together across national boundaries. Examples: export agents, commission houses, customs brokers, freight forwarders, import agents, export agents, import firms, and export firms.

As mentioned earlier, one of Sunnymead Supply Company's principal problems was that it was actually several businesses under one roof, each with special problems. The owners of Sunnymead Supply did not fully recognize this. As a result, they suffered severe operational problems and poor profits in spite of their many years of business experience and exceptional sales abilities.

UNDER-STANDING

To understand fully how a company can stumble into the multiple-business trap, you need to recognize the major types of businesses and familiarize yourself with the special opportunities and problems of each type. You will then understand the special effort required to run two or more different kinds of businesses at once and be able to judge whether or not you can handle more than one business.

Major Types of Small Business and Their Problems and Opportunities

What are the major types of small businesses? There are three categories: retail, manufacturing, and service. The last category, service, includes such a broad spectrum of businesses that, in addition to discussing service firms in general, we will review some special opportunities and pitfalls of three specific kinds of service companies: wholesaling, contracting, and export-import. This subdivision should make it easier for you to understand what can happen when, for example, a manufacturer begins exporting its products or a retailer contracts to install its products for its customers. Exhibit 19.2 briefly defines each type of business we will discuss in this chapter. In the section that follows we will look at the special opportunities and problems each type of business holds in store for you.

Retailing

Special Opportunities.   A retailer has the opportunity to be in direct contact with the final consumer at the moment the consumer decides to buy. If the retailer has what the consumer needs at an attractive price and can demonstrate to the consumer that the product meets the consumer's needs, a sale will be made. Friendly and helpful service at the retail level can lead to high markups and excellent profits for the small business owner who is skilled at adapting to the conditions of the local marketplace. Indeed, since most retail sales are made at the end of long channels of distribution, these markups can appear enormous to a manufacturer or wholesaler, leading to the temptation to sell direct to the public. Selling products directly to the public, however, requires special skills and resources that the manufacturer or wholesaler may not possess. Since the manufacturer or wholesaler has only a limited amount of time and money, acquiring these skills and resources almost inevitably undermines existing business. Is it worth it? Only you can decide after considering the special problems of retailing.

Special Problems.   Retailers have six special problems:

1. What assortment of goods should be carried?
2. Where should the store be located?
3. What prices should be charged?
4. How should the goods be displayed in the store?
5. How will the consumer be attracted to the store?
6. How will the product be sold to customers once they enter the store?

In retailing, perhaps more than in any other category of small business, none of the special problems faced by the small business has a final solution. The retailer must deal with a dynamic, constantly changing world. Consumers' tastes change, competitors come and go, the economic fortunes of a neighborhood rise and fall. It often takes incredible flexibility on the part of the small business retailer to survive and profit from such changes. The retailer is at the end of a long pendulum that swings as dictated by the marketplace.

The profits are greatest at the end, but the swings are greatest too. Other types of business, such as manufacturing or wholesaling, are further up the pendulum toward the fulcrum. For them, the swings are normally less violent and easier to adapt to. The key to deciding when to change your retail strategy and how much to change it lies in remembering that a small business has certain natural advantages that, combined with effective management techniques, can give it a competitive edge.

What is the exact nature of each of the six special problems found by the retailer, and why are they problems? Further details about each will help you to understand.

Selection of an assortment of goods for a retail store is both an art and a science. The goods selected contribute to the store's image. If there is a mismatch between the merchandise you stock and the customers you want, you may lose not only today's sale but tomorrow's sale too. Even if you have a knack for selecting the right merchandise, you still have to understand the science of inventory management. Understanding techniques for determining what to order, calculating when and what to restock, and figuring when to have clearances on slow-moving merchandise, can make the difference between big profits and big losses. You can be sure the big chain down the street pays careful attention to inventory management. As a retailer, you must also.

For the small business retailer, store location is absolutely critical. Since the small business retailer typically starts with only one store and is locked into the store's location by lease agreements, choosing the wrong location often leads to business failure. The key element of the retail location decision is customer convenience. The store must be easy to reach and highly visible to target customers. For the retailer, customer convenience is far more important than other location factors, such as rent per square foot, or accessibility to distribution channels, which are more important to wholesalers and manufacturers.

Pricing for a retail store can be a real challenge. Markups have to be determined, and special sales have to be planned. Further, since a store's price structure often contributes to its image, sales or discounts may have to be planned with care. A fancy men's store that routinely discounts its merchandise, for example, is saying the wrong thing about the quality of its merchandise.

Retailing is also unique in the demands it makes on the business owner's knowledge of store layout and displays. Many retail sales are made by attractive displays and by neat and orderly store layouts that encourage browsing. A large investment in store fixtures may be required to create the desired image for your store. Contrast this with the manufacturer whose plant has concrete floors and a tin roof!

Since a retailer sells directly to the public, the decision on how to advertise in the store's trade area is probably more complicated for the retailer than for any other type of business. Decisions have to be made about how best to spend scarce advertising dollars to reach those particular people most likely to buy from the store. It is often far easier for wholesalers or manufacturers to create a list of potential customers and to direct advertising to them. Customers for their products are fewer in number and easier to identify since they are typically businesses also. Even service businesses have a somewhat easier time than retailers in reaching customers since the services they offer can often be sold to commercial customers. Also, consumers looking for a service will often seek service companies out in advertising media such as telephone books.

An aspect of attracting customers that is unique to retail stores is the design of the exterior of the store. The storefront display windows and signs must give a favorable impression to the buying public, or few shoppers will walk in the front door.

Selling also presents some special problems for retailers since almost all sales must be closed in the store. The retailer, by and large, has to wait for the potential customer to enter the store before a sale can be made. This is in contrast to most other kinds of small businesses, which can go to the customer to make the sale. Further, unlike other types of small businesses, the number of sales made by a small retail business is typically too large to be handled by one salesperson. These characteristics of retail selling require the store to be amply staffed with friendly, courteous sales personnel who know how to sell, know the store's products, and know how the store's products can best be used. Successfully operating a retail business therefore requires you to know not only how to sell to the buying public but also how to select and train salespersons.

Manufacturing

Special Opportunities. Small business manufacturers can turn product dreams into realities. Often people with no manufacturing experience turn to a manufacturer to design and produce their product idea for them. In many cases, the manufacturing costs of the product represent a relatively small portion of the final sales price to the consumer. This permits an efficient manufacturer to enjoy a comfortable markup on the product. Small manufacturers with considerable skill in making a certain type of product may find that large companies will buy from them rather than trying to make the product themselves. Often the large companies simply do not need enough of the product to justify the investment in equipment and trained personnel required to make it themselves. Indeed, most small manufacturers start out by making small quantities of a product following specifications custom tailored to a particular customer's needs. The profit per unit in this type of business can be very good. The trick is to find enough customers with somewhat similar manufacturing needs to keep the small business manufacturer's specialized equipment and personnel busy.

Special Problems. For a manufacturer, many problems arise between the placing of an order and the delivery of the product that most other types of small business do not have to worry about. This is because other types of businesses deal in finished goods, and manufacturers deal with the making of finished goods. Manufacturers have six special problems:

1. How should the product be designed and manufactured?
2. What materials will be needed, and when will they be needed?
3. How can labor and equipment best be used to make the product?
4. Which product should be made first?
5. How can the quality of the product be assured?
6. What price should be charged for the product?

Selling is not on the list as a special problem. Although this critical function must be performed, it is not unusually complicated, even though several industries might have to be searched to find sufficient customers to keep your manufacturing company operating full time.

Just how do the above six problems affect the manufacturer? Why are they of special concern for this type of business? We will now take a closer look at each.

There is a lot more to the design and manufacture of a product than meets the eye. Consider, for example, a simple product such as a cigarette lighter. How many parts does it have? How is each part made? Does its design help it light easily, stay lighted in the wind, and be miserly with fuel? Is it safe? Is it compact so that it doesn't make a big bulge in a purse or pocket? Will it last a long time without breaking? Is it attractive? Is the price what you would expect to pay? Questions like these and myriad others must be answered when designing a product. There is more to product design than the product itself, however. For example, the best material may be too costly or unavailable. Changes in design may be necessary to permit a product to be made efficiently by your people on your equipment at a reasonable cost. The answer to the special problem of how to design and manufacture your product is the creation of a comprehensive plan that balances product price, function, reliability, production efficiency, and consumer needs.

A manufacturer must also decide what materials will be needed and when they will be needed. Once an order is taken, it must be broken down into its component parts or materials. Ideally, these components and materials will be purchased in the exact amounts needed for production from the lowest bidder, and this supplier will provide the specified parts on time to allow your production process to flow smoothly. The reality is usually far from the ideal, however. Purchasing strategies are designed to try to approach the ideal.

Whan a small manufacturer gets an order, a decision has to be made about which people will work on it and which machines they will use. This planning process is called routing. Careful routing can often save considerable labor time and make the use of equipment much more efficient. Since many different routes may be possible, even an experienced manufacturer man make costly mistakes if it does not systematically plan production.

Typically, a small manufacturer works on several orders at once. In a plant where each order is slightly different, using a production plan to determine the sequence of orders worked on can make a big difference in terms of overall efficiency. Conscious planning to balance the labor time, materials, and equipment required for each order with what is available to produce all orders is nearly always a good idea.

Even when you have a firm purchase order, simply making a product does not assure that you have sold it. If the product is not made according to the customer's specifications the customer can legally refuse to accept it. The cost of remaking or repairing product defects can easily turn a profitable order into a financial disaster. Even if the customer accepts the product, you may be sued if the product fails while being used by the final consumer, causing economic or personal injury. In many cases, you may be required to guarantee a product for a given period of time. If too many warranty repairs are necessary, you may be put in a financial bind. It is not surprising, therefore, that quality assurance is very important to the manufacturer. The product must be inspected and tested at each step of the production process to assure that it will perform as you say it will. This does not mean the product must be indestructible. Most people cannot afford to pay for indestructibility. Rather, what it means is that the product must perform as promised and must last long enough to be considered a good value, given its price.

The last problem, setting a price for the product, is a special problem for manufacturers because it is more difficult for them to determine their true costs than it is for retailers, for example, which simply buy finished products from wholesalers at a given price. In addition to calculating the overhead and including it in markups to cover the cost of the business operation and a reasonable profit, the manufacturer must also determine and recover the cost of raw materials, expenditures for machinery, labor costs, the cost of the plant itself, and the cost of any other facility used in the production process. Effective product-costing procedures therefore require keeping careful cost records on each and every product the company manufactures.

As you might expect, an experienced retailer would probably find itself totally overwhelmed by the careful planning and controls required for efficient production. Similarly, the small manufacturer is typically naive about how best to sell to the complex web of consumer target markets. It is rare to find a small business that both manufactures and sells all its products directly to final consumers through its own retail outlets.[2] The two types of business *can* complement each other nicely, but it is almost impossible for a *small* business to efficiently run both types of business at once.

Service

Special Opportunities. Of all the types of businesses, service companies seem to be the best designed for the small businessperson. Since the service is generally taken to the customer, a fancy store location is not needed. Since the company performs activities for customers on a fee or contract basis rather than making or stocking merchandise, inventories can be kept down. This means start-up costs are low and operating costs are low. Further, many customers expect to pay cash for services, and those who do receive credit either use credit cards or expect to pay when the bill arrives at the end of the month. No wonder small service companies can easily show better financial results than the large corporations that contract for their services!

A service company can generate an excellent return by repairing expensive or key equipment, freeing people's time by doing their chores for them, or providing special skills and knowledge to handle technical problems that must be solved before a deadline.

Still, despite this rosy picture, a great many service firms barely make ends meet. The number of service firms that yield mediocre profits for their owners is far too large to blame on bad luck. If getting into a service business is so cheap and simple to do, why do so many fail?

Special Problems.   Perhaps the biggest problem with a service business is that it is so easy to start and so cheap to run. Prospective service business owners tend to forget that a service business is still a business. Squeezing good profits out of a service business opportunity requires management skill. It is not enough to know your trade. You must also know how to run a business efficiently. More than one small business book has suggested it is possible to convert a hobby, such as electrical appliance repair, into a business enterprise overnight. It is possible, but will it be profitable? Profits will largely depend on how well you handle the special problems noted below.

The special problems of a service business vary somewhat depending on the type. Still, the following special problems can be said to apply to most service businesses:

1. How do you get to your customers and sell to them?

2. How do you efficiently "manufacture" services?

3. How do you build your reputation?

If you are the hobbyist seeking to cash in on your hobby, one of the first problems you have to deal with is how to get to your customers and sell to them. Typically, a service business requires missionary selling to be successful. By this we mean that you have to go out and find your customers. Once you find them, you have to sell your services on the spot. This type of selling is made easier by solving the third special problem of service firms—reputation building. Once you build a favorable reputation, people may come to you. Still, the ability to go out into the field and sell without the credibility provided by a retail store or a manufacturing plant is a necessity. Consider, for example, someone opening a small plumbing business. A yellow page ad may attract some requests for emergency repairs, but will any more business develop once these repairs are made? How will profitable installation jobs be obtained?

Many service businesses have even less to work with than the plumber described above. They offer concepts or ideas to their customers. It may be difficult to show that these services will really benefit the customer. Even when you can, there often is a time lag between the implementation of an idea and concrete evidence of its success. This can cause a crisis of confidence on the part of your client, who is paying out money and getting no results. Therefore, even after you convince the client that you can deliver what he or she needs, the sales process must continue.

The second type of special problem many service companies face is really one of nonrecognition. They do not realize that they are manufacturers of services. A service firm produces services. Even though its service may be getting buyer and seller together, the service firm's activities can be viewed as a production process. This means that a service firm must plan and schedule like a manufacturer to be efficient. Therefore, the six special problems of manufacturers must also be answered by the efficient service firm. The answers are of course different. They can also be tougher. How do you estimate, for example, how long it will take to create an advertising campaign? How do you judge the performance of a creative individual? How do you control the activities of a field salesperson?

The third special problem faced by a service firm is reputation building. How do you create credibility? How do you generate repeat business? How do you get referrals? As noted above, a good reputation makes selling easier. It can bring people to you that have already decided to buy from you. When you deal in services, your reputation is your stock in trade. Good reputation alone will not make you profitable, but a good reputation sold effectively will keep the order books full.

Before proceeding to solutions for the problems of retail, manufacturing, and service companies raised so far, three specific types of service companies merit discussion. These are wholesaling, contracting and export-import businesses. Each type has special problems and opportunities requiring special attention.

Wholesaling. A wholesaler is a middleman that links a buyer and seller in a product distribution channel. Some wholesalers are similar to retailers in that they stock and sell merchandise, provide credit, and arrange delivery. Other wholesalers are simply brokers, bringing buyer and seller together and receiving a commission for arranging the sale. The distinguishing characteristic of wholesalers is that they sell to profit-oriented businesses rather than to the general public. This distinction provides an opportunity, but it also sets a trap. The opportunity is to focus on the buyer's profit motive, making the sale's impact on the customer's bottom line a central feature of the sale. If the wholesaler can demonstrate that the profit potential of a product is exceptional to the customer, the customer is not likely to quibble over the fact that the wholesaler makes a good profit also. The trap arises when the small business wholesaler treats its products as commodities and focuses on low price. Large wholesalers may be able to do this with some products since they deal in large volumes and receive quantity discounts from manufacturers that can be passed on to their customers, who buy smaller quantities. This process is known as "breaking bulk." However, small business wholesalers must focus on the other services a wholesaler can provide that have a favorable impact on the customer's bottom line. These services will be discussed in detail in the solutions section.

Contracting.   Of all types of service businesses, contracting is probably the one where the underlying production process is most obvious. The steps involved in completing a job closely parallel what goes on in a manufacturing plant. In certain fields like construction, the job is manufacturing. The big difference is that the labor, equipment, and materials necessary to produce the product are brought to the construction site rather than kept in a centrally located manufacturing plant.

All types of contracting must deal with the complexity of handling an assortment of one-time projects in a variety of locations. A successful small business contractor can easily end up with a more complex scheduling problem than its small business manufacturing counterpart since the contractor, in effect, puts together a manufacturing plant for each job and disassembles the plant when the job is done. Further, the contractor may be operating several of these plants scattered over a wide geographical area. Getting labor, equipment, and supplies to the right place at the right time can be a real challenge.

The contractor can often operate with much less capital than a manufacturer. Since the contractor is providing a service, it is often the person contracting for the service who pays the contractor's out-of-pocket costs. The cost of materials may be advanced to the contractor. Progress payments may be made by the customer, which in turn can be used to pay subcontractors without the contractor having to carry these wage costs on its books. Equipment needed for the job can be rented or purchased directly by the customer. Still, careful controls are necessary to insure that the work that is supposed to be done is being done and that customer billings for work in progress are justified properly and processed rapidly. Without such controls, rapidly growing contractors can easily find themselves in cash flow crisis with little financial reserves to fall back on.

Export-Import.   The export-import business brings buyers and sellers together across national boundaries. The special problems in this field center about time, distance, and culture. As the marketplaces of the world become more sophisticated, many of these problems are shrinking. Advancing communications technologies make it possible to complete financial transactions that used to take weeks in moments. Transportation technologies now exist that markedly reduce product travel time and the risk of theft and damage. Even cultural differences between sophisticated economies have become less pronounced. Still, each of these special problem areas can make the difference between profit and loss for the export-import business. There are still a myriad of details to be handled knowledgeably: financing, insurance, shipping arrangements, preparation for shipment, billing, credit, collections. Cultural differences are often critical, with factors ranging from technological compatibility to the effect of superstition on the salability of a product. Some of the most profitable marketing opportunities involve bridging wide gaps in the three export-import problem areas.

Solutions to Special Problems of Small Businesses

Now that we have reviewed the special problems and opportunities of the major types of small businesses, it is time to consider how to overcome the special problems so that the special opportunities can be exploited.

Many books have been written about each of the types of small business discussed in this chapter. It is impossible in a few pages to provide a detailed strategy for handling each special problem of each type. We can, however, give you an overall picture of how each problem can be solved and refer you to more detailed discussions of strategy and tactics in other parts of this book and in other sources.

As you read the rest of this chapter, keep in mind how different the various types of small business can be. You can be an established success in one type of small business and still quickly find yourself in serious difficulty when you enter another. The new problems encountered tend to absorb much of your time, which leads to the neglect of your existing business. This tends to decrease the profitability of your established business at the same time that the problems with your new business are gobbling up your cash.

Given the inevitable problems, your entry into a new type of business must be planned with care. Haphazard, opportunistic diversification will in most cases dilute your profitability, if not bankrupt you. If you do get in trouble due to lack of planning, don't expect sympathy or financial help from your banker. A banker can easily see the mistake you made and knows it is your fault. Why should the bank back someone who appears to be a poor risk because he or she is not businesslike?

Let's now review each type of business and discuss how to handle its special problems.

Retailing.   Six special problems were highlighted for retailers:

1. What assortment of goods should be carried?
2. Where should the store be located?
3. What prices should be charged?
4. How should the goods be displayed in the store?
5. How will customers be attracted to the store?
6. How will the product be sold to customers once they enter the store?

As noted in the "Understanding" section, decisions concerning assortment involve both art and science. The art involves the selection of merchandise you think your customers will buy. To do this well, you must keep in touch with both the current trends in your lines of merchandise and your customers.

Keeping in touch with current trends in your lines involves visiting merchandise marts, attending trade shows, scanning catalogues of major suppliers, visiting leading stores in trend-setting cities, and joining and keeping active in trade associations. In brief, you need to keep in touch with your industry and keep up to date on new fashions. What you are looking for are reliable leading indicators of fashion trends or product innovations. Normally, you do not have enough time to do all these things. We recommend you focus on what the leading stores in your area are doing, study trade publications (both advertisements and articles), and pick the brains of your suppliers. Also, select at least one supplier who provides sound advice in addition to merchandise and who works for you rather than for the makers of your products. Good examples of middlemen who work for you are resident buying offices or purchasing agents (depending on your industry). You contract with them to provide you marketing advice and assist you in your buying. Fees of these paid buying offices may look large if your sales volume is small (usually one to two thousand dollars minimum per year), but they more than pay for themselves since you save travel time and expense, get expert advice, and make smarter purchases with their help. There are literally thousands of this type of middleman scattered in major markets across the United States. Your trade association should be able to steer you to those with the best reputations. Stick to a few major buying sources, and establish a close relationship with them.

There are some things your buying sources cannot tell you about selecting merchandise your customers will buy. They can tell you about national sales trends and about new products, but they cannot tell you what your customers will buy. You must keep in touch with your customers. Observe your customers in your store, and talk with them about their preferences and needs. Conduct formal surveys from time to time of your key customers to see if their needs and preferences are changing. The techniques and strategies discussed in chapters 9 and 10 can help you plan such surveys to insure that you keep in touch.

The science of selecting merchandise typically involves review of sales records to determine what to stock and how much to stock at various times of the year. If your store sells staples that are in steady demand, sales records should be analyzed weekly using the inventory analysis techniques discussed in chapter 18. Today's microcomputers make it economical and feasible for even the small retailer to automate much of the tedium involved in these calculations. If you deal in fashion merchandise, you must keep a much closer watch on sales. You need to know on an almost daily basis both the number of sales and whether the sales rate is increasing or decreasing. Again, the techniques discussed in chapter 18 and a microcomputer can help you to compile the information you need so that you can quickly reorder merchandise that is moving and discount and close out merchandise with dwindling sales. The science of assortment selection allows you to squeeze the maximum profits out of the good buying decisions you have made and minimize losses on your bad choices. The science makes being good at the art of selection really pay off.

The question of store location is a critical one for retailers. Because of this, we have discussed it in detail in chapter 12, Appendix A. You should review our discussion carefully before deciding on your retail location.

The third special problem for retailers is determining what price to charge. Chapter 13 is dedicated to pricing. The key point to remember is that for small retailers, as well as for small businesses in general, price competition with larger competitors should be avoided. The object is to mark up your goods sufficiently to yield a good profit and to make them worth this price to the consumer by providing personal attention and exceptional service. The branding of a small business is not based on the price of its products. It is based on the overall value of its product service system. Any fine tuning of your pricing system beyond using traditional markups, loss leaders, and sales is therefore probably not worth the time and effort.

Display of goods is the fourth special problem of retailers. This problem is closely related to the fifth problem of attracting customers by means of the store's exterior image. Once you have determined who your target customer is, we recommend that you visit several stores catering to your type of customer. Observe the percentage of passers by who enter the store and the number of browsers relative to the number who buy. This will help you to determine what works. Pick the best ideas and copy them. If you already are operating your store, you can also survey your customers as they leave the store to determine what they like and dislike about your interior and exterior store layout and what image it gives them of your store.

If you want advice on store design, architects specializing in store design, store planners, fixture specialists, and free-lance window dressers can be consulted. Again, trade associations and noncompetitive stores outside your trade area that have had good jobs done for them can provide you referrals to the specialized help you need for your particular kind of store.

The problem of attracting customers to retailers also involves advertising. Advertising is discussed in detail in chapter 11. The key point to remember is that the effectiveness of all advertising should be monitored using the techniques described in chapter 11 to insure that your advertising dollars are well spent.

In-store selling is of special importance to the retailer. Small business retailers need friendly sales people with good product knowledge who attempt to help customers as well as to sell to them. They need sales people knowledgeable in customer psychology and selling techniques. Stability in the sales force is highly desirable so that salespersons can get to know customers by name and show a genuine personal interest in them. However, retailing is known for wide variations in the need for personnel. Busy periods tend to be extremely busy, and slow periods tend to be very slow. Customers expect prompt service whether they enter the store at a busy time or a slow time, however. The techniques described in chapters 12, 14, and 15 will help you to develop a stable part-time and full-time sales force to meet your needs. You should have a core of full-time personnel and schedule part-time personnel as needed. Remember, though, part-time employees need to be trained and given incentives to sell just like full-time employees.

Manufacturing.   Six special problems were highlighted for manufacturers:

1. How should the product be designed and manufactured?
2. What materials will be needed and when?
3. How can labor and equipment best be used to make the product?
4. Which product should be made first?
5. How can the quality of the product be assured?
6. What price should be charged for the product?

The science of dealing with these problems is well established and well documented for almost every conceivable manufacturing situation. If you are new to manufacturing or want to hone your skills, we recommend that you read three books for an overview of good techniques to use to deal with each problem.[3] We also recommend you join two associations: American Production and Inventory Control Society (APICS) and American Institute of Industrial Engineers (AIIE). APICS offers a variety of helpful literature and training courses. AIIE offers forty computer programs in forms ready to use on microcomputers that will do your calculations for you. Both associations publish journals that will give you innumerable ideas about how to improve your manufacturing operations. Both associations will serve to introduce you to the marketplace for the expert help you need.

After you have explored the above resources, you will know whether or not you are really prepared to be a manufacturer. If you decide to proceed, equipment suppliers are excellent sources of information about plant setup and operation (once their biases have been allowed for). Another good source of advice is production managers of similar operations, who can often be induced to moonlight as consultants on the setup of your operation. You will not, however, be able to exploit the advice of these people to your best advantage until you have trained yourself in the principles of efficient production using the resources listed above.

Service.   Service businesses in general have three special problems:

1. How do you get to your customers and sell to them?
2. How do you efficiently "manufacture" services?
3. How do you build your reputation?

The solution to the first problem is discussed in chapters 9 and 10, where marketing strategy is reviewed, and in chapters 12, 14, and 15, where selling and the hiring and motivation of sales personnel are discussed.

The solution to the second problem involves applying the scheduling and control strategies used by manufacturers to your business. The sources recommended above for manufacturers are also helpful for service businesses. Pay special attention to the topics of master scheduling, capacity requirements planning, production control, and project management.

The third special problem of service firms, reputation building, merits close examination. How do you create credibility? How do you generate repeat business? How do you get referrals? The basic goal of your reputation-building strategy is to become recognized as one of the very few companies that can solve your customers' problems. Whether you are selling specific skills that your customers do not have or simply providing services that they do not have the time or a sufficient workforce to provide themselves, it is a safe bet that just being good at what you do will not sell your services. You will have to market your services (chapters 9 and 10). However, reputation building goes beyond the topics discussed in chapters 9 and 10. It also goes somewhat beyond the topics discussed in chapter 11 on selling. Reputation building is a very sophisticated form of selling. It is more than advertising. It is more than overcoming client objections. It is selling by demonstrating your competence without giving away free services.[4]

How do you get in the door to do this? Howard Shenson suggests seven low-cost ways to build your reputation.[5] One or more of these will work for you. Pick the ones you are most comfortable with.

1. *Lectures.* Give lectures at local professional and civic meetings. Pick groups with members that can use your services. Your subject does not have to be new, but it should be presented in a new way. You should speak as an authority or expert. The goal is to be seen as an intelligent resource who is accessible to deal with problems.

2. *Directories.* Make sure you are listed in the yellow pages and in directories related to your field.

3. *Newsletters.* Use newsletters as your direct mail vehicle rather than brochures. Newsletters build reputations when they combine important information about your field with subtle promotion highlighting your availability to provide service. Your newsletter will often get read and saved when the brochures and flyers of your competitors are being thrown out.

4. *Public and Professional Meetings.* Attend and participate in the one public or professional organization that will best expose you to your potential customers. Speak out and get active. Contribute your time to the committees that make the organization work.

5. *Write.* Write short articles for the trade magazines read by your customers. Make sure your articles let them know you are available. Offer free how to literature to those who write to you. Include your photograph and a biography. If articles are not your style, try writing letters to the editor on controversial subjects.

6. *Use the Press.* Manufacture publicity and make sure it is made available to trade journals. Do interviews on local TV and radio stations. Don't sell on the air, but offer free informative literature to open doors. Remember that pictures get published.

7. *Teach.* Adult or continuing education programs, YMCAs and YWCAs, and chambers of commerce often provide opportunities for you to teach people about your business. For example, you might teach a class on how to select an auto mechanic or how to pick a contractor. Useful handouts with your company name on them are bound to generate business.

Wholesaling. As noted above, the small business wholesaler must avoid the trap of treating its products as commodities and focusing on low price to sell. Rather, the small business wholesaler must focus on the other services that it can provide that have a favorable impact on the customer's bottom line. What are these services, and how can you profit from providing them? Since a wholesaler is a middleman, the services you can provide can either be directed at your buyers or your sellers. Exhibit 19.3 summarizes these services.

Exhibit 19.3 Wholesaler Services You Can Capitalize On

Services Provided:

To Your Buyers	To Your Sellers
1. Buying for forecasted needs	1. Help in selling
2. Specialized bulk breaking	2. Storage space
3. Offering assortments	3. Carrying inventory
4. Stocking inventory	4. Help in collecting debts
5. Speedy delivery	5. Market information
6. Credit	
7. Market information and buying advice	

Reviewing the services you can provide to buyers, buying for forecast needs refers to anticipating what your customers will order and when they will order it and having it in stock at the right time. This strategy can be risky, but the risk is reduced if you keep in close touch with your customers and focus on nonfad, nonseasonal demand items. Specialized bulk breaking refers to focusing on a specific market of several buyers and buying in large quanities to meet the pooled needs of these buyers. Offering assortments refers to giving buyers a wide choice of a specific type of merchandise. Again, a specialized niche can earn you a good living but is not big enough for large wholesalers to bother with. One small company, for example, specializes in batteries—everything from flashlights to calculators. Another specializes in athletic windbreakers with team logos and gym shorts and gym socks trimmed with team colors. Stocking inventory for buyers relieves buyers of the expense of carrying inventory themselves. Again, this can be risky if you do not know your customers well. However, providing speedy delivery by knowing where to find products your customers want and expediting delivery once an order is placed can be a low-risk way to do the same thing. Credit terms can also be offered to customers. Again, this strategy has its risks; they can be minimized, but not eliminated, by sound credit administration (see Chapter). The final service you can provide to buyers, market information and buying advice, is a low-cost way of exploiting the knowledge you naturally acquire in a middleman position. Conscious efforts to survey your market and to relay this information to your buyers in an organized, professional manner will make you a valued resource. Newsletters, lectures, and teaching can reinfore your reputation as the wholesaler to deal with in your specialized market.

Turning now to services you can provide your sellers, you can help them to sell by showing them how to package and advertise their products and suggesting sales promotions. You can also provide storage space for seller-owned merchandise or carry inventory of a seller's product. Both of these cost you money, the latter being the riskier since you are in effect acting as a banker for the seller by purchasing in advance of the actual sale to your buyers. You can also use your credit administration capabilities to collect monies owed to your seller, even if you never actually own the goods sold. By qualifying buyers and aggressively pursuing collections, you can make sure sales turn into profits for your seller. Finally, sellers need market information too, and your middleman status puts you in a good position to collect and distribute this information, thereby building your reputation.

Contracting. A contracting business can easily get out of control. Complex scheduling problems for scattered projects, slow payments of accounts receivable, and poor relationships with accounts payable can often sap financial reserves and lead to business failure. Because of this, a detailed control system must be established to insure that:

1. Jobs are planned and bid based on realistic costs and realistic estimates of labor, material, and equipment availability;

2. The job plan is translated into a master schedule for completion that is realistic and that labor, materials, and equipment are ordered and dispatched to jobs according to this plan;

3. Information is recorded on daily operations in the field for each job, detailing progress, special conditions, use of labor, subcontractors, materials, and equipment; etc.

4. Daily information is used to post payroll, accounts receivable (for progress payments from clients), and accounts payable (for payments for authorized work by subcontractors, equipment rentals, etc.), as well as to update cost information used for bidding;

5. Daily operations and their costs are checked and confirmed by you to make sure they occurred and by the client to make sure billings will be speedily paid;

6. All extras requested by the client are acknowledged in writing by the client before work is begun to make sure extras will lead to extra profits rather than extra costs;

7. Billings to the client are submitted in the proper form and with the proper field authorization to insure prompt payment;

8. Accounts payable owed from each billing are paid when the client pays you.

As you can readily see, even a relatively small contracting business requires a sophisticated, but not necessarily complex, set of books. If such books are not kept, you will not be able to bid jobs accurately. Also, you will lose money in a myriad of little ways as each job progresses. Also, sloppy bookkeeping and control documentation will promptly lead to unhappy clients who pay slowly or not at all and even unhappier suppliers and subcontractors. Expert advice on how to keep your books is necessary. If your expert wants to give you balance sheets and income statements but does not suggest a system to help you handle the eight key control areas listed above, we recommend you find another expert.[6]

Export—Import. The three special problems for export-import businesses are time, distance, and culture. Since there are a myriad of details involved in export-import, we feel there is no substitute for firsthand knowledge about the specific market you are seeking to enter or seeking to get goods from. General background information is available to you through the U.S. Commerce Department, particularly on exporting. To get specific, up-to-date information on how to reach and sell to foreign markets or how to get goods from a foreign market, however, you will need the assistance of those involved in the business. A good way to start is to contact export agents or export firms in your area. These companies often act as middlemen for both exports and imports. Sometimes they will buy your product. They might help you license your product (franchise it) to a foreign company. Sometimes they can find a foreign company that will license their products to you or will form a joint venture with you to get a toehold in the United States market. If your company is too small to conduct international marketing efficiently, an export-import firm can help you to form a joint venture with producers of other related products and thereby keep your marketing costs down. The possibilities are endless.

How do you find export-import agents, and how do you make sure they can help you? A good way to contact major companies in the business is to correspond with the Federation of Export Management Companies, P.O. Box 7612, Washington, D.C. 20044. It will tell you the kind of product information you should compile and, once you supply it, will refer it to members in your region. Remember, though, just because a firm expresses interest in what you are doing does not mean you should deal with it. Dealing with an export-import firm is like dealing with any other consultant (see appendix to chapter 14). Does the firm have good references? Does it market complementary, rather than competing, products? Is its sales staff large enough to do a good job for you?

CASE
SOLUTION

Sunnymead Supply Company

Sunnymead Supply Company grew from a janitorial supply wholesaler into several different, not totally compatible businesses. These diverse businesses are listed below:

Janitorial Supplies—Wholesaling

Packaging Supplies—Wholesaling

Liquid Cleaners—Manufacturing

Carpets and Draperies—Retailing

Tape Cutting—Manufacturing

Running these businesses was further complicated by the fact that three entrepreneurs were involved, each with his own established customers. While there was some justification for adding each of these businesses to Sunnymead Supply, company efficiency suffered due to the lack of recognition of the problems involved.

The solution to Sunnymead's problem lies in divestiture and focus. The company must divest itself of operations that do not focus on its primary target markets. Products unrelated to janitorial supplies and packaging should be dropped. The company needs to stay in one kind of business. Unless the production process is extremely simple, private-label liquid cleaners and tape cutting should be subcontracted to an experienced manufacturer. The company can then sell these products without getting into the manufacturing business. If the products do not sell, they can be dropped.

Similarly, the retail carpet and drape business should be sold if possible or simply closed. Lastly, the janitorial and packaging operations should be viewed as separate profit centers, or businesses, and the costs and profitability of each should be watched carefully.

It may very well make economic sense for the two specialized wholesaling operations to share warehousing facilities and front office overhead due to similarities in the mechanics of ordering, transportation, and billing. However, since janitorial supplies are a lot less bulky than packaging supplies, the warehouse space, rent, and transportation costs are bound to be less for the janitorial supplies. Average order size in dollars and profitability of each order will also differ. Separate promotional literature is also appropriate for each type of business due to the different target markets. Only by carefully keeping the two businesses separate will management ever be able to determine which is contributing the most to profits. Determining this has obvious implications for profit sharing.

This chapter has a threefold purpose. First, it permits you to define what type of business you are in. Next, it reviews the special problems and opportunities that characterize the type of business you are in. Finally, it refers you to solutions to the special problems you are likely to encounter in your type of business. The major types of businesses discussed in this chapter are retailing, manufacturing, and service. Three special types of service businesses are discussed: wholesaling, contracting, and export-import.

    One common problem many small business owners have is the lack of a clear-cut mission, or market focus. This often leads the opportunistic entrepreneur to enter two or more incompatible types of business at once. This chapter discusses the problems this can cause and explains how you can avoid these problems.

CHAPTER SUMMARY

1. **Short Case: Southern California Diesel**

   Southern California Diesel (SCD) was formed by two partners to distribute diesel parts for two major brands of commercial diesel engines. One partner ran a distribution center for one of the two engine manufacturers for several years. The other partner ran the same company's warranty repair department. SCD sells parts on a wholesale and retail basis and repairs diesel engines. Recently, the partners have been exploring the possibility of refurbishing commercial vehicles for fleets.

   a. What businesses is SCD in?

   b. Are the businesses compatible in this case?

   c. What key problems does each kind of business present that appear relevant in this case?

   d. Are there any special opportunities created by being in all these businesses at once that would not exist if SCD were in only one type of business?

2. Describe one small business in your neighborhood that appears to be in more than one type of business. What kind of problems is it likely to encounter? Explain. (Hint: Fill out the questionnaire in Exhibit 19.1 as if you were the owner of the business.)

3. Explain how one retailer in your neighborhood has dealt with the special problems faced by a retailer and exploited the retailer's special opportunities.

4. Explain how one manufacturer in your neighborhood has dealt with the special problems faced by a manufacturer and exploited the manufacturer's special opportunities.

DISCUSSION QUESTIONS

5. Explain how one service firm in your neighborhood has dealt with the special problems faced by a service firm and exploited the service firm's special opportunities.

REFERENCES   Chase, Richard B. and Aquilano, Nicholas J. *Production and Operations Management*, 3rd ed. Homewood, Ill.: Richard D. Irwin, Inc., 1981.

Dilworth, James B. *Production and Operations Management*. New York: Random House, 1979.

George, Claude S. *Management for Business and Industry*, rev. ed. Englewood Cliffs, N.J.: Prentice-Hall, Inc., 1970.

FOOTNOTES   1. This case was prepared by one of the authors based upon a Small Business Institute counseling report completed under his supervision. In order to maintain client confidentiality, the facts given here differ somewhat from the original case.

2. A major exception is the restaurant business. Still, because this business does combine attributes of both manufacturing and retailing, it is far more complex than it first appears. As a result, failure rates of independently owned restaurants are high.

3. In order of increasing complexity, the books are: George, Claude S. *Management for Business and Industry*, rev ed. Englewood Cliffs, N.J.: Prentice-Hall, Inc, 1970; Dilworth, James B. *Production and Operations Management*, New York: Random House, 1979; Chase, Richard B., and Aquilano, Nicholas J. *Production and Operations Management*, 3rd ed. Homewood, Ill.: Richard D. Irwin, Inc., 1981.

4. This definition was suggested by Howard L. Shenson in his seminar entitled, "How to Build and Maintain Your Own Part-Time—Full-Time Consulting Practice," given on April 14, 1981 in Anaheim, California, seminar outline, p. 6.

5. *Ibid.*, p. 7.

6. Several accounting systems are available that are oriented to contractors. See the yellow pages for your area under the heading "Business Forms and Systems." You will have to custom tailor such systems to meet your own needs. Still, they are far less expensive than having an accountant set up a set of books for you from scratch. Further, reviewing a few of these systems will give you a quick education on what you need to know to keep up-to-date, usable accounts for your business.

Index